Research Agenda for Mathematics Education

The Teaching and Assessing of Mathematical Problem Solving

Volume 3

Editors

Randall I. Charles
San Jose State University

Edward A. Silver
University of Pittsburgh

LAWRENCE ERLBAUM ASSOCIATES

NATIONAL COUNCIL OF
TEACHERS OF MATHEMATICS

Copyright © 1988 by
THE NATIONAL COUNCIL OF TEACHERS OF MATHEMATICS, INC.
1906 Association Drive, Reston, Virginia 22091
All rights reserved

ISBN: 0-87353-267-8 (Vol. 3, paper)
ISBN: 0-8058-0355-6 (Vol. 3, cloth)
ISBN: 0-87353-256-2 (5-vol. set, paper)

Printed in the United States of America

CONTENTS

Preface

This volume is the product of one of four NCTM Research Agenda Project conferences held during 1987. The conference from which this monograph emerged was initiated because of needs that exist in schools related to the focus of the conference—teaching and evaluation of problem solving—and because of the paucity of research-based knowledge in these areas. The topics of teaching and evaluating problem solving are high interest topics for teachers, teacher educators, curriculum developers, and administrators. Since 1980, many educators as a result of in-service programs, changes in curriculum guidelines, and changes in textbooks, have come to accept the important role problem solving can play in the curriculum and are interested in ways of improving their instructional programs. Furthermore, achievement test data have suggested that immediate attention need be given to the teaching of problem solving. Research related to problem solving over the past ten years has focused almost exclusively on analyses and characterizations of problem-solving competence and performance. Very little research has been conducted on issues more closely concerned with teaching and assessing problem solving. Indeed the time seems ripe to open new lines of attack on fundamental issues related to the teaching and evaluation of problem solving.

Since a major purpose of the conference was to open new lines of attack on fundamental issues related to teaching and evaluating problem solving, we sought a diverse group of conference participants and monograph authors. Representatives were chosen from many fields including anthropology, reading, cognitive psychology, mathematics, and mathematics education. At the conference major presentations were made by John Bransford, Ann Brown, Tom Carpenter, Jean Lave, Sandra Marshall, Nel Noddings, Lauren Resnick, George Stanic, and Rich Shavelson. These presentations provided the stimulus for rich discussions of issues. Each of these presenters incorporated some aspects of these discussions into the revised papers that appear in this monograph. Other aspects of the discussions were incorporated into companion papers written after the conference by Randy Charles, Jeremy Kilpatrick, Jim Greeno, Frank Lester, Alan Schoenfeld, Ed Silver, Larry Sowder, and Alba Thompson. Some of the companion papers were written specifically as a response to one of the papers presented at the conference while others address issues not directly raised during the conference.

The development of an adequate research agenda for teaching and assessing mathematical problem solving cannot emerge from a brief conference with but a few representatives of all those concerned about research in these areas. The major purposes of this monograph are to bring to the attention of researchers the need for coordinated and collaborative research efforts related to teaching and assessing problem solving and to hopefully influence the beliefs, methodologies, and perspectives that will be used in conceptualizing this research. The papers in this monograph do not present a listing of the most pressing researchable questions related to the teaching and assessing of mathematical problem solving. Furthermore, it would probably be inappropriate to provide such a listing. The advancement of knowledge in these areas can best be promoted by encouraging a variety of theoretical perspectives and research methodologies. The papers in this monograph provide a sampling of perspectives and methodologies. Also evident in these papers are examples of issues and themes that need to be considered in building a research agenda relative to teaching and evaluating problem solving, including, for example, one's perspective as to the nature of problem solving and the nature of schooling. Furthermore, this conference reaffirmed the need for and potential benefits that might emerge from collaborative efforts among mathematicians, mathematics teacher educators, classroom teachers, anthropologists, school administrators, cognitive psychologists, and others in building and implementing a research agenda.

Schools will change without waiting for research to set directions. Yet we cannot allow change to occur without attempting to influence that change through knowledge gleaned from research. The papers in this monograph serve as a start in building a research agenda for the teaching and assessment of mathematical problem solving. Our hope is that the ideas presented here will lead to abundant research activities with results that ultimately influence practice in the schools.

If this volume succeeds in influencing directions for research related to the teaching and evaluation of problem solving, there are many people who need to share the credit. Naturally, we are grateful to all of the authors for their willingness to prepare thoughtful chapters for this collection. We also wish to acknowledge all of the participants at the conference; their collective contribution is substantially represented in this volume. We want to thank the many people that played a role in helping with the conference and in finalizing this monograph. We are particularly grateful to Verna Adams for her assistance with local arrangements and conference logistics and to Wendy Metzger and Joseph Schanberger for their assistance during the conference. We want to acknowledge the editing assistance of Ann Roper and the typing efforts of Karen Sabin. Finally, we wish to thank Judy Sowder for her patience and assistance in the completion of this monograph.

R.I.C.
E.A.S.

Series Foreword

We clearly know more today about teaching and learning mathematics than we did twenty years ago, and we are beginning to see the effects of this new knowledge at the classroom level. This is possible in part because of the financial support that has become available to researchers. If theory building and knowledge acquisition are to have a basis broad enough to inform policy and influence educational practice, such support is essential. Although funding levels remain low in comparison to existing needs, there are several research projects either completed or in progress that could not have been undertaken without support.

In particular, we can point to several significant sets of studies based on emerging theoretical frameworks. For example, young children's early number learning and older children's understanding of rational numbers have been the subject of several recent research programs. Most of us who do research would agree that our work is more likely to be profitable when it results from an accumulation of knowledge acquired through projects undertaken within a coherent framework rather than through single, isolated studies. To establish such a framework, researchers must be provided with the opportunity to exchange and refine their ideas and viewpoints. Conferences held in Georgia and Wisconsin during the seventies serve as examples of the role such meetings can play in providing a vehicle for increased communication, synthesis, summary, and cross-disciplinary fertilization among researchers working within a specialized area of mathematical learning.

Over the past few years, the members of the Research Advisory Committee of the National Council of Teachers of Mathematics (NCTM) have observed specializations emerge that could benefit from collaborative efforts. We therefore proposed to the National Science Foundation that funding be provided for the purpose of establishing research agendas in several areas where conceptual and methodological consensus seemed possible. We believed that such a project was needed at this time for two reasons: first, to direct research efforts toward important questions, and second, to encourage the development of support mechanisms essential to collaborative chains of inquiry. Four such specialized areas were selected for this project: the teaching and assessing of problem solving, the teaching and learning of algebra, effective mathematics teaching, and the learning of number concepts by children in the middle grades.

The plan for the project included a working group conference in each of the four areas, with monographs of conference proceedings to be published by the National Council of Teachers of Mathematics. An overview monograph, written by advisory board members, was also planned. The advisory board consisted of F. Joe Crosswhite, James G. Greeno, Jeremy Kilpatrick, Douglas B. McLeod, Thomas A. Romberg, George Springer, James W. Stigler, and Jane O. Swafford, while I served as project director. For each of the four selected areas, two researchers were named to serve as conference co-directors and as co-editors of the monograph of conference proceedings. These pairs were Edward A. Silver and Randall I. Charles for teaching and assessing problem solving; Sigrid Wagner and Carolyn Kieran for learning and teaching algebra; Douglas A. Grouws and Thomas J. Cooney for effective mathematics teaching; and Merlyn J. Behr and James Hiebert for number learning in the middle grades.

The project began in May of 1986 with a planning meeting of advisory board members and conference co-directors. Issues to be addressed and possible paper topics for each conference were first identified by the group. Tentative lists of invitees for each conference were drawn up to include researchers from mathematics education and relevant fields of psychology and social science, as well as mathematicians and practitioners. The names of promising young researchers were included along with names of established researchers. An international perspective was considered important, and so the list also included names of scholars from abroad. The concept of working group conferences funded for 25 people precluded expanding the conference to all interested persons. We therefore decided to invite people to attend only one conference, thus maximizing the total number of persons involved in the project. The final participant lists follow this report.

The first of the four working conferences, on teaching and assessing mathematical problem solving, was held in January, 1987, in San Diego. Several approaches to teaching problem solving were advanced and discussed: teaching *as* problem solving, the teacher as coach versus teacher as manager, modeling master teachers, viewing students as apprentices, the use of macro-contexts to facilitate mathematical thinking, consideration of mathematics as an ill-structured discipline. Discussion of assessment issues focused on process rather than outcome, and questions of evaluating processess and schema structures were explored. Considerable attention was given throughout the conference to associated problems of teacher preparation.

The conference on effective mathematics teaching was held in March in Columbia, Missouri. The first paper delivered there, on teaching for higher-order thinking in mathematics, tied this conference to the first one. A paper on the functioning of educational paradigms set a stage for much of the discussion at the conference. The question of what makes a good mathematics teacher was explored in discussions ensuing from presentations on expert-novice studies, on cross-cultural studies, and on teacher professionalism. Concern for the content in mathematics classes and the manner in which this is determined also received attention. The lack of funding necessary for observational research was strongly noted.

The conference on teaching and learning algebra, also in March, was held in Athens, Georgia. The papers and discussions focused on four major themes: what is algebra and what should it become, in light of continuing technological advances; what has research told us about the teaching and learning of algebra; what is algebraic thinking and how does it relate to general mathematical thinking; and what is the role of representations in the learning of algebra. Research questions from the perspectives of content, of learning, of instruction, and of representations were formulated.

The final conference, on number concepts in the middle grades, was held in May in DeKalb, Illinois. A theme permeating many of the papers at this conference was that number concepts related to topics taught at this level are qualitatively different from those in lower grades, both in terms of the number systems studied and the operations involved. The papers explored the new conceptions and complexities that students encountered, and examined the effects of conventional and experimental instructional programs. It was acknowledged that the differences between early and later number concepts need to be recognized and more adequately understood before instructional programs can be developed to enhance number learning in the middle grades.

The brevity of these descriptions does not do justice to the diversity and richness of the papers and discussions. Each of the conferences was indeed a working conference. Participants addressed difficult questions and discussions were lively and intense. Consensus was elusive, as might be expected with a group of people with such diverse backgrounds. Even so, there was agreement on many fundamental issues, and individual researchers, representing different disciplines and viewpoints, were able to reach new understandings.

There are five monographs being published as a result of this project, all under the general title *Research Agenda in Mathematics Education*. Four of the monographs contain conference proceedings and are subtitled as follows: *The Teaching and Assessing of Mathematical Problem Solving, Perspectives on Research on Effective Mathematics Teaching, Research Issues in the Learning and Teaching of Algebra,* and *Number Concepts and Operations in the Middle Grades*. The proceedings include revised conference papers, some discussion, response, and summary papers by other conference participants, and chapters by the co-editors. They will be of particular interest to researchers interested in the learning and teaching of mathematics. The fifth monograph, *Setting a Research Agenda,* is intended for a wider audience, including policy makers, mathematics supervisors, and teachers. In this monograph the project advisory board discusses the past and present state of research in mathematics education and cognitive science, the relation of reform movements to research efforts, the role of this project in guiding future research in mathematics education, major issues addressed at the conferences and other issues still needing to be addressed, and resources needed to facilitate research. We are fortunate to have Lawrence Erlbaum Associates, Inc., join with the National Council of Teachers of Mathematics in publishing this series of monographs.

This project was funded by the National Science Foundation under Grant No. MDR-8550614. The advisory board and monograph editors join me in an expression of gratitude to Raymond I. Hannapel of the National Science Foundation for his continued support throughout the term of this project. We also wish to thank James D. Gates and Charles R. Hucka of the National Council of Teachers of Mathematics for their assistance with the publication of these monographs, and Julia Hough of Lawrence Erlbaum Associates for her work in facilitating joint publication between NCTM and Erlbaum. Finally, we wish to acknowledge the assistance of administrators at San Diego State University, University of Missouri, University of Georgia, and Northern Illinois University, and thank them for the many amenities they provided to conference participants.

I personally want to express my appreciation to the members of the advisory board for all the assistance they have given me during these past two years. My largest debt of gratitude is owed to the conference co-directors and co-editors for their work in directing four outstanding conferences and for providing all of us with sets of proceedings that will guide research efforts in the years to come.

Judith T. Sowder
San Diego State University

Historical Perspectives on Problem Solving in the Mathematics Curriculum

George M. A. Stanic
Jeremy Kilpatrick
University of Georgia

Problems have occupied a central place in the school mathematics curriculum since antiquity, but problem solving has not. Only recently have mathematics educators accepted the idea that the development of problem-solving ability deserves special attention. With this focus on problem solving has come confusion. The term *problem solving* has become a slogan encompassing different views of what education is, of what schooling is, of what mathematics is, and of why we should teach mathematics in general and problem solving in particular.

This confusion is exemplified in the *Agenda for Action* of the National Council of Teachers of Mathematics (1980), which asks that "problem solving be the focus of school mathematics" (p. 1). In the *Agenda,* problem solving is characterized as one of 10 "basic skill areas." The *Agenda* assumes that there is a direct relationship between problem solving in the mathematics classroom and problem solving in other parts of our lives. There is no adequate clarification of what problem solving is, why we should teach it, or how the position taken fits into a historical context.

In this paper, various themes are identified that historically have characterized the role of problem solving in the school mathematics curriculum. These themes have intertwined and remained largely unexamined. What mathematics educators are saying to each other today about problem solving is linked to several different traditions in the fields of psychology, curriculum, and mathematics education.

PROBLEMS IN THE CURRICULUM

Problems in the curriculum go back at least as far as the ancient Egyptians, Chinese, and Greeks. For example, the Ahmes Papyrus, copied by the scribe Ahmes in about 1650 B.C. from an older document, is an Egyptian mathematical manuscript that consists of a collection of problems. In one of the problems (see Figures 1 and 2), the student is asked to sum the geometric progression of five terms, where the first term and the multiplier are both 7 (Chase, 1979, pp. 59, 136–137). In the papyrus itself, only an abbreviated form of the problem is given, with two methods of solution and the answer provided. The fact that the problem refers to houses, cats, mice, spelt, and hekat being summed suggests that it was a recreation problem or puzzle.

1

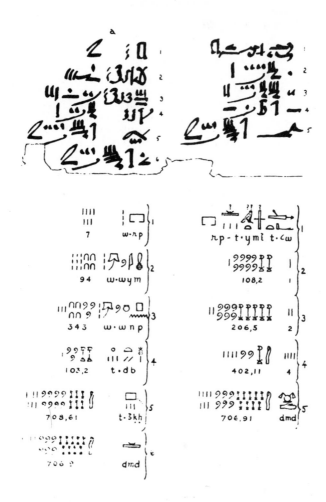

Figure 1. A geometric progression problem from the Ahmes Papyrus. (Chase, 1979, p. 17)

A second example comes from *Nine Sections*, a Chinese document dating back to about 1000 B.C.:

> Of two water weeds, the one grows 3 feet and the other 1 foot on the first day. The growth of the first becomes every day half of that of the preceding day while the other grows twice as much as on the day before. In how many days will the two grow to equal heights? (cited in Sanford, 1927, p. 7)

And from the ancient Greeks we get an early version of the cistern problem:

I am a brazen lion; my spouts are my two eyes, my mouth and the flat of my right foot. My right eye fills a jar in two days, my left eye in three, and my foot in four. My mouth is capable of filling it in six hours; tell me how long all four together will take to fill it. (cited in Sanford, 1927, p. 69)

w'·t[1]	imy·t- pr (?)[2]	pr·w	7
A	*house-inventory* (?)	*houses*	
1	2,801	myw·w	49
2	5,602	*cats*	
4	11,204[3]	pnw·w	343
		mice	
dmd	19,607.	bd·t	2,301[4]
Total		*spelt*	
		ḥkȝ·t	16,807
		hekat	
		dmd	19,607.
		Total	

[1] This heading is very corrupt. The phonetic part of w'·t is clear but either the usual stroke determinative is absent or the imy-sign is not here. We agree with Peet (page 122) that w'·t imy·t-pr is as likely a reading as anything that can account for the hieratic as it stands, but we do not see how the stroke and the imy-sign can both be present as on Peet's Plate W. When the word w', *one*, precedes its noun the two are always connected at this period by the genitive n and one wonders whether the light horizontal stroke of the sign tentatively read imy is possibly an n added later. This would, of course, make the reading imy·t-pr impossible while it would restore the stroke to w'·t. The form used here would be most unusual for imy at this time. Elsewhere in the Rhind (Problems 65, 82-84, and 86, where it has the value wnm) the sign has two vertical strokes.

[2] The compound means *that which is in a house* and came to be the regular word for an *estate* in the legal sense. The first part of the word is an adjective from the preposition m.

[3] Note the sign for 10,000.   [4] Mistake for 2,401.

Figure 2. Translation of the geometric progression problem from the Ahmes Papyrus. (Chase, 1979, p. 16)

Particular methods of solving problems also have a long history. For example, a technique much like the Rule of False Position appeared in the Ahmes Papyrus. In her history of algebra problems, Vera Sanford (1927) gave an example of the Rule of False Position using the following problem from a 15th century work by Phillipo Calandri:

The head of a fish weighs 1/3 of the whole fish, his tail weighs 1/4 and his body weighs 30 ounces. What does the whole fish weigh? (p. 19)

Sanford explained that the Rule of False Position was used to solve the problem as follows:

If the whole fish weighs 12 oz., then the head would weigh 4, the tail 3, and the body 5. Evidently the weight of the fish is the same multiple of 12 that 30 is of 5, and thus the fish weighs 72 ounces. (p.19)

One finds similar problems in mathematics textbooks from the 19th and 20th centuries. The important point to be made about these examples is that a very limited view of the learning of problem solving is assumed. Until relatively recently, teaching problem solving meant presenting problems and perhaps including an example of a specific solution technique. A page from William J. Milne's 1897 text entitled *A Mental Arithmetic* reflects this view of teaching problem solving (see Figure 3). G. A. Wentworth's 1900 text entitled *New School Algebra* is similar (see Figure 4).

Clifford B. Upton, in his 1939 text entitled *Social Utility Arithmetics,* tried to make children think about the process of solving a problem by presenting problems without numbers (see Figure 5), but he did not go on to discuss what one can learn from such problems.

Even texts written specifically for teachers presented limited views of problem solving. A good example is H. O. R. Siefert's *Principles of Arithmetic,* published in 1902 (see Figures 6 and 7). Also consider the page from Edward Brooks's *Normal Elementary Algebra,* published in 1871 (see Figures 8 and 9). Brooks at least talked about "the method of solving a problem."

There are examples of more detailed discussions of how to solve problems, as the page from Wentworth's *Plane and Solid Geometry,* published in 1899, shows (see Figure 10). The *Strayer-Upton Arithmetics—Higher Grades,* published in 1928, has some advice on "how to solve hard problems" (see Figure 11).

Today's attention to developing students' problem-solving abilities can be seen in Figure 12, which shows a page from Book 5 of *Addison-Wesley Mathematics* (Eicholz, O'Daffer, Fleenor, Charles, Young, & Barnett, 1987).

THE CHANGING ROLE OF PROBLEM SOLVING

As these examples show, problems have a long history in the mathematics curriculum. However, primarily within the last century, discussions of the teaching of problem solving have moved from advocating that students simply be presented with problems or with rules for solving particular problems to developing more general approaches to problem solving. Although the teaching of problem solving is now receiving a greater emphasis, mathematics educators have not fully examined the issue of why we should teach problem solving at all. The role of problem solving in the school mathematics curriculum is the result of conflicting forces tied to ancient and enduring ideas about the benefits of the study of mathematics and to a variety of interacting events that took place near the beginning of the 20th century.

The main reason for the greater emphasis given by mathematics educators to the teaching of problem solving is that until this century, it was assumed that the study of mathematics—of any mathematics, not just what we would now consider problems—would, in some general way, improve people's

24. A and B can do a piece of work together in 3 days, A and C in 4 days, B and C in 4½ days. How long will it take each alone to do the work?

Let x, y, z = the number of days in which A, B, C can do the work, respectively.

Then, $\frac{1}{x}$, $\frac{1}{y}$, $\frac{1}{z}$ = the parts A, B, C can do in 1 day, respectively.

And $\frac{1}{x} + \frac{1}{y}$ = the part A and B together can do in one day.

But $\frac{1}{3}$ = the part A and B together can do in 1 day.

Therefore, $\frac{1}{x} + \frac{1}{y} = \frac{1}{3}$, (1)

Likewise, $\frac{1}{x} + \frac{1}{z} = \frac{1}{4}$, (2)

and $\frac{1}{y} + \frac{1}{z} = \frac{2}{9}$, $\left(\frac{1}{4\frac{1}{2}} = \frac{2}{9}\right)$ (3)

Add, and divide by 2, $\frac{1}{x} + \frac{1}{y} + \frac{1}{z} = \frac{29}{72}$ (4)

Subtract (1), (2), and (3), separately from (4), and we have

$$\frac{1}{z} = \frac{5}{72}, \quad \frac{1}{y} = \frac{11}{72}, \quad \frac{1}{x} = \frac{13}{72}$$

Therefore, $z = 14\frac{2}{5}$, $y = 6\frac{6}{11}$, $x = 5\frac{7}{13}$.

Therefore, A can do the work in $5\frac{7}{13}$ days, B in $6\frac{6}{11}$ days, and C in $14\frac{2}{5}$ days.

25. A cistern has three pipes, A, B, and C. A and B will fill the cistern in 1 hour 10 minutes, A and C in 1 hour 24 minutes, B and C in 2 hours 20 minutes. How long will it take each pipe alone to fill it?

26. A and B can do a piece of work in $2\frac{1}{3}$ days, A and C in $3\frac{1}{3}$ days, B and C in 4 days. How long will it take each alone to do the work?

27. A and B can do a piece of work in a days, A and C in b days, B and C in c days. How long will it take each alone to do the work?

Figure 4. A page from G. A. Wentworth's *New School Algebra.* (Wentworth, 1900)

---

52. How much will it cost to plow 32 acres of land at $3.75 per acre?

SOLUTION: — $3.75 is ⅜ of $10. At $10 per acre the plowing would cost $320; but since $3.75 is ⅜ of $10, it will cost ⅜ of $320, which is $120. Therefore, etc.

53. How much will 72 sheep cost at $6.25 per head?

54. A baker bought 88 barrels of flour at $3.75 per barrel. How much did it all cost?

55. How much will 18 cords of wood cost at $6.66⅔ per cord?

56. How much must be paid for a case of boots containing 24 pairs at $3.33⅓ per pair?

57. The hats purchased for a company consisting of 64 men cost $1.25 each. How much did they all cost?

58. A clothier sold 48 boys' overcoats at $8.75 apiece. How much did he receive for all of them?

59. The railroad fare from Brantford to Hazelton is $8.75. How much must be paid for tickets for a party of 16?

60. The wages of a machinist were $3.75 per day. How much did he earn in 24 days?

61. The porter on a sleeping car was paid $37.50 per month for 16 months. How much did he earn?

SUGGESTION: — $37.50 is ⅜ of $100.

62. The charge for tuition at a certain school was $62.50 per quarter. If 40 pupils attended the school, to how much did the tuition fees amount?

63. A party of 32 went to Europe for the summer, paying $87.50 each for their passage tickets. How much did they all pay?

MILNE MENTAL—7

Figure 3. A page from William J. Milne's *A Mental Arithmetic.* (Milne, 1897)

PROBLEMS AND PRACTICE

PROBLEMS WITHOUT NUMBERS

1. If you know the cost of a coat, a hat, and a suit, how do you find the cost of all of them?

2. If you know the length of a piece of ribbon and the number of equal parts into which you will cut it, how do you find the length of each part?

3. If you know the amount of money you make on each magazine you sell, how do you find how much you make on all the magazines that you sell?

*4. If you know the weight of a truck loaded with coal and also the weight of the empty truck, how do you find the weight of the coal?

5. If you know the number of rooms in a school building, the number of seats in one room, and that each room has the same number of seats, how do you find the number of seats in the building?

MIXED PRACTICE

Find the answers to the following:

1. 6 × 186	3. 5814 − 2931	5. ⅓ of 294
2. 500 + 5	4. 79 + 58 + 63	6. ⅓ of 165

7. Find the product of 4 and 93.

8. How many times is 3 contained in 309?

9. Find the sum of 296, 385, 477, and 108.

10. Find the difference between 6000 and 2104.

11. Multiply 75 by 4.   Add 98 to the product.

Figure 5. A page from Clifford B. Upton's *Social Utility Arithmetics.* (Upton, 1939)

PRINCIPLES OF ARITHMETIC

EMBRACING COMMON FRACTIONS, DECIMAL FRACTIONS, PERCENTAGE, PROPORTION, INVOLUTION, EVOLUTION AND MENSURATION

A MANUAL FOR TEACHERS AND NORMAL STUDENTS

BY

H. O. R. SIEFERT,

SUPERINTENDENT OF PUBLIC SCHOOLS, MILWAUKEE

BOSTON, U.S.A.

D. C. HEATH & CO., PUBLISHERS

1902

Figure 6. Title page of H. O. R. Siefert's text for teachers. (Siefert, 1902)

---

4. EXERCISES.

1. A street car runs 35 miles in 5 hours; how far will it run in 7 hours?

Construct a triangle ABC, in which the side AB shall be equal to the side AC. The third side may have any convenient length. (Such a triangle is called an isosceles triangle.)

Fig. 8.

Draw DE making $AD = AE$.

Since $AB = AE$, and $AB = AC$, it is obvious that

$$AD : AE :: AB : AC.$$

Interchanging the means, we have

$$AD : AB :: AE : AC.$$

Now if only the first three terms are given, we can find the fourth term, for

$$AD : AB :: AE : x.$$

Multiplying the means together, and dividing by the given extreme, we have,

$$x = \frac{AB \times AE}{AD}.$$

Now let us apply this general demonstration to the given problem.

Let

$$
\begin{aligned}
AB &= 7 \text{ hours} \\
AD &= 5 \text{ hours}
\end{aligned}
\right\} \text{ time measured along the same line.}
$$

$$
\begin{aligned}
AE &= 35 \text{ miles} \\
AC &= x \text{ miles.}
\end{aligned}
\right\} \text{ distance measured along the same line.}
$$

Figure 7. A page from H. O. R. Siefert's *Principles of Arithmetic.* (Siefert, 1902)

Left page (title page)

THE

NORMAL

ELEMENTARY ALGEBRA:

CONTAINING THE

First Principles of the Science,

FOR

DEVELOPED WITH CONCISENESS AND SIMPLICITY,

FOR

COMMON SCHOOLS, ACADEMIES, SEMINARIES AND NORMAL SCHOOLS.

By EDWARD BROOKS, A.M.,

PRINCIPAL OF PENNSYLVANIA STATE NORMAL SCHOOL, AND AUTHOR OF THE NORMAL SERIES
OF ARITHMETIC, NORMAL GEOMETRY, ETC.

"*Mathematical studies cultivate clearness of thought, acuteness of analysis, and accuracy of expression.*"

PHILADELPHIA:

SOWER, POTTS & CO.,

530 MARKET ST., AND 523 MINOR ST.

Figure 8. Title page of Edward Brooks's normal school text. (Brooks, 1871)

Right page (page 106)

PROBLEMS IN SIMPLE EQUATIONS.

173. A **Problem** is a question requiring some unknown result from things which are known.

174. The **Solution** of a problem is the process of finding the required unknown result.

175. The solution of a problem in Algebra consists of two distinct parts—

1st. The formation of the equation;

2d. The solution of the equation.

176. The **Method of Solving** a problem cannot be stated by any general or precise rule. The following directions may be of some value:

1. *Represent the unknown quantity by one of the final letters of the alphabet.*

2. *Form an equation by indicating the operations necessary to verify the result were it known.*

3. *Solve the equation thus derived.*

NOTE.—The formation of the equation is called the *concrete* part of the solution; the reduction of the equation the *abstract* part. The first part is also called the *statement* of the problem. It is merely a translation of the problem from common into *algebraic* language.

PROBLEMS.

CASE I.

1. A farmer bought a cow and a horse for $375, paying 4 times as much for the horse as for the cow; required the cost of each.

SOLUTION. Let x represent the cost of the cow; then, since he paid 4 times as much for the horse as for the cow, $4x$ will represent the cost of the horse; and since both cost $375, we have the equation $x + 4x = 375$; uniting the terms, we have $5x = 375$; dividing by 5, we have $x = 75$; and multiplying by 4, we have $4x = 300$. Hence, the cow cost $75, and the horse $300.

OPERATION.

Let x = the cost of the cow.

Then $4x$ = the cost of the horse.

$$x + 4x = 375 \qquad (1)$$
$$5x = 375 \qquad (2)$$
$$x = 75, \text{ cost of cow.} \qquad (3)$$
$$4x = 300, \text{ cost of horse.} \qquad (4)$$

Figure 9. A page from Edward Brooks's *Normal Elementary Algebra.* (Brooks, 1871)

SOLUTION OF PROBLEMS.

319. If a problem is so simple that the solution is obvious from a known theorem, we have only to make the construction according to the theorem, and then give a synthetic proof, if a proof is necessary, that the construction is correct, as in the examples of the fundamental problems already given.

320. But problems are usually of a more difficult type. The application of known theorems to their solution is not immediate, and often far from obvious. To discover the mode of application is the first and most difficult part of the solution. The best way to attack such problems is by a method resembling the analytic proof of a theorem, called the analysis of the problem.

1. **Suppose the construction made,** and let the figure represent all parts concerned, both given and required.

2. Study the relations among the parts with the aid of known theorems, and try to find some relation that will suggest the construction.

3. If this attempt fails, introduce new relations by drawing auxiliary lines, and study the new relations. If this attempt fails, make a new trial, and so on till a clue to the right construction is found.

321. A problem is *determinate* if it has a *definite* number of solutions, *indeterminate* if it has an *indefinite* number of solutions, and *impossible* if it has *no* solution. A problem is sometimes determinate for certain relative positions or magnitudes of the given parts, and indeterminate for other positions or magnitudes of the given parts.

322. The **discussion** of a problem consists in examining the problem with reference to all possible conditions, and in determining the conditions necessary for its solution.

Figure 10. A page from G. A. Wentworth's
Plane and Solid Geometry. (Wentworth, 1899)

CHAPTER II

HOW TO SOLVE HARD PROBLEMS

A dealer buys 28 doz. oranges at 24¢ a dozen. He sells 24 doz. of them at 35¢ a dozen. The rest of them spoil. Allowing 15% of the selling price for overhead expenses, what per cent of the selling price is his profit?

To solve a problem like this, which requires careful thinking, it is helpful to ask yourself these six questions:

1. *Do I understand every word and phrase in the problem?* What do "dealer," "overhead expenses," and "profit" mean?

2. *What am I asked to find?* You are here asked to find the per cent of profit on the selling price.

3. *What facts are given that will help me to find the answer?* There are five such facts in the above problem. What are they?

4. *By what steps can I find the answer?* For this problem, use the following steps:

(1) Find the total cost. $28 \times 24¢ = \$6.72.$
(2) Find the total selling price. $24 \times 35¢ = \$8.40.$
(3) Find the overhead expenses.   15% of $\$8.40 = \$1.26.$
(4) Find the profit. $\$8.40 - (\$6.72 + \$1.26) = \$.42.$
(5) Find the per cent of profit on the selling price. $\$.42$ is 5% of $\$8.40.$ Hence the answer is 5%.

5. *Have I found what was asked for?* Read the problem again to make sure that you have answered the question asked.

6. *Is my work right?* Go over your work to see if your thinking has been correct and if you have used the right steps. Then check your computations. Whenever possible, estimate the answer roughly to see if your result is sensible.

101

Figure 11. A page from Strayer-Upton Arithmetics—
Higher Grades. (Strayer & Upton, 1928)

Figure 12. A page from *Addison-Wesley Mathematics* (Book 5). (Eicholz, O'Daffer, Fleenor, Charles, Young, & Barnett, 1987) Reprinted by permission.

thinking. Plato said that "those who are by nature good at calculation are, as one might say, naturally sharp in every other study, and . . . those who are slow at it, if they are educated and exercised in this study, nevertheless improve and become sharper than they were" (Grube, 1974, p. 18). So from at least as far back as Plato, we get the idea that studying mathematics would improve one's ability to think, to reason, to solve problems that one will confront in the real world. In a sense, solving problems in the curriculum was simply a means to get students to study mathematics. Problems were a given element of the mathematics curriculum that contributed, like all the other elements, to the development of reasoning power.

During the 19th century, mental discipline theory provided the framework for expressing these ideas. The theory was a result of a not entirely smooth merger between faculty psychology and the liberal arts tradition. Faculty psychology made people look at the possibility that a person's mind was composed of various abilities, or faculties, such as perception, memory, imagination, understanding, and intuition or reason. As a curriculum theory, mental discipline was based on the idea that it was the job of the school to help students develop these faculties (and that the traditional liberal arts—i.e.,—mathematics and the classical languages—were the best vehicles for developing these faculties). According to mental discipline theory, mathematics, especially higher level mathematics, provided the primary vehicle for developing the reasoning faculty.

Although the tradition reflected in mental discipline theory continues to endure, events that took place near the turn of the 20th century led to significant changes in how the study of mathematics was viewed. The work of Edward L. Thorndike is generally accepted as refuting the basic notions of mental discipline theory. Although Thorndike's work clearly played a major role in the decline of the theory, he never completely rejected the idea of mental discipline and actually extended the idea of breaking down the intellect into its components. Thorndike essentially argued that the various categories of abilities or faculties were too general and that particular subjects did not have far greater disciplinary value than others. According to Thorndike and R. S. Woodworth, in their classic transfer-of-training experiment published in 1901, "It is misleading to speak of sense discrimination, attention, memory, observation, accuracy, quickness, etc." because "multitudinous separate individual functions are referred to by any one of these words. These functions may have little in common" (p. 249). And in a study Thorndike published in 1924, he came to the following conclusion:

> The intellectual values of studies should be determined largely by the special information, habits, interests, attitudes, and ideals which they demonstrably produce. The expectation of any large difference in general improvement of the mind from one study rather than another seems doomed to disappointment. The chief reason why good thinkers seem superficially to have been made by having taken certain school studies, is that good thinkers have taken such studies, becoming better by the inherent tendency of the good to gain more than the poor from any study. . . . Disciplinary values may be real and deserve weight in the curriculum, but the weights should be reasonable. (p. 27)

The fact that Thorndike was still dealing with the issue in 1924 shows that mental discipline theory did not disappear at the turn of the century. However, Thorndike's work, when combined with other developments, clearly led to a decline in importance of mental discipline theory. More and more psychologists, sociologists, and educators took stands against the theory.

These critics looked at a society changing under intense industrialization, urbanization, and immigration; worried about a school population that would increase twentyfold between 1890 and 1940; and concluded that the school curriculum had to change. They argued that a person needed to study only that which was directly functional to his or her future societal role. Activity analyses of various societal roles were used to set up specific objectives for the school curriculum. And the mental measurements movement grew as people looked to intelligence tests to decide who should have access to what knowledge in the school curriculum. Mathematics, which was such a crucial element in the curriculum based on mental discipline theory, came under direct attack. The critics agreed that mathematics was very important but argued that most people needed to know no more than sixth-grade arithmetic (Stanic, 1983/1984).

Thus the turn of the century witnessed two very different ways of looking at people, education, and the school curriculum. Mental discipline theory (which is, ironically, often associated with an elitist view of education) yielded a fundamentally optimistic view of human intelligence. Although mental disciplinarians recognized the obvious differences that exist between people, what was more important to them was that all people were born with the same faculties; and it was the job of the school to develop those faculties that everyone had. Because all people have the same faculties, the mental disciplinarians argued that when it came to deciding what should be taught to whom, what was good for one student was good for all students. All students were to have access to the same knowledge and methods of instruction.

The alternative view based on Thorndike's work does not present such an optimistic picture of human intelligence. People like Thorndike and Granville Stanley Hall, who spoke of "the great army of incapables" in schools (Hall, 1904, p. 50), provided the foundation for the idea that individual differences dictated the need to expose different children to different subject matter and methods of instruction.

No longer was it assumed that the study of mathematics inevitably improves one's thinking. This view set the stage for a greater emphasis by mathematics educators on how, exactly, students might improve their thinking ability, or reasoning ability, or problem-solving ability, through the study of mathematics. Many of our professional forebears, however, were reluctant to give up the tradition going back to Plato that gave such a prominent place to mathematics in the school curriculum.

By the beginning of the 20th century, people like David Eugene Smith at Teachers College, Columbia University, and Jacob William Albert Young at the University of Chicago were establishing mathematics education as a legitimate professional field of study at colleges and universities around the country. Smith, Young, and most of our other professional forebears saw mathematics, including higher level mathematics, as appropriate for all students and as an essential vehicle for developing students' reasoning power.

It is ironic that as the number of professional mathematics educators at colleges and universities around the country began to grow, the place of mathematics in the school curriculum came under attack. Mathematics educators tried to adjust to the changing times and ideas, some even embracing the ideas of the critics, but the conflict embodied in the competing traditions led to a crisis in mathematics education in the 1930s, a crisis that has not yet been resolved (Stanic, 1983/1984, 1986).

It is especially ironic that partly because of this attack on the place of mathematics in the school curriculum, many of our forebears, while advocating the benefits of mathematics for one's thinking, were leery of giving problems too large a role in the curriculum. Mathematicians such as Felix Klein in Germany, John Perry in England, and Eliakim Hastings Moore in the United States were discussing the relationship between pure and applied mathematics in the school curriculum and, in essence, advocating a greater role for applications. But many mathematics educators, particularly Smith, did not want to give too large a role to applications because the critics of the school curriculum who were not mathematicians were also calling for making school mathematics more relevant to real life. In essence, Smith was afraid to give up what he saw as the role and essential content of mathematics for the sake of applications, and he was afraid to give too much support to the cause of the critics.

Klein, Perry, and Moore were not asking for applications to take over the curriculum. Moore (1903/1926) called for the unification of pure and applied mathematics, and Klein warned of overreacting to the benefits of applications:

> It is possible that through the mere mass of interesting applications, the real logical training may be crippled, and under no circumstances may this happen, for then the real marrow of the whole is lost. Hence: We desire emphatically an enlivening of instruction in mathematics by means of its applications, but we desire also that the pendulum which in earlier decades perhaps swung too far in the abstract direction, should not now swing to the other extreme, but we wish to remain in the just mean. (Klein, cited in Young, 1903, p. 54)

Smith, however, was unconvinced. Of Moore's famous presidential address delivered in 1902 before the American Mathematical Society, Smith (1905) said "it was a fact apparent to all who heard it that the address was not favorably received by many of those present" (p. 135). In a 1909 article, Smith expressed concern about the "tendency throughout the country to make arithmetic, as other subjects, more interesting to children," arguing that "we should do all in our power to make arithmetic interesting or even attractive to the children, but that we must not hope to attain this result by offering a sickly substitute for the vigorous subject that has come down to us" (p. 39). Smith simply did not want to give up the idea that any work in mathematics could contribute to a person's ability "to attack the every-day problems of life" (Smith, 1900, p. 2); for Smith, calculating a greatest common divisor was as valuable as solving an "applied problem."

Therefore, events surrounding the decline of mental discipline theory may have set the stage for mathematics educators to begin to give more specific emphasis to the development of problem-solving ability, but the clash of basic ideas about human intelligence, education, and the school curriculum still permeates discussions of problem solving. And as one looks at problem solving in the curriculum from the ancient Egyptians to the present, different themes are revealed.

PROBLEM-SOLVING THEMES

Three general themes have characterized the role of problem solving in the school mathematics curriculum: problem solving as context, problem solving as skill, and problem solving as art.

Problem Solving as Context

The context theme has at least five subthemes, all of which are based on the idea that problems and the solving of problems are means to achieve other valuable ends.

Problem solving as justification. Historically, problem solving has been included in the mathematics curriculum in part because the problems provide justification for teaching mathematics at all. Presumably, at least some problems related in some way to real-world experiences were included in the curriculum to convince students and teachers of the value of mathematics.

Problem solving as motivation. The subtheme of motivation is related to that of justification in that the problems justify the mathematics being taught. However, in the case of motivation, the connection is much more specific, and the aim of gaining student interest is sought. For example, a specific problem involving addition with regrouping might be used to introduce a series of lessons leading to learning the most efficient algorithm for adding the numbers.

Problem solving as recreation. The subtheme of recreation is related to that of motivation because student interest is involved, but in the case of recreation, problems are provided not so much to motivate students to learn as to allow them to have some fun with the mathematics they have already learned. Presumably, such problems fulfill a natural interest human beings have in exploring unusual situations. The problem shown earlier from the Ahmes Papyrus is a good illustration. The recreation subtheme also differs from the first two in that puzzles, or problems without any necessary real-world connections, are perfectly appropriate.

Problem solving as vehicle. Problems are often provided not simply to motivate students to be interested in direct instruction on a topic but as a vehicle through which a new concept or skill might be learned. Discovery techniques in part reflect the idea that problem solving can be a vehicle for learning new concepts and skills. And when the mathematics curriculum consisted exclusively of problems, the problems obviously served as vehicles.

Problem solving as practice. Of the five subthemes, problem solving as practice has had the largest influence on the mathematics curriculum. In this subtheme, problems do not provide justification, motivation, recreation, or vehicles as much as necessary practice to reinforce skills and concepts taught directly. A page from an 1854 text by Nelson M. Holbrook entitled *The Child's First Book in Arithmetic* shows a good example of this subtheme. Notice that the "mental exercises" on division follow work on the division table (see Figure 13).

Figure 13. Pages from Nelson M. Holbrook's *The Child's First Book in Arithmetic.* (Holbrook, 1854)

Problem Solving as Skill

Problem solving is often seen as one of a number of skills to be taught in the school curriculum. According to this view, problem solving is not necessarily a unitary skill, but there is a clear skill orientation.

Although problem solving as context remains a strong and persistent theme, the problem-solving-as-skill theme has become dominant for those who see problem solving as a valuable curriculum end deserving special attention, rather than as simply a means to achieve other ends or an inevitable outcome of the study of mathematics.

The skill theme is clearly related to the changes that took place near the turn of the century, although not all advocates of this point of view would claim an association with, for example, the work of Thorndike. Nonetheless, largely because of Thorndike's influence (as well as the other changes discussed earlier), most educators no longer assumed that the study of mathematics improved one's thinking and made one a better solver of real-world problems. Especially because many of our professional forebears were reluctant to give up their claims about mathematics and to include more applied problems in the curriculum, they essentially allowed educational psychologists like Thorndike to define the new view of problem solving.

Putting problem solving in a hierarchy of skills to be acquired by students leads to certain consequences for the role of problem solving in the curriculum. One consequence is that within the general skill of problem solving, hierarchical distinctions are made between solving routine and nonroutine problems. That is, nonroutine problem solving is characterized as a higher level skill to be acquired after skill at solving routine problems (which, in turn, is to be acquired after students learn basic mathematical concepts and skills). This view postpones attention to nonroutine problem solving, and, as a result, only certain students, because they have accomplished the prerequisites, are ever exposed to such problems. Nonroutine problem solving becomes, then, an activity for the especially capable students rather than for all students.

Problem Solving as Art

A deeper, more comprehensive view of problem solving in the school mathematics curriculum—a view of problem solving as *art*—emerged from the work of George Polya, who revived in our time the idea of heuristic (the art of discovery). Mathematicians as far back as Euclid and Pappus, and including Descartes, Leibnitz, and Bolzano, had discussed methods and rules for discovery and invention in mathematics, but their ideas never made their way into the school curriculum. It remained for Polya to reformulate, extend, and illustrate various ideas about mathematical discovery in a way that teachers could understand and use.

Polya's experience in learning and teaching mathematics led him to ask how mathematics came to be—how did people make mathematical discoveries? Won't students understand mathematics better if they see how it was created in the first place and if they can get some taste of mathematical discovery themselves? Polya's experience as a mathematician led him to conclude that the finished face of mathematics presented deductively in mathematical journals and in textbooks does not do justice to the subject. Finished mathematics requires demonstrative reasoning, whereas mathematics in the making requires plausible reasoning. If students are to use plausible reasoning, they need to be taught how.

Like our professional forebears Smith and Young, Polya argued that a major aim of education is the development of intelligence—to teach young people to think. In the primary school, children should be taught to do their arithmetic insightfully rather than mechanically because although insightful performance is a more ambitious aim, it actually has a better chance of success. It yields faster, more permanent results. In the secondary school, mathematics should offer something to those who will, and those who will not, use mathematics in their later studies or careers. The same mathematics should be taught to all students because no one can know in advance which students will eventually use mathematics professionally.

> If the teaching of mathematics gives only a one-sided, stunted idea of the mathematician's thinking, if it totally suppresses those "informal" activities of guessing and extracting mathematical concepts from the visible world around us, it neglects what may be the most interesting part for the general student, the most instructive for the future user of mathematics, and the most inspiring for the future mathematician. (Polya, 1966, pp. 124–125)

In Polya's view, mathematics consists of information and know-how. Regardless of how well schools impart mathematical information, if they do not teach students how to use that information, it will be forgotten. "To know mathematics is to be able to do mathematics" (Polya, 1969/1984, p. 574). "What is know-how in mathematics? The ability to solve problems" (Polya, 1981, p. xi).

To Polya, problem solving was a practical art, "like swimming, or skiing, or playing the piano" (1981, p. ix). One learns such arts by imitation and practice. Polya assumed neither that simply solving problems by itself with no guidance leads to improved performance nor that the study of mathematics by its very nature raises one's general level of intelligence. Instead, he recognized that techniques of problem solving need to be illustrated by the teacher, discussed with the students, and practiced in an insightful, nonmechanical way. Further, he observed that although routine problems can be used to fulfill certain pedagogical functions of teaching students to follow a specific procedure or use a definition correctly, only through the judicious use of nonroutine problems can students develop their problem-solving ability.

In Polya's formulation, the teacher is the key. Only a sensitive teacher can set the right kind of problems for a given class and provide the appropriate amount of guidance. Because teaching, too, is an art, no one can program or otherwise mechanize the teaching of problem solving; it remains a human activity that requires experience, taste, and judgment.

There are those today who on the surface affiliate themselves with the work of Polya, but who reduce the rule-of-thumb heuristics to procedural skills, almost taking an algorithmic view of heuristics (i.e., specific heuristics fit in specific situations). A heuristic becomes a skill, a technique, even, paradoxically, an algorithm. In a sense, problem solving as art gets reduced to problem solving as skill when attempts are made to implement Polya's ideas by focusing on his steps and putting them into textbooks. Although distortion may not be inevitable when educators try to capture within textbooks and teachers' guides what is essentially an artistic endeavor, the task is clearly a difficult one.

Of the three themes, we see problem solving as art as the most defensible, the most fair, and the most promising. But at the same time it is the most problematic theme because it is the most difficult to operationalize in textbooks and classrooms. The problem for mathematics educators who believe that problem solving is an art form is how to develop this artistic ability in students.

Because of the caricature most people hold of John Dewey, we are reluctant to bring his work into the discussion. But we believe that Dewey's ideas about problem solving complement those of Polya. Dewey does not provide all the answers; in fact, he demonstrates that the situation is even more complex than one might think. But he does give valuable direction and another way to think about problem solving.

Although Dewey is clearly the major 20th century American philosopher of education and although he is blamed often and by various people for all that is wrong with American education, his influence on the school curriculum in general, and the mathematics curriculum in particular, has been minimal. A host of educators and psychologists ranging from Moore to Thorndike have praised Dewey's ideas; however, except for the lab school at the University of Chicago at the turn of the century, there is no example of his ideas being implemented as they were intended. What has been called progressive education did have an influence on the school mathematics curriculum, but the critique of progressive education Dewey (1938/1963) provided in *Experience and Education* shows how far from his basic ideas most other reformers were. Nonetheless, Dewey remains a major figure in American education because so many people have claimed a link with his work, including a few people who have actually taken the time to read Dewey's own writing rather than second-hand distortions.

Dewey did not often use the term *problem solving*, but it is clear that problems and problem solving were crucial in Dewey's view of education and schooling. What we refer to as problem solving Dewey usually called *reflective thinking*. Rather than being one way in which human beings deal with the world, problem solving was for Dewey the essence of human thought: Being able to think reflectively makes us human. Dewey distinguished among several types of thinking, but when he wrote *How We Think* in 1910 and revised it in 1933, to think meant to think reflectively.

Better than anyone else, Dewey combined the ideas of problem solving as means and problem solving as an end worthy of special attention. Dewey used much of *How We Think* to discuss how thought can be trained, so developing people's problem-solving ability was an important end for Dewey. But it was not an end separate from the progressive organization of subject matter that is a direct result of reflective thinking. That is, the same experiences that lead to the development of reflective thinking also lead to learning important subject matter. As simple and obvious as this may sound, our history of failures to accomplish the twin goals of helping students to develop problem-solving ability and organize the subject matter of mathematics is convincing evidence of how complex the task is.

Perhaps the greatest single misconception about John Dewey is that he was concerned with the child and not with subject matter. The problem, said Dewey (1902/1964), "is just to get rid of the prejudicial notion that there is some gap in kind (as distinct from degree) between the child's experience and the various forms of subject-matter that make up the course of study" (p. 344). Dewey argued that the child's experience "contains within itself elements—facts and truths—of just the same sort as those entering into the formulated study . . . and [even more important] the attitudes, the motives, and the interests which have operated in developing and organizing the subject matter to the place which it now occupies" (p. 344).

For Dewey, experience was central, problems arise naturally within experience, teaching and learning consist of the reconstruction of experience which leads to the progressive organization of subject matter, and the reconstruction of experience requires reflective thinking (or problem solving).

Like Polya, Dewey placed a great deal of emphasis on the teacher. Dewey did not reject the idea of teachers transmitting information to students. In fact, he said that "no educational question is of greater importance than how to get the most logical good out of learning through transmission from others" (Dewey, 1910, p. 197). Dewey said that the problem was how to convert such information into an intellectual asset. "How shall we treat the subject-matter supplied by textbook and teacher so that it shall rank as material for reflective inquiry, not as ready-made intellectual pabulum to be accepted and swallowed just as supplied by the store?" (pp. 197–198). Dewey answered his own question by saying that the transmitted information should not be something students could easily discover through direct inquiry; that the information "should be supplied by way of stimulus, not with dogmatic finality and rigidity"; and that the information "should be relevant to a question that is vital in the student's own experience" (pp. 198–199). According to Dewey,

> Instruction in subject-matter that does not fit into any problem already stirring in the student's own experience, or that is not presented in such a way as to arouse a problem, is worse than useless for intellectual purposes. In that it fails to enter into any process of reflection, it is useless; in that it remains in the mind as so much lumber and debris, it is a barrier, an obstruction in the way of effective thinking when a problem arises. (p. 199)

Teachers, then, can justifiably transmit information, according to Dewey, but only if the information is linked to the child's experience and problems that arise within experience. In a sense, subject matter is even more important for the teacher than for the student. The teacher needs to use her or his knowledge of subject matter in order to help the child reconstruct experience so that subject matter becomes progressively more organized for the child.

In "The Child and the Curriculum," Dewey (1902/1964) compared logically-organized subject matter to a map. The map, said Dewey, is a "formulated statement of experience" (p. 350). As students reconstruct their experience, they make a map of subject matter. They can also use maps constructed by others as guides to future journeys, but no map can "substitute for a personal experience" (p. 350). A map "does not take the place of an actual journey" (p. 350). Like Polya, Dewey was concerned with transforming logically organized subject matter into psychologically meaningful experience for students.

The process of thinking reflectively, of solving problems that arise within experience, was for Dewey, an art form. Dewey (1910) said that "no cast iron rules [for reflective thinking] can be laid down" (p. 78). He believed students should be "skilled in methods of attack and solution" (p. 78), but he expressed concern about an "overconscious formulation of methods of procedure" (p. 112). So, according to Dewey, skill is involved in reflective thinking, or problem solving, but reflective thinking itself is not a skill. In fact, Dewey expressed concern about too great an emphasis on skill acquisition. "Practical skill, modes of effective technique, can be intelligently, non-mechanically *used*," he said, "only when intelligence has played a part in their *acquisition*" (p. 52).

Furthermore, Dewey (1910) believed not only that students should be "skilled in methods of attack and solution" but also that they should be "sensitive to problems" (p. 78). That is, proper *attitudes* were very important to Dewey:

> Because of the importance of attitudes, ability to train thought is not achieved merely by knowledge of the best forms of thought. Possession of this information is no guarantee for ability to think well. Moreover, there are no set exercises in correct thinking whose repeated performance will cause one to be a good thinker. The information and the exercises are both of value. But no individual realizes their value except as he is personally animated by certain dominant attitudes in his own character. (Dewey, 1933, p. 29)

What is necessary, said Dewey (1933), is the union of attitude and skilled method. Dewey believed that the three most important attitudes to be cultivated are open-mindedness, whole-heartedness, and responsibility.

Developing such attitudes was so important to Dewey that he said if he were forced to make a choice between students having these attitudes and students having knowledge about principles of reasoning and some degree of technical skill in reasoning, he would choose the attitudes. "Fortunately," he said, "no such choice has to be made, because there is no opposition between personal attitudes and logical processes. . . . What is needed is to weave them into unity" (p. 34).

Dewey's connection to Polya seems clear. Polya (1981) suggested that "instead of hurrying through all the details of a much too extended program, the teacher should concentrate on a few really significant problems and treat them leisurely and thoroughly" (Vol. 2, p. 123). Dewey (1933) said that "fewer subjects and fewer facts and more responsibility for thinking the material of those subjects and facts through to realize what they involve would give better results" (p. 33).

Polya's and Dewey's belief that mathematics and problem solving are for everyone ties them to our professional forebears in mathematics education and the basic faith they had in human intelligence. Smith and Young could not or would not see in Dewey the opportunity to recast their view of the benefits of the liberal arts in light of a changing society. In a sense, we need to use the work of Dewey and Polya to recapture and revise the tradition embodied in the work of Smith and Young.

CONCLUSION

One consequence of recapturing this tradition is to take seriously the notion that problem solving really is for everyone. We need to look more at what children can actually do and to insist on broad evidence of what counts as ability to solve problems. In other words, we must study more carefully the role of context in problem solving. Some recent research shows that children who have trouble solving mathematical problems in school can solve comparable problems in out-of-school situations that are more meaningful to them. Taking seriously the notion that problem solving is for everyone means studying children in a variety of situations and providing examples to teachers of what children can do when an attempt is made to link subject matter to experience.

Again, neither Dewey nor Polya has all the answers, but they do help us with the basic issues of what problem solving is, why we should teach it, and how it is related to the progressive organization of subject matter. And their work provides for us a vehicle through which we might "critically examine our heritage as a field of study" by carrying on "a dialogue . . . with our professional forebears" (Kliebard, 1968, p. 83).

REFERENCES

Brooks, E. (1871). *The normal elementary algebra: Containing the first principles of the science, developed with conciseness and simplicity, for common schools, academies, seminaries and normal schools.* Philadelphia: Sower, Potts.

Chase, A. B. (1979). *The Rhind mathematical papyrus.* Reston, VA: National Council of Teachers of Mathematics.

Dewey, J. (1964). The child and the curriculum. In R. D. Archambault (Ed.), *John Dewey on education: Selected writings* (pp. 339–358). Chicago: University of Chicago Press. (Original work published 1902)

Dewey, J. (1910). *How we think.* Boston: Heath.

Dewey, J. (1933). *How we think: A restatement of the relation of reflective thinking to the educative process.* Boston: Heath.

Dewey, J. (1963). *Experience and education.* New York: Collier. (Original work published 1938)

Eicholz, R. E., O'Daffer, P. G., Fleenor, C. R., Charles, R. I., Young, S., & Barnett, C. S. (1987). *Addison-Wesley mathematics* (Book 5). Menlo Park, CA: Addison-Wesley.

Grube, G. M. A. (Trans.). (1974). *Plato's Republic.* Indianapolis: Hackett.

Hall, G. S. (1904). *Adolescence* (Vol. 2). New York: Appleton.

Holbrook, N. M. (1854). *The child's first book in arithmetic.* Portland, ME: Sanborn & Carter.

Kliebard, H. M. (1968). The curriculum field in retrospect. In P. Witt (Ed.), *Technology and the curriculum* (pp. 69–84). New York: Teachers College Press.

Milne, W. J. (1897). *A mental arithmetic.* New York: American Book.

Moore, E. H. (1926). On the foundations of mathematics. In R. Schorling (Ed.), *A general survey of progress in the last twenty-five years* (First Yearbook of the National Council of Teachers of Mathematics, pp. 32–57). New York: Columbia University, Teachers College, Bureau of Publications. (Original work published 1903)

National Council of Teachers of Mathematics. (1980). *An agenda for action: Recommendations for school mathematics of the 1980s.* Reston, VA: Author.

Polya, G. (1966). On teaching problem solving. In E. G. Begle (Ed.), *The role of axiomatics and problem solving in mathematics* (pp. 123–129). Boston: Ginn.

Polya, G. (1981). *Mathematical discovery: On understanding, learning, and teaching problem solving* (Combined ed.). New York: Wiley.

Polya, G. (1984). Fundamental ideas and objectives of mathematical education. In G. C. Rota (Ed.), *George Polya: Collected papers: Vol. 4. Probability; combinatorics; teaching and learning in mathematics* (pp. 569–578). Cambridge, MA: MIT Press. (Reprinted from *Mathematics in Commonwealth Schools,* 1969, pp. 27–34)

Sanford, V. (1927). *The history and significance of certain standard problems in algebra.* New York: Columbia University, Teachers College, Bureau of Publications.

Siefert, H. O. R. (1902). *Principles of arithmetic: Embracing common fractions, decimal fractions, percentage, proportion, involution, evolution and mensuration. A manual for teachers and normal students.* Boston: Heath.

Smith, D. E. (1900). *The teaching of elementary mathematics.* New York: Macmillan.

Smith, D. E. (1905). Movements in mathematical teaching. *School Science and Mathematics, 5,* 134–139.

Smith, D. E. (1909). *The teaching of arithmetic.* New York: Columbia University, Teachers College.

Stanic, G. M. A. (1984). Why teach mathematics? A historical study of the justification question (Doctoral dissertation, University of Wisconsin-Madison, 1983). *Dissertation Abstracts International, 44,* 2347A.

Stanic, G. M. A. (1986). The growing crisis in mathematics education in the early twentieth century. *Journal for Research in Mathematics Education, 17,* 190–205.

Strayer, G. D., & Upton, C. B. (1928). *Strayer-Upton arithmetics—Higher grades.* New York: American Book.

Thorndike, E. L. (1924). Mental discipline in high school studies. *Journal of Educational Psychology, 15,* 1–22, 83–98.

Thorndike, E. L., & Woodworth, R. S. (1901). The influence of improvement in one mental function upon the efficiency of other functions (I). *Psychological Review, 8*, 247–261.

Upton, C. B. (1939). *Social utility arithmetics—First book.* New York: American Book.

Wentworth, G. A. (1899). *Plane and solid geometry.* Boston: Ginn.

Wentworth, G. A. (1900). *New school algebra.* Boston: Athenaeum.

Young, J. W. A. (1903). What is the laboratory method? *Mathematical Supplement of School Science, 1*, 50–56.

For the Study of Mathematics Epistemology[1]

James G. Greeno

Stanford University

The topic of this conference, problem solving, is considered by many individuals as a separate issue from basic knowledge of mathematics. A common view held by many teachers is that the primary task of mathematics education is the transmission of knowledge of mathematics, and that learning to solve problems in mathematics is an important but secondary goal.

A different view is taken by most of the contributors to this volume. While we were asked to discuss various aspects of the teaching and evaluation of problem solving, we have taken this topic to involve the core of mathematical knowledge. Mathematical problem solving, in our discussions, has been considered broadly, as involving understanding of mathematics in ways that enable students to reason meaningfully with and about mathematical concepts and principles.

The contributions in this volume, therefore, raise the nature of mathematical knowledge as a crucial and central issue for research. Concern with the epistemology of mathematics is not new, of course. As Stanic and Kilpatrick (this volume) point out, alternative goals for the teaching of mathematical problem solving have been proposed and discussed for many decades.

The main point of my commentary is to suggest that questions in the epistemology of mathematics are of crucial importance for research in mathematics education. There are two sets of questions that overlap. One set of questions involves the nature of mathematical knowledge. The second set involves the beliefs and understandings that individuals have about mathematical knowledge and about themselves as learners or teachers of mathematics.

The study of mathematical epistemology can be an important research topic now, partly because some very significant new scientific resources for its study are being developed. Until about 1975, discussions of mathematical knowledge were conducted primarily by mathematicians and mathematics educators, and dealt mainly with the content of mathematics, methods of instruction, and general properties of mathematical understanding and reasoning. In the most recent decade or so, methods of cognitive science have been added to the tools used to analyze mathematical knowledge, and detailed analyses of cognitive processes involved in mathematics have been developed. Results of the analyses of cognitive processes are reflected in several papers in the conference, especially those of Bransford, Brown and Campione, Marshall, and Resnick.

A third set of methods for the scientific study of mathematical knowledge is being developed, and is reflected especially in the papers by Lave and Noddings in this volume. These papers, and some other recent writing that I will mention, are beginning to provide methods of understanding mathematical knowledge and learning in a broad context of personal and social factors. These discussions are beginning to develop a third way of thinking about mathematical knowledge, considering it as a collaborative practice.

My commentary is divided into two main sections. The first deals with the concept of a practice, considered as an idea in the epistemology of mathematics. This idea provides a theme that could organize research into the nature of mathematical knowledge. The second section discusses a question that concerns students' and teachers' understanding of knowledge and learning, which I call the question of personal epistemologies. This idea is concerned with what different individuals believe mathematical knowledge is, and how they understand themselves as learners and teachers.

THE CONCEPT OF A COLLABORATIVE PRACTICE

The idea of a practice contrasts with our standard ways of thinking about knowledge. We generally think of knowledge as some content in someone's mind, including mental structures and procedures. In contrast, a practice is an everyday activity, carried out in a socially meaningful context in which activity depends on communication and collaboration with others and knowing how to use resources that are available in the situation.

In her contribution to this volume, Lave begins to develop the idea of knowledge of school mathematics as a practice. Lave points out that the common view of school mathematics is knowledge that is deliberately decontextualized; its point is to be abstract so that it might be applied anywhere, but its learning is unrelated to contexts in which it might be used. As Lave has pointed out elsewhere (Lave, Murtaugh, & de la Rocha, 1984), everyday activities are organized by social and environmental structures, while mathematical knowledge from school is organized by a logic of definitions, axioms, and derivations.

An important complementary view is discussed by Noddings in her contribution to this volume and elsewhere (1984). Noddings develops a view of morality in which the fundamental human commitment is to situated, interpersonal caring, rather than to abstract principles of ethics. Crucial aspects of this commitment include engrossment and displacement of motivation, in which the individual appreciates another person's situation for its own sake and works on behalf of the other's needs and accomplishments. Noddings also considers an attitude of receptivity toward ideas in which the individual works intuitively by appreciating a set of ideas and allowing himself or herself to be influenced by the ideas and their structure. Teaching, in her view, is a caring relation in which the primary commitment is to students as individuals, and their growth through the conduct of intellectual projects in which the teacher plays a facilitating role.

An important idea in Lave's and Noddings's discussions, as well as in Schoenfeld's (this volume and 1987), is that the learning of mathematics in schools should be thought of as becoming skilled in the collaborative practice of mathematical thinking, and that the teaching of mathematics is primarily an engagement with students and a fostering of their receptivity to mathematical ideas and ways of thinking. The goal of teaching students to think mathematically is not a new idea, as Stanic and Kilpatrick document, but there is much more about it that we need to understand.

Analyses of Mathematical Practice

First, we need to understand what "thinking mathematically" really is. At this point the information we have about that is almost entirely anecdotal, consisting of the reflections of some mathematicians (e.g., Hadamard, 1945; Poincare, 1948), and some discussions of mathematics teachers whose instructional goals have been to provide their students with abilities to think mathematically (Fawcett, 1938; Lampert, in press; Polya, 1962; Schoenfeld, this volume). We need much more thorough analyses of the characteristics of the practice of mathematical thinking to develop goals and methods of teaching that will be productive.

One kind of analysis that will be helpful is philosophical and historical. An important example has been contributed by Kitcher (1984). Kitcher's goal was to develop an epistemology of mathematics. The key concept in his epistemology is an idea of a mathematical practice, and mathematical knowledge is to be understood as knowledge of mathematical practice. A mathematical practice includes knowledge of the language of mathematics and the results that are currently accepted as established. It also includes knowledge of the currently important questions in the field, the methods of reasoning that are taken as valid ways of establishing new results, and metamathematical views that include knowledge of general goals of mathematical research and appreciation of criteria of significance and elegance. Kitcher used this idea of a practice to account for important developments in the history of mathematics, showing that changes in questions, methods of reasoning, and general goals all occurred in reasonable ways during periods of important historical development.

Kitcher's analysis can be especially useful for thinking about education because he attended to ways in which mathematical knowledge changes. The task of education, of course, is to bring about changes in children's mathematical thinking. If we decide to adopt the goal of teaching the practice of mathematics, Kitcher's discussion can provide the beginning of a consideration of ways that mathematical practice changes and develops, which can be at least suggestive of patterns of growth that could be fostered in children's ability to think mathematically.

We also need to conduct analyses of the mathematical thinking that students can achieve in the kinds of learning settings that are provided by teachers such as Balacheff, Fawcett, Lampert, and Schoenfeld (see Schoenfeld, this volume). The use of cognitive-science methods has led to definite models of cognitive structures and processes involved in doing routine instructional tasks. Definite analyses also are needed of students' thinking when they construct new concepts or arguments, generate questions, or relate mathematical ideas to general intellectual goals.

Collaboration and Caring

A second set of questions involves interpersonal relations and social settings that bring about productive collaborative learning. Fawcett's (1938) and Lampert's (in press) teaching provide examples that seem to have the features of teachers' engrossment in students' thinking and students' engagement with ideas that Noddings (1984) emphasized in her discussion of teaching characterized by caring. We need careful study of such examples, including exploration of ways to develop skills of teaching in this way in the education of teachers, as well as ways to characterize and assess the personal and intellectual outcomes of teaching that depends on collaboration among students and their receptivity to the structure of ideas.

Levels of Mathematical Content

A third set of questions is in the domain of genetic epistemology; we need a genetic epistemology of mathematical thinking. This would provide analyses of the kinds of knowledge and understanding children need in order to learn to think generatively and collaboratively about topics in the curriculum.

We have a technology for analyzing the prerequisites of learning mathematics when that is viewed behaviorally (e.g., Resnick, Wang, & Kaplan, 1973), and there is a developing technology for analyzing prerequisites when mathematical knowledge is viewed as a set of cognitive structures and processes (e.g., Anderson, Boyle, Farrell, & Reiser, 1984). If we decide to adopt the teaching of mathematical practice as a goal, we will need to investigate the prerequisites of learning the various components of that curriculum.

The sequence of topics in the curriculum might look quite different if we considered prerequisites for learning the practice of mathematics, rather than its content. As an example, consider the learning of operations on rational numbers. The prerequisites for the procedure of testing whether two rational numbers are equivalent include multiplication of integers and knowledge of the rational-number notation. Appropriately, the curriculum introduces multiplication of integers and rational-number notation before equivalence of rational numbers is taught. What would be the prerequisites for generating the idea of equivalence of rationals and questions about different methods of testing equivalence? One interesting possibility might involve another equivalence relation on pairs of integers, the relation of equal difference. Constructing the idea of that equivalence relation would be an interesting addition to the curriculum in its own right, and could include generating tests in which (a,b) and (c,d) are equivalent if $a+d$ and $b+c$ are equal, or if c and d are obtained from a and b, respectively, by adding or subtracting a single whole number. Perhaps analyses of this additive equivalence relation would be an important component of background experience for students to be able to generate the idea of equivalent rational numbers and tests of equivalence. It also would allow for interesting questions about the parallel structure of the two relations, the need for negative numbers to obtain closure in one case but not in the other, and other quite general mathematical properties. In the curriculum that we use at present, negative integers are usually introduced well after rational numbers, and the equivalence of differences is given little or no emphasis.

Relation of Classroom and Everyday Practices

A fundamental research question in mathematical epistemology is the question of how the practices of school mathematics and everyday quantitative reasoning can be related. Lave, in this volume, gives an eloquent account of the chasm that separates them in their present forms. A growing body of research results provides many examples of skillful reasoning about quantities in everyday settings that are unrelated to the mathematics that individuals may have learned in school (e.g., Carraher, Carraher, & Schliemann, 1985; Lave, in press; Scribner, 1984). As Lave points out, application of school mathematics in everyday activity requires more than simply transferring an item of knowledge from one situation to another. It requires transforming a dilemma that arises in the everyday structure into terms that make the relevance of a mathematical concept apparent, and that concept is embedded in its own structure.

One important research question involves methods of teaching that could result in knowledge that students would be more likely to apply in ordinary situations. Traditionally, this has been understood as the problem of transfer, and significant progress has been made recently toward understanding ways in which instruction can lead to more transferable knowledge. Important contributions to this progress have been made by Bransford, including his contribution to this volume, by Brown (in press), and by Holland, Holyoak, Nisbett, and Thagard (1986). Holland and others (1986) have provided an especially provocative discussion of relations between formal rules for inference and everyday reasoning, especially in the domains of statistics and logic.

A second research question involves consequences of teaching mathematics as a practice, rather than as a body of content. Students who acquire a practice will have mathematical knowledge that is more generative than students who only acquire the content of mathematics in the form of concepts and procedures. We might hope that this greater generativity of their knowledge will result in a greater ability and disposition to use the concepts and principles of mathematics in their everyday reasoning. Whether this hope is realistic has to be evaluated in research. It is notable that in Fawcett's (1938) course in geometry, designed on the principle that students should construct a deductive geometry collaboratively, a significant effort was made in using the methods of deductive reasoning to evaluate claims made in everyday situations, including advertisements and application of statutes.

A third research question is harder to formulate in our present state of understanding, but might be very important. Anthropologists have taught us that the world that a person sees and understands is culturally determined in many ways. Groups of individuals within a society have different views of reality that we can call subcultures. It might be that effective education in the practice of mathematical thinking could result in individuals becoming members of subcultures in which their views of everyday situations would be imbued with mathematical structure. Professional mathematicians seem to find mathematical structure ubiquitously in their everyday experience. Perhaps significant levels of that kind of structuring could occur for all persons, if we could find appropriate ways to teach mathematical thinking in schools.

PERSONAL EPISTEMOLOGIES

In the first section, I discussed research issues concerning epistemology of mathematics itself. This involves ideas about what mathematical knowledge is and what is involved in learning it. In this section I address some questions about what individual students and teachers believe and feel about mathematical knowledge.

My discussion here rests on a conjecture that the epistemological beliefs that individuals have about knowledge, learning, and teaching have profound effects on the activities that they carry out in their efforts to learn and teach. This seems to be a plausible conjecture, but it is largely unsupported by evidence.

There are two published examples that support the point. In one example, diSessa (1985) found two students in a project physics course with sharply contrasting beliefs about knowledge of physics. One student understood physics knowledge to be largely procedural, involving ability to find correct answers to the problems given in the text. The other understood physics knowledge to be much more conceptual, involving grasping the meanings and relations of concepts. These two students spent their time and energy in quite different ways, as would be expected. The other example is given by Schoenfeld (in press), and involves a geometry teacher whose instruction for construction problems emphasized memorized sequences of operations and technical accuracy in placing marks used in the construction, and neglected constraints or relations with propositions proved in other parts of the course. The result was a strong belief by students that constructions and proofs reside in different compartments of geometry, and a resulting lack of use of theorems to guide work on construction problems.

A significant study of personal epistemologies was conducted recently by Belenky, Clinchy, Goldberger, and Tarule (1986). Belenky and others interviewed 135 women, 90 of whom were students in colleges and 45 of whom were clients of family agencies who were seeking information or advice about their roles as mothers. Interview questions included a wide range of topics, including inquiries about the participants' beliefs about knowledge and their learning. Examples included:

> "When learning about something you want to know (for example, how to bring up children, deciding who to vote for, and so on), do you rely on experts?"

> "How do you know what is right/true?"

> "Has your learning here [being in this program] changed the way you thnk about yourself or the world?"

Belenky and others (1986) identified a startling range of epistemological positions. These included silent knowing, where knowledge is limited to activities that one knows how to perform and learning is being shown how to perform them. A second position, called received knowledge, views knowledge as being held by experts and considers learning as reception from an expert. Subjective knowing involves judgments of validity by the learner, but justifications or rejections are based on intuitive responses that are relatively inarticulate. Procedural knowledge is obtained by definite methods, and has two varieties: separate knowing in which the focus is on ideas or information in themselves, and connected knowing in which the focus is on interpersonal acquaintance and relationship, including use of information about a person's ideas and opinions to come to know that person. Constructed knowing has a variety of sources and justifications, forming an integration of different positions.

The implications of distinctions like those made by Belenky and others (1986) have yet to be investigated in research, but it seems very likely that such differences are important. For example, it seems likely that students who view learning as a purely receptive process engage in quite different activities from those with an epistemology in which knowledge is the outcome of constructive procedures. As another example, individuals for whom knowledge supports interpersonal relations and knowledge of other persons probably are less engaged by presentations of information and activities in which knowledge is presented for its own sake, rather than forming a basis for interpersonal interaction.

Noddings's contribution to this volume includes a provocative suggestion regarding a possible source of gender differences in the learning of mathematics, involving personal epistemologies, when she suggests that young women learn that they are expected to be rule followers, while young men are expected to be rule makers. This could reinforce an epistemology of received knowledge and inhibit development of procedural knowing in mathematics and other domains. Belenky and others' (1986) discussion of connected knowing is related to Noddings's (1984) view of teaching as being primarily interpersonal, with the subject matter providing opportunities for intellectual growth, rather than the subject matter dominating concerns about students' personal welfare.

Another important program of investigation related to personal epistemologies is the research that Dweck (e.g., 1987) is conducting on children's theories of intelligence. Children differ in the extent to which they believe that how smart they are is a fixed quantitative entity, versus a quality that results from their activities and experiences. The fixed-entity theorists view intellectual tasks as occasions for exposure of their intellectual weaknesses, while the malleable-quality theorists view intellectual tasks as opportunities for intellectual growth. This has predictable effects on the children's tendencies to choose and engage in difficult intellectual tasks.

The research that has been done has barely scratched the surface of questions about the relation of individuals' beliefs about learning, the kinds of activities that they engage in as learners, and the consequences for the knowledge and capabilities they acquire. Some of the most intriguing questions may lie in the interactions between personal epistemologies and the social contexts of learning that are developed to foster students' acquisition of collaborative practices. But in any case, a new horizon of research and potential for educational effectiveness seems to be in view, as the resources of social science are combined with those of cognitive science, mathematics, and mathematics education for the study of the teaching and learning of mathematics.

FOOTNOTE

1. Supported by the National Science Foundation through NSF grant MDR–8550332.

REFERENCES

Anderson, J. R., Boyle, C. F., Farrell, R., & Reiser, B. J. (1984). *Cognitive principles in the design of computer tutors* (Technical Report #ONR–84–1). Pittsburgh: Advanced Computer Tutoring Project, Carnegie-Mellon University.

Belenky, M. F., Clinchy, B. McV., Goldberger, N. R., & Tarule, J. M. (1986). *Women's ways of knowing: The development of self, voice, and mind.* New York: Basic Books.

Brown, A. L. (in press). Analogical learning and transfer: What develops? In S. Vosniadou & A. Ortony (Eds.), *Similarity and analogical reasoning.*

Carraher, T. N., Carraher, D. W., & Schliemann, A. D. (1985). Mathematics in the streets and in schools. *British Journal of Developmental Psychology, 3,* 21–29.

di Sessa, A. A. (1985). Learning about knowing. In E. L. Klein (Ed.), *Children and computers. New directions for child development,* no. 28. San Francisco: Jossey-Bass.

Dweck, C. (1987). *Children's theories of intelligence.* Paper presented at a meeting of the American Educational Research Association, Washington, DC.

Fawcett, H. (1938). *The nature of proof.* National council of teachers of mathematics, thirteenth yearbook. New York: Teachers College, Columbia University.

Hadamard, J. (1945). *The psychology of invention in the mathematical field.* Princeton: Princeton University Press.

Holland, J. H., Holyoak, K. J., Nisbett, R. E., & Thagard, P. R. (1986). *Induction: Processes of inference, learning, and discovery.* Cambridge, MA: MIT Press.

Kitcher, P. (1984). *The nature of mathematical knowledge.* New York: Oxford University Press.

Lampert, M. (in press). Knowing, doing, and teaching multiplication. *Cognition and Instruction.*

Lave, J. (in press). *Cognition in practice: Mind, math and culture in everyday life.* Cambridge: Cambridge University Press.

Lave, J., Murtaugh, M., & de la Rocha, O. (1984). The dialectic of arithmetic in grocery shopping. In B. Rogoff & J. Lave (Eds.), *Everyday cognition: Its development in social context* (pp. 67–94). Cambridge, MA: Harvard University Press.

Noddings, N. (1984). *Caring: A feminine approach to ethics and moral education.* Berkeley, CA: University of California Press.

Poincare, H. (1948). Mathematical creation. *Scientific American, 179,* 54–57.

Polya, G. (1962). *Mathematical discovery: On understanding, learning, and teaching problem solving.* New York: John Wiley & Sons.

Resnick, L. B., Wang, M. C., & Kaplan, J. (1973). Task analysis in curriculum design: A hierarchically sequenced introductory mathematics curriculum. *Journal of Applied Behavior Analysis, 6,* 679–710.

Schoenfeld, A. H. (1987). What's all the fuss about metacognition? In A. H. Schoenfeld (Ed.), *Cognitive science and mathematics education* (pp. 189–215). Hillsdale NJ: Lawrence Erlbaum Associates.

Schoenfeld, A. H. (in press). When good teaching leads to bad results: The disasters of "well taught" mathematics courses. *Educational Psychologist.*

Scribner, S. (1984). Studying working intelligence. In B. Rogoff & J. Lave (Eds.), *Everyday cognition: Its development in social context* (pp. 9–40). Cambridge, MA: Harvard University Press.

Treating Mathematics as an Ill-Structured Discipline

Lauren B. Resnick

University of Pittsburgh

Educators and cognitive scientists commonly think of mathematics as the paradigmatic "well-structured discipline." Mathematics is regarded as a field in which statements have unambiguous meanings, there is a clear hierarchy of knowledge, and the range of possible actions in response to any problem is both restricted and well defined in advance. Cognitive scientists frequently contrast mathematics and mathematical logic problems—which must and can be solved within the narrow constraints of accepted postulates and transformations—with problems in such domains as the social sciences, where large amounts of external knowledge must be brought to bear, texts draw alternative interpretations, and conclusions can be defended rationally but not always strictly proven. Educators typically treat mathematics as a field with no open questions and no arguments, at least none that young students or those not particularly talented in mathematics can appreciate. Consider in evidence how little discussion occurs in typical mathematics classrooms compared with English, social studies, and some science class-rooms. Even when we teach problem solving, we often present stereotyped problems and look for rules that students can use to decide what the right interpretation of the problem is—so that they can find the single appropriate answer.

One result of this common way of teaching mathematics is that many children come to think of mathematics as a collection of symbol manipulation rules, plus some tricks for solving rather stereotyped story problems. They do not adequately link symbolic rules to mathematical concepts—often informally acquired—that give symbols meaning, constrain permissible manipulations, and link mathematical formalisms to real-world situations (Resnick, 1987a). Widespread indications of this problem include children's use of *buggy* arithmetic algorithms and algebra malrules and their general inability to use mathematical knowledge for problem solving. There is some evidence, however, that strong mathematics students are less likely than other students to detach mathematical symbols from their referents. These students seem to use implicit mathematical principles and knowledge of situations involving quantities to construct explanations and justifications for mathematical rules, even when such explanations and justifications are not required by teachers.

Research in other fields of learning supports this conjecture. Studies show, for example, that good readers are more aware of their own level of comprehension than poor ones; good readers also do more elaboration and questioning to arrive at sensible interpretations of what they read (e.g., Brown, Bransford, Ferrara, & Campione, 1983). Good writers (e.g, Flower & Hayes, 1980), good reasoners in political science and economics (e.g., Voss, Greene, Post, & Penner, 1983), and good science problem solvers (e.g., Chi, Glaser, & Rees, 1982) all tend to treat learning as a process of interpretation, justification, and meaning construction. As in these other fields, students who understand mathematics as a domain that invites interpretation and meaning construction are those most likely to become flexible and inventive mathematical problem solvers.

All of this suggests that we urgently need to begin investigating possibilities for teaching mathematics as if it were an ill-structured discipline. That is, we need to take seriously, with and for young learners, the propositions that mathematical statements can have more than one interpretation, that interpretation is the responsibility of every individual using mathematical expressions, and that argument and debate about interpretations and their implications are as natural in mathematics as they are in politics or literature. Such teaching would aim to develop both capability and disposition for finding relationships among mathematical entities and between mathematical statements and situations involving quantities, relationships, and patterns. It would aim to develop skill not only in applying mathematics but also in thinking mathematically.

To embark on such a venture requires an analysis of the various possible meanings of mathematical expressions. From one perspective the meaning of a mathematical expression is entirely contained within the formal proof system of postulates and acceptable derivations from those postulates. We establish the truth of a mathematical statement by proving it. If the initial assumptions and rules of proof are accepted, there is no ambiguity about whether a mathematical statement is true (although some statements may be "not yet proven" and, therefore, not yet of established truth). The meaning of the statement lies in its place within a system of statements—nothing less. Mathematical statements need not refer to objects or concepts as the statements of ordinary language normally do. This is the essence of the *formalist* position on the nature of mathematical knowledge (cf. von Neumann, 1985).

In its purest form, the formalist position would deny any necessary relationship between mathematics and physical reality. But viewed from another perspective, if mathematical statements really had no meaning beyond their relationship to other statements in the same formal system, mathematics could not be used to describe patterns or relations in the world or to draw inferences of new, not yet observed patterns and relations. Mathematics would be merely an intricate game, entrancing to those who loved it, but of no general value to society. Like music, it would be valued for emotional and aesthetic qualities, without reference and "utility." But mathematics is useful. It helps us describe and manipulate real objects and real events in the real world. Mathematical expressions, therefore, must have some *reference*. Numerical expressions refer to numbers—abstract entities which, in turn, stand in some regular relationship to actual physical quantities or enumerable events. A useful essay by Carnap (1956) explores the complications of a language that refers to abstract entities. Statements in a geometry proof refer to points, lines, angles, and triangles-abstract entities which stand in some regular relationship to actual physical shapes. Algebra equations refer to functional relationships between numbers and between the quantities or events to which numbers can be reliably mapped. These *referential meanings* of mathematical statements are what allow mathematics to be used.

Accepting as the reference of mathematical statements only abstract (but still *real*) entities such as numbers, points, and lines would permit alternatives of interpretation for mathematical statements, but their number would be limited. We encounter an explosion of interpretations, however, when we include as potential referents for mathematical statements the actual things in the world to which abstract mathematical entities can be reliably mapped—what we might term "situations that we can mathematize." If we are willing to treat mathematizable situations as in some sense the potential referents of mathematical statements, we must take seriously this explosion of possible interpretations. In other words, we must recognize that there is no single meaning for a mathematical expression and no single reason the relationships it expresses are true.

We usually regard mathematical problem solving, or at least the part of it that treats real-world problems, as a process of building a mathematical interpretation of a situation and then using a formal, fully determined system to manipulate relationships that have been "mathematized" by this interpretation. Our ability to do this depends upon treating the mathematizable situation as part of the potential referential meaning of mathematical expressions and doing so opens mathematics to interpretation and meaning construction of the kind that is an inherent part of all language use. Children initially learn mathematics by interpreting mathematical symbols in terms of situations about which they already know certain defining relations. And people who become good mathematics learners continue for some time to build justifications for mathematical statements and algorithmic rules that are couched in terms other than mathematical proof (cf. Resnick, 1986). They do this even though their teachers do not demand it, in fact may even discourage it because it seems to be a form of thinking too imprecise for mathematics. Could all children be taught to regularly think about mathematics in this justificatory, "ill-structured" way? What would be the effects?

THE NATURE OF MEANING CONSTRUCTION FOR MATHEMATICAL LANGUAGE

If mathematical expressions refer to real things, both abstract and physical, not just to a system of other mathematical expressions, it makes sense to think of them as a language. In this case our knowledge of natural language understanding can guide our thinking about mathematical language understanding. People do not understand natural language statements by simply registering the words. Instead they use a combination of what is said, what they already know, and various inference processes to construct a plausible mental representation of what the statement refers to. This representation omits material that does not seem central to the message; it also *adds* information needed to make the message coherent and sensible. The process of understanding natural language is an inferential, meaning *construction* process. So is the process of understanding mathematical language. As already noted, there are two domains of reference for mathematical language: the world of abstract mathematical entities and the world of mathematizable situations. The next two sections explore ways in which children might come to treat these two domains as spaces in which to construct plausible mental representations of the meaning of mathematical statements.

Mathematical Entities as the Referents for Mathematical Language

Constructing representations that involve mathematical entities can be difficult, because the mathematical entities are themselves abstract mental constructions. Furthermore, informal discussions about mathematical entities can be difficult, because, other than the mathematics symbols themselves, we do not usually develop vocabularies for discussing mathematics. Nevertheless, children sometimes can describe the meaning of formal statements and expressions in ways that show they think of the symbols as referring to these abstractions. Here is an example of a seven-and-a-half-year-old explaining why 2×3 and 3×2 both equal 6:

> What's two times three? Six. How did you get that? Well, two threes . . . one three is three; one more equals six. Okay, what's three times two? Six. Anything interesting about that? They each equal six and they're different numbers. . . .I'll tell you why that happens. . . .Two has more ways; well it has more adds . . . like two has more twos, but it's a lower number. Three has less threes but it's a higher number. . . . All right, when you multiply three times two, how many adds are there? Three . . . and in the other one there's two. But the two—that's two threes—but the other one is three twos, 'cause twos are littler than threes but two has more . . . more adds, and then the three has less adds but it's a higher number.

In the following example, the same child explains his strategy for making the quantity, 64, from various combinations of numbers. Asked how $23 + 41$ (written vertically on paper) could be rewritten but still equal 64, he first wrote $24 + 40$ and then continued:

I'm going one less than 40 and this one more . . . 25 plus 39. Tell me what you're doing now to get that. I'm just having one go lower; take one away and put it on the other. . . .I'm taking the 3 [from 23] away and making that 2 and putting it on the 41 to make it 42. Like that, I was going lower, lower, higher, higher. Okay, you gave me three examples of how you could change the numbers. Now why do all those numbers equal the same amount? Because this is taking some away from one number and putting on the other number. And that's okay to do? Yes. Why is that okay to do? Why not? Well, can you give me a reason? No, anyone can do that . . . Because you still have the same amount. You're keeping that but putting that on something else. . . .You're not just taking it away.

These examples reveal an awkwardness of expression characteristic of children discussing mathematical ideas. The child struggles to find—even invent—words to express his knowledge about the mathematical objects to which the formal statements refer. In part this reflects his lack of practice in talking about these mathematical entities. His knowledge of them is largely implicit, expressed more in the variety of things he can do with numbers than in a developed ability to talk about them (cf. Gelman & Greeno, in press).

Other examples of children talking about the mathematical objects to which formal statements refer appear in Magdalene Lampert's (1986) descriptions of her fourth grade mathematics classes. In those classes, children *argue* about the meaning of mathematical expressions, attempting to convince each other (and Lampert) that various arithmetic algorithms they invent are correct. This is an important ingredient of Lampert's classes. The children are not just *doing* mathematics. They are *discussing* mathematics, arguing about it, disagreeing about it. In short they are, within some important limits, treating mathematics as an ill-structured discipline in which multiple points of view are legitimate and proposals must be justified, not so much on the basis of their being correct as of their being sensible.

Situations as Referents for Mathematical Statements

Even more room for argument and discussion exists in the relationship between mathematical language and real-world situations, because the same mathematical expressions can refer to different situations. A simple subtraction sentence ($5 - 3 = 2$ for example) illustrates the three classes of situations that have become familiar to us from research on early story problems (e.g., Riley & Greeno, in press): *Change* situations in which a starting quantity (5) is modified by removing a certain quantity (3) from it; *Combine* (and *decomposition*) situations in which a whole (5) is broken into two parts (3 and 2); *Compare* situations in which two quantities (5 and 3) are compared and their difference found. The numbers in the expression refer to different kinds of entities in each of the three situations. Decomposition situations require only cardinal numbers. That is, the 5, the 3, and the 2 in a decomposition story problem all derive from measurement or counting operations. In change situations, the 5 and 2 are both measures (cardinals), but the 3 describes an operator, i.e., a number that transforms other numbers. And in the comparison situation, the 5 and the 3 are both cardinals, but the 2 refers to a third kind of number, one that represents a difference, a relationship between measures.

We have conducted several studies examining students' abilities to interpret simple algebra and arithmetic expressions in terms of situations. In the first of these studies (Resnick, Cauzinille-Marmeche, & Mathieu, 1987), we asked French middle school children to make up stories that could be represented by expressions such as $17 - 11 - 4$ or its equivalent, $17 - (11 + 4)$. Initially we were interested in whether we could use children's knowledge of the relationship between stories and expressions to help them understand the reasons for symbolic algebra rules such as the "sign change rule." We never reached the algebra goal, however, since many of the children were not able to relate arithmetic expressions reliably to stories. The most interesting aspect of the data for the current context of discussion is that many children were reluctant to treat the numbers in the written expression as anything other than expressions of cardinals. Some of the youngest children (11–12 years old) could not construct a simple story in which a child went out to play with 17 marbles in his pocket and lost 11, then 4 of them, in two successive games. For example, they told stories in which 6 marbles were lost, so that the child could have 11 marbles after the first game. Older children could generally construct the two-step marble-losing story, but many did not believe that they could combine the two operator numbers (11 and 4) to determine how many marbles had been lost in all. This difficulty, which echoes earlier findings by Vergnaud (1982, 1983) and Escarabajal, Kayser, Nguyen-xuan, Poitrenaud, & Richard (1984), suggests that by middle school the children had not reliably constructed interpretations of numbers as referring to anything other than cardinalities.

Our more recent studies (Putnam, Lesgold, Resnick, & Sterrett, 1987) attempt to confirm these surprising findings and extend the work on relationships between expressions and story situations to multiplicative as well as additive numbers. We interviewed 28 students from each of grades 5, 7, and 9. Both studies included three interview phases. In Phase 1 the child read several sets of three-story situations. In each set, two stories could be represented by equivalent formal expressions, but the expressions were not presented. The child was asked to decide which stories were equivalent and why, without actually solving the problems. Phase 2 assessed the child's knowledge of the equivalence of the formal expressions. The child was asked to judge as equal or not equal, pairs of expressions representing correct and incorrect transformations and then to justify each judgment. Phase 3 examined the child's ability to link the story situations with the formal expressions. Given a story situation and a set of three expressions, the child was asked to choose the expression best describing the situation and justify that choice. For the other expressions, the child was asked to modify the situation to fit the expression.

In both studies, the students successfully judged the equivalence of the story situations and justified the equivalences (Phase 1). Students were very poor, however, at judging the equivalence of the formal expression pairs (Phase 2). When explicitly asked (in Phase 3) to link stories with expressions, students could often do so, even when they had not spontaneously used stories to help them reason in Phase 2. This pattern of results suggests that many students have relevant informal knowledge that they do not normally draw upon in thinking about formal expressions, although difficulties like those in the earlier French study persisted. For these students, instruction focused on the task of interpreting mathematical expressions as mathematizations of possible real-world situations seems essential to their development as mathematical problem solvers. In such instruction, as in practice on more typical problem solving in which students are given situations to interpret mathematically, the key is learning to identify the mathematical entities that map to elements in the situation. In all such instruction, both the processes of meaning construction and the relevant situational and mathematical knowledge should be the focus of attention.

SOCIALIZING MATHEMATICS LEARNING

Several lines of cognitive theory and research point toward the hypothesis that we develop habits and skills of interpretation and meaning construction through a process more usefully conceived of as *socialization* than *instruction*. Psychologists use the term *socialization* to refer to the long-term process by which personal habits and traits are shaped through participation in social interactions with particular demand and reward characteristics. Theorists such as George Herbert Mead (1934) and Lev Vygotsky (1978) have proposed that thought is an internalization of initially social processes. Mead refers to thinking as *conversation with the generalized other.* Vygotksy describes learning as a process in which the child gradually takes on characteristics of adult thought as a result of carrying out activities in many situations in which an adult constrains meaning and action possibilities.

A small but growing number of psychologists, anthropologists, linguists, and sociologists have begun to study the nature of cognition as a social phenomenon. (See Resnick, 1987a, for a review and interpretation of some of this research.) In education, the best developed line of work on socialized learning is in the field of reading. Palincsar and Brown (1984), broadly following a Vygotskian analysis of the development of thinking, proposed that extended practice in *communally* constructing meanings for texts would eventually produce an internalization of the meaning construction processes in each individual. They used a highly organized small-group teaching situation in which children took turns playing the teacher's role by posing questions about texts, summarizing them, offering clarifications, and making predictions. These four activities are thought to induce the kinds of self-monitoring of comprehension that are characteristic of good readers. The adult's role in these reciprocal teaching sessions, although informal in style, is highly structured. In addition to facilitating the general process, the adult is expected to model problem-solving processes and provide careful reinforcement for successively better approximations of good self-monitoring behaviors on the part of the children.

Using a social setting to practice problem solving is a method shared by other investigators, at least some in the field of mathematics learning. (See Resnick, 1987 b; and Collins, Brown, & Newman, in press, for a more general review.) I have already mentioned the work of Lampert, who conducts full-class discussions in which children invent and justify solutions to mathematical problems. Lampert's discussions, like those in reciprocal teaching, are carefully orchestrated by the teacher and include considerable modeling of interpretive problem solving by the teacher. Schoenfeld's (1985) work with college students shares many features of the Lampert class lessons. In Schoenfeld's problem-solving sessions, groups of students work together to solve mathematics problems. The instructor works with them, often stepping in when students reach an impasse to restart the problem-solving process. The instructor's special role is to "think aloud" while solving problems, thereby modeling for students heuristic processes usually carried out privately, hidden from view. To facilitate this modeling, students sometimes generate problems for the instructor, and the instructor occasionally pretends more puzzlement than actually experienced in order to show how several candidate solutions may be developed and evaluated. In contrast, Lesh's (1982, 1985) problem-solving sessions share reciprocal teaching's small-group format for collaborative problem solving but have no teacher present. This means that Lesh's problem-solving groups benefit from children's debate and mutual critiquing, but children do not have the opportunity to observe expert models engaging in the process and are not taught any specific techniques for problem analysis or solution.

Another line of work, this one rooted in a convergence of Piagetian and European social psychology theory, offers further support for the idea that collaborative problem-solving experience ought to promote general cognitive development. The research of Genevan social psychologists (Mugny, Perret-Clermont, & Doise, 1981) has shown that peer discussion of certain classical Piagetian problems (e.g., conservation) can improve performance *even when both discussants begin at the same low level*. The importance of this finding is that it eliminates the possibility that a more advanced child simply taught a new response to a more backward child. Instead something in the conflict of opinions apparently sets constructive learning processes in motion (cf. Murray, 1983).

Socially shared problem solving, then, apparently sets up several conditions that may be important in developing problem-solving skill. One function of the social setting is that it provides occasions for *modeling* effective thinking strategies. Thinkers with more skill—often the instructor, but sometimes more advanced fellow students—can demonstrate desirable ways of attacking problems, analyzing texts, constructing arguments. This process opens to inspection mental activities that are normally hidden. Observing others, the student can become aware of mental processes that might otherwise remain entirely implicit. When Palincsar and Brown compared modeling alone with modeling embedded in the full reciprocal teaching situation, however, modeling alone did not produce very powerful results. Thus there is more to the group process than just the opportunity to watch others perform.

Something about *performing* in social settings seems to be crucial to acquiring problem solving habits and skills. "Thinking aloud" in a social setting makes it possible for others—peers or an instructor—to *critique and shape* a person's performance, something that cannot be done effectively when only the results, but not the process, of thought are visible. It also seems likely that the social setting provides a kind of *scaffolding* (Wood, Bruner, & Ross, 1976) for an individual learner's initially limited performance. Instead of practicing bits of thinking in isolation so that the significance of each bit is not visible, a group solves a problem, writes a composition, or analyzes an argument together. In this process, extreme novices can participate in solving a problem that would be beyond their individual capacities. If the process goes well, the novices can eventually take over all or most of the work themselves, with a developed appreciation of how individual elements in the process contribute to the whole.

Yet another function of the social setting for practicing thinking skills may be what many would call *motivational*. Encouraged to try new, more active approaches, and given social support even for partially successful efforts, students come to think of themselves as capable of engaging in interpretation. The public setting also lends social status and validation to what may best be called the *disposition* to meaning construction activities. Here the term *disposition* does not denote a biological or inherited trait, but rather a *habit* of thought, one that can be learned and, therefore, taught. Thus, it seems possible that engaging in problem solving with others may teach students that they have the ability, the permission, and even the obligation to engage in a kind of independent interpretation that does not automatically accept problem formulations as presented (cf. Resnick, 1987b).

There is good reason to believe that a central aspect of developing problem-solving abilities in students is a matter of shaping this disposition to meaning construction. There is surprisingly little research linking cognitive skills and disposition to use them. On the whole, research on cognitive ability has proceeded separately from research on social and personality development, and only the latter has attended to questions of how dispositions—often labeled *traits* in the social and personality research literature—develop or can be modified. Some recent work takes important steps toward creating links between the quality of thinking and dispositions. For example, Dweck (in press; Dweck & Elliot, 1983) propose that individuals differ fundamentally in their conceptions of intelligence and that these conceptions mediate very different ways of attacking problems. They distinguish between two competing conceptions of ability or "theories of intelligence" that children may hold. One, called the *entity* conception, treats ability as a global, stable quality. The second, called the *incremental* conception, treats ability as a repetoire of skills that can be expanded through efforts to learn. Entity conceptions orient children toward performing well so that they can display their intelligence and toward not revealing lack of ability by giving "wrong" responses. Incremental conceptions orient children toward learning goals, seeking to acquire new knowledge or skill, mastering and understanding something new. Most relevant to the present argument, incremental conceptions of ability and associated learning goals lead children to analyze tasks and formulate strategies for overcoming difficulties. We can easily recognize these as close cousins of the interpretive, meaning construction activities discussed here. Such analyses suggest that participation in socially shared problem solving should, under certain circumstances, produce dispositional as well as cognitive ability changes.

COLLABORATIVE PROBLEM SOLVING

We have begun a line of research that attempts to adapt the principles of reciprocal teaching, as developed by Palincsar and Brown (1984), to teaching mathematics problem solving. Using the reciprocal teaching procedure for mathematics problem solving is not the straightforward process it might initially seem, primarily because mathematics problem solving is more strictly knowledge-dependent than reading. Part of what makes reciprocal teaching work smoothly in reading is that the same limited set of activities (summarizing, questioning, predicting, clarifying) is carried out over and over again. Finding repeatable activities of this kind in mathematics is not easy. Polya-like heuristics (Polya, 1973), as Schoenfeld points out, are so general they provide little guidance for people who are not already good at solving mathematics problems. In reading activities, furthermore, children are rarely totally *wrong* but are more likely to be just weak—that is, while responses may not enhance comprehension very much, they do not turn it off course, either. In mathematics problem solving, however, children frequently come up with incorrect formulations that do actively interfere with problem solving. Another difficulty lies in our inability to calibrate mathematics problems to increase the value of practice and assessment, because nothing equivalent to readability or grade-level difficulty allows us to group problems according to difficulty, as we do texts for reading.

We have, then, three main problems to solve in adapting the reciprocal teaching strategy to mathematics problem solving. First, we need to find a set of repeatable (thus general) yet adequately constraining (thus specific) activities that children can use and develop over many practice problems. Second, we need to find an appropriate balance between attention to general problem-solving strategies and processes and attention to the specific mathematical knowledge required for problem solving. Third, we need to find ways of grouping and calibrating problems for instructional and assessment purposes. My colleagues and students and I have been working on these problems in the context of a series of exploratory studies discussed briefly below. Although none of the work is definitive at this time, it is helping us to refine questions and develop research methods that will allow us to move into the relatively uncharted waters of research lying at the intersection of social and cognitive processes.

Knowledge-Dependence of Mathematical Problem Solving

In a series of four sessions, we asked a group of five fifth-grade children to solve collaboratively word problems involving some aspect of rational numbers, with children alternating as discussion leader. Sessions were tape recorded, with full transcriptions prepared. Study of the protocols revealed that two fundamental problems must be resolved if we are to adapt the principles of reciprocal teaching to mathematics. Both problems are rooted in the fact that mathematics problem solving is more strictly knowledge-dependent than reading.

First, in our problem-solving sessions, children frequently foundered because they lacked knowledge of relevant mathematical content, despite our efforts to match session content to what children were studying in their regular mathematics classes. Insecure basic mathematical knowledge at times dramatically blocked successful problem solving in our group. In one such instance the children drew a "pizza" and divided it into six parts, each called "a sixth"; they shaded three of those parts and then asserted that each shaded part was "a third." In such situations, the adult must either interrupt problem-solving processes to teach basic mathematics concepts or allow the children to continue with fundamental errors of interpretation. Neither choice seems likely to foster the proper development of appropriate meaning construction abilities.

Second, since part of what makes reciprocal teaching work smoothly in reading is the repetition of the same limited set of activities (summarizing, questioning, predicting, clarifying) and since it is not as easy to find such activities in mathematics, we had the adult leader introduce and repeat some very general questions, e.g., "What is the question we are working on?" "Would a diagram help?" "Does that [answer] make sense?" and "What other problem is like this one?" As is also often the case for more mathematically sophisticated Polya-like heuristics, however, these questions appeared to be too general to constrain adequately the children's efforts. They did not know *what* diagram to draw, for example, or they drew it incorrectly, or could not decide if an answer was sensible because they had misunderstood basic concepts.

Using Strategies Versus Talking About Them

In a second effort, we attempted to respond to each of these problems in a systematic way. The children involved were fourth graders who were asked to work in a group of 5 for 13 sessions, each led by the same adult. To control for children's lack of specific relevant mathematical knowledge, we used problems that invoked concepts from the previous year of mathematics instruction rather than the current year. With this control for unmastered mathematical content, we encountered very few occasions in which fundamental mathematical errors or lack of knowledge impeded problem solving.

Based on cognitive theories of problem solving, we identified four key processes that should be repeated in each new problem-solving attempt: (a) planning—i.e., analyzing the problem to determine appropriate procedures; (b) organizing the steps for a chosen procedure; (c) carrying out those steps; and (d) monitoring each of the above processes to detect errors of sense and procedure. For each problem to be solved, these functions were assigned to four different children. The Planner was charged with leading a discussion of the problem in order to set forth applicable strategies and procedures. Once the group chose a procedure, the Director's task was to state explicitly the steps in the procedure. These steps were then to be carried out by the Doer at a chalkboard visible to all. The Critic's role was to intervene if any unreasonable plan or error in procedure was detected.

The tactic of dividing mental problem-solving processes into overt social roles was not initially successful. Although our research community has specific meaning for such terms as *planning, directing,* and *critiquing/monitoring,* with the exception of the Doer role, these meanings were not conveyed to children by the labels, and we were not successful in verbally explaining them to the children. As a result, the roles became instruments for controlling turn-taking and certain other social aspects of the sessions, but did not give substantive direction to problem solving. And while children discussed the roles a great deal, they did not become adept at performing them. This points to a fundamental problem with certain metacognitive training efforts that focus attention on knowledge *about* problem solving rather than on guided and constrained practice in *doing* problem solving. Such efforts may be more likely to produce ability to talk about processes and functions than to perform them.

In session 6, we attempted a modification of the Critic role in order to deal with this problem. The Critic's function was now shared by two children, who received "cue cards" to use in communicating their criticisms. The cue cards read:

1. Why should we do that? [request for justification of a procedure]
2. Are you sure we should be adding (subtracting, multiplying, dividing)? [request for justification of a particular calculation]
3. What are we trying to do right now? [request for clarification of a goal]
4. What do the numbers mean? [insistence that attention focus on meanings rather than calculation and symbol manipulation]

The cue cards served to scaffold the Critic function by limiting the possible critiques and providing language for them. At first the children used the cue cards almost randomly and rather intrusively. During the seven succeeding sessions, however, children's use of the cue cards became increasingly refined, i.e., used on appropriate occasions and in ways that enhanced rather than disrupted the group's work. Nevertheless, at the end of 13 sessions there was no strong evidence that the overall level of problem-solving activity had improved substantially. It seemed appropriate, therefore, to turn away from this global approach to collaborative problem solving and try to develop more targeted forms of scaffolded problem-solving experience.

Forms of Scaffolding

A continuing problem in this research has been finding adequately controlled methods of study. Just recording and transcribing conversations among five children is a daunting task. Finding systematic ways to analyze these conversations that enable us to go beyond the anecdotal without losing their essential character in the service of quantification is even more challenging. One way of solving these problems is to conduct an interrelated series of studies, each designed to answer particular questions. With such a strategy, the program of research as a whole instead of any one study should produce strong conclusions. We are now conducting several studies in this spirit, each aimed at exploring how specific aspects of scaffolded problem-solving practice, together with discussion and argument, may shape the dispositions and skills of problem solving.

An initial study examined pairs of children solving problems particularly suited to classical means-ends strategies (cf. Newell & Simon, 1972). The limitation to pairs of children allowed us to record all conversation and develop a way of analyzing the conversation that captured key aspects of both the problem-solving structure and the social interaction. The problems given to the children, highly structured arithmetic story problems, were suitable for developing our method of analysis, although they limited the range of discussion and interpretation we would eventually like to develop in problem-solving groups. For the problems used, we were able to determine the probable paths of solution and points of difficulty in advance, and this guided our data analysis.

Participants in the study were 12 pairs of children, 3 pairs each from grades 4, 5, 6, and 7. Each pair of children met 3 times for 40 minutes and solved from 2 to 6 problems. To scaffold the means-ends problem-solving strategy, children were given a Planning Board on which to work. The board provides spaces for recording what is known (either stated in the problem or generated by the children) and what knowledge is needed (goals and subgoals of the problem). Using the board, children can work both "bottom-up" (generating "what we know" entries) and "top-down" (generating "what we need to know" entries). A space at the bottom is provided for calculation. Figure 1 shows a Planning Board with some typical entries. Each child writes on the board with a different color pen to facilitate tracking the social exchange.

At each grade level, one pair of children was assigned to each of the following three conditions:

1. Planning Board with Maximum Instruction. The children solved problems using the Planning Board. The adult demonstrated use of the Planning Board during the first session and then participated in the first two sessions by providing hints and prompts to further scaffold the problem-solving process and increase use of the board.

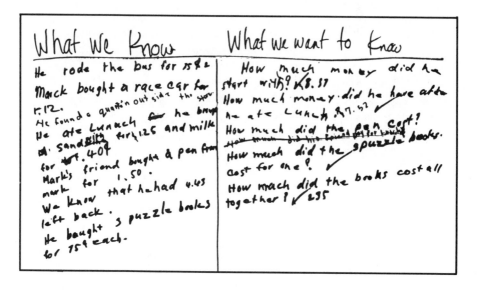

Figure 1. Planning board with typical entries

2. Planning Board with Minimum Instruction. The children solved problems using the Planning Board. The adult demonstrated use of the board and provided hints and prompts during the first session only.
3. Control. The children solved problems without the Planning Board during all three sessions.

Since this was a pilot study, we have results on only a few problems and can draw no strong conclusions about processes of interaction under the three conditions of scaffolding. It is possible, however, to use these initial data to demonstrate some possibilities for detailed analysis of collaborative problem solving. In the following paragraphs we examine data on the final problem of the third session in the study—a problem that all dyads worked without adult intervention.

Efficiency in using the board. We rated efficiency in use of the Planning Board on a three-point scale reflecting the extent to which the children reduced the language in the problem statement to a more succinct form. *Table 1* shows the results of this coding for the children who used the Planning Board with minimum and maximum instruction. As can be seen, fourth graders, regardless of amount of instruction, and fifth graders with minimum instruction mostly recopied the words of the problem onto the Planning Board. In contrast, seventh graders with maximum training tended to reduce the information to a symbolic form that could be entered directly into calculations. Not surprisingly, older children used the planning board more efficiently. It is encouraging that even the very brief training and practice in this study seemed to produce more efficient use of the board among all but the youngest children. With more extended practice all children could conceivably become very efficient—in the limited sense thus far considered—at using the board.

The board as a scaffold for goal analysis. The Planning Board was not meant simply as a recording device for students, however. It was intended

Table 1
Mean planning board efficiency by level of training and grade

	Grade			
Level of Training	4	5	6	7
Minimum	0	0	1	1.5
Maximum	0	1	1.5	2

Scale

0–children expressed information on planning board in full sentences, or, as worded in the problem;
1–children paraphrased, or expressed phrases with quantities and referents;
2–children expressed information symbolically

to prompt and support them in identifying goals and subgoals and clarifying the relationship of the given information to these goals. We wanted to examine the extent to which children in the different groups carried out such problem analysis. We began by delineating the goal-given structure of a problem in "expert" terms. *Figure 2* shows both this structure and the problem statement given to the children. Although apparently simple, this problem is deceptive. The basic structure of the problem requires *adding* the amount of money spent to the amount left at the end of the day to determine the money in hand at the beginning of the day. In basic structure the problem is a Riley/Greeno (in press) Change–3 problem, one of the most difficult additive story problems. The problem can be stated algebraically as $? - b = c$. But it is complicated by the fact that Mark also *gains* money during his outing, and this money must be *subtracted* from the amount spent before the amount spent is *added* to the amount left at the end of the day. The algebraic structure thus becomes $? - (b - d) = c$. Our research on children's ability to connect additive story problems with arithmetic statements (Putnam, Lesgold, Resnick, & Sterret, 1987) has shown this composition-of-transformation type problem to be among the most difficult for children to interpret. Thus this problem provides extensive complex material for fourth through seventh graders.

In the goal analysis shown in Figure 2, direct statements from the problem are shown without brackets; statements in brackets contain information the problem solver must generate (either implicitly or explicitly) to solve the problem. G_0 represents the "top goal" which, when reached, means that the whole problem has been solved. To meet this goal it is necessary to find out how much money Mark spent (G_1), how much he received in the course of the day (G_2), and how much he had left at the end of the day (G_3). G_1 has several subgoals (G_{11}, G_{13}, G_{14}), each asking for a specific portion of the day's expenditure. Information provided to help satisfy goals is coded as V (for givens); the subscripts specify the relevant goal or subgoal for each piece of information.

With this analysis in hand, it was possible to use the typed protocol of each dyad's problem-solving session to construct a record similar to a problem behavior graph (cf. Ericsson & Simon, 1984) showing the sequence in which the dyad generated and used the goals and givens of the problem. In our working records, we enter statements made by each subject in the same color as the subject's pen. This color coding enables us later to recapture information about the social aspects of the joint problem solving.

From the problem behavior graphs, different kinds of information can be extracted. For example, we examined the extent to which each of the dyads in the study noted the necessary information (goals and givens) in the problem statement and the extent to which they generated explicitly (in writing or orally) the necessary subgoals. For the problem under consideration here, all dyads specified at least 7 of the 9 pieces of given information,

Problem Statement:

One Saturday, Mark went shopping with some friends. He rode the bus to the shopping center for $.75. Mark bought a miniature race car for $1.12 and 3 puzzle books for $.75 each. He found a quarter outside one of the stores. The boys ate lunch while they were out. Mark bought a sandwich for $1.25 and milk for $.40. Mark's friend, Denny, talked him into selling his pen. Denny paid Mark $1.50 for it. After lunch, Mark rode back home on the bus. The ride cost $.75. After Mark got home, he counted his money. He had $4.43 left. How much money did he start out with?

Goal Analysis:

G_0: How much money did he start out with?

[G_1: How much did he spend?]

[G_{11}: How much did he spend on bus rides?]

V_{111}: He rode the bus to the shopping center for $.75

V_{112}: [He] rode back home on the bus [for] $.75

V_{12}: [He] bought a miniature race car for $1.12

[G_{13}: How much did he spend on puzzle books?]

V_{131}: [He bought] 3 puzzle books

V_{132}: Puzzle books [cost] $.75 each

[G_{14}: How much did he spend on lunch?]

V_{141}: [He] bought a sandwich for $1.25

V_{142}: [He bought] milk for $.40

[G_2: How much did he receive along the way?]

V_{21}: He found a quarter outside one of the stores [$.25]

V_{22}: Denny paid Mark [him] $1.50 for [his pen]

[G_3: How much did he have left?]

V_{31}: He had $4.43 left

G = Goals
V = Givens
[ ] = implicit

Figure 2. Saturday shopping analysis

exhibiting no differences due to grade level or treatment. This high level of noting the given information was common to all problems studied. The children were not so good, however, at generating goals. As shown in Figure 2, six subgoals could be specified for this problem. *Table 2* shows how many of these each dyad specified. As can be seen, no dyad was complete in its goal specification. It must be noted, however, that it is possible to properly use the information in V_{111}, V_{112}, V_{131}, V_{132}, V_{141}, and V_{142} without specifying the intermediate subgoals, i.e., without explicitly asking how much was spent on the subcategories of bus rides, puzzle books, and lunch. Thus it is only absolutely necessary to specify three subgoals (G_1, G_2, and G_3) in order to solve the problem. Both the Planning Board and the level of training apparently affected the number of goals specified. Groups with the board and with maximum training on it generated a much higher proportion of the goals.

Solution structures. Despite the greater proportion of goal generation, no dyad gave exactly correct responses to the Saturday Shopping problem. Our goal analysis and algebraic analysis of the problem allow us to examine the points of difficulty and nature of errors for each group. *Table 3* shows a structural analysis of the responses to this problem and characterizes each dyad's responses.

We have described the problem as being of the form $? - (b - d) = c$, where b = the amount spent, d = the amount received along the way, and c = the amount left at the end of the day. Since the amount left at the end of the day is directly stated in the story, the problem can be rerepresented as $? - (b - d) = \$4.43$. Correct solution requires adding the quantity $(b - d)$ to $\$4.43$. We look first at which dyads correctly *added* the result of their calculations on spending and receiving to the $\$4.43$, despite the minus sign in front of this quantity. All responses above the midline in *Table 3* were of this kind; those below the midline subtracted rather than added or carried out no arithmetic linking b and d to $\$4.43$. *Table 4* shows the data organized by grade and treatment. While we cannot determine statistical significance, it appears that the Planning Board with maximum instruction may have had some effect in supporting students' analyses of the problem at this level.

Table 2
Number of goals generated by dyads on "Saturday Shopping"

		Grade			
Condition	4	5	6	7	Mean
PB-Maximum	2	1	2	3	2.67
PB-Minimum	0	0	0	3	.75
Control	x	0	1	0	.33
Mean	1	.3	1	2	

Note: x = data not available

Table 3
Structural analysis of responses to "Saturday Shopping"

Problem Structure: ? − [b−d] = 4.43

Solution Structure[1]	Dyad										
	4C²	4M	5Mi	5C	5M	6Mi	6C	6M	7Mi	7C	7M
[b + d] + 4.43								X			X
[b + d₁] + 4.43	X		X								
[b + d₂] + 4.43					X						
[b] + 4.43							X			X	
[b − d] + 4.43											
[b + d] 4.43									X		
[b + d] (−4.43)				X³							
[b + d] − 4.43		X									
[b] 4.43					X						

[1]d_1 and d_2 refer to 1.50 and .25 respectively
[2]C—control, M—maximum, Mi—minimum
[3]Stated in protocol that answer is [b + d] but subtracted 4.43 from [b + d] on planning board.

Table 4
Dyads that added their (d) result to 4.43 in "Saturday Shopping"

Condition	Grade				Mean
	4	5	6	7	
PB-Maximum	0	1	1	1	.73
PB-Minimum	1	0	1	1	.67
Control	X	1	0	0	.33
Mean	.5	.67	.67	.67	

Note: x = data not available

We can also examine the extent to which students understood that the amounts received during the day (*d*) reduced the amount spent. They could show this understanding either by subtracting *d* from *b* before adding the result to $4.43 (following the form we have given: $(? − (b − d) = \$4.43)$ or by converting the problem to the equivalent form $(? − b + c = \$4.43)$, which requires adding *b* to $4.43 and subtracting *d*. No dyad did this correctly by either method. The arguments and elaborations children provided for each other, however, showed that for several of the dyads the question of what to do with the *d* quantities constituted a major point of discussion. Thus most of the dyads located the difficult aspect of the problem but could not resolve their questions successfully.

Social collaboration. We have been considering the problem-solving processes of the dyad as those of an individual. Now we turn to the examination of social interaction between the pairs of children, unpacking their performance according to which child engaged in various parts of the shared problem-solving process. This is possible because our sequential coding of each dyad's problem-solving process retained information about which child was responsible for each statement or written operation.

A question often raised in considering the effects of discussion and interaction on learning concerns whether children adopt highly specialized roles in such interactions and thus fail to practice all of the different activities that comprise successful problem solving. The result of consistent, long-term specialization in these situations might be that, while the group becomes effective at problem solving, individual members (or at least some individual members) could not function independently. According to the theory of scaffolded learning, early in their learning individuals ought to succeed in jointly solving problems that they cannot solve individually, but eventually they should take on more components of problem solution and function independently. Presumably then, in successfully scaffolded learning, specialization would be apparent during early phases but less so later.

Our present data do not follow dyads over long enough periods to track changes in specialization, but we can show how our analyses would permit us to determine such specialization. *Table 5a* (columns 1–3) shows overall utterances by the two children in each dyad and the number of utterances by each child (H for the child with the higher math achievement score, L for the child with the lower math achievement score). The amount of overt activity by the dyads varies considerably, with the total number of utterances ranging from 5 (dyad 7 Con) to 106 (dyad 6 Min). We examined the per-

Table 5
Analysis of verbal instructions

a. By Dyads

	Number of Utterances			Givens		Goals		Calculations	
Dyads	H	L	Total	H	L	H	L	H	L
4 Con	x	x	x	x	x	x	x	x	x
4 Min	7	4	11	0	1	0	2	2	3
4 Max	43	31	74	8	3	7	5	6	0
5 Con	8	2	10	0	2	0	1	1	1
5 Min	21	13	34	8	10	1	2	0	2
5 Max	20	31	51	4	0	1	1	2	12
6 Con	6	22	28	4	3	1	1	0	7
6 Min	49	57	106	11	18	1	0	14	4
6 Max	9	15	24	4	5	1	1	6	8
7 Con	5	0	5	0	0	1	0	2	2
7 Min	20	11	31	3	8	0	3	0	8
7 Max	7	4	11	7	3	4	1	3	0

b. Total Utterances by Condition by Grade

	Grade				
	4	5	6	7	Mean
Control	x	10	28	5	14.33
Minimum	11	34	106	31	45.50
Maximum	74	51	24	11	40.00
	42.5	31.67	52.67	15.67	

centage of talk by the dominant member of each dyad, but for this problem no clear pattern seemed attributable to either grade level or treatment condition. Table 5b shows that there was somewhat more total talk by the two Planning Board groups, especially by the more intensively trained group.

The remaining columns of Table 5a break down the interaction more specifically according to who states the givens in the problems (columns 4–5), who makes the goal statements (columns 6–7), and who does calculations (columns 8–9). There were wide variations among the dyads, but again no clear pattern seemed attributable to grade level or treatment condition. Given more problems, more stable assessments for each dyad might be made, and some pattern might emerge. In addition, studies following subjects over many sessions of shared problem solving could track changes in degree of specialization.

We are interested not only in role specialization, but also in the quality of the shared interaction over problem solving. One way to examine this is to identify statements by one member of the dyad showing some level of direct response to the other's problem-solving effort. These direct responses can then be contrasted with simple division of labor (such as we examined in the last paragraph) and purely parallel work, where each student solves the problem separately, despite the shared work space. In one analysis, we identified three kinds of direct response—repetition, argument, and elaboration. Of the three, arguments and elaborations correspond roughly to the two main ways in which socially shared problem solving is thought to facilitate learning—peer conflict and peer scaffolding.

Only a small minority of all utterances made while working on the problem were coded as arguments or elaborations. This is characteristic of other data we have examined and represents one of the difficulties of both studying shared intellectual activity and using it as a pedagogical method. There is a very low density of the kind of activity we believe is most instrumental in producing learning. Shared problem solving looks inefficient by usual pedagogical standards. These children, for example, could very probably work on more problems in a similar amount of time if they worked alone. Shared problem solving also requires tremendous patience from the researcher who would study it. Not only are the data harder to collect and transcribe and the sessions longer, but also the density of "interesting" events—events probably worth detailed scrutiny and qualitative analysis—is very low. Nevertheless much can be learned from such scrutiny. Important to our research agenda will be establishing what patterns of challenge and elaboration exist and how givers and receivers of challenges and elaborations benefit from the exchange.

ISSUES FOR FURTHER INVESTIGATION

In this chapter I have suggested a broad point of view on the nature of mathematical problem solving and illustrated some of the research questions and strategies such a point of view generates. To explore more fully the possibilities for and the difficulties of teaching mathematics as an ill-structured discipline, we need continuing research of several kinds. My concluding statements identify some of the questions requiring additional research.

Natural Language and Mathematical Language

At the heart of the suggestion that we teach mathematics as an ill-structured discipline lies the proposal that talk about mathematical ideas should become a much more central part of students' mathematics experience than it now is. This will inevitably entail greater use of ordinary language, rather than the specialized language and notation of mathematics, in mathematics classrooms. The ways in which ordinary language expresses mathematical ideas have been little studied. We know that under current teaching conditions students have little opportunity to develop a vocabulary that expresses their implicit knowledge of mathematical concepts. In what ordinary language terms can mathematical ideas be discussed? What complications can we expect as we begin to talk more with students about mathematics?

Recent work by Kintsch and Greeno (1985) uses the rich body of cognitive theory about how people interpret and make sense of texts to explain how children understand arithmetic story problems. Kintsch's work shows how children at different levels of linguistic and mathematical competence use story problem texts to construct representations of quantities and their relationships. This work represents a valuable first joining of cognitive research on mathematics problems and on language understanding. It focuses on a narrow band of problems, however, and on textual forms that are so stereotyped as to function almost as quasi-formalisms. To solve these problems, students must learn to interpret the special linguistic code in which story problems are expressed. But this kind of special code is unlikely to be the vehicle for active discussions of mathematical relationships or concepts.

When students themselves generate linguistic expressions of mathematical arguments, we move closer to natural language discussion of mathematics. A recent book by Eleanor Wilson Orr (1987), a teacher who has for many years required students studying algebra and geometry to develop informal, natural language justifications for problems they work, describes some of the difficulties that may be encountered in such a program. Orr's book documents the ways in which some students' language may fail to encode precisely key mathematical relationships. These relationships include distinctions between distances and locations, between directions of movement, and between quantities and differences among quantities. Orr is concerned that some students may be particularly poor at expressing these mathematical relationships linguistically. Researchers interested in mathematics problem solving should consider this fundamental question about the relationship between natural language and mathematical thought. The success and difficulties of a mathematics teaching program that has been grounded in natural language expression will suggest many new questions for systematic investigation.

Social Engineering

How can we profitably organize collaborative problem solving and other forms of mathematical talk and discussion, given typical teacher-student ratios of 1 adult to 25 or 30 students? An apparently simple answer—having groups of students work problems independently of the teacher—seems unlikely to prove successful as the sole or even the major mode in which students talk about mathematical ideas. There does not yet exist a body of research that examines patterns of students' activity over extended periods of collaborative work. It seems likely, however, that left to themselves students will often fail to generate productive ideas and may allow one or two strong students to do the group's work rather than supporting everyone's learning needs. Most cooperative learning efforts have found it necessary to carefully engineer ways of posing questions, grouping students, and providing incentives in order to develop productive patterns of cooperative intellectual behavior. Slavin (1983), for example, has developed a successful system of cooperative team learning. Children are organized into heterogeneous ability teams that study together and coach each other; individuals then compete against others of about the same ability from other teams to earn points for their study teams. The homogeneous ability competitions allow even the weaker students to earn points for their teams and thereby motivate the study teams to help each student learn. This system works well for highly-structured learning tasks where students can easily tutor one another through drill and rehearsal. Might it also work for much more ill-structured problem solving, where what is to be learned is a general approach and a set of heuristics that cannot be so easily specified and rehearsed? We do not know. We must find out.

Edward A. Silver (personal communication, June 1987) has suggested another form of classroom social engineering that seems promising and particularly well suited to open-ended problem solving. In Silver's plan, a problem is posed to an entire class. Students initially try to work it alone. Then they work in pairs; then pairs are joined to make quartets of students who compare, share, and rework ideas. A whole class discussion of the problem can next be used to merge and rework the quartets' ideas, but the final solutions are left to quartets, pairs, and, eventually, individual students. This organization forces individual students to formulate initial ideas but uses successively larger groups as vehicles for confrontation and enlargement of ideas. The whole class discussion allows the teacher to help students organize ideas, suggest new approaches, raise questions, and otherwise orchestrate and nurture the problem solving of groups and individuals. Effective use of this and similar schemes will require detailed investigation of the nature of student interactions in various work phases and of the outcomes of extended participation in such activities for children of different characteristics.

Integrating Strategy and Content in Problem Solving

Future research must also concentrate on how to integrate teaching fundamental mathematical concepts with teaching problem solving. As indicated earlier, if students do not know key concepts on which a solution might be based, their problem-solving efforts can go badly awry. In our research, we found that one solution was to base problem-solving sessions on concepts that had been well learned a year or two earlier. This allowed students to focus on strategies of problem analysis and interpretation, key components of problem solving. Yet long-term or exclusive reliance on such a pedagogical technique might lead students to view problem solving as a game or application that is optional for those who have learned the "real" content and not as an integral part of mathematics.

One way to avoid this difficulty and to integrate problem-solving and sense-making activites fully with the main body of students' mathematics learning is to use discussion and sense-making activities to introduce and develop basic mathematical content. Lampert has taken this approach in her classroom work. It is typical there to base an entire class lesson on working out only one to three problems. In the course of a class period, children propose and evaluate multiple solutions under the teacher's careful guidance. In classes I have observed, the discussion was punctuated with periods in which children worked out solutions individually and recorded some of the solutions agreed upon by the group. We need research on lessons such as Lampert's and those of the Japanese, research that tells us how expert teachers direct and manage discussions, how children of differing abilities and learning characteristics participate in the discussions, and what children of various types learn from their participation. We also need experimentation and analysis that will provide sharper pedagogical guidelines for conducting lessons in this discussion/problem-solving mode, including a careful working out of the kinds of problems and concepts that can profitably be taught in this way. We need, in other words, a much more extensive base of pedagogical lore for discussion-based conceptual teaching than now exists, supported by the kind of theoretical analyses that researchers can provide.

Contextualizing Problem Solving

Another approach to integrating conceptual and problem-solving activities is to try to develop more contextualized problems for classroom use. Some of what appear to be conceptual deficiencies may derive more from children's difficulty in working in a decontextualized classroom situation than from complete lack of mathematical understanding. As Lave, Smith, and Butler (this volume) suggest, people often engage in successful mathematical reasoning when working within a specific context of action and decision. In such cases, they often use mathematical knowledge that they do not—perhaps cannot—bring to bear on the kind of decontextualized problems presented in the classroom. Can ways be found to make classroom mathematics approximate the contextualized mathematics in which people engage outside school?

Traditionally story problems have been used with this intent. In such use, the stories are intended to evoke familiar situations in which mathematics might be applied. Students are, in effect, invited to imagine themselves elsewhere and consider how the mathematics they know might be used in that situation. Considerable evidence now exists, however, that story problems do not effectively simulate the out-of-school contexts in which mathematics is used. As already noted, the language of story problems is highly specialized and functions as almost a quasi-formalism, requiring special linguistic knowledge and distinct effort on the part of the student to build a representation of the situation described. Furthermore, this representation, once built, is a stripped down and·highly schematic one that does not share the material and contextual cues of the real situation.

If we are to engage students in contextualized mathematics problem solving, we must find ways to create in the classroom situations of sufficient complexity and engagement that they become mathematically engaging contexts in their own right. Several of the approaches to mathematical problem solving described in this chapter and elsewhere in this volume represent efforts in this direction. Some of Lesh's extended and not fully defined problems, for example, can be thought of not as stories containing mathematics problems, but as settings in which planning a project (e.g., wallpapering a room) engages a substantial amount of mathematical knowledge and strategy. Similarly Bransford's and his colleagues' (this volume) proposal for using videodisc presentations can be viewed as an effort to bring complex situations into the classroom. The realism and engaging character of the filmed sequences should more fully contextualize mathematical activity than verbal presentations of the same story line would. They should also permit students to develop their own questions, not only solve problems posed by others.

Computerized simulation environments can also provide settings for highly contextualized mathematical activity. College students who work in simulated microeconomic environments, for example, do mathematical work in the context of the simulation world. To the extent that they engage with this world, accepting its rules and constraints, they are doing contextualized mathematics in much the same way that Lave's supermarket shoppers and weightwatcher cooks are. Computer and board games in which calculation, estimation, or other mathematical processes are required also can be thought of as contextualizing devices. Such games do not so much simulate external environments as provide fully engaging environments in their own right. Children who play computer games such as "How the West Was Won" or board games such as "Parchisi"—both games that require strategic use of number combinations—are engaging in highly contextualized arithmetic problem solving. In much the same way, students captivated by the equation/graph problems of Dugdale's (1982) "Green Globs" game engage in highly contextualized algebra problem solving. These various forms of contextualized mathematical problem solving in the classroom need further development and study.

Scaffolding Supports for Problem Solving

As discussed earlier in this chapter and elsewhere in this volume, students can often engage successfully in thinking and problem solving that is "beyond their capacities," if their activity receives adequate support either from the social context in which it is carried out or from special tools and displays that scaffold their early efforts. In current cognitive theory, scaffolding is a provocative but not fully developed idea. As introduced by Wood and Middleton (1975), the term *scaffolding* referred to the support for a child's cognitive activity provided by an adult when child and adult performed a task together. In that original use, scaffolding described a natural way that adults interact with children; little could be said prescriptively. Brown and others have expanded the meaning of the term to include the support provided by other children in joint problem-solving activity. This is a significant extension, for it implies that several individuals, none of whom are expert at a task, can nevertheless scaffold each other's inexpert performance, eventually resulting in independent performance by all individuals. This idea has not yet been rigorously tested. In the Palincsar and Brown (1984) interventions, an adult worked with each group of children. Research on groups of children working without an adult has not usually included pretests that establish the entering competence of individual members of the group. As a result, the group members may not be strictly peers; instead, some children may serve as expert scaffolders for the less expert in the group. These various forms of socially mediated scaffolding need thorough investigation if the notion of scaffolding is to move from a description of a natural phenomenon to a prescription for teaching in which details of scaffolding strategies and their conditions of application can be specified.

Our own recent work has introduced yet another extension of the scaffolding metaphor. We have proposed that record-keeping and other tools can also be viewed as scaffolds for learning. This conception, thus far tried with only the simple planning board tool, suggests that many pedagogical devices can be considered and treated as learning scaffolds. Representational devices that display an underlying theoretical structure, for example, can be treated as tools for supporting problem solving in early phases of learning. A number of *microworlds*—graphic displays that "objectify" mathematical entities such as numbers and operators (e.g., Ohlsson, 1987; Peled & Resnick, 1987)—can function as scaffolds. These displays can also support conversation between two or more individuals about mathematical ideas, thus allowing two forms of scaffolding—social and tool—to function together. In an example drawn from physics rather than mathematics, Behrend, Singer, and Roschelle (1988) have described in some detail the growth of concepts about projectile motion in two 9-year-olds as the result of their joint investigation of a graphic system that represents trajectories as a function of force vectors. Scaffolding tools of these types need to be developed and explored more fully as part of a full agenda of research on mathematical problem solving.

Socializing Problem Solving: A Long-Term Agenda

As suggested earlier in this chapter, the reconceptualization of thinking and learning that is emerging from the body of recent work on the nature of cognition suggests that becoming a good mathematical problem solver—becoming a good thinker in any domain—may be as much a matter of acquiring the habits and dispositions of interpretation and sense-making as of acquiring any particular set of skills, strategies, or knowledge. If this is so, we may do well to conceive of mathematics education less as an instructional process (in the traditional sense of teaching specific, well-defined skills or items of knowledge), than as a socialization process. In this conception, people develop points of view and behavior patterns associated with gender roles, ethnic and familial cultures, and other socially defined traits. When we describe the processes by which children are socialized into these cultural patterns of thought, affect, and action, we describe long-term patterns of interaction and engagement in a social environment, not a series of lessons in how to behave or what to say on particular occasions. If we want students to treat mathematics as an ill-structured discipline—making sense of it, arguing about it, and creating it, rather than merely doing it according to prescribed rules—we will have to socialize them as much as to instruct them. This means that we cannot expect any brief or encapsulated program on problem solving to do the job. Instead we must seek the kind of long-term engagement in mathematical thinking that the concept of socialization implies. This challenge is larger than those normally confronted by any single discipline of the school curriculum. It is, however, a challenge whose time has come. The theoretical bases for a conceptualization of mathematics as a way of thinking, rather than a set of skills, now exist, along with an emerging body of research and theory on the links between social and cognitive aspects of thought and learning. Building on these foundations, research and development on teaching mathematics problem solving may well lead the way in stimulating important changes in educational practice.

REFERENCES

Behrend, S., Singer, J., & Roschelle, J. (1988). *A methodology for the analysis of collaborative learning in a physics microworld.* Unpublished manuscript, University of Pittsburgh, Learning Research and Development Center.

Brown, A. L., Bransford, J. D., Ferrara, R. A., & Campione, J. C. (1983). Learning, remembering, and understanding. In J. H. Flavell & E. M. Markman (Eds.), *Cognitive development* (Vol. III of P. H. Mussen, Ed., *Handbook of child psychology,* pp. 77–166). New York: Wiley.

Carnap, R. (1956). Empiricism, semantics, and ontology. In R. Carnap (Ed.), *Meaning and necessity* (2nd ed.). Chicago: University of Chicago Press.

Chi, M. T. H., Glaser, R., & Rees, E. (1982). Expertise in problem solving. In R. Sternberg (Ed.), *Advances in the psychology of human intelligence* (Vol. 1). Hillsdale, NJ: Lawrence Erlbaum & Associates.

Collins, A., Brown, J.S., & Newman, S. E. (in press). Cognitive apprenticeship: Teaching the craft of reading, writing, and mathematics. In L. B. Resnick (Ed.), *Knowing and learning: Issues for a cognitive science of instruction.* Hillsdale, NJ: Erlbaum.

Dugdale, S. (1982). Green globs: A microcomputer application for the graphing of equations. *Mathematics Teacher,* 208–214.

Dweck, C.S. (in press). Motivation. In A. Lesgold & R. Glaser (Eds.), Cognitive psychology of education: tutorial essays. Hillsdale, NJ: Erlbaum.

Dweck, C.S., & Elliot, E.S. (1983). Achievement motivation. In E. M. Hetherington (Ed.), *Socialization, personality, and social development* (Vol. IV of P.H. Mussen, Ed., *Handbook of child psychology,* pp. 643–692). New York: Wiley.

Ericsson, K. A., & Simon, H. A. (1984). *Protocol analysis: Verbal reports as data.* Cambridge, MA: MIT Press.

Escarabajal, M. C., Kayser, D., Nguyen-xuan, A., Poitrenaud, S., & Richard, J. F. (1984). *Comprehension et resolution de problemes arithmetiques additifs. Les Modes De Raisonnement.* Association Pour La Recherche Cognitive, Orsay, France.

Flower, L. S., & Hayes, J. R. (1983). The dynamics of composing: Making plans and juggling constraints. In L. Gregg & E. Sternberg (Eds.), *Cognitive processes in writing: An interdisciplinary approach* (pp. 31–50). Hillsdale, NJ: Erlbaum.

Gelman, R., & Greeno, J. G. (in press). On the nature of competence: Principles for understanding in a domain. In L. B. Resnick (Ed.), *Knowing and learning: Issues for a cognitive science of instruction.* Hillsdale, NJ: Erlbaum.

Kintsch, W., & Greeno, J. G. (1985). Understanding and solving word arithmetic problems. *Psychological Review,* 92, 109–129.

Lampert, M. (1986). Knowing, doing, and teaching multiplication. *Cognition and Instruction,* 3, 305–342.

Lesh, R. (1982). *Metacognition in mathematical problem solving.* Unpublished manuscript, Northwestern University.

Lesh, R. (1985). Processes, skills, and abilities needed to use mathematics in everyday situations. *Education and Urban Society,* 17 (4), 439–446.

Mead, G. H. (1934). *Mind, self, and society.* Chicago: University of Chicago Press.

Mugny, G., Perret-Clermont, A., & Doise, W. (1981). Interpersonal coordinations and sociological differences in the construction of the intellect. In G. M. Stephenson & J. M. Davis (Eds.), *Progress in applied social psychology* (Vol. 1, pp. 315–343). New York: Wiley.

Murray, F. B. (1983). Learning and development through social interaction and conflict: A challenge to social learning theory. In L. Liben (Ed.), *Piaget and the foundation of knowledge* (pp. 231–247). Hillsdale, NJ: Erlbaum.

Newell, A., & Simon, H. A. (1972). *Human problem solving*. Englewood Cliffs, NJ: Prentice-Hall.

Ohlsson, S. (1987). Sense and reference in the design of interactive illustrations for rational numbers. In R. W. Lawler & M. Yazdani (Eds.), *Artificial intelligence and education. Volume One. Learning environments and tutoring systems*. Norwood, NJ: Ablex.

Orr, E. W. (1987). *Twice as less*. New York: Norton.

Palincsar, A. S., & Brown, A. L. (1984). Reciprocal teaching of comprehension-fostering and comprehension-monitoring activities. *Cognition and Instruction, 1,* 117–175.

Peled, I., & Resnick, L. B. (1987). Building semantic computer models for teaching number systems and word problems. In J. C. Bergeron, N. Herscovics, & C. Kieran (Eds.), *Proceedings of the 11th International Conference of the Psychology of Mathematics Education, 2,* 184–190.

Polya, G. (1973). *How to solve it* (2nd ed.). New York: Doubleday.

Putnam, R. T., Lesgold, S. B., Resnick, L. B., & Sterrett, S. G. (1987, July). *Understanding sign change transformation*. Paper presented at the Eleventh Annual Conference of the International Group for the Psychology of Mathematics Education, Montreal.

Resnick, L. B. (1986). The development of mathematical intuition. In M. Perlmutter (Ed.), *Perspectives on intellectual development: The Minnesota Symposia on Child Psychology* (Vol. 19, pp. 159–194). Hillsdale, NJ: Erlbaum.

Resnick, L. B. (in press,a). Constructing knowledge in school. In L. S. Liben & D. H. Feldman (Eds.), *Development and learning: Conflict or congruence?*. Hillsdale, NJ: Erlbaum.

Resnick, L. B. (in press,b). Learning in school and out. *Educational Researcher.*

Resnick, L. B. (1987a). *Education and learning to think*. Washington, D.C.: National Academy Press.

Resnick, L. B., Cauzinille-Marmeche, E., & Mathieu, J. (1987b). Understanding algebra. In J. A. Sloboda & D. Rogers (Eds.), *Cognitive processes in mathematics* (pp. 169–203). New York: Oxford University Press.

Riley, M. S., & Greeno, J. G. (in press). Developmental analysis of understanding language about quantitatives and solving problems. *Cognition and Instruction.*

Schoenfeld, A. (1985). *Mathematical problem solving*. New York: Academic Press.

Slavin, R. (1983). *Cooperative learning*. New York: Longman.

Vergnaud, G. (1982). A classification of cognitive tasks and operations of thought involved in addition and subtraction problems. In T. P. Carpenter, J. M. Moser, & T. A. Romberg (Eds.), *Addition and subtraction: A Cognitive perspective* (pp. 39–59). Hillsdale, NJ: Erlbaum.

Vergnaud, G. (1983). Multiplicative structures. In H. P. Ginsburg (Ed.), *The development of mathematical thinking* (pp. 128–174). New York: Academic Press.

von Neumann, J. (1985). The formalist foundation of mathematics. In P. Benacerraf & H. Putnam (Eds.), *Philosophy of mathematics: Selected readings* (2nd ed., pp. 61–65). New York: Cambridge University Press.

Voss, J. F., Greene, T. R., Post, T. A., & Penner, B. C. (1983). Problem-solving skill in the social sciences. In G. H. Bauer (Ed.), *The psychology of learning and motivation: Advances in research learning* (Vol. 17, pp. 165–213). New York: Academic Press.

Vygotsky, L. S. (1978). *Mind in society*. Cambridge, MA: Harvard University Press.

Wood, D., Bruner, J. S., & Ross, G. (1976). The role of tutoring in problem solving. *Journal of Child Psychology and Psychiatry, 17,* 89–100.

Wood, D., & Middleton, D. (1975). A study of assisted problem-solving. *British Journal of Psychology, 66* (2), 181–191.

Problem Solving as an Everyday Practice

Jean Lave, Steven Smith and Michael Butler
University of California, Irvine

Suppose we approach the next decade of research on the teaching and evaluation of problem solving by noting certain promising trends for research in the social sciences more generally. Some of these converge in common concepts, problems, and theoretical approaches. This seems a good sign, given the inherently interdisciplinary character of research on the teaching of problem solving. But these trends converge in ways that seem directly relevant to the subject at hand, offering new perspectives on teaching, learning, cultural transmission, the social organization of schooling, and relations between what goes on in the classroom and the world outside and after school.

In the broadest theoretical terms there is interest within anthropology and sociology in theories of practice (Bourdieu, 1977; Ortner, 1984), approaches that focus attention on relations between the situated construction of activity and knowledge in everyday settings and the political, economic, and social structuring in relation to which experience is formed. Within the sociology and anthropology of science much research is now focused on exploration of the practice of scientists at work, and new metaphors describe science as a craft (Krieger, n.d.; John-Steiner, 1985; Traweek, in press). The idea of mathematical proof is treated as the social practice of mathematical argumentation (Schoenfeld, 1985; Livingston, 1983). There is greater interest in the everyday problem-solving practices of the alumni of schooling (Carraher, Carraher, & Schliemann, 1982, 1983; Carraher & Schliemann, 1982; Scribner & Fahrmeier, 1982; Scribner, 1984a, 1984b; Brenner, 1985; de la Rocha, 1986; Murtaugh, 1985a, 1985b; Lave, in press). And in educational research, several developments point in similar directions to those above: The present political climate is one of reaction to the serious loss of initiative by teachers in the classroom. There is concern about the damaging effects of exam-driven instruction (e.g., Schoenfeld, 1985; Kilpatrick, 1986) and the unintended lessons about what constitute problem solving and mathematics that emerge in the course of standard-test-oriented instruction(Schoenfeld, 1985, 1987, in press). The need for mathematics teachers is increasing while their numbers are declining, and there is evidence of their lack of preparation. Constructivists are developing critiques of content-free analyses of teaching (e.g., Confrey, 1986). Those who have studied the teaching and learning of problem solving most closely express great dissatisfaction with the superficial level of understanding of fundamental principles of mathematics problem solving and have done much to characterize their sources.

A number of recent proposals that express concern about these issues suggest that we might want children to learn to do what mathematicians do (Schoenfeld, 1985, 1987; Brown, Collins, & Newman, in press; Butler & Lave, in preparation). Such proposals emphasize the situated character of problem-solving practice (Brenner, 1985; Brown, Collins, & Newman, in press; de la Rocha, 1986; Lave, in press; Murtaugh, 1985a, 1985b; Suchman, in press). All of this converges on a possible unifying concept for new research on children's problem-solving practice, focusing on their day by day engagement in doing/learning, in terms of apprenticeship.

We will discuss here what such research might involve, for there are far reaching differences in assumptions about how learning takes place, what constitutes powerful and efficacious knowing, what relations properly characterize the interface between schooling and real life, what changes might lead to improved teaching and evaluation of the learning of problem solving, and even research practices. Research on craft apprenticeship as a form of education, and on everyday mathematics practices among adult alumni of schooling, cross-cultural and alternative models of learning, and creation of the UCI Farm School and its approach to mathematics have led us to think about relations between educational forms, everyday activities, and cognitive and educational theory.

PROBLEM SOLVING: WHAT IS IT; WHY TEACH IT?

The characterization of mathematics education in terms of problem solving reflects a trend, which at the same time is a reaction to past characterizations of mathematics as a set of facts, algorithmic procedures, knowledge to be mastered by rote or by mental exercise. The trend is to characterize learners as more active, problems as less precisely and narrowly defined, and to view problem-solving activity as a complex coordination of several levels of activity at once. Current interest in problem solving as *practice,* is an extension of this trend, and has generated a new goal for mathematics learning: that children might learn, by becoming apprentice mathematicians, to do what master mathematicians and scientists do in their everyday practice.

This agenda reflects a willingness on the part of mathematics learning researchers to enlarge the scope of their conceptions of mathematical problem solving, raising for us the question of what new vision of problem solving they have in mind. Greeno and others (1986) provide an elegant example of the difference between being taught a body of mathematical principles and learning to do what mathematicians do. They contrast different ways of presenting relations between arithmetic and algebra. The first is to impart a compendium of the algebraic relations formerly encountered in arithmetic (e.g., evaluate expressions) with the central activity of manipulating equations in algebra. Schoenfeld, (1985) provides another example. When he reflects on his practice as a mathematician doing problem solving with students, he describes four dimensions of good practice, all of which must be assembled at the same time if problem-solving activity is to proceed: resources of mathematical knowledge, heuristic strategies, control over the process of working on problems, and a deep understanding of the nature of mathematical argumentation. He comments that his understanding of what it means to invent, discover, and solve problems developed during an advanced educational apprenticeship in graduate school. Brown, Collins, & Newman (in press) suggest that students should learn "not so much . . . conceptual knowledge, but rather, . . . the processes that experts use to handle complex tasks. The new apprenticeship focuses on teaching knowledge situated in the context of its use." And, "among the critical skills that people learn from apprenticeship are: recognizing opportunities or problem finding, knowing when and how to apply skills that have been learned in other contexts, and exploiting properties of the presenting situation. These skills are not emphasized much in school learning." Implicitly then, the answer to the question, "why teach problem solving in school?" for those who have emphasized its value in contrast to rote procedural and performance-oriented approaches to mathematics instruction, is that they believe learners have a greater probability of coming to understand mathematical principles when they learn in a manner that enables them to engage in mathematical practice.

We may also ask the more searching question, "Why teach mathematics in school?" in order to lay out in a preliminary way differences between conventional views and those reflected in conceptions of mathematics as practice and learning as apprenticeship. There are a number of conventional responses. Mathematics should be taught in school in order to replace the inferior informal procedures of the everyday lives of just plain folks (jpfs). Mathematics, like Latin, is a form of mental exercise that should improve the ability to reason generally. Mathematics is important because great scientists think mathematically, and ability at mathematics is a great screening device for native intelligence. Math is important because in this highly technical world, it is required in important jobs, and even just to survive.

An exploration of the social logic of apprenticeship as a model of teaching and learning leads to a different answer to the question. The research referred to earlier, on the practice of science and the everyday practice of just plain folks, calls the conventional justifications for teaching mathematics into question, as we shall see.

One of the strengths of an apprenticeship model of learning may be its embedded challenges to old views. There are other general strengths of such a model to mention before discussing apprenticeship as a form of learning process. In particular, in current complaints and concerns about research on the teaching of problem solving, a pair of problems stands out which point to a general critique of standard research practice. One concern is that researchers who study mathematical problem-solving processes in the laboratory do not ground their research in studies of educational processes in the classroom. But the other side of this academic division of labor is equally narrow. Those who study the effectiveness of different forms of teaching and learning in the classroom do so without reference to the substance of what is being taught. An apprenticeship model of learning does not recognize, much less depend on, this division of theory and labor. If one studies learning as activity in process, with master practitioners who are also in the process of doing what they do, the line between the content to be taught and transmission procedures disappears.

Another general advantage of learning-as-apprenticeship is that it assumes that knowing, thinking, and indeed, problem-solving activity, are generated in practice, in situations whose specific characteristics are part of the practice as it unfolds. The conventional way of putting this idea has pejorative connotations. In apprenticeship, learning is conventionally characterized as informal, context embedded, concrete and specific. The point is that there is no disagreement between old and new research genres about the situated character of learning and knowing where apprenticeship is concerned. But there are sharp differences of opinion as to whether this is an advantage or a disadvantage.

It is useful to explore a particular form of craft apprenticeship, among Vai and Gola tailors in Liberia. We have selected features of this version of craft apprenticeship that seem relevant to the present discussion and will not attempt here a full account of the tailors' approach to education (Lave, in preparation). The tailors have a clear curriculum to be mastered. At the same time, there are a number of masters present who are models of what it means to be a master tailor—running a business, tailoring, and supervising apprentices. There are few formal lessons. Apprenticeship, averaging five years, involves a sustained, rich structure of opportunities to observe masters, journeymen, and other apprentices at work, to observe the full process of producing garments and the finished products. Learning processes do not merely reproduce the sequence of production processes. Apprentices begin by learning the finishing stages of producing a garment, go on to sewing it, and only after this do they learn to cut it out. This pedagogical ordering has the effect of first focusing apprentices' attention on the details of garment construction, as they handle garments repeatedly while attaching buttons and hemming cuffs. Their attention is then turned to the logic by which different pieces are sewn together, which in turn explains why they are cut out as they are. Once apprentices have a conceptual grasp of the particular production segment they are trying to learn (e.g., to sew a hat), and can construct a first approximation, they have rich opportunities to practice. They do so in a particular way. They reproduce the production segment from beginning to end (doing what masters do), though they might have quite different levels of skill at different parts of the process. Whole-activity practice is viewed as more important in long term mastery than consistent correct execution of decomposed parts of the process. Further, apprentices have means of gauging their own skill. They know whether they can complete a garment or not, and whether they have made mistakes. They must ask themselves whether the things they make are good enough to sell and what price to set, and they discover how much customers are willing to pay.

A very important structural feature of apprenticeship learning is that the increasing skill of the apprentice is of value to both apprentices and their masters. A very high percentage of apprentices become masters (85% of the apprentices Lave observed over a period of years). Those who quit seemed to do so for lack of motivation, or for reasons that had nothing to do with aptitude for learning the craft.

Other simple but crucial differences between craft apprenticeship and schooling help to account for their differently patterned distributions of accomplishment. Apprentices have the privilege of learning from masters. Apprentices know that there is a legitimate field for the use of what they are learning as they progress towards masterhood. Neither of these circumstances characterizes the structure of learning in schools. Instead, the organization of teaching and learning in schools is governed by a paralyzing contradiction between goals of universal socialization on the one hand, and intensive selection and ranking, in order to groom potential elite practitioners on the other. Tests are a means for accomplishing and legitimizing the latter, by documenting failure in the former (e.g., McDermott, 1982; McDermott & Goldman, 1983). That there are no formal tests to punctuate, legitimate, or screen out learners at any stage appears to reflect the structural commitment of apprenticeship forms of education to equal accomplishment for all learners. The implications of these claims will be elaborated further. For the moment, the point is that apprenticeship as a form of education is appealing in its outcomes both for apprentices and for a society that benefits from widespread, high levels of mastery. But it is at odds with prevailing theories about how and why problem solving should be taught, and diagnoses of why there is a high degree of failure in attempts to learn (and teach) mathematical problem solving in school.

To make this clearer, we contrast the manner in which, respectively, an apologist for current school practices, a critic, and a craft master might each assess problem-solving instruction in school classrooms today. First, a conventional, programmatic view. Those who defend current educational practice take the view that teaching is a conduit for cultural transmission; what is taught is what is learned. Thus, only degree of acquisition, or types of faulty acquisition, account for differences among learners. Explicit, detailed instruction, decomposition of tasks into small component steps, and imitative, repetitive practice on substeps, lead to skill. The less knowledgeable the learners, the more precisely teachers must try to provide direction in exactly what they are to do. The classroom is a privileged context. It is the only one that takes children out of the contexts of everyday activity and of the workplace. Only by abstracting from experience, distancing learners from their direct experience in the world, can they acquire the general principles necessary to equip them efficiently for the varied situations of real life.

Second, we may review the same scene from the point of view of school critics. Those who assess the results of conventional classroom practices negatively argue that what's going on in the classroom is ineffective, partial, distorted cultural transmission in the face of active reconstruction of, and resistance to, what is transmitted in a compartmentalized world where general procedures, even if learned, do not go often or far beyond the classroom. Further, children tend to conceal from their teachers problem-solving strategies they bring into or invent in the classroom, having learned that they are not valued in that context. It is possible to add to this description evidence that, in spite of failures in teaching/learning in the classroom, problem-solving activity outside school is remarkably effective (Lave, Murtaugh, & de la Rocha, 1984; Lave, in press).

Finally, we may take a third view of the same scene, asking how a craft master or a new proponent of apprenticeship might describe it. From the vantage point of apprenticeship as an educational form, it appears that teachers who have no claim to mastery, are mandated to teach children something for which almost none of them will ever have a legitimate field of serious use. In school classrooms there are neither masters, nor fields of practice for children. Blame is a major motivator, errors diagnose wrong thinking rather than marking way-stations in problem-solving processes. Rationalizations for highly prescriptive curricula and for the failure of children to learn, are based on misrepresentations of the goals of the educational form (Smith, n.d.).

It follows from these scenarios, as well as from earlier discussion of the issues, that a central difference between apprenticeship models and the conventional view concerns the manner in which they provide theoretical specification of relations between situations of learning and situations of use. The seamless merging of apprenticeship into master-practice provides a very different view of the relations between learning and doing than the gulf in time, setting, and activity that separates school learning from the application of school knowledge. A number of conventional dichotomous divisions generated in assumed distinctions between school, work, and daily life emerge as obvious distinctions in the latter model, but not in the former. Thus the conventional view assumes that situations of learning and situations in which learned knowledge is applied are quite different, and stand in a sequence, separated in time. Schooling is further thought to stand in contrast with real life, implying that schooling is somehow unreal, a connotation not lost on the young. Schooling is also treated as the locus of formal intellectual activity, presumed to be out-of-context learning. School prepares children for work, while work lies elsewhere.

Diagnoses of difficulties with current efforts to teach problem solving revolve around the question of what constitutes the proper relations between schooling and the everyday world. This division is drawn into debates about the teaching of problem solving at three levels: at the general level at which schooling is justified with arguments that high level problem-solving skills are needed in the workplace and everyday life; in the course of theorizing about how schooling works to change cognitive skills; and in ongoing debates about how to enhance th effectiveness of learning processes. Several examples of the first were mentioned earlier, and we suggested that they were under challenge. The other two require discussion as well. It seems important to review each of them carefully (in the next three sections), partly because recent research and critical analyses suggest an alternative view of existing relations between everyday and school worlds. This in turn raises the question of how closely assumptions underlying an apprenticeship model of education are compatible with an alternative assessment of current educational practice.

PROBLEM SOLVING AND TECHNOLOGY IN EVERYDAY LIFE AND IN THE WORKPLACE

Let us begin with broad beliefs about how school and the real world are related to each other. There is a very general first assumption that it is the responsibility of schooling to replace the (presumably) faulty and inefficient mathematical knowledge acquired by people in the real world. This project is viewed as especially urgent in a highly technical world. But there is an increasing body of research on mathematics in domestic life that challenges the view that school is the central source of everyday mathematics practice. This research suggests that quantitative relations are dealt with inventively and effectively in everyday situations, without employing school-taught mathematics in any obvious way. These activities seem to be independent of age and number of years of schooling.

Some conclusions from this research may be quickly summarized (Lave, in press). In everyday settings people look efficacious as they deal with problems of number and space. Their mathematics activity is structured in relation to ongoing activity and its settings. Its structure unfolds in a situated way. People do not stop to perform canonical, school-taught mathematics procedures and then resume activity; such activity is structured into and by ongoing activity. In the supermarket and kitchen jpfs have more than sufficient resources of mathematical knowledge to meet the exigencies of their activities. (The Weight Watchers study makes this especially clear, de la Rocha, 1986). They have such good control over the process that they almost never arrive at wrong answers, while abandoning problems they recognize they cannot solve in the time, and for the reasons, available. Many relations of quantity have closer relations with other aspects of activity than with each other, so there are many more relations of quantity in activity than there are well formed mathematics problems. There are no tests, grades, failure, or blame. Being free to generate problems for themselves, jpfs are also free to change a problem, resolve it, transform it, or abandon it, as well as solve it. People are walking histories of their own past calculations, but not of procedures for solving problems. Results are carried around but procedures are invented on the spot, as part of situated ongoing activity. Problem-solving activity in everyday situations looks, in these respects, rather like the problem-solving practice of mathematicians and scientists engaged in their everyday practices. Jpfs who are not mathematicians appear to take away from school the belief that they don't know and are unable to do "real mathematics." They are unaware of their own abilities. It is doubtful that attempts to imitate or integrate the mathematical relations of everyday life in classroom contexts, even in elaborate realistic word problems, bears any continuity with those experiences. Nor does it appear that everyday life is a good place to learn mathematics as such, given its structuring into higher priority ongoing activity. In short, it is not at all clear that schooling has succeeded in replacing one kind of practice with another.

Mathematics, as formally taught in the classroom, does not resemble everyday problem-solving forms as these have just been described. On the other hand, there are theoretical grounds for claims that problem solving in everyday mathematics practice and the everyday practice of mathematicians have common characteristics. I have argued elsewhere that what constitutes "the everyday" is a category which would embrace both. Its customary use in the parlance of both academics and jpfs obscures this point. Thus,

> . . . the label "everyday" is heavy with negative connotationsemanating from its definition in contrast to scientific thought. Its customary use encompasses the unmarked, unsung category of humble domestic activities and their associated social roles (e.g., housewives, running errands) . . . "Everyday" is not a time of day, a social role, nor a set of activities, particular social occasions, or settings for activity. Instead, the everyday world is just that: what people do in daily, weekly, monthly, ordinary cycles of activity. A schoolteacher and pupils in the classroom are engaged in everyday activity in the same sense as a person grocery shopping in the supermarket after work and a scientist in her laboratory. (Lave, in press, chapter 1, p. 21).

The definition of everyday activity applies directly to the classroom: for children do mathematics lessons everyday, to go to school on an everyday basis. An analysis of schooling that does not treat it as everyday activity misses its essential character. But this leaves open a major question as to what constitutes everyday practice in mathematics classes in school. We shall return to this question below.

This description suggests several observations relevant to discussions of contrasting relations between everyday and educational experience in school and apprenticeship. We might relieve those in charge of mathematics problem-solving instruction in school of the burden of teaching children mathematics as preparation for their everyday lives. In so doing we might relieve pupils of the belief that what they do in everyday situations is of no value. If they were able to recognize the inventiveness of their own practice, it might also help to mitigate the belief that only geniuses can discover and invent mathematics. There is one further general point. We are proposing that school mathematics problem-solving procedures are not, in fact, generalized, powerful forms of everyday problem solving, but form a specialized practice with conventions, occasions, organizations, and concerns of their own. We shall return to this observation shortly.

Schooling, especially mathematical training, is often justified in functional, utilitarian terms as a means to the world of work and its pressing necessity to meet the needs of a technologically sophisticated society. The distinction between everyday life and the world of work makes clear the conflicting goals of school as a public site of universal socialization and as the locus of the production of a legitimate elite in a meritocracy. We are as skeptical about the urgent needs of widespread, advanced mathematics skills in the workplace as about claims concerning everyday practice. It seems likely that where mathematics is routinely needed in work situations workers are furnished with jigs, instruments, formulae, tables, programs, and routine experiences that get the job done. Hutchins (personal communication) gives an elegant example of the organization and instrumentation that makes "on-line" mathematical problem solving and calculational work unnecessary for navigating an aircraft carrier. Scribner & Fahrmeier (1982) and Scribner (1984a, 1984b) have shown that when novices apply school mathematics procedures to the routine calculational dilemmas of blue-collar workers in a commercial dairy they are grossly inefficient compared with the invented, situated units of quantity, and heuristics for resolving recurrent problems, of experienced dairy workers who presumably initiate each other over the years. Job supervisors report that advanced mathematics qualifications are necessary for specific jobs which workers consistently report to involve nothing more complicated than simple arithemtic. Serious mathematical activity in the workplace is almost certainly an extraordinarily specialized activity-in-setting. In a small number of work circumstances the capacity to relearn or reinvent mathematical principles might occasionally and conceivably be valuable. But we suspect that more often than not this involves codiscovery sessions with experienced hands, focused on "how we do it" as opposed to the structure of relevant mathematical fields. If true, desirable skills would include just those of discovery and reinvention attributed by Schoenfeld and others to good mathematical practice, and hence an apprenticeship approach to the learning of problem solving might provide learners with relevant experience for future work situations. But current pedagogical practices for inculcating mathematical expertise, justified in the name of preparation for the workplace, seem very unlikely to produce the desired effect; discovery and reinvention skills are just what exam-driven education will not teach.

Together, the discussion of mathematics practice for everyday living and for the workplace suggest several observations and questions. The assumption that school is a mode of preparation for real life devalues engagement in schooling. The assumption that school teaches real mathematics devalues everyday mathematics practice. It appears that the distinction between the real and the ersatz itself generates pernicious comparisons, sometimes in one direction, sometimes in the other. It has already been suggested, by contrast, that this distinction is not generated when apprenticeship is the form of education under discussion. This introduces the question of whether it is possible to adapt the latter model to the teaching of problem solving in school.

SCHOOLING AND COGNITIVE SKILLS

Debates about how to teach problem solving effectively in the classroom also take a stance on relations between schooling and other aspects of the everyday world. Proper relations between daily activity and educational activity are taken to be a key source of the difficulties children experience in school as they try to become good mathematical problem solvers. The particular assumption addressed here is the belief that cognitive benefits follow only from taking the process of learning out of the fields of its application. This belief underlies the standard distinctions between formal and informal learning, or context-free and context-embedded learning. Schooling is viewed as the institutional locus for decontextualizing knowledge so that, abstracted, it may become general and hence generalizable, and therefore transferable to many situations of use in the real world.

Arguments about school as a—privileged—noncontext, as a "universal donor" site for the acquisition of knowledge and skill, treat schooling as if it was not the locus of particular situated activities, organized in ongoing activity in relation with its settings. But if ongoing, day-to-day activity in school is everyday practice, if schooling involves specialized forms of situated everyday activity, then there is a distinction to be made between schooling as a privileged setting and schooling as a specialized setting. We would argue that those who go through any specialized educational process, including schooling, come out with specialized forms of knowledge and skill. This calls into question claims that what is learned in school should be generally applicable across the varied situations of daily life.

PROBLEM-SOLVING PROCESSES

Further assumptions about relations between situations of learning and situations of use underlie approaches to the teaching and evaluation of problem solving more directly. There seems to be general agreement in recent problem-solving research (as opposed to research on teaching) that children actively construct theories at all times, including conceptions about the manipulation of quantity and how the physical world works. These have been characterized as intuitive, implicit, and informal in everyday settings, in sharp contrast to what are presumed to be formal, explicit, and intentional constructions in school. This leads to notions that children's difficulties in school are due to the absence of relevant everyday experiences or to their faulty conceptualization in nonschool settings. Thus, Resnick (1986) suspects that everyday life presents opportunities for dealing with quantity by additive composition but not in terms of (mathematically) functional relations, and DiSessa (1985) worries about children's inadequate conceptions of the physical world. There have been three common characterizations of learning difficulties in the research literature on problem solving. Everyday life provides too little relevant experience, making it difficult for children to grasp the meaning of new concepts in the classroom. Everyday life provides erroneous experience, or children actively construct erroneous concepts of it, and so everyday experience interferes with classroom learning. Classroom learning difficulties reflect too little and too weak a connection between what is being taught and the intuitive, everyday experience of learners (e.g., Brown, Collins, & Newman, in press). These views have had direct impact on recommendations for pedagogical innovations. In sum, these researchers propose that greater connectedness of mathematical experience in everyday and school settings might strengthen mathematics learning in school.

Until quite recently it has been assumed that an unavoidable chasm existed between the privileged world of school instruction, and the informal, intuitive, context-embedded, everyday world. But there are two alternative views, both consonant with an apprenticeship model of learning, that characterize recent research. First, in the paper quoted above, Resnick questions the existence of the gulf:

> There may be less difference than we have often thought between formal and informal learning, between intentional knowledge acquisition in school and unintentional knowledge acquisition elsewhere.

While Resnick questions the conventional devaluation of learning possibilities in situ, (as do Brown, Collins, & Newman, in press), Schoenfeld (1987) questions the value of traditional classrooms as learning situations. He concludes that we need to "engender a culture of schooling that reflects the use of mathematical knowledge outside the school context."

In the early 19th century mathematics curricula in school were drawn from the denominate mathematics of branches of commerce introduced into the school from the marketplace (Cohen, 1982). Since that time the locus of definition of appropriate mathematics has shifted from the everyday world into the school. In the contemporary view it is the formal mathematics of the classroom that should constitute the proper practice of mathematics in all life situations, replacing the inferior practices of intuitive and nonintentionally invented everyday mathematics. An apprenticeship approach takes a different view of this relation: that the practice on which classroom instruction might be modeled is that of mathematicians at work.

How is a classroom alien (in Schoenfeld's terms) to the learning and practice of mathematics? How have results of research on mathematical learning led to these recommendations that we rethink existing and desirable relations between educational forms and other aspects of the lived-in world? And what relevant conceptions of problem solving have emerged from studies of everyday mathematical practice?

Resnick (1986) points out that there is good evidence that active construction and invention of mathematical procedures by learners is no guarantee that they will understand mathematical procedures. In fact, by her assessment, school learners have reasonably correct calculational rules. They learn, in the classroom, rules for manipulating the syntax of symbolic notation systems. But they fail to learn the meaning of symbols and the principles by which they represent quantity and its permissible constrained transformations. Wrong answers are likely to look right, in other words, while at the same time conceptual errors betray a lack of mathematical understanding. This description of everyday practice in the classroom surely is not a close approximation to the mathematical practice of master mathematicians. Nor is the practice of the high school and college mathematics students Schoenfeld studied. He characterizes them as naive empiricists, who plunge into geometry problem solving with straightedge and compass in constant play, without planning, without making sure they understand the problem, believing that mathematical proof is irrelevant. They do not bring their mathematical resources to bear, have no control over the process, believe themselves unable to invent or discover procedures (because they aren't mathematical geniuses) and so on.

Schoenfeld argues that these beliefs are not based on erroneous everyday mathematics activities but rather are unintended consequences of classroom lessons (1985). Well taught lessons by well meaning teachers aimed at preparing students to pass state and national standardized examinations often lead to routinized procedures at the expense of understanding. Lessons place emphasis on the form of presentation of results at the expense of mathematical argumentation. Students expect problems to take less than two minutes to solve, and they believe that if they can't solve a problem in about ten minutes, they will never be able to do so. They believe that mathematics is to be received, not discovered, and that it is a body of knowledge rather than a form of activity, argumentation, and social discourse. Schoenfeld concludes that mathematics is taught as what experts know to be true rather than as a process of scientific inquiry (what mathematicians might be said to do). The decomposition of skills—a major structuring device in curricula design—strips problem-solving activity of its relation to mathematical practice.

Another example in which diagnosis of students' weaknesses locates the difficulties in the organization of mathematics lessons in the classroom (rather than in links with the everyday world) comes from the work of Hass (n.d.), who has been observing mathematics lessons in a bilingual Spanish/ English third grade classroom in Santa Ana, California. His ethnographic study offers some insight into how children learn symbol manipulation without understanding, at the same time they are successful in day to day terms in the classroom. Hass focused on a group of 11 children, the upper mathematics group within the classroom. The children brought to the three-week unit on multiplication and division facts almost as much knowledge as when they finished. They could solve, on average, half of the problems on a 40-problem test given before and after the unit. There were differences in pretest scores between children in the group, but the performances of the less successful converged over time with those of the more adept, so that all finished with roughly the same level of performance on the final test.

In that three-week period the children were deeply engaged in mathematics work during drill and practice time (about 75% of class time), while they invested minimal attention and involvement in ongoing activity during the teacher's instruction sessions (about 25% of class time). During the three weeks the children gave no evidence of having adopted any of the specific strategies demonstrated by the teacher during general instruction time.

The children sat around a table for individual work and the teacher moved about between their table and two others, helping children with work, or sat at her desk checking workbook exercises as the children finished their assignments. There was a great deal of interaction among the children at the table. (The three who interacted least were the least able in mathematics. One improved sharply after being placed between two highly interactive students who drew him into much greater participation.) The children began their group work sessions by making sure they agreed on what they were supposed to do. They concerted the timing of their activity, so as to work on approximately the same problems at the same time. They asked each other for help and helped each other without being asked. They collaborated and invented procedures. They discovered that the multiplication table printed in their book could be used to solve division problems, an opportunity for mathematical discussion of which the teacher was unaware. Each of the 11 turned in errorless daily practice assignments. On the rare occasions when one of the students consulted the teacher for individual help, the information gleaned in the interaction quickly spread around the table. Essentially all problems were solved using counting and regrouping strategies. These were not being taught, and were not supposed to be in use.

So the children got much practice in the problem-solving methods they brought with them to the classroom, but employed them so as to produce the appearance of having used the formal procedures being taught, for which the teacher took a correct answer as evidence. The end product was correct answers to problems that had been designed to teach a particular procedure which was not used by the children. And finally, interviews with the teacher suggested that she was unaware of the interactive mathematics activity of the children; the majority of the children reported that they consulted the teacher when they had difficulty solving problems.

Let us go back to Resnick's characterization of children's mathematics practice. First, how does the everyday practice of the children observed by Hass lead to the outcome that they are reasonable at integer arithmetic calculation? These children used home-grown procedures for calculation whose laborious character was offset by their known familiarity and reliability. When asked to learn new forms of calculation, they did not risk using the new form, for fear of failing to get it right, but used familiar skills instead. Second, Resnick points to the lack of relationship between children's understanding of basic principles of arithmetic and their manipulation of the formal notational system and formal procedural algorithms in school. We suspect that Hass has been looking at the social organization of what could be called a "veneer of accomplishment" (a term that fits the performance of the geometry students observed by Schoenfeld as well) and the reasons why it is disassociated from basic understanding. Furthermore, it appears that the distinction jpfs make between real mathematics and their everyday practice, may not be generated as they move back and forth from school to other settings but, like other beliefs and practices we have documented, arises in the classroom itself. For the clear understanding of the children as they worked out answers using their own techniques, and then translated them into acceptable classroom form on their worksheets, was quite sufficient to generate the categorical distinction between "real" and "other" mathematics.

The question was raised earlier as to what constitutes the everyday practice of learning in mathematics classes. On the basis of these descriptions it appears that, for the most part, such practice is constituted cautiously out of known quantities. It is aimed at success or at least survival in the classroom rather than focused on deep understanding of mathematics. In more general terms, the everyday practice of mathematics learning is a specialized activity, but not a privileged, value-neutral, decontextualized transmission of general knowledge. The dilemmas that motivate activity are ones of performance and blame-avoidance to a strong degree. Learners must infer that the practice itself is of little value to society, since they are taught by texts and evaluated by grades. There exists no legitimate field of practice other than the classroom itself, and there is no masters' practice to be found there.

That the classroom promotes a working repertory of mathematical practices which are not themselves taught, but which are brought into play in order to produce proper appearances of successful problem solving, is supported by other research. Brenner (1985) carried out research in Liberia on primer, first, and fourth grade arithmetic classes in Vai schools in Grand Cape Mount County. The Vai number system (which tallies at 5, 10, and 20) and arithmetic procedures are different from those taught in school where English is the language of mathematics instruction. U.S. textbooks are used, a base–10 number system, and Arabic place holding arithmetic. The children routinely employ a syncretic form of Vai and Arabic arithmetic, and become increasingly skilled in its use over time, though it is never taught. Presumably the urge to manufacture a successful performance in the classroom is important there as well.

In short, the work of Schoenfeld, Hass, and Brenner suggests that the problems which genuinely engage even enthusiastic mathematics learners in school classrooms are, at an important level, dilemmas about their performance rather than mathematical dilemmas. These give shape to learners' everyday mathematical activity in the classroom as they strive to succeed, and in the process generate appearances of understanding. It is this classroom organization, the kind that leads Schoenfeld (1987) to call for new cultural design of classrooms, that generates forms of everyday practice in school that are alien to the everyday mathematical practice of working mathematicians and regular people. A general question grows out of this analysis that may be addressed to apprenticeship models of learning: How might we establish dilemmas in the classroom that lead children to engage in mathematical practice (Butler and Lave, in preparation)? A partial answer lies in reducing or abandoning dilemmas in the classroom that are not themselves mathematical.

In sum, problem solving is dilemma motivated, and ongoing activity in response to whatever issues are lively and problematic for learners will shape the form of arithmetic activity in unintended ways and into unintended forms, unless arithmetic provides the central dilemmas in ongoing activity. Decreeing that mathematics is the central activity is not sufficient to make it problematic in substantive, mathematical ways for other people. Teachers cannot stipulate that it is the central activity for pupils, though they might be able to enhance that possibility by engaging with children in mathematical argumentation about mathematical dilemmas. Where reproducing procedures is the central activity, then learners should be expected to generate a veneer of accomplishment through everyday activity of a dependable and effective kind—self-generated everyday mathematics practices.

We have by now developed a number of contrasts between school-based and apprenticeship-based views of learning, set out in schematic form here:

SCHOOL

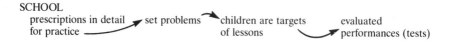

prescriptions in detail → set problems children are targets evaluated
for practice of lessons performances (tests)

APPRENTICESHIP
    opportunities for   →   dilemmas   ↖children are periph-   everyday
    activity   eral participants in   ↗ practice
                                       masters' activities ↗

This diagram points to an interesting theoretical contrast: The organization of a curriculum for apprenticeship may well specify what is to be learned at a different, less specific level than school lessons. The former aims to create opportunities for problem-solving activity, marshalling, a la Schoenfeld's scheme, knowledge resources, heuristics, and control of the process, in coactivity with a master who has clear curricular goals and is good at problem solving. The goal would be to generate dilemmas, opportunities for invention, discovery, and understanding in patterns of activity, rather than to prescribe exercises on specific problem types and procedures.

It is now time to summarize and draw some conclusions from this discussion of relations between schooling and the everyday world, and the impact of their assumed relations on research on the teaching of mathematical problem solving. We have argued that apprenticeship and schooling as models for instruction in mathematical problem solving depend, centrally, on different assumptions about proper relations between institutionalized learning experiences and the ultimate uses of knowledge so generated. A number of conclusions along the way may now be brought together. If everyday practice seems to combine adequate resources of mathematical knowledge, heuristics, and control, without apparent recourse to school mathematics; if mathematical practice in work settings is primarily a matter of interaction with instruments and procedures in which relations of quantity and their transformations are stored, and only rarely occasions on which mathematics is relearned, discovered or reinvented; if school is children's everyday activity; if school is not a privileged, but only one among many specialized settings for activity, a number of questions arise. What specialized (rather than general, preparatory) activities do we want children to engage in every day and why? How do we make children good at discovering and reinventing mathematics when they need it? (We shall return to these questions shortly.)

Next, if there is no open field for the employment of mathematical problem-solving skills, and very few children can feel that there is any probability that they will engage in serious mathematical practice during their lives or ever have legitimate claim to mastery as a goal, and if, further, we recognize as significant the situated, specialized, everyday character of activity in school classrooms, perhaps there is a basis for redesigning our view of the purposes of schooling in such a way as to create, at least for a time in children's lives, a field for mathematical action. We can act on the recognition that school is what children do every day, that schooling creates a field for action for mathematics problem-solving activity in its own right. That is, the fact that schooling is the institutional arrangement in this society for organizing a major portion of children's lives and activities may be treated seriously; it is in some sense more robust than conflicting claims that school is only a mode of preparation for real life.

Doesn't it matter whether children need to learn mathematics on utilitarian grounds? Otherwise how are we to justify it in a rational, utilitarian society? Easily; ours may well be the only culture still in existence where transmitting culture from one generation to the next is not considered a crucial end in itself. Mathematics is a valued part of our cultural heritage, and to know and understand it is of intrinsic value; mathematics has a special kind of beauty of the best our culture offers. Mathematics represents, intuitively, a kind of play, something our species is good at. Were this the experienced state of affairs in school classrooms, it would surely be perceived to be of general value.

MATHEMATICAL APPRENTICESHIP IN REAL LIFE IN SCHOOL?

Let us review what we mean by apprenticeship learning. Schoenfeld reports that:

> A significant part of what I attempt to do (in my problem solving courses . . .) is to create a microcosm of mathematical culture—an environment in which my students create and discuss mathematics in much the same way that mathematicians do (1987).

In this view, the central goal for apprentice learners is to learn the situated practice of mathematical work. Schoenfeld has suggested that mathematical problem solving requires several kinds of resources, including an understanding of what it is all about—what's called "proof," a special form of discourse, that of mathematical argumentation. As envisioned, the "new apprenticeship" involves invention and discovery, the emphasis on doing mathematics rather than being taught the experts' compendium of mathematical truths. Such an approach implies that the teacher be someone with a strong mastery of the practice of mathematics, someone with the autonomy to engage with learners in the practice of problem solving in inventive ways.

Given this approach, and the underlying assumption that all practice is situated, we have found it useful to analyze the classroom as a socially situated production of everyday activity. Several analyses of children's difficulties in producing mathematics in everyday school practice implicate everyday classroom practices, rather than faulty cognition or inadequate everyday experience, in explanations for the poor mathematical practices of children. They imply that a new cultural design for learning mathematical problem solving is needed, including new conceptions of curriculum, what it means to teach and to learn, and the nature of motivation and reward— that is, if we want learners to participate in practice, concern themselves with mathematical dilemmas, and learn with masters whose very mastery conveys the message that it is important to learn what they do. This view moves away from narrow cognitive models of problem solving to thinking as part of culturally organized activity; away from decomposing tasks for purposes of instruction, to arranging opportunities for practice; away from a teacher and pupils to a community of practitioners that includes apprentices, journeyfolk, and masters. Understanding, the resolution of dilemmas, and the aesthetics of mathematics are sources of impetus for learners to continue and get better at problem solving.

But there are several important questions raised that have yet to be addressed. What form would a curriculum for mathematical apprenticeship in school take? Can an apprenticeship model be translated to early mathematical learning? What new research questions does this suggest? These questions may be considered in order, beginning with that of the form of a curriculum.

The productive level of specification in the tailors' curriculum lies between a commitment to the—too general—proposition that learners will learn mathematics if they engage in mathematics practice, on the one hand, and a set of prescriptive recipes for executing small steps in canonical procedures, on the other hand. If masters are not going to specify surface features of practice, it is very important that they be quite clear about both long term and immediate goals for learning. On the other hand, for learners to be successful in the everyday practice of problem solving, they must engage in choice, judgement, control processes, problem formulation, and in making wrong choices and wild goose chases. Learners cannot have such experiences if practice is specified at the detailed levels of conventional lessons. To develop curricula, then, involves answers to two questions: What should those sequences of mathematical practices consist of? (This question, among other things, should be addressed to the mathematical learning research of the last decade.) And how can they be specified at the level of projects and dilemmas rather that at the level of problems and procedures?

The notion of apprenticeship learning may appear more obviously relevant to college and advanced high school classes than to grade school. What would a curriculum for young children look like, that: (a) had a strong view of what children should learn; (b) specified what was to be learned at a level that created opportunities for children to formulate the problems deemed desirable for them to address as their own; and (c) addressed the fundamental character of quantity and its expression in symbolic forms? There is an example close at hand, in the Farm School at UCI, developed by its director, Michael Butler. Farm School children (who receive no grades) are exposed to many mathematical dilemmas, and the goal is deep understanding of mathematical principles and mathematical practice.

Farm School teachers want children at the School to come to think like good mathematical thinkers. So the children, aged 5–12, are systematically asked to: (a) find interesting patterns in numbers, shapes, and procedures, compare the patterns, extend them until they fail, and make them plausible; (b) vary problems they are given; (c) invent their own problems, and to invent problems for others; (d) turn their own mathematically promising noticings into investigations and pursue them across days or weeks; (e) develop more than one solution to a problem, and more than one formulation of a solution; (f) consider the character and strength of their understanding and how they came to that understanding; (g) use the world to provoke and exemplify mathematical notions; and, finally, (h) teach other children the way they are taught. Algorithms for arithmetic operations are approached through child-devised physical and numerical decompostions and recombinations, at first quite free, then under series of teacher introduced, puzzle-like constraints. Along the way the standard American recipes for adding, subtracting, multiplying, and dividing appear as choices among many, choices with particular and interesting but not magical advantages. Against this background of child experimentation, they can readily be seen as successively more complex variations on a single meta-procedural theme: given a two-number problem involving a certain operation, break up the numbers to form a set of little problems of the same type, solve the little problems, and sum the results. To those oldest children who reach them, the polynomial computations in algebra seem almost transparent summaries of these discoveries. In these and other ways the Farm School acts on the assumption that children should learn to do what mathematicians do, not simply memorize some of the things they have found out, so that children will also have a chance to learn what it is about mathematics that delights practitioners.

The original goal of this paper was to propose new directions for research on the teaching and evaluation of problem solving. This seems, therefore, an appropriate place to conclude. An approach which emphasizes the learning of practice, in practice, makes certain research questions and methods salient. It surely recommends research on practice in situ, whether this be the practice of mathematicians at work, children at learning, or jpfs in everyday life. It would be useful to pay closer attention to the literature on the practice of science and mathematics, not necessarily in order to seek models for classroom activities (which might effectively develop out of the training of teachers as masters of their subject), but rather, as a basis for revising our assumptions about what constitutes the mathematics and mathematical practice that we want children to learn.

Within the classroom, the study of teaching has often been taken as an appropriate approach to analyzing learning. In apprenticeship, the relevant ongoing activity is learning rather than teaching. And it follows from the analysis of this paper that learning always occurs in everyday activity, whatever that activity might be. Together, these observations recommend that the focus of investigation should fall on the activity of learners in the classroom, with an emphasis on what's actually going on and being learned. We are in the habit of thinking about how children's cognitive and metacognitive skills get stronger, or why they are weak, in mathematics learning research. We like to argue about how to arrange things so that children will (or won't) find their real-world experience relevant to learning mathematics in school. The comparable question for a theory of practice is, "What does it mean to become more powerful in practice, in situ?

A number of questions follow. What happens to the organization of classroom activity when practice involves no grades, unfolding in cooperative work in small groups, in coached sessions of problem-solving activity? What kinds of dilemmas and fields for action get children involved? What happens if curricula are reformulated so that children come to believe that they can reinvent and discover mathematics, argue mathematically, marshall their mathematical resources heuristically and with control over sustained bouts of mathematical work? What methods will help children (especially beginning learners) generate mathematical knowledge resources in ways that at all times involve heuristics and control at levels they can manage? That is, in what senses can the holistic character of problem solving be preserved across early learning where essential mathematical resources are initially being established? What does it mean to invent dilemmas rather than problems?

REFERENCES

Bourdieu, P. (1977). *Outline of a theory of practice.* Cambridge: Cambridge University Press.

Brenner, M. (1985). *Arithmetic and classroom interaction as cultural practices among the Vai of Liberia.* Unpublished doctoral dissertation, University of California, Irvine.

Brown, J. S., Collins, A. & Newman, S. E. (in press). Cognitive apprenticeship: teaching the craft of reading, writing, and mathematics. In L. B. Resnick (Ed.). *Cognition and instruction: Issues and agendas.* Hillsdale, NJ: Lawrence Erlbaum Associates.

Butler, M. & Lave, J. (in preparation). *Learning to think mathematically.*

Carraher, T., Carraher, D. & Schliemann, A. (1982). Na vida dez, na escola, zero: Os contextos culturais da aprendizagem da matimatica. Sao Paulo, Brazil. *Caderna da Pesquisa* 42: 79–86.

Carraher, T., Carraher, D. & Schliemann, A. (1983). Mathematics in the streets and schools. Unpublished manuscript, Universidade Federal de Pernambuco, Recife, Brazil.

Carraher, T. & Schliemann, A. (1982). *Computation routines prescribed by schools: Help or hindrance.* Paper presented at NATO conference on the acquisition of symbolic skills, Keele, England.

Cohen, P.C. (1982). *A calculating people: the spread of numeracy in early America.* Chicago: University of Chicago Press.

Confrey, J. (1986). A critique of teacher effectiveness research in mathematics education. *Journal for Research in Mathematics Education,* 17 (5), 347–360.

de la Rocha, O. (1986). *Problems of sense and problems of scale: An ethnographic study of arithmetic in everyday life.* Unpublished doctoral dissertation, University of California, Irvine.

DiSessa, A. (1985). *Final report on intuition as knowledge.* Spencer Foundation.

Greeno, J., Brown, J. S., Foss, C., Shallin, V., Bee, N., Lewis, M. & Vitolo, T. M. (1986). *Cognitive principles of problem solving and instruction.* Final report, Office of Naval Research. (Project NR154–497).

Hass, M. (n.d.) Cognition-in-context: *The social nature of the transformation of mathematical knowledge in a third grade classroom.* Social Relations graduate program. University of California, Irvine.

John-Steiner, V. (1985). *Notebooks of the mind.* Albuquerque: University of New Mexico Press.

Kilpatrick, J. (1986). Editorial. *Journal of Research in Mathematics Education.* 17 (5): 322.

Krieger, M. (n.d.) *The physicist's toolkit.* University of Southern California.

Lave, J., Murtaugh, M. & de la Rocha, O. (1984). The dialectic of arithmetic in grocery shopping. In B. Rogoff and J. Lave (Eds.), *Everyday cognition: Its development in social context* (pp. 67–94). Cambridge, MA: Harvard University Press.

Lave, J. (in press). *Cognition in practice: Mind, math and culture in everyday life.* Cambridge: Cambridge University Press.

Lave, J. (in preparation). *Tailored learning: Apprenticeship and everyday practice among craftsmen in West Africa.*

Livingston, E. (1983). *An ethnomethodological investigation of the foundations of mathematics.* Unpublished doctoral dissertation, University of California, Los Angeles.

McDermott, R. P. (1982). Institutionalized psychology and the ethnography of schooling. In P. Gilmore and A. Glatthorn (Eds.). *Children in and out of school* (pp. 232–49). Arlington, VA: Center for Applied Linguistics.

McDermott, R. P. & Goldman, S. V. (1983). Teaching in multicultural settings (pp. 145–63). In L. van de Berg-Elderling (Ed.). *Multicultural education.* Dortrecht: Foris.

Murtaugh, M. (1985a). *A hierarchical decision process model of American grocery shopping.* Ph.D. dissertation. Irvine, CA: University of California, Irvine.

Murtaugh, M. (1985b). The practice of arithmetic by American grocery shoppers. *Anthropology and Education Quarterly* 16 (3): 186–192.

Ortner, S. B. (1984). Theory in anthropology since the sixties. *Comparative Studies in Society and History.* 26 (1): 126–166.

Resnick, L. B. (1986). Constructing knowledge in school. In L. S. Liben and D. H. Feldman (Eds.). *Development and learning: Conflict or congruence?* (pp. 19–50). Hillsdale, NJ: Erlbaum.

Schoenfeld, A. H. (1985). *Mathematical problem solving.* New York: Academic Press.

Schoenfeld, A. H. (1987). What's all the fuss about metacognition? In A. Schoenfeld (Ed.). *Cognitive science and mathematics education* (pp. 189–215). Hillsdale, NJ: Erlbaum.

Schoenfeld, A. H. (in press). When good teaching leads to bad results: The disasters of "well taught" mathematics courses. *Educational Psychologist.*

Scribner, S. & Fahrmeier, E. (1982). *Practical and theoretical arithmetic: Some preliminary findings* (Industrial Literacy Project, Working Paper No. 3). Graduate Center, CUNY.

Scribner, S. (1984a). (Ed.). Cognitive studies of work. Special issue of the *Quarterly Newsletter of the Laboratory of Comparative Human Cognition,* 6 (1&2).

Scribner, S. (1984b). Studying working intelligence. In B. Rogoff and J. Lave (Eds.). *Everyday cognition: Its development in social context* (pp. 9–40). Cambridge, MA: Harvard University Press.

Smith, S. (n.d.) *Blame, criticism, and the manufacture of error.*

Suchman, L. (in press). *Plans and situated actions: The problem of human-machine communication.* Cambridge: Cambridge University Press.

Traweek, S. (in press). Discovering machines: Nature in the age of its mechanical reproduction. In F. A. Dubinskas (Ed.). *Chronos' children: Anthropologies of time in science and high technology organizations.* Philadelphia: Temple University Press.

Problem Solving in Context(s)[1]

Alan H. Schoenfeld

University of California, Berkeley

During the past two decades the research community has made significant advances toward an understanding of the cognitive support structures that underlie mathematical problem solving. Further explorations of mathematical cognition (see, e.g., Schoenfeld, 1985), of the "nuts and bolts" of cognition, with instructional implications (Greeno, 1987; Hiebert, 1986; Silver, 1987), of metacognition (Brown & Campione, this volume), and of students' belief systems, teachers' beliefs, and classroom ecology (Peterson & Carpenter, in press) will, in all likelihood, continue to be profitable in the coming years. Since it is clear that such work will be actively pursued, it will not be discussed here. This article focuses on an emerging area of research which, in my opinion, will prove to be equally important. Broadly speaking, that research deals with the cultural transmission of knowledge in mathematics classrooms. Related explorations of this topic may be found in Collins, Brown, and Newman (in press) and Lave (this volume).

The argument advanced in this paper is based on two major assumptions. My first assumption is about the nature of schooling. I believe that school mathematics learning is most appropriately viewed as simultaneously comprising both cultural and cognitive phenomena, and that the two are not separable. In most of the educational research that has learning as the "bottom line," classrooms are considered merely as the sites in which learning takes place; the research focuses on the cognitive aspects of the exchanges that happen within them. Classrooms, however, are also cultural milieux in which—as in all cultural microcosms—there are (most often tacit) sets of beliefs and values that are perpetuated by the day-to-day practices and rituals of the cultures. In the case of any specific discipline, those beliefs and values are about the nature and purposes of that discipline. Hence the knowledge about mathematical facts and procedures that the students receive in their formal mathematics instruction comprises only one component of what the students learn about mathematics. Whether or not it is intended, the students' sense of "what mathematics is really all about" is shaped by the culture of school mathematics—the environment in which they learn those facts and procedures. In turn, that sense of what mathematics is really all about determines how (if at all) the students use the mathematics they have learned. My second assumption is about the nature of mathematics. I believe that at its core, doing mathematics can be and should be an act of sense-making—and moreover, that the facts and procedures students learn in mathematical instruction should be a means to that end, rather than an end in themselves.

Implications for both research and practice follow from these assumptions. At the philosophical and phenomenological levels—to be able to explain what students really learn in our mathematics classrooms, and how and why they use (or will not use) what they have learned outside those classrooms—we will need to develop theories and methodologies that encompass cultural and cognitive phenomena, and the dialectic between them. The next section of this paper makes a preliminary attempt at dealing with those issues. At the level of curriculum design, we may need to rework our ideas entirely. Typically, curriculum design means creating materials that "work." However, given the assumptions above, it is untenable to conceive of designing curricula without taking classroom culture into account. The central issue for instruction thus becomes the following: How can we help to create classroom environments in which the "right" kinds of interactions take place, so that students develop the right sense of what mathematics is all about, as well as mastering the formal mathematics they need to know? Fortunately, there exist some case studies that serve both as existence proofs (that it is possible to create classroom mathematical microcultures that support mathematical thinking) and as sources of ideas. A discussion of those case studies comprises the second half of this paper.

ON CULTURE AND COGNITION: SCHOOL MATHEMATICS SHAPES MATHEMATICAL BEHAVIOR

Consider the following nonsense problem:

There are 26 sheep and 10 goats on a ship. How old is the captain?

The problem has achieved folklore status in European mathematics education circles, for the following reason: Although it is clearly absurd, students will try to solve it. French mathematics educators found that more than three students in four who were given the problem in a school setting produced a numerical answer to it. (The most frequent answer given is 36, the most plausible numerical combination of 26 and 10.) In Switzerland, Reusser (1986) replicated the French results and explored related problems. He gave students a number of similar problems, for example: "There are 125 sheep and 5 dogs in a flock. How old is the shepherd?" The following quote from a fourth grade student working the problem out loud speaks for itself:

> $125 + 5 = 130$ . . . this is too big, and $125 - 5 = 120$ is still too big . . . while . . . $125/5 = 25$. That works . . . I think the shepherd is 25 years old.

Also, he asked 101 fourth and fifth grade students to work the following problem:

Yesterday 33 boats sailed into the port and 54 boats left it. Yesterday at noon there were 40 boats left in the port. How many boats were still in the port yesterday evening? (Reusser, 1986, p. 37)

He reports that all but one of the 101 students produced a numerical solution to the problem, and that only one student complained that the problem was ill-defined and unsolvable. Admittedly the teachers' authority might inhibit overt negative reactions from the students. Afterwards, however, students were asked to comment on the problem and to evaluate the correctness of their solution. Only 28 of the 100 students who produced a numerical solution expressed doubts about their solution, and only 5 of the 101 students expressed the opinion that the problem was the least bit out of the ordinary.

Of course, one need not travel to Europe to find such behavior. Our own most notable example comes from the third National Assessment of Educational Progress (Carpenter et al., 1983):

An army bus holds 36 soldiers. If 1128 soldiers are being bussed to their training site, how many buses are needed?

Of the students who worked the problem 29% wrote that the number of buses needed is "31 remainder 12," while only 23% gave the correct answer to the problem. And as should be clear, the examples given here barely represent the tip of an enormous iceberg. For more examples and a more extended discussion, see Schoenfeld (in press).

My purpose in giving these examples is not to provide an illustrated catalogue of horrors. It is, rather, to point to the systematicity that lies behind them. In every one of these examples, it is impossible to arrive at the indicated answers if you insist that the problem (and your solution) make sense. To obtain the answers given above, you must either suspend, or be unable to implement, the sense-making requirement. Now, no one in his or her right mind would claim that mathematics teachers around the world are engaged in a conspiracy to subvert sense-making in mathematics. Indeed, the rhetoric—which mathematics teachers believe as much or more than anyone else—is that "mathematics helps you think." Where, then, are the origins of the students' behavior?

The explanation, I believe, lies in the practices of mathematics classrooms—the web of everyday activities that constitute classroom mathematics culture. One striking example of how classroom practice affects cognition was provided by Paul Cobb at the research presessions to the 1984 NCTM annual meetings. Cobb asked students from four different schools to solve a list of simple equations given on dittoed worksheets. A typical worksheet listed problems like "$9 - x = 6$," "$x - 5 = 7$," and "$8 = x - 3$" in sequence. Students from three of the four schools produced the standard miscellany of errors. However, some of the students from the fourth school produced answers that were both consistent and, at first glance, almost bizarre. Given the worksheet problems listed above, for example, these students would produce the answers 3, 2, and 5 to the three problems. They usually got the first problem right, but many of the others wrong.

A visit to the students' class resolved the dilemma. Like the students in the other classes, these students solved problems on worksheets every day. But in this class, all the problems on each worksheet (which were produced by the classroom teacher) were equivalent in form. That is, if the first problem was of the form "9 − 1 = 6," which can be solved by subtracting the smaller given number from the larger, then every other problem on the worksheet could be solved by the same method. Having worked these problem sheets day after day, some of the students clearly developed the following method for doing worksheet assignments: Figure out how to solve the first problem, and then apply that procedure to all of the remaining problems.

Their method worked. They got 100% on their assignments, and praise for getting the correct answers. As far as they could tell, they had learned the mathematics they were supposed to learn. Only when one looks at their work in a broader context does one see that their (perfectly rational) behavior resulted in significant mis-learning.

In one sense, the incident just described was an aberration. The worksheets were poorly designed, the misconceptions the students developed were blatant, and the normal feedback process was likely, in the near future, to result in the identification and remediation of those misconceptions. In another sense, however, the incident is so typical as to be almost generic. It illustrates quite dramatically that students learn what mathematics is all about by immersion in the routine, day-by-day practices of their mathematics classrooms. More precisely, the students' behavior, in this case, what appears to be "purely cognitive" behavior, their solutions to arithmetic problems, is shown to be shaped by the day-to-day classroom rituals in which they engage.

Perhaps the most important observation about this particular example is that sense-making is contextually bound, and is defined in the cultural microcosm by the practices of the microculture. From the outside we can clearly see that the application of the same procedure to a set of problems, without stopping to study the individual problems, doesn't make very much sense. However, the view from the outside doesn't count. What counts is the view from inside. In this particular microcosm that procedure described above produced the right results consistently, so it did make sense. And hence it came to be used.

Herein lies the explanation to the suspension of sense-making described in the examples at the beginning of this section. In the context of school mathematics, word problems always have answers. Those answers are almost always integers, which are obtained by manipulating the integers that appear in the problem statements. Thus, in classroom practice, one learns to combine the numbers, whether or not doing so makes sense in other contexts. Indeed, mathematics instruction generally provides support for the idea that students need not try to make sense of problems: The "key word" algorithm for working word problems, for example, allows students to "solve" problems without reading them. Hence the fact that 75% of the students either add or subtract the number of sheep and goats to get the age of the captain should come as no surprise. That behavior is entirely consistent with (and ultimately derived from) classroom practice. If sense-making does enter the picture, it does so by way of imposing constraints on the solution. For example, the student working Reusser's shepherd problem rejected 120 and 130 as people's ages, but settled on 25 because that seemed reasonable. As the NAEP bussing problem indicates, however, sense-making constraints are not always applied. The plurality of students who obtained the answer "31 remainder 12" did so by implementing the following four-step procedure: (1) Read the problem; (2) Select the numbers and the relevant operation; (3) Perform the operation; and (4) Write down the answer. That procedure is derived from classroom practice; it usually works, and is rewarded, in the classroom context.

To sum up, this section presents a first and very tentative step toward the elaboration of a theoretical perspective incorporating a theory of practice with a theory of cognition. I have tried to outline an argument about the cultural origins of cognitive structures, an argument based on (a) the epistemological assumption that much of our knowledge is "local" and contextually bound, and that much knowledge development is tied to the contexts in which the learning takes place; and (b) a theory of practice that points to the development of understandings about certain domains as being shaped by the practices of those domains (in addition to, or sometimes rather than, the rhetoric of the domains).

ON SENSE-MAKING IN THE MATHEMATICS CLASSROOM

One of the classical, and frequently disparaged, arguments in favor of teaching mathematics is that "mathematics helps you think." In a technical sense that argument is false; as the previous section shows, students may master the formal procedures of mathematics but may fail to use them sensibly. Mastering the formal procedures of mathematics is a far cry from learning mathematics. To be clear, I shall refer to the latter as learning to think mathematically.

For anthropologists it is axiomatic that members of radically different cultures will see and interpret the same things in different ways; those people's world views are shaped by their cultures (see, e.g., Geertz, 1983). I wish to argue here that the same holds for subcultures, in particular, for the subculture of mathematicians. There is a cultural component to learning to think mathematically: Becoming a mathematician involves a process of acculturation, in which initiates become members of, and accept the values of, a particular community. A large part of what apprentice mathematicians pick up, in addition to their formal mathematical skills, is what might be called the mathematician's aesthetic. In Schoenfeld (1987), for example, I described one particularly vivid memory of a teacher about to write the statement of a probability theorem on the board.

> When she got to the statement of the main result she stopped and said, "I never remember this result, but that's no problem; it's so easy to derive." She did just that, showing us why it made sense; then she finished writing the statement of the theorem. At that moment I saw how mathematics should be: If you really understand it, you don't have to memorize a lot, because you can figure it out. That became part of my sense of what mathematics is all about. (p. 213)

Indeed, "figuring it out" is what mathematics is all about. At its core, doing mathematics is fundamentally an act of sense-making, an act of taking things apart (mathematically) and seeing what makes them tick. From the outside this may be clearest in applied mathematics, where mathematical models are used to explicate the structures of physical (or other) systems. But it's also very much the case in pure mathematics. Every theorem is, in essence, a statement of the following type: "Things fit together in a particular way, for the following reasons." In short, mathematicians spend most of their time making sense of things. Doing mathematics is sense-making, and becoming a mathematician includes developing (or internalizing) the mathematician's aesthetic, a predilection to analyze and understand, to perceive structure and structural relationships, to see how things fit together. Developing this aesthetic is a fundamental aspect of learning to think mathematically. Here we come to the crux of the matter, which, once again, is cultural. As the examples in the previous section indicated, you don't develop this aesthetic simply by mastering the formal procedures of the domain. You certainly don't develop it by having it preached at you, in classic platitudes (e.g. "Mathematics helps you think."). To put things simply, you pick it up by internalizing it, that is, by living in a culture in which the appropriate values are reflected in the everyday practices of the culture.

I have argued that learning to think mathematically involves both mastering the mathematical "tools of the trade" and developing a sense of the discipline—a view of mathematics as a sense-making activity, and the habit of using mathematics in that way. The former is within our grasp. Helping students master the tools of the trade (various mathematical facts and procedures) is by no means a trivial enterprise, but it is relatively straightforward. Moreover, this task will become easier as our understanding of the cognitive support structure of mathematical cognition deepens. Helping students develop the appropriate sense of the discipline is, however, quite something else. For students to see mathematics as a sense-making activity, they have to internalize it as such. That is, they need to learn mathematics in classrooms which are microcosms of mathematical culture, classrooms in which the values of mathematics as sense-making are reflected in everyday practice. For mathematics education, then, the issue is a cultural one: How can we create classroom environments which are microcosms of the right mathematical culture?

There are no easy answers to this question. I pose it as a research challenge, with the expectation that answering it will be an extremely difficult but rewarding enterprise over the decades to come. Much of that work will be inductive, finding instances of classroom cultures that work and abstracting from them the elements that contribute to their success. At present I can point to four case studies that (a) prove the enterprise is feasible, and (b) provide the richness of descriptive detail necessary for the inductive task. The oldest of the four, and in some ways the most interesting, because it explicitly deals with the transfer of mathematical ideas to nonmathematical situations, is nearing its fiftieth birthday. I shall discuss it at some length, and merely assert that the other three (Balacheff, 1987; Lampert, in press; Schoenfeld, 1985 & 1987) are consistent in spirit and substance with the discussion.

Harold Fawcett's (1938) *The Nature of Proof* provides "a description and evaluation of certain procedures used in a senior high school to develop an understanding of the nature of proof." Fawcett taught a two-year-long course in plane geometry, focusing on developing in his students an understanding of the logical deductive procedures used in geometric arguments. He took quite seriously the idea that mathematics should help you think.

Quoting John Dewey, Fawcett (p. 7) identifies one of the major goals of instruction as helping students to develop "reflective thinking"—"active, persistent and careful consideration of any belief or supposed form of knowledge in the light of the grounds that support it and the further conclusions to which it tends." Quoting H.C. Christofferson, Fawcett (p. 5) claims that geometry reaches its highest possibilities if "it can develop an attitude of mind which tends always to analyze situations, to understand their interrelationships, to question hasty conclusions, to express clearly, precisely, and accurately non-geometric as well as geometric ideas." His goals for his two-year course in geometry were that, after the course, his student would:

> select significant words and phrases in any statement that is important to him and ask that they be carefully defined; require evidence in support of any conclusion he is pressed to accept; analyze the evidence and distinguish fact from assumption; recognize stated and unstated assumptions; . . . evaluate the assumptions; . . . evaluate the argument, accepting or rejecting the conclusion. [Moreover, he would] constantly re-examine the assumptions which are behind his beliefs and which guide his actions. (pp. 11–12)

It is impossible to convey the flavor and substance of Fawcett's approach in a few pages, and I recommend that the reader seek out the original for details. Fawcett sought transfer, and he believed that you have to prepare the groundwork for transfer if you expect to get it. Hence it was essential to discuss definitions, logical reasoning, etc., in real-world as well as mathematical contexts. Early in the term, for example, all his students agreed with the statement that "Abraham Lincoln spent very little time in school." He then asked the students to define "school." Twelve students defined school as the building set aside for formal instruction, ten considered school as a place for learning things, and three considered school to be "any experience from which one learns." The students were then given this exercise:

> If you agree to define "school" as "any experience from which one learns," do you agree or disagree with the proposition that "Abraham Lincoln spent very little time in school?"

All the students present then disagreed with the proposition. In such ways, Fawcett pointed out the role of definitions in drawing conclusions. He had students suggest terms that might be defined by them, and then discussed the definitions. Issues discussed included: Is the librarian a teacher? What is 100% Americanism? How do I know when I am tardy? (A student had been punished for particular behavior in one class, and not another.) What is a foul ball in baseball? What is an obscene book? Such discussions pointed out the importance of definition (a) for purposes of drawing conclusions, and (b) as a matter of social convention. At the same time, Fawcett pursued issues of mathematical definition. For example, the class argued over definition of "adjacent angles." "Two angles that share a common side" was considered, but was ruled out by a zigzag figure. "Two angles that share a common vertex" was ruled out by another sketch. "Two angles that share a common vertex and a common side" was accepted for a while, but was then ruled out when the students realized that a figure in which one angle includes another satisfied their definition, but not their intention. Ultimately, a student proposed that, "Adjacent angles are angles that have a common vertex and a common side between them." This definition was accepted by the class.

In a similar way, mathematical and nonmathematical arguments were objects of classroom discussion. The class read and analyzed newspaper editorials, finding inconsistencies in the logic advanced. They read advertisements, looking for implicit assumptions. They discussed supreme court decisions, mulling over the fact that justices who were supposed to be arguing on the basis of "pure logic" reached split decisions about important issues. And, of course, they discussed mathematical arguments as well. What made arguments convincing? What made them complete? Could you always believe the results of an inductive argument? Of a deductive argument? Is the converse of a true result always true?

Most important, however, was the structure of the classroom mathematics discussions. Fawcett specifically refrained from giving students the statements of results to be proved. That is, he would not give students problems in the form "Prove that the diagonals of a parallelogram bisect each other," or "Prove that the diagonals of a parallelogram are perpendicular." Instead, he gave the students problem situations. For the two theorems stated above, he might have phrased his assignment as follows.

1. Consider the parallelogram ABCD, with diagonals AC and BD. State all the properties of that figure you are willing to accept.
2. Suppose you assume in addition that AB = CD, so ABCD is a rhombus. State all additional properties of the figure you are willing to accept.

Having given this assignment, Fawcett would ask the students to list their assertions ("properties of the figure you are willing to accept"). Some of these would turn out to be true, some of them not. He listed all the assertions, and then the class discussed each one—whether it seemed plausible, whether there might be a counterexample, why a result should be accepted if they believed it was true. Ultimately, the class produced proofs of the ones they accepted. Similarly, the class generated (and proved the validity of) various geometric constructions—but in answers to questions of the form: If (as the class had asserted) "a line segment can be bisected by one and only one point," how may this point be determined? Though the students "covered" less geometry than they would have covered in a standard class, Fawcett argued that they discovered a good deal of meaningful information. He also presented evidence of what the students learned.

In summing up what he had done, Fawcett focused on the ways that his students built up the mathematics in ways that made it meaningful. The students proved their own theorems. Undefined terms and terms to be defined were selected by the pupils, and definitions were an outgrowth of student discussions rather than the basis for them. Rather than being told what to prove, students were given problem situations in which they guessed and proved results. In their mathematical and nonmathematical work, the detection of implicit or tacit assumptions was encouraged and recognized as important. Moreover, the logic of their inquiry was an object of discussion and reflection. All this seems reasonable, but I suggest that there is another and equally essential dimension to Fawcett's success. As you might expect at this point, my explanation is cultural in nature.

It is clear from reading *The Nature of Proof* that Fawcett provided his students with much of the cognitive support structure required for doing geometry, and for the transfer of logical reasoning to tasks outside of formal mathematics. But he did more. In Fawcett's classroom, a critically important set of mathematical values, beliefs, and predilections was induced and reinforced by the daily rituals and practices in which the students engaged. In essence, his classroom environment was a culture of sense-making. The climate was one of reason. Statements were not taken on authority, but were evaluated and negotiated. Conjecture was encouraged, but the bottom line was that for a statement to be accepted as valid, the class had to accept the reasoning process that justified it. The standards were high, but they were not artificial or dogmatically imposed from the outside; indeed, the standards themselves were objects of discussion. The class negotiated its definitions, working over them until their precise statements captured the intended meanings; it negotiated its theorems, working over them until the statements were clear and the proofs convincing. Asking tough questions was not only appropriate, but was encouraged and rewarded by full participatory membership in the culture. The students lived mathematics, in much the way that practicing mathematicians do.

As far as I can tell, Fawcett's high school students experienced mathematics in a way that I first experienced it as an advanced graduate student. Independent of subject matter, that is the common thread that links Fawcett's course with Balacheff's (1987) geometry classes for seventh graders, Lampert's fourth grade class sessions on multiplication, and my (1985; 1987) problem-solving classes for undergraduates. Each course, in its own way, was a microcosm of (certain aspects of) mathematical culture. Each was an environment in which the day-to-day rituals and practices made it natural to think mathematically—in which the mathematical aesthetic (the predilection to analyze and understand) permeated the atmosphere, and was reflected in and supported by the ongoing activities within the culture. As the examples in the previous section indicated, it is all too easy for students to internalize the wrong sense of mathematics from their classroom experiences. The three studies cited here indicate that it is possible to create classroom environments in which students can internalize a reasonably appropriate sense of mathematics. To sum up this section, the issue for research is to understand and abstract the commonalities in these isolated examples, to understand how to create classroom environments in which it is natural to think mathematically. To the degree that we succeed in this endeavor, the "transfer problem" will become less and less of a problem.

FOOTNOTES

1. The work described in this paper was supported by the National Science Foundation through NSF grant MDR–8550332. NSF grant support does not necessarily imply NSF endorsement of the ideas expressed in this paper.

REFERENCES

Balacheff, N. (1987). Devolution d'un probleme et construction d'une conjecture: Le cas de "la somme des angles d'un triangle." [Evolution of a problem & construction of a conjecture: The case of "the sum of the angles of a triangle."] Cahier de didactique des mathematiques No. 39, IREM Universite Paris VII.

Carpenter, T.P., Lindquist, M.M., Matthews, W., & Silver, E.A. (1983). Results of the third NAEP mathematics assessment: Secondary School. *Mathematics Teacher,* 76 (9), 652–659.

Collins, A., Brown, J. S., & Newman, S. (in press). The new apprenticeship: teaching students the craft of reading, writing, and mathematics. In L.B. Resnick (Ed.), *Cognition and instruction: Issues and agendas.* Hillsdale, NJ: Erlbaum.

Fawcett, H. P. (1938). *The nature of proof (1938 Yearbook of the National Council of Teachers of Mathematics)* New York: Columbia University Teachers College Bureau of Publications.

Geertz, C. (1983). *Local knowledge.* New York: Basic Books.

Greeno, J.G. (1987). Instructional representations based on research about understanding. In A.H. Schoenfeld (Ed.), *Cognitive science and mathematics education* (pp. 61–88). Hillsdale, N.J.: Erlbaum.

Hiebert, J. (Ed.). (1986). *Conceptual and procedural knowledge: The case of mathematics.* Hillsdale, N.J.: Erlbaum.

Lampert, M. (in press) Knowing, doing, and teaching multiplication. *Cognition and Instruction.*

Peterson, P.L., & Carpenter, T.L. (in press). Learning through instruction: The study of students' thinking during instruction in mathematics, a special issue of *Educational Psychologist.*

Reusser, K. (in preparation) *Problem solving beyond the logic of things.*

Schoenfeld, A.H. (1985). *Mathematical problem solving.* New York: Academic Press.

Schoenfeld, A. H. (1987). What's all the fuss about metacognition? In A. H. Schoenfeld (Ed.), *Cognitive science and mathematics education* (pp. 189–215). Hillsdale, NJ: Erlbaum, in press.

Schoenfeld, A.H. (in press). When good teaching leads to bad results: The disasters of "well taught" mathematics courses. *Educational Psychologist.*

Silver, E.A. (1987). Foundations of cognitive theory and research for mathematics problem solving instruction. In A.H. Schoenfeld (Ed.), *Cognitive science and mathematics education* (pp. 33–60). Hillsdale, N.J.: Erlbaum, in press.

Metacognition: On the Importance of Understanding What You Are Doing[1]

Joseph C. Campione, Ann L. Brown, and Michael L. Connell
University of Illinois, Urbana-Champaign

Our charge in this chapter is to discuss the implications of research on metacognition for practice in mathematics education. In this context, our major argument is that standard educational practices, with regard to both instruction and assessment, have not made provision for the incorporation of metacognitive skills, with negative consequences for students. In the paper, we outline what we see as some of the limitations of current educational practices. Using that analysis as a starting point, we elaborate some alternative approaches to instruction and assessment that emphasize metacognition, and we illustrate the new methods in the contexts of reading and mathematics.

In the remainder of this section, we discuss some of the issues that have arisen in the work on metacognition, and proceed to an analysis of traditional instructional practice that leads to the conclusion that metacognitive factors have been in good part neglected.

In the next two sections, we discuss in more detail the limitations of instructional practices, and the development of an alternate program, reciprocal teaching of comprehension skills. We first describe the results produced by a major program in reading comprehension, and then present some initial data extending the procedures to mathematics instruction.

Following that, we consider assessment practices, where we argue that features of standard assessment approaches reinforce some of the less desirable features of instructional programs. Finally, we outline an alternative approach to testing, a form of dynamic assessment, and illustrate it with examples drawn from research on inductive reasoning skills and early mathematics.

METACOGNITION

One of the most salient features about metacognition is that the term means different things to different people, with the result that there is considerable confusion in the literature about what is and what is not metacognitive. This confusion leads to apparently contradictory viewpoints, ranging from claims that the concept is too ill-defined or fuzzy to be the object of scientific inquiry to assertions that things metacognitive are the driving force of learning, and therefore the major aspects of learning we should be studying.

To understand this confusion, it may be worthwhile to review the history of this term. The recent surge of interest in metacognition stems originally from a paper by Tulving and Madigan (1970), in which they criticized the state of research on memory. They particularly noted that no one was looking at that which is uniquely human about human memory, the fact that people have knowledge and beliefs about their memory processes. John Flavell (e.g., 1971; Flavell, Friedrichs, & Hoyt, 1970) picked this up and began studying children's metamemory, i.e., what do children know about memory, and when do they come to know it? Much of this work demanded that children reflect on their own memory processes. This is work emphasizing knowledge about cognition.

At the same time, but from a somewhat different perspective, other researchers, ourselves among them, became interested in taking charge of one's learning, or the management processes of learning (Brown, 1974, 1975, 1978). The prime reason for this interest was the typical outcome of instructional studies aimed at improving students' learning and memory skills. Although performance indeed improved when it was under the experimenter's control, students repeatedly failed to use their newly acquired competence on their own volition (Campione & Brown, 1977). They did not seem to grasp the significance of the skills they had been taught and subsequently applied them only when prompted to do so by the experimenter (e.g., Brown & Barclay, 1976; Brown, Campione, & Barclay, 1979). This awkward fact led to work on teaching students methods of self-regulation, and to a concentration on monitoring and overseeing the use of strategic resources (Brown et al., 1981). This thrust reflected concern primarily with control of cognition.

Thus, there are several aspects to the study of metacognition. One concerns students' conscious and statable knowledge about cognition, about themselves as learners, about the resources they have available to them, and about the structure of knowledge in the domains in which they work. Another centers on self-regulation, students' monitoring and orchestration of their own cognitive skills. A further emphasis that cuts across the above is the ability to reflect upon both their knowledge and their management processes. These somewhat different emphases can be confusing, but taken together combine to paint a rich picture of how well students can learn independently in a domain. Successful learners can reflect on their problem-solving activities, have available powerful strategies for dealing with novel problems, and oversee and regulate those strategies efficiently and effectively. They find learning challenging and see themselves as in control of their destiny. Weaker students, in contrast, acquire fewer problem-solving strategies, are less aware of the utility of those strategies, and do not use them flexibly in the service of new learning. They are not convinced that they can control their performance and tend to be relatively passive in learning situations.

Although the majority of our work in metacognition has centered on learning from texts, we believe the principles of learning and instruction we have developed are general and relevant to many academic disciplines, including mathematics. The problems encountered in teaching and evaluating students are consistent across domains, as are the potential solutions to some of those problems. We argue that attention to metacognitive aspects of learning can play a central role in upgrading both instructional programs and methods of assessment and evaluation. In the next sections, we present an analysis of typical instructional programs and their weaknesses, and indicate the ways in which metacognition in its various guises could and possibly should be interjected into those programs.

AN ANALYSIS OF THE CURRENT STATUS

There is considerable converging evidence that by sixth grade, children have some success at mastering basic skills of reading, writing, and arithmetic. But there are also disturbing signs that many students lack a firm conceptual grasp of the goal of the activities in which they engage. They can perform the necessary subskills or algorithms on demand, but do not grasp their significance. In Table 1 we make some superficial comparisons of aspects of traditional instruction that might be responsible for this state of affairs.

Table 1
Traditional Education

READING	MATH	WRITING
Direct Instruction	Direct Instruction	Direct Instruction or No Instruction
Decoding before comprehension	Algorithms before understanding	Mechanics before communication
Strategies are rarely taught or made explicit		
When attacking understanding, practice decomposed skills		
Differential treatment effect		
(slow learners get heavier skills emphasis)		
LEADS TO METAPROBLEMS		
The child believes that the goal is syntax not semantics, i.e.,		
Reading is decoding	Algorithms and correct answers are math	Writing is neatness
Leads to "Inert" encapsulated knowledge		
Leads to trouble with control structures		
SUGGESTED REMEDIES		
Cognitive Modelling, Apprenticeship System, etc.		
Example		
Reciprocal teaching	Modeling and group discussion	Seminar and soloing

As indicated in Table 1, in the three major "domains" of grade school learning, there is an emphasis on direct instruction with strong teacher control. Lower level skills are taught before higher level understanding, causing predictable problems of metacognition. Students fundamentally misunderstand the goal of early education; they come to believe that reading is decoding, that math consists *only* of running off well-practiced algorithms, etc. This emphasis on skill training is stressed to an even greater degree for low achieving students, those for whom explicit instruction in understanding is particularly necessary. Strategies are rarely taught. When practice in understanding is finally provided, frequently it too is treated as consisting of decomposed skills (summarizing, inferring, etc.). Such activities are presented as ends in themselves, rather than as a means to a more meaningful end. Little attention is paid to the flexible or opportunistic use of strategies in appropriate contexts. This common approach leads to the acquisition of "inert knowledge" (Whitehead, 1916) that cannot be applied flexibly. We argue below that one major reason for this state of affairs is that traditional educational practice rarely incorporates metacognitive and contextual factors in learning.

METACOGNITION AND INSTRUCTION

A consideration of Table 1 suggests that much of the instruction students receive in school involves what we have referred to. as blind instruction, in that students are rarely told about why they practice the activities they do. This contrasts with informed, self control instruction, in which students are informed of the reasons why the skills are taught, and are further encouraged to monitor, regulate, and control their own learning (Brown, Campione, & Day, 1981; Brown, Bransford, Ferrara, & Campione, 1983). One clear consequence of blind instruction is a lack of ensuing transfer. Students taught strategies blindly do not apply these strategies to related problems. If flexible use of instructed strategies is the goal, students need to be informed of the purposes of the skills they are taught, and given instruction in the monitoring and regulation of those resources.

On the positive side, there is growing consensus that interactive learning environments, in which the goal is to enhance students' conceptual understanding of the semantics, or the meaning, of procedures (Resnick, 1982) and to confront the metacognitive issues directly, produce more insightful intentional learners (Bereiter & Scardamalia, in press). Leading examples of such approaches are reciprocal teaching of reading comprehension (Brown & Palincsar, 1982, in press; Palincsar & Brown, 1984), procedural facilitation in writing instruction (Scardamalia, Bereiter, & Steinbach, 1984), and Schoenfeld's (1983, 1985) discussion-based approach to instruction in mathematical problem solving.

LIMITATIONS OF TRADITIONAL INSTRUCTIONAL PRACTICES

In this section, we expand upon the points made in Table 1 with illustrations from the work in reading comprehension that influenced the development of reciprocal teaching and from comparable data emerging in the field of mathematics education. The suggestion is that the philosophy of education underlying the reading program might carry over to mathematics instruction.

Limitations of Standard Instructional Practices

The major problems in reading and mathematics are that although the majority of school-aged children acquire the ability to decode texts or run off algorithms, significantly fewer come to understand what they are doing; they fail to learn efficiently from reading or to understand the logic of, for example, place value notation. We believe this pattern is the result the educational practices listed in Table 1 and elaborated below.

Emphasis on direct instruction. The typical mode of instruction is one in which the teacher lectures, and the students listen. The general conception is of the students as passive, rather than active, participants. And the idea is that the knowledge the teacher has can be transmitted directly to the students—the metaphor is that of pouring information from one container (the teacher's head) to another (the student's head). This tendency is, if anything, even clearer in mathematics. Stodolsky's (1988) observations indicate that the typical pattern is for teachers to work out problems on the board and for students to practice further examples of the same type, as seatwork. She finds less discussion and argument in mathematics classes than in, e.g., social studies classes, even when the same teacher is working with the same students.

Lack of on-line diagnosis. As a partial result of the emphasis on direct instruction, the teacher does not expend much effort in making on-line diagnoses of individual student processing capabilities. The instruction proceeds at a predetermined rate and sequence, dictated by the curriculum employed in the particular classroom. For example, Durkin (1984), in reviewing research on the teaching of reading comprehension, noted that:

> . . . none of the 15 teachers appeared to be diagnostically oriented. That is, none seemed to look for evidence of instructional needs which, presumably, could then meet with appropriate instruction and practice. Instead, as Duffy (1981) has suggested, they moved their students through materials in a way that indicated they were more concerned about 'a smooth flow of activities' than about learning who knew what and doing something about what was missing. (Durkin, 1984, p. 743)

This practice can also be seen in mathematics education. Putnam (1987) evaluated the activities of teachers working in the context of multiple-digit addition with actual second grade students and with computer-simulated students. The computer-simulated students featured one systematic error pattern, or bug (Brown & Burton, 1978). In evaluating the teachers' performance, Putnam was led to reject a diagnostic/remedial model featuring on-line diagnosis of student problems. Rather, he concluded that a better account of teacher behavior featured the concept of a curriculum script, prescribing the sequence of skills and activities through which students are expected to progress. Although the teachers did engage in some evaluation of student responses, their major aim was to ensure progress through the curriculum-driven agenda. The similarity with reading is striking.

Basic skills before understanding. Reading instruction in the early grades focuses almost exclusively on decoding skills. The argument is that students need to be able to identify the words in the text before they can begin to understand it, a reasonable point. But an overemphasis on decoding results in few opportunities for learning comprehension-fostering skills, with the attendant problem that students get the impression that reading is decoding—believing that the aim of reading is to be able to identify the words appearing in the text. Similarly, early instruction in mathematics emphasizes the acquisition of essential mathematical facts and algorithmic procedures. The use of these facts and procedures in solving mathematical problems is put off to a later time.

Emphasis on subskills. Reading for meaning is a compiex task, and for purposes of instruction it is necessary to render it somewhat more manageable for non-expert learners. The most frequent approach is to analyze the task into sets of elementary subskills that together provide the means for dealing with the more global task. These subskills then become what is taught. Thus, even when comprehension is the target of instruction, students are given practice in isolated, decontextualized skills such as finding topic sentences, selecting summaries, finding the main idea, etc. It is important to note that these skills are practiced in relative isolation, both from each other and from the task of reading and comprehending intact text. The task of selecting and combining the subskills and bringing them to bear on the task of understanding while actually reading is then left as an exercise for the student. A comparable example in mathematics instruction is the introduction of multiplication as an enterprise in itself, rather than an example of repeated addition.

Absence of explicit strategy instruction. This emphasis on subskills is accompanied by a lack of explicit instruction regarding the more complex strategies that expert studiers deploy flexibly when attempting to learn from texts. For example, analyses of the comprehension process have identified an impressive array of such tactics, ones that are acquired by extremely capable students in the absence of explicit instruction. These activities, such as summarizing and paraphrasing what one has just read, anticipating the author's argument, etc., allow students both to extend their comprehension and to monitor its progress. (If one cannot summarize or if anticipations are disproved, this is evidence that comprehension is not occurring.) However, there is by now considerable evidence that less capable students do not acquire a variety of such cognitive strategies unless they are given detailed and explicit instruction in their use (e.g., Campione, Brown, & Ferrara, 1982; Rohwer, 1973). It is also true that the more complex the strategy in question, the more explicit the instruction needed, even for more capable students (Brown et al., 1983; Day, 1986). An excellent example of this point with highly selected students is the finding by Schoenfeld (1985) that in order to induce college mathematics students to make effective use of Polya-like heuristics, such as examining special cases and establishing subgoals, it was necessary for him to present a detailed description of the operation of the heuristics, together with considerable directed practice in their use. The idea that complex comprehension strategies will emerge from instruction aimed at instilling their constituent subskills is difficult to defend.

Differential treatment effect. These general emphases on "basic" skills and subskills are even more extended in time and pronounced in the case of weaker students. Those perceived by their teachers as poor readers get extensive decoding practice at the expense of instruction aimed at higher level processing (e.g., Brown, Palincsar & Armbruster, 1985). Teachers interrupt reading more often when poor readers are involved than when the same errors are made by good readers. Further, teachers are likely to interrupt poor readers as soon as an error is made, thereby disrupting the flow and impeding comprehension; but with good readers, they wait until the end of a meaning-chunk before interrupting (Allington, 1980; Brophy & Good, 1969). Good readers tend to be questioned about the meaning of what they are reading. In contrast, poor readers are given practice primarily in pronunciation (Collins, 1980; McDermott, 1978). Similarly, in the case of mathematics, teachers introducing new topics (for example, remainder division) structure their feedback and emphases differently with groups of higher and lower ability students (Petitto, 1985). The weaker the students, the more pronounced the tendency to emphasize basic over higher-level skill instruction. And the weaker the students, the less likely they are to acquire those higher-level skills without explicit instruction.

Metacognition and self-regulation. We have argued that explicit instruction is needed before important comprehension strategies become a part of a learner's repertoire. Even if such instruction is included, however, problems remain. Having a strategy available does not mean that it will be accessed appropriately when needed, nor does it guarantee that it will be executed optimally when accessed. The literature is replete with examples of students' inability to retrieve strategies appropriate to a task even when it is clear that those strategies are available (e.g., can be elicited with a minimal prompt) and can be used effectively on the particular task. In the case of open-ended domains like comprehension, the situation is complicated by the fact that the use of various strategies depends upon a number of factors, including the reader's relevant knowledge, the complexity of the text, the purposes of reading, etc. (Brown et al., 1983). Fluent readers (studiers) apply their strategies opportunistically, reacting swiftly to changing circumstances. And it is necessary to deal with the control of instructed strategies as well as to provide for their availability.

In the case of reading instruction, this is simply unlikely to occur. For example, Durkin characterized the reading lessons she observed by noting that:

> . . . 15 of the 16 teachers in the present research:
>
> (1) Never told the children why a particular assignment was being given.
> (2) Went over an assignment only if the written directions were unclear or if the format was different from any used before.
> (3) Never explained how the topic of an assignment and the ability to read were related.
> (4) Seemed most concerned that students finish assignments and get the right answers. (Durkin, 1984, p. 741)

The parallel with mathematics instruction, with its emphasis on working swiftly and getting the right answers, is obvious.

Consequences of Traditional Practice

Given this educational history, it is not surprising that there are a number of metaproblems that arise. Many students acquire a distorted view of what the academic tasks are, i.e., they come to believe that reading is decoding, that math is executing procedures, that writing is neatness, etc. They come to view the syntax of the domain, rather than its semantics, as its core concept (Resnick, 1982).

The knowledge and skills many students acquire tend to be encapsulated and inert, available when clearly marked by context (as they are, for example, on many standardized tests) but not serviceable in other circumstances as tools for learning. Although skills may be learned, the control structure needed to apply them flexibly and appropriately can be notably absent from the repertoires of even talented students (Davis, 1984; Schoenfeld, 1983, 1985).

In the context of metacognition, students suffer from problems in the two main arenas included under that rubric. Their knowledge of the domains is faulty, and they experience particular difficulties attempting to monitor and regulate their on-line learning and problem-solving attempts.

ALTERNATIVES TO TRADITIONAL INSTRUCTION

As illustrated in Table 1, there have been several attempts to design instructional programs that avoid these difficulties. They share the feature that they involve cooperative learning groups in which students and a teacher work together to improve some target performance (understanding a text, producing a composition, solving a mathematics problem, etc.); they have been dubbed cognitive apprenticeship programs by Collins, Brown, and Newman (in press). In this section, we describe the reciprocal teaching program developed by Palincsar and Brown (Brown & Palincsar, 1982, 1987, in press; Palincsar & Brown, 1984) to teach comprehension skills to academically weak grade school students, illustrate the effects it generates, and present some initial data on extensions of the procedures to early algebra.

Reciprocal Teaching

Philosophy and background. The reciprocal teaching program was developed specifically to overcome the difficulties highlighted in Table 1. Reciprocal teaching takes place in a cooperative learning group that features guided practice in applying four concrete strategies (questioning, clarifying, summarizing, and predicting) to scaffold a discussion concerning the meaning of expository texts. These particular strategies both promote comprehension and provide the student with concrete methods of monitoring their understanding. All members of the group, in turn, serve as the learning leader, responsible for orchestrating the discussion, and supportive critics, whose job it is to encourage the learning leader to explain the content and help resolve misunderstandings. The strategies provide concrete heuristics for getting the discussion going. Teacher modeling provides examples of expert performance. And the reciprocal nature of the procedure guarantees student engagement.

This is how it works. The dialogue leader begins the discussion by asking a question on the main content and ends by summarizing the gist. If there is disagreement, the group rereads and discusses potential candidates for question and summary statements until they reach consensus. Summarizing provides a means by which the group can monitor its progress, noting points of agreement and disagreement. Particularly valuable is the fact that summarizing at the end of a period of discussion helps students establish where they are in preparation for tackling a new segment of text. Opportunistic attempts to clarify any comprehension problems that might arise are also an integral part of the discussions. And finally, the leader asks for predictions about future content. Throughout, the adult teacher provides guidance and feedback tailored to the needs of the current discussion leader and the respondents.

Reciprocal teaching is a form of guided cooperative learning because of the provision of expert scaffolding by the adult teacher. It is the teacher's job to see that responsibility for the comprehension activities of the group is transferred to the students as soon as possible. As students master one level of involvement, the teacher increases his or her demands so that students are gradually called upon to function at a more challenging level, finally adopting the leader/critic role fully and independently. The teacher then fades into the background and acts as a sympathetic coach, allowing the students to take charge of their own learning.

Main findings. Since 1981 when the program began, 287 junior high school students and 366 first to third grade children have taken part in reading and listening comprehension programs respectively. These interventions were conducted by regular classroom teachers working with small groups (the ideal group size is six, but the teachers have handled much larger groups). Students enter the study scoring approximately 30% correct on independent tests of comprehension and continue in the program for at least 20 instructional days. We count as successful any student who achieves an independent score of 75% correct on five successive days. With this as the criterion, approximately 80% of the students at both ages are judged to be successful. Furthermore, they maintain their independent mastery for up to six months to a year after instruction ceases (Brown & Palincsar, 1982), generalize to other classroom activities, notably science and social studies, and improve approximately two years on standardized tests of comprehension (Palincsar & Brown, 1984). In one school district alone, 50 teachers and 700 students are using the procedure as their regular reading comprehension instruction.

Reciprocal teaching and coherent content. In the majority of our work on reciprocal teaching we have followed the typical pattern of classroom "reading groups," that is, each day the children read a text in their "readers" that is unrelated to the previous texts; passage follows passage with no coherent link between them (a story about volcanoes, follows one on dinosaurs, follows one on aquanauts, etc.). Skill training in basal readers is also arranged this way. For example, Durkin (1984) noted that successive lessons dealt with exaggeration, multiple meanings, bar graphs, vowel sounds, and main ideas. Further, there was little relation between the topic of an assignment and the text students were reading at the time. This use of unrelated material has several drawbacks if one is interested in the accumulation of knowledge, as well as process. It encourages encapsulated knowledge acquisition; topic follows topic with little opportunity for cumulative reference. Such measures positively encourage the child to build up encapsulated "inert" knowledge (Whitehead, 1916), rarely used again after the test hurdle has been surmounted. If one is interested in reading as a process of decoding text and grasping the meaning, any text will do, but if one is interested in learning with understanding in the sense of acquiring a usable, flexible body of knowledge, such procedures are unsatisfactory.

In a recent study, we used the reciprocal teaching method to encourage third grade minority students to acquire coherent knowledge about biological themes concerning animal adaptation (camouflage, mimicry, protection from elements, parasites, extinction, and natural pest control).

Twenty days of discussions of such themes led to dramatic improvements in both process and theme understanding. On daily independent measures of comprehension, reciprocal teaching groups increased their performance by 32 percentage points from the pre to the posttest (40%—72%). And even twelve months later the effect of instruction was apparent. Although the students started off poorly, scoring an average of 51% correct on the first two days, on the third and fourth day they had jumped to 89% and by the last two days of follow-up they scored 92% correct.

Not only did the children remember how to conduct the reciprocal teaching dialogues, and scored well on independent tests, they also remembered the content. Asked to sort pictures of the animals into the six themes, they scored 85% correct immediately after being in the study and 82% correct one year later. Scored as correct were responses that the child could justify in terms of why the example was a member of a theme. On both the long- and short-term tests the children were able to classify novel exemplars of the themes. Reciprocal teaching experience enables the children both to learn a body of coherent, usable, knowledge and to develop a repertoire of strategies that will enable them to learn new content on their own.

Extension to mathematics. We are working on a number of projects involving an extension of the principles underlying the reciprocal-teaching reading/listening program to mathematics. Here we will describe one of those attempts, involving beginning algebra word problems. The students were selected because they showed considerable ability to run off algorithms correctly, but did not give evidence of understanding the concepts underlying those algorithms. For example, students who got the right answer but could not defend themselves from seductive countersuggestions would be ideal candidates (see example below).

As in the reading work, the students work together with an instructor in small cooperative groups. The students and adult teacher again take turns being learning leaders and supportive critics responsible for leading a discussion aimed at understanding algebra word problems. The procedure embodies expert modeling, scaffolding, and coaching on the part of the teacher; the method forces externalization of strategies, monitoring of progress, and attempts to impose meaning. What differs is that the strategies selected to scaffold the discussion are appropriate to the domain. Just as the strategies used in promoting reading comprehension are different from those that facilitate writing (Scardamalia & Bereiter, 1985), so too we needed domain-specific control structures for mathematics.

In our mathematics modifications, learning leaders guide the group in working on three successive chalkboards designed to help students proceed systematically. In addition, these procedures generate an external record of the group's problem solving, which can then be monitored, evaluated, and reflected upon. The three boards are: (1) The Planning Board, where the group extracts the relevant facts embodied in the word problem; (2) The Representation Board, where the students draw diagrams illustrating the problem; and (3) The Doing Board, where they translate the drawings into the appropriate equation(s) and compute the answer. Students throughout discuss their approaches and help each other reflect upon the visual trace of their joint work.

Text of Problem:

Harry ate a hamburger and drank a glass of milk which totaled 495 calories. The milk contained half as many calories as the sandwich. How many calories were in the sandwich and how many in the milk?

PLANNING BOARD	DRAWING BOARD	DOING BOARD
A hamburger and a glass of milk totaled 495 calories The milk contained half as many calories than the hamburger H = calories of hamburgers M = calories of milk	495 H M	$H + M = 495$

PLANNING BOARD	DRAWING BOARD	DOING BOARD
A hamburger and a glass of milk totaled 495 calories The milk contained half as many calories than the hamburger H = calories of hamburgers M = calories of milk	495 H M 495 M M M H	$H + M = 495$ $M + M + M = 495$ $\begin{array}{r} 165 \\ 3\overline{\smash{)}495} \\ \underline{3} \\ 19 \\ \underline{18} \\ 15 \\ \underline{15} \\ 0 \end{array}$

Figure 1. Sample boards

In Figure 1 are some intermediate states in the problem-solving process that illustrate the use of the boards. In the top panel, the students have extracted the relevant information and have begun to develop a representation of the problem. They have also translated it into an equation (on the Doing Board). However, the equation does not have a unique solution, so they are forced to go back to the drawing board and elaborate their sketch. In the next panel, we see additional work that leads to an appropriate equation, and the computational stage is begun (they solve for the number of calories in the milk). Later in the sequence they finish the problem and engage in some checking activities to make sure that the result makes sense and is consistent with the problem statement.

The group worked on three different types of problems over the course of the 20 days of instruction—those involving: (1) a single-variable linear equation; (2) two-variable linear equations; and (3) monomial by binomial equations. The design included several pretests evaluating computational skill as well as entering ability to deal with these kinds of problems; essentially, the students could not solve these problems independently when the intervention was begun. A posttest assessed improvement on the target problems, as well as performance on some very open-ended transfer problems. A control group received the same introduction to the problem types as the experimental group and samples of worked out examples. They also took the same tests as did the experimental group.

The main results are shown in Figure 2, where it can be seen that the experimental group outperformed the control group on both the target and transfer problems. This pattern of results is encouraging. The discussions do proceed smoothly; student engagement does result; the Planning, Drawing, Doing routine does become established. The students are enthusiastic and willing to spend considerable periods of time working on individual problems, both in class and at home. And, their performance does improve significantly more than a control group's given equivalent practice and feedback on the main problem types but no discussions. We should point out, however, that so far the procedure has been attempted only by an experienced mathematics teacher, while the reading comprehension methods can be handled by average teachers. We are currently engaged in replicating and extending the study, noting the vicissitudes of the procedure when it is handed over to regular classroom mathematics teachers.

LIMITATIONS OF TRADITIONAL ASSESSMENT PRACTICES

It is believed that testing drives teaching, and there is little doubt that assessment procedures influence instruction. Students, teachers, and school districts are evaluated against performance on standardized tests, and considerable time is spent preparing students to take those tests. Consider first

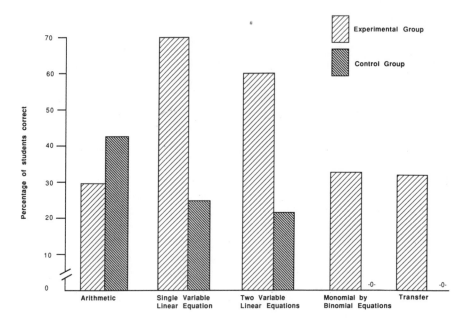

Figure 2. Group performance by problem type

reading assessment. In line with the properties of reading instruction outlined above, tests at the earlier grades are heavily oriented toward phonics, as compared with comprehension. It is not until around fourth grade that this bias begins to change, and it is around this time that weaker students' performance begins to look particularly poor. Students with comprehension problems can do reasonably well on reading tests until this time, but beyond the fourth grade level, their performance begins to diverge rapidly from that of more capable readers.

Even at the upper grade levels, test structures continue to reinforce the subskills emphasis. The items designed to evaluate comprehension tend to tap skills, such as summarizing, finding the main idea, etc., in settings divorced from actually reading and understanding large segments of text. That is, the activities are tested as ends in themselves, rather than as means to the end of understanding what is being read. Students are asked to perform on items similar to those that appear on worksheets that go along with basal reader series; and it is quite possible to master those exercises without actually being able to read with understanding. Stated in another fashion, students are tested on their ability to perform the requisite activities, but are not tested on their understanding of those activities, for example, in terms of when or why they would be appropriate adjuncts to learning.

Similarly, mathematics evaluations are based on static tests assessing students' ability to run off algorithms, to solve problems displayed in a recognizable format, etc. They do not tap the extent of student understanding of the procedures they are asked to execute. There is a tendency to assume that children who get the right answers know what they are doing, and that those who fail do not. In addition, it is assumed that what a child does *now* on a test is a reasonable reflection of his or her knowledge, and that knowledge predicts or is equivalent to readiness to learn. As reasonable as those assumptions may sound, we quarrel with both of them.

One major set of criticisms leveled against standard test procedures centers about their static, product-based nature. They are static in that they afford a glimpse of what students can do at a given point when asked to work independently. They are product based, in that scores are based on the number and/or pattern of items answered correctly. In this way, they provide an estimate of degree of current knowledge, but little insight into the processes underlying the acquisition of that competence. An alternative approach involves dynamic assessment (e.g., Campione & Brown, 1987, in press), where the aim is to correct this imbalance by evaluating the operation of these key processes. In the limited space available, we will outline the specific approach to dynamic assessment we have been developing, and illustrate it in the context of early mathematics. As background, we illustrate some of the difficulties associated with standard static tests.

Static Tests

A major problem with standard static tests featuring problems presented in canonical form is that getting the right answer does not necessarily indicate that a child knows what he or she is doing (Erlwanger, 1973). For example, Peck, Jenks, and Connell (in press) interviewed fourth to sixth graders who had just taken a standardized mathematics test used by their school district for placement in appropriate instructional groups. On the basis of the interviews, they found four types of students: (1) Those who got the answers right and knew why; (2) Those who produced incorrect answers and did not know why—the two categories that tests are meant to separate. But there were large numbers of students who fell into the other two classifications: (3) Those who got the right answer but did not understand what they were doing; and (4) Those who were wrong but did show evidence of understanding. On the basis of these interviews, Peck et al. report that 41% of the students were inappropriately placed.

Of the two groups, those in group (3) are the more interesting. Group (4) consists of children who are scored wrong primarily because they don't conform to the strict rules of the game (1/2 is correct, 3/6 is incorrect). Of more interest are students who appear to work out the problem correctly, e.g.,

$$3 \, 1/3 - 2 \, 5/6 =$$
$$10/3 - 17/6 = 20/6 - 17/6 = 3/6 = 1/2$$

This child is in control of the algorithm. However, what happens if he is asked to discuss the answer a little, for example by being asked if 1/2 or 3/6 is larger? This student insisted that 1/2 is larger because:

> "the denominator of 1/2 is smaller, so the pieces are larger and one of the great big pieces (1/2) is more than 3 of the tiny (sixth) pieces."

Having been suitably confused, the student had difficulty reworking the problem. This student, like a significant number of his peers, recognizes the problem type when presented in canonical form and can run off the algorithm correctly. However, he cannot resist countersuggestions because he does not have a firm grip on the meaning of what he is doing.

ALTERNATIVES TO TRADITIONAL ASSESSMENT PRACTICES

Dynamic Tests

How might one measure understanding? In our work, we take the knowledge that students apparently possess as a starting point, but then supplement that information with assessments of how readily they can acquire and understand new skills or procedures that are just beyond their current competence level. That is, we ask not only how much a student knows, but in addition, how readily he can progress beyond that point. We also have assumed that this latter, dynamic, information will provide more sensitive diagnostic information about individual students than does their current knowledge. We have conducted a series of studies, involving an array of task domains and students varying widely in age and ability. Encouragingly, the results are extremely consistent across those variations.

The initial studies (Bryant, Brown, & Campione, 1983; Campione, Brown, Ferrara, Jones, & Steinberg, 1985; Ferrara, Brown, & Campione, 1986) were set in the context of inductive reasoning problems. In those studies, students were given a pretest establishing their entering competence in the particular domain, followed by instructional sessions in which we estimated how quickly they could learn new sets of rules and how flexibly they could apply them to novel problems. They were then given a posttest to see how much they had learned from that exposure. These learning and transfer scores were shown to have both concurrent and predictive validity (Campione & Brown, 1987, in press). They distinguished groups of students differing in academic success. And, more importantly, they were the best predictors of gain from pre to posttest.

For example, Bryant et al. (1983) worked with five- and six-year-olds solving two kinds of inductive reasoning problems, one involving variants of the Raven Progressive Matrices and the second a series completion task involving objects of different sizes and shapes. Summaries of multiple regression analyses of the pre to posttest gain scores are shown in Table 2. As can be seen, the dynamic scores accounted for more variance than estimates of general ability (IQ) and entering competence. Further, the learning and transfer scores accounted for additional variance in gain scores even after the effects of ability and competence were removed. Finally, the transfer scores were consistently more powerful predictors than the learning scores.

Table 2
Multiple Regression Summaries

Multiple Regression Summary Table for Series Completion Gain Scores				
Predictor Variable	Zero-Order Correlation	Multiple Correlation	R2	Change in R2
Estimated IQ	.52*	.52	.27	.272*
Ravens	.35	.58	.34	.062
Training	− .46*	.60	.36	.020
Transfer	− .69*	.75	.56	.221*
Far Transfer	− .56*	.75	.56	.000

*p < .05

Multiple Regression Summary Table for Matrices Gain Scores				
Predictor Variable	Zero-Order Correlation	Multiple Correlation	R2	Change in R2
Estimated IQ	.49*	.49	.24	.235*
Ravens	.47*	.61	.37	.135*
Training	− .61*	.77	.59	.224*
Transfer	− .60*	.88	.77	.173*
Far Transfer	− .70*	.88	.77	.014

*p < .05

Multiple Regression Summary Table for Mathematics Gain Scores				
Predictor Variable	Zero-Order Correlation	Multiple Correlation	R2	Change in R2
Background Knowledge	.47*	.47	.222	.222*
IQ	.28	.47	.222	.000
Learning	− .41*	.49	.239	.017
Transfer	− .73*	.75	.559	.320*

*p < .05

To illustrate the approach in more depth, we review a recently conducted Ph.D. dissertation conducted by Roberta Ferrara (1986), who worked with five-year-old children learning to solve word arithmetic addition and subtraction problems. The basic procedure begins with a series of pretests to assess entering competence. For each student, Ferrara obtained IQ scores, standardized mathematics scores, initial indices of their ability to solve the targeted problems, and a test of arithmetic understanding based on current cognitive developmental theory and research.

The student and tester then worked collaboratively to solve problems that the student could not solve independently. During the learning phase of the study, the problems were simple two- digit addition problems, $3 + 2 = ?$, presented as word problems, such as:

"Cookie Monster starts out with 3 cookies in his cookie jar, and I'm putting 2 more in the jar. Now how many cookies are there altogether in the cookie jar?"

When the student encountered difficulties, the tester provided hints or suggestions about how he or she should proceed. These hints are standardized and proceed from general to specific, with the general hints being of the metacognitive type, "Is this problem like one you have seen before?" "Are you sure you remember the main facts?" "Can you restate the problem?" "Can you represent the problem with these tokens?" These are followed by hints suggesting appropriate strategies, and eventually by a full demonstration and explanation of the solution if needed. The interaction continues until the student can solve a series of such problems without help, and we measure the amount of aid needed to achieve mastery.

Following this, a variety of transfer problems was presented, in the same interactive, assisted format. These problems required the children to apply the procedures learned initially to a variety of problems that differ in systematic ways from those on which they had worked initially; some were quite similar (near transfer: 2-digit addition problems involving new quantities and different toy and character contexts), others more dissimilar (far transfer: $3 + 2 + 5 = ?$), and some were quite different indeed (missing addend problems: $3 + ? = 8$). Again, what is scored is the amount of help students need before they can solve these transfer problems on their own. The goal here is to evaluate understanding of the learned procedures. That is, in our dynamic assessment approach, the aim is to program transfer and to use the ease of application of routines to novel contexts as the measure of understanding. In other words, can the students use only what they have been taught and only in the context in which it was taught, or can they go further and apply what they know intelligently?

After these learning and transfer sessions were completed, a posttest was given to determine how much the student had learned during the course of the assessment/instruction, the gain from pre to posttest. The question of interest again concerns which variables best predict the gain scores. The major data are summarized in Table 2. The main features are that the dynamic measures are better predictors of gain (mean correlation = $-.57$) than are the static, knowledge and ability, scores (mean correlation = $.38$). Further, in a hierarchical regression analysis, although the static scores when extracted first did account for 22.2% of the variance in gain scores, addition of the dynamic scores accounted for an additional 33.7% of the variance, with transfer performance doing the majority of the work; it accounted for 32% of that variance.

Summary

The results from the mathematics study are consonant with those gleaned from the earlier ones involving inductive reasoning. Although measures of general ability and entering knowledge do predict the amount of gain individuals achieve, the dynamic measures are: (1) better individual predictors of gain; (2) account for significant additional variance in those gain scores beyond general ability and knowledge; with (3) transfer, or understanding, scores being significantly more diagnostic than learning scores. If the interest is in predicting the learning trajectories of different students, the best indicant is not their IQ or how much they know originally, nor even how readily they acquire new procedures, but how well they understand and make flexible use of those procedures in the service of solving novel problems. Static tests do not necessarily measure understanding, or readiness to learn.

OVERALL SUMMARY

Metacognitive components of learning involve students' awareness and control of their cognitive resources. We have argued that traditional educational practices, in both instruction and assessment, tend to ignore these aspects. Specifically, students are not made aware of the reasons for the skills and procedures they are taught. They are seldom given explicit teaching regarding the orchestration, management, and opportunistic and appropriate use of those skills. And they are seldom required to reflect upon their own learning activities. These factors help to induce in students a flawed understanding of themselves as learners and of the academic domains they are called upon to master.

In the light of this analysis, we have designed alternative approaches incorporating metacognitive factors into both instruction and assessment. In each case, students and adults work collaboratively to solve problems. In the course of these collaborations, the adult models appropriate problem-solving strategies, along with the selection and monitoring of those approaches. In each case, the adult also provides feedback tuned to the child's need at any point.

Reciprocal teaching features a group of individuals working together to solve a problem, be it a case of extracting the meaning of a text they are reading, or attacking an algebra word problem. At the outset, the teacher does the lion's share of the cognitive work, with that contribution decreasing as the students become progressively more able to orchestrate the problem-solving process for themselves. The main feature is that a set of domain-appropriate strategies or heuristics is used to scaffold the discussion. It is important to note that those strategies are never practiced as independent activities, but always in the context of actual on-line problem solving. In reciprocal teaching of either reading or mathematics, the teacher models, and the students practice, the metacognitive, self-regulatory skills associated with the flexible and opportunistic application of those strategies as means for learning.

Dynamic assessment methods present children with problems just one step beyond their existing competence. The tester begins by providing as little help as possible but then provides help as needed for the child to reach independent mastery. The degree of aid needed, both to learn new principles and to apply them, is carefully calibrated and measured. The required amount of help provides a much better index of students' future learning trajectories than static pretests. In particular, the ease with which students apply, or transfer, principles they have learned is regarded as an indication of student understanding of those principles; and this transfer performance is the most sensitive index of a student's readiness to proceed within a particular domain.

Common to the new look in both diagnosis and instruction is the key notion of supportive contexts for learning. Four main principles are involved: (1) Understanding procedures rather than just speed and accuracy should be the aim of assessment and instruction; (2) Expert guidance should be used to reveal as well as promote independent competence; (3) Microgenetic analysis permits estimates of learning as it actually occurs over short periods of time; and (4) Proleptic teaching is involved in both assessment and instruction, for both aim at one stage beyond current performance, in anticipation of levels of competence not yet achieved individually but possible within supportive learning environments (Brown & Campione, 1986).

FOOTNOTE

1. Preparation of this manuscript and the research reported therein were supported by Grants HD–05951 and HD–15808 from the National Institute of Child Health and Human Development.

REFERENCES

Allington, R. (1980). Teacher interruption behavior during primary-grade oral reading. *Journal of Educational Psychology, 72*, 371–377.

Bereiter, C., & Scardamalia, M. (in press). Intentional learning as a goal of instruction. In L. B. Resnick (Ed.), *Knowing and learning: Issues for a cognitive science of instruction.* Hillsdale, NJ: Erlbaum.

Borkowski, J. G., & Cavanaugh, J. C. (1979). Maintenance and generalization of skills and strategies by the retarded. In N. R. Ellis (Ed.), *Handbook of mental deficiency: Psychological theory and research* (pp. 569–617). Hillsdale, NJ: Erlbaum.

Brophy, J. E., & Good, T. L. (1974). *Teacher-child dyadic interaction: A manual for coding classroom behavior.* Austin, TX: The Research and Development Center for Teacher Education, The University of Texas.

Brown, A. L. (1974). The role of strategic behavior in retardate memory. In N. R. Ellis (Ed.), *International review of research in mental retardation* (Vol. 7, pp. 55–111). New York: Academic Press.

Brown, A. L. (1975). The development of memory: Knowing, knowing about knowing, and knowing how to know. In H. W. Reese (Ed.), *Advances in child development and behavior* (Vol. 10, pp. 103–152). New York: Academic Press.

Brown, A. L. (1978). Knowing when, where, and how to remember: A problem of metacognition. In R. Glaser (Ed.), *Advances in instructional psychology* (Vol. 1, pp. 77–165). Hillsdale, NJ: Erlbaum.

Brown, A. L. (in press). Analogical transfer and learning in children. What develops? To appear in S. Vosniadou (Ed.), *Similarity metaphor and analogy.* Hillsdale, NJ: Erlbaum.

Brown, A. L., & Barclay, C. R. (1976). The effects of training specific mnemonics on the metamnemonic efficiency of retarded children. *Child Development, 47,* 71–80.

Brown, A. L., Bransford, J. D., Ferrara, R. A., & Campione, J. C. (1983). Learning, remembering, and understanding. In J. H. Flavell & E. M. Markman (Eds.), *Handbook of child psychology* (Vol. 3, pp. 77–166). New York: Wiley.

Brown, A. L., & Campione, J. C. (1986). Psychological theory and the study of learning disabilities. *American Psychologist, 41,* 1059–1068.

Brown, A. L., Campione, J. C., & Barclay, C. R. (1979). Training self-checking routines for estimating test readiness: Generalization from list learning to prose recall. *Child Development, 50,* 501–512.

Brown, A. L., Campione, J. C., & Day, J. D. (1981). Learning to learn: On training students to learn from texts. *Educational Researcher, 10,* 14–21.

Brown, A. L., & Palincsar, A. S. (1982). Inducing strategic learning from texts by means of informed, self-control training. *Topics in Learning and Learning Disabilities, 2,* 1–17.

Brown, A. L., & Palincsar, A. S. (1987). Reciprocal teaching of comprehension strategies: A natural history of one program for enhancing learning. In J. D. Day & J. G. Borkowski (Eds.), *Intelligence and exceptionality: New directions for theory, assessment, and instructional practices.* New York: Ablex.

Brown, A. L., & Palincsar, A. S. (in press). Guided, cooperative learning and individual knowledge acquisition. In L. B. Resnick (Ed.), *Cognition and instruction: Issues and agendas.* Hillsdale, NJ: Erlbaum.

Brown, A. L., Palincsar, A. S., & Armbruster, B. B. (1984). Inducing comprehension-fostering activities in interactive learning situations. In H. Mandl, N. Stein, & T. Trabasso (Eds.), *Learning from texts* (pp. 255–287). Hillsdale, NJ: Erlbaum.

Brown, J. S., & Burton, R. R. (1978). Diagnostic models for procedural bugs in basic mathematical skills. *Cognitive Science, 2,* 155–192.

Bryant, N. R., Brown, A. L., & Campione (1983). *Preschool children's learning and transfer of matrices problems: Potential for improvement.* Paper presented at the Society for Research in Child Development meetings, Detroit.

Campione, J. C., & Brown, A. L. (1977). Memory and metamemory development in educable retarded children. In R. V. Kail, Jr. & J. W. Hagen (Eds.), *Perspectives on the development of memory and cognition* (pp. 367–406). Hillsdale, NJ: Erlbaum.

Campione, J. C., & Brown, A. L. (1978). Toward a theory of intelligence: Contributions from research with retarded children. *Intelligence, 2,* 279–304.

Campione, J. C., & Brown, A. L. (1987). Linking dynamic assessment with school achievement. In C. Lidz (Ed.), *Dynamic assessment: An interactional approach to evaluating learning potential* (pp. 82–115). New York: Guilford.

Campione, J. C., Brown, A. L., & Ferrara, R. A. (1982). Mental retardation and intelligence. In R. J. Sternberg (Ed.), *Handbook of human intelligence* (pp. 392–490). New York: Cambridge University Press.

Campione, J. C., Brown, A. L., Ferrara, R. A., Jones, R. S., & Steinberg, E. (1985). Breakdowns in flexible use of information: Intelligence-related differences in transfer following equivalent learning performance. *Intelligence, 9,* 297–315.

Collins, J. (1980). Differential treatment in reading groups. In J. Cook-Gumperz (Ed.), *Educational discourse.* London: Heinemann.

Collins, A., Brown, J. S., & Newman, S. E. (in press). Cognitive apprenticeship: Teaching the craft of reading, writing, and mathematics. In L. B. Resnick (Ed.), *Cognition and instruction: Issues and agendas.* Hillsdale, NJ: Erlbaum.

Davis, R. B. (1984). *Learning mathematics: The cognitive science approach to mathematics education.* Norwood, NJ: Ablex.

Day, J. D. (1986). Teaching summarization skills: Influences of student ability level and strategy difficulty. *Cognition and Instruction, 3,* 193–210.

Durkin, D. (1984). Is there a match between what elementary teachers do and what basal reader manuals recommend? *The Reading Teacher, 37,* 734–745.

Erlwanger, S. H. (1973). Benny's conception of rules and answers in IPI Mathematics. *Journal of Children's Mathematical Behavior, 1,* 7–26.

Ferrara, R. A. (1987). *Learning mathematics in the zone of proximal development: The importance of flexible use of knowledge.* Unpublished Ph.D. dissertation, University of Illinois.

Ferrara, R. A., Brown, A. L., & Campione, J. C. (1986). Children's learning and transfer of inductive reasoning rules: Studies in proximal development. *Child Development, 57,* 1087–1099.

Flavell, J. H. (1971). First discussant's comments: What is memory development the development of? *Human Development, 14,* 272–278.

Flavell, J. H., Friedrichs, A. G., & Hoyt, J. D. (1970). Developmental changes in memorization processes. *Cognitive Psychology, 1,* 324–340.

Harris, P. L., Kruithof, A., Terwogt, M. M., & Visser, P. (1981). Children's detection and awareness of textual anomaly. *Journal of Experimental Child Psychology, 31,* 212–230.

McDermott, R. P. (1978). Some reasons for focusing on classrooms in reading research. In P. D. Pearson & J. Hansen (Eds.), *Reading: Disciplined inquiry in process and practice* (Twenty-seventh Yearbook of the National Reading Conference). Clemson, SC: National Reading Conference.

Palincsar, A. S., & Brown, A. L. (1984). Reciprocal teaching of comprehension-fostering and monitoring activities. *Cognition and Instruction, 1,* 117–175.

Peck, D. M., Jenks, S. M., & Connell, M. L. (in press). Improving instruction via brief interviews. *Arithmetic Teacher.*

Petitto, A. L. (1985). Division of labor: Procedural learning in teacher-led small groups. *Cognition and Instruction, 2,* 233–270.

Polya, G. (1973). *How to solve it: A new aspect of mathematical method* (2nd ed.). Princeton, NJ: Princeton University Press.

Putnam, R. T. (1987). Structuring and adjusting content for students: A study of live and simulated tutoring of addition. *American Educational Research Journal, 24,* 13–48.

Resnick, L. B. (1982). Syntax and semantics in learning to subtract. In T. Carpenter, J. Moser, & T. Romberg (Eds.), *Addition and subtraction: A cognitive perspective* (pp. 136–155). Hillsdale, NJ: Erlbaum.

Rohwer, W. D., Jr. (1973). Elaboration and learning in childhood and adolescence. In H. W. Reese (Ed.), *Advances in child development and behavior* (Vol. 8, pp. 1–57). New York: Academic Press.

Scardamalia, M., & Bereiter, C. (1985). Fostering the development of self-regulation in children's knowledge processing. In S. Chipman, J. Segal, & R. Glaser (Eds.), *Thinking and learning skills: Current research and open questions* (Vol. 2, pp. 563–577). Hillsdale, NJ: Erlbaum.

Scardamalia, M., Bereiter, C., & Steinbach, R. (1984). Teachability of reflexive processes in written composition. *Cognitive Science, 8,* 173–190.

Schoenfeld, A. H. (1983). Beyond the purely cognitive: Belief systems, social cognitions, and metacognitions as driving forces in intellectual performance. *Cognitive Science, 7,* 329–363.

Schoenfeld, A. H. (1985). *Mathematical problem solving.* New York: Academic Press.

Stodolsky, S. (1988). *The subject matter: Classroom activity in math and social studies.* Chicago: University of Chicago Press.

Tulving, E., & Madigan, S. A. (1969). Memory and verbal learning. *Annual Review of Psychology, 21,* 437–484.

Whitehead, A. N. (1916). *The aims of education.* Address to the British Mathematical Society. Manchester, England.

Reflections about Mathematical Problem-Solving Research[1]

Frank K. Lester, Jr.
Indiana University

"Mathematics is the Queen of the Sciences."
(C. F. Gauss)

"My main goal in teaching math is to introduce my students to the Queen."
(a respected math teacher)

Several years ago, early in my teaching career, a respected colleague advised me never to lose sight of the fact that mathematics is not a pedestrian discipline made up of routine facts, formulas, definitions, and procedures. Rather, he said, it is a regal, multifaceted subject, limitless in extent and depth. He insisted that although mathematics can be a tool for the manual laborer, the office worker, the draftsman, and the mechanic, to mention only a few areas of application, it is so much more as well. He warned me that if I ever lost sight of this truth, I would not only find teaching to be a boring, unchallenging job but, much worse, I would inculcate in my students the notion that mathematics is only a tool, and for many, a useless tool at that. Moreover, I would not have given these students a chance to meet the "Queen of the Sciences." Since my first years in the classroom, the standard I have used to judge a teacher's performance is to consider whether or not the students involved "met the Queen" as a result of their teacher's efforts. Furthermore, my concern for helping students meet the Queen has had a very strong influence on my research on problem solving. That is, my perception of mathematics has played a dominant role in my choice of questions to investigate and how to study them. But what has all this talk about "meeting the Queen" have to do with research on mathematical problem solving? Simply this—there are signs that mathematics educators, at least those of us involved in problem-solving research, have relinquished to others (psychologists, computer scientists, anthropologists, etc.) the responsibility for establishing direction for future research in mathematics education. In my view this is an intolerable situation. Since I regard this issue as central to the creation of a research agenda for the next decade, let me begin with a brief discussion of it. Then, I will turn my attention to the role of metacognition in problem solving and will conclude with some suggestions for future research emphasis.

ON DIFFERING VIEWS OF THE NATURE OF MATHEMATICS

A researcher's view of a phenomenon (or of reality) of necessity affects the way in which that phenomenon will be investigated. Lin (1979) has provided a good illustration of this point:

> Consider a student and a teacher in a room . . . being observed by a behaviorist, a Piagetian, and a psychoanalyst. When they record a significant event in the interaction, they ring a bell. Under these circumstances, they probably will not ring their bells in synchronization; each person has his own views of what constitutes a significant interaction and what is irrelevant (p. 15).

Similarly, a researcher who has taught mathematics and studied it seriously will necessarily have a different perspective about the nature of mathematics and of problem solving than someone who has neither taught nor studied mathematics in any depth. It is natural to expect that non-mathematics educators would introduce views about the nature of mathematics that are quite different from those held by mathematicians or mathematics teachers.

Psychologists have a long history of looking to mathematics as a medium through which to study human learning and instruction, and there is no doubt that mathematics education has benefited tremendously from their involvement. In recent years, sociologists, anthropologists and other social/behavioral scientists have joined this group in studying questions associated with the learning and teaching of mathematics. For the most part this is a very healthy development, but because these non-mathematics educators typically have rather restricted views of the nature and value of mathematics, they are likely to ask different questions, draw different conclusions, and use different methodologies than mathematics educators.

My concern is that too many of the individuals who are now doing research on mathematical problem solving seem to view mathematics as nothing more than a practical tool. Furthermore, some of them seem not to understand that mathematical problem solving involves much more than the application of previously learned rules and procedures. Unfortunately, despite having such a restricted sense of what mathematics and problem solving are, some of these researchers have been quick to offer "research-based" suggestions for classroom practice and curriculum reform. I have been particularly distressed by reports of their research dealing with algorithm and skill learning in which suggestions are provided to teachers about how to teach problem solving. Mathematics educators should be willing to look to disciplines such as psychology, sociology, and anthropology for advice and ideas, but they must not allow researchers in these fields to dictate the directions in which the research will go. Unfortunately, I see signs that this is exactly what is happening.

METACOGNITION AND MATHEMATICAL PROBLEM SOLVING

I have been interested in mathematical problem-solving instruction since the early 1970s, and I developed a special interest in studying how to help students "take charge of their own learning" (to use Brown's phrase) during my involvement with a large-scale research and development project at Indiana University during 1974–76. In particular, it was during that period that I became convinced that training in the use of a collection of skills and heuristics without attention to affective and metacognitive aspects of problem solving is inadequate. I was quite pleased to discover a few years later that Brown and her colleagues had been doing some groundbreaking work in the area of metacognition and that in their minds executive skills (e.g., monitoring, coordinating) are "the basic characteristics of thinking efficiently in a wide range of learning situations" (Brown, 1978, p. 80). In 1981 when Joe Garofalo and I undertook a preliminary investigation of young children's metacognitive awareness as it relates to mathematical performance, we were already very much impressed with Brown's work and it served as a basis for our initial conceptualization of our study (Lester & Garofalo, 1982). I am particularly interested in her ideas about reciprocal teaching of comprehension monitoring strategies because I think she directly addresses some of the key research questions about problem-solving instruction. In a later section I relate reciprocal teaching to the work I have been doing with Randy Charles and Joe Garofalo (Charles & Lester, 1984; Lester & Garofalo, 1986; Garofalo, Kroll, & Lester, 1987).

METACOGNITION IN MATHEMATICS VS. METACOGNITION IN READING

Much of Brown's work has been done with reading tasks, although recently she has turned her attention to biology and computation tasks. The question arises: Are the metacognitive behaviors used in solving mathematics problems the same as those used to comprehend a passage of written prose? Her answer is that while there are similarities between the metacognitive demands made on the individual in the two areas, metacognitive activities probably are driven by domain-specific knowledge. I agree with this position. There is no question but that in both domains decisions must be made about: choice of representation, strategy selection, what and how to monitor, how to evaluate progress, and so forth. However, because of the fundamental interconnections among a problem solver's mathematical resources (e.g., knowledge of facts, algorithms and heuristics), the control mechanisms used to marshall these resources, and the belief systems and affective factors that influence performance, it is essential that metacognition be studied extensively with respect to specific domains; in particular, it is important that we study metacognition as it relates to mathematical activity (Garofalo & Lester, 1985; Lesh, 1983; Lester, 1987; Schoenfeld, 1985). It would be folly to expect the research on text comprehension to provide us with much specific guidance.

Table 1 is a first attempt at speculating about the similarities and differences between reading and mathematics tasks with respect to the cognitive and metacognitive demands made upon the individual. Space limitations on this paper prevent me from elaborating on the information provided in the table. It will suffice to say that a primary activity of mathematical problem-solving researchers who are interested in metacognition should be to focus attention on those aspects of metacognitive behavior that seem to distinguish mathematical problem solving from other kinds of intellectual activity, in particular from reading comprehension.

Table 1
Comparison of reading and mathematics with respect to cognitive and metacognitive demand on the individual

Phase	Prose Reading	Mathematical Problem Solving
Understanding (Comprehending)	Usually the primary goal	Initial goal only
	Amount and complexity of content influences difficulty and number & kinds of strategies used	Same as for reading
	Individual may have a schema for the situation	Individual may have a problem-type schema
Planning & Exploring	Only involved insofar as it is needed to aid comprehension	At times needed for comprehension, but mostly after at least partial comprehension is attained (individual may be "lost at sea" even with comprehension)
Monitoring	Monitoring of progress toward comprehension (ongoing evaluation of outcome of strategic actions)	Same as for reading
		Adequacy of comprehension assessed with respect to: progress toward solution, and plan used
		Consistency of plans with goals
		Performing of local actions (e.g., performing calculations, keeping track of steps in algorithms)
		Making trade-off decisions (e.g., speed vs. accuracy, degree of elegance)
Evaluating	Recall, inference, or recognition used to assess adequacy of comprehension	Same as for reading
		Assessing reasonableness of answer
		Consistency of final results with problem conditions
Other Factors	Prognosis of success often can be made relatively early	Prognosis of success often cannot be made until an attempt is made to solve the problem
	Out-of-school reading is somewhat like school reading	Out-of-school math is often very unlike school math
	Familiarity with context often aids comprehension	Familiarity with problem context may help or may hinder success
	Not socially acceptable to read poorly	It often is socially acceptable to do poorly in math

TEACHING STUDENTS TO TAKE CHARGE
OF THEIR OWN LEARNING

Brown (this volume) makes the important point that it is wrong to assume that metacognitive skills (and other "higher order thinking skills") are acquired relatively late in an individual's mental development. My own research on problem-solving instruction has been based on two assumptions: (a) metacognitive processes evolve over time in domain-specific contexts, and (b) there is a dynamic interaction between mathematical concepts and the processes (including metacognitive ones) used to solve problems involving those concepts. That is, control processes and awareness of cognitive processes develop concurrently with the development of an understanding of mathematical concepts (cf., Lesh, 1982). Consequently, if children are to learn how to take charge of their own problem solving, it is important to give direct attention in instruction at every level to metacognitive aspects of the learning of mathematical ideas.

Reciprocal teaching (Brown, this volume) is a promising approach to metacognition-based instruction. This method has five features that make it especially appropriate for mathematical problem-solving instruction: (a) instruction takes place in the context of learning specific content; (b) the student's attention is focused on solving a specific problem, not on monitoring, regulating, or evaluating actions per se; (c) students are not protected from error in their solution efforts; (d) the teacher is allowed to be fallible; and (e) the teacher's role as a guide and model diminishes as students become more confident and competent.

Several of these features are prominent ingredients of the problem-solving teaching strategy created in the mid–1970s by the Mathematics Problem Solving Project at Indiana University (Stengel, LeBlanc, Jacobson, & Lester, 1977) and refined by Randy Charles and me (Charles & Lester, 1982). In a study of the effectiveness of this approach, we (Charles and Lester, 1984) found significant growth in students' problem-solving abilities with respect to comprehension, planning, and execution strategies. While this teaching strategy has a very definite metacognitive flavor, features d and e above are not prominent. Consequently, when Joe Garofalo and I were designing the instructional treatment for our study of the role of metacognition in the problem-solving performance of seventh graders, we decided to develop a treatment incorporating aspects of reciprocal teaching and the approach developed earlier by Charles and me. The result was an approach having three components: (a) teacher as an external monitor; (b) teacher as facilitator of students' development of metacognitive awareness; and (c) teacher as a model of a metacognitively-aware problem solver. The "teacher as monitor" component consists of a set of teaching actions for the teacher to engage in: (a) to direct whole-class discussions about a problem to be solved; (b) to observe, question, and guide students as they work either individually or in small groups to solve the problem; and (c) to lead whole-class discussions about solution attempts. The second component involves the teacher: (a) asking questions and devising assignments that require students to analyze their mathematical performance; (b) pointing out aspects of mathematics that have bearing on performance; and (c) helping students build a repertoire of heuristics and control strategies, along with knowledge of their usefulness. The "teacher as model" component involves the teacher explicitly demonstrating regulatory decisions and actions while solving problems for the students in the classroom (Garofalo, Kroll, & Lester, 1987).

Rather than elaborate upon the comparability of our and Brown's reciprocal teaching approaches, I will point out some observations about the use of instructional methods of this sort (refer to Brown's discussion in her paper of the similarities between reciprocal teaching and Schoenfeld's method). More specifically, I will report some of the observations we have made with regard to the three components of the instructional treatment we used in our study.

The Teacher as External Monitor

Students often are lacking in adequate conceptual understanding or are weak in certain basic skills (e.g., understanding of percents or adding fractions). Thus, much of the "external monitoring" time during the students' solution efforts is likely to be spent explaining the meaning of a concept or how to do a calculation, rather than discussing metacognitive-level considerations. Teachers probably should expect to provide instruction in the meaning of concepts and how to perform various basic skills simultaneously with instruction in metacognitive awareness.

The Teacher as Facilitator

One way in which we directed students to reflect upon their own cognition was to have them complete self-inventory sheets on which they listed their own strengths and weaknesses in doing mathematics. Many students have considerable difficulty reflecting on their own thought processes and otherwise analyzing their own performance. Furthermore, some students are reticent to discuss their own capabilities and limitations; they may view such an activity as a threat to their self-concepts. A way around this difficulty that we have found promising is to have the students view a videotape of someone else solving a problem and to discuss with them the good and not so good behaviors they see.

The Teacher as Model

The notion of having teachers solve problems in front of their classes is anything but novel. Many teachers regularly explain the solutions of problems by pointing out the importance of reading carefully, by discussing why a particular strategy was chosen, by openly checking their work, and by comparing the final answer with the conditions of the problem. The distinguishing feature of this component was that students would have an opportunity to observe the monitoring strategies used by an expert problem solver as he (in actuality I was the teacher for all sessions in our study) solved a problem he had never solved before. There are two limitations to this idea. First, under the best of circumstances, when teachers engage in modeling good problem-solving behavior, they should actually be solving a problem, not pretending to solve a problem. However, most problems suitable for seventh graders' level of mathematical sophistication are not real problems for their teacher. And, problems for the teacher are likely to be far too difficult for the students. Consequently, modeling of true problem solving by the teacher necessitates very careful selection of problems.

The second limitation of teacher modeling lies in my difficulty in maintaining the role of expert problem solver. That is, I tended to fall back into my role of teacher, and soon I was explaining, questioning, and guiding, rather than modeling. Not surprisingly, the students found it hard to focus on me as an expert problem solver, rather than as a teacher. A modification of the modeling procedure, in which the students viewed a videotape of my research assistant solving a problem at a desk worked much better. The students had no expectations that the assistant should "explain clearly," "talk slowly," and "write neatly on the board," since she was obviously simply writing while talking to herself, not to them.

Near the beginning of this section I indicated that reciprocal teaching is a promising approach to instruction. Preliminary analysis of the data gathered on the effectiveness of our instructional approach suggests that it too holds considerable promise. But, as encouraging as the results of our and Brown's research may be, much more study is needed into the nature and extent of the effectiveness of approaches such as these.

DIRECTIONS FOR FUTURE STUDY

The suggestions I make here about the directions future research in this area should take must be considered in light of my interests and expertise. When I am asked by a new acquaintance what it is that I do for a living, I usually reply that I am a mathematics teacher. Throughout my 21 years as a professional educator I have always considered myself a teacher first, a researcher second. Also, although I do not consider myself a mathematician, I enjoy doing mathematics, reading about mathematics, and talking with others about things mathematical. These interests, together with the fact that I studied mathematics throughout my 20 years of formal schooling, strongly color my perceptions about what sorts of research studies are needed. As one reads what follows, these perceptions should be kept in mind.

In my thinking, five themes should guide our research during the next several years. Of course, these themes are not the only important ones, but we would do well to give them top priority in designing an agenda for research.

Needed: Adequate Theories of Instruction

Sternberg (1986) argues convincingly that, among the trouble spots in the relationship between cognition and instruction, one occurs at the level of theory. He suggests that the link between cognition and instruction requires a compatibility between a theory of cognition and theory of instruction and that these theories must apply at two levels: the classroom unit and the individual. In my mind current theories of cognition apply primarily to individual problem-solving performance and theories of instruction are concerned mostly with classroom processes. It is imperative that greater attention be given to the development of instructional theories that, to use Sternberg's words, can serve as "the link between cognitive theory . . . and educational practice" (Sternberg, 1986, p. 378). Extant theories of instruction that have relevance for mathematical problem solving are woefully inadequate.

What Factors Influence Problem-Solving Performance?

Our current infatuation with cognitive science has contributed greatly to what I consider to be a very narrow view of the sorts of factors that influence problem-solving performance. Elsewhere I have argued that an individual's success or failure in solving a problem when the individual possesses the necessary knowledge stems from the presence not only of cognitive factors that affect the utilization of this knowledge, but also of noncognitive and metacognitive factors (Lester & Garofalo, 1987, April; Lester, 1987, July). These factors can be placed in five broad, interrelated categories: knowledge, control, affects, beliefs, and socio-cultural conditions. Future efforts must be cognizant of the close link among these categories.

Teachers' Knowledge, Affects, and Beliefs: A Much-Ignored Issue

It is clear that the teacher's knowledge, affects, and beliefs can strongly influence both the nature and effectiveness of instruction. Unfortunately, what the teacher brings to a mathematics lesson has been ignored by most researchers interested in problem-solving instruction. Much more work is needed of the kind done by Thompson (1985) on teachers' conceptions of teaching problem solving and by Brown, Brown, Cooney, and Smith (1982) on teachers' beliefs about teaching mathematics.

Teaching Experiments: An Underexploited Methodology

The rather recent acceptance of the use of various clinical methods such as structured and semi-structured interviews and observations of individual and small-group problem solving has been a major development in mathematical problem-solving research. These methodologies, as valuable and important as they are, are more applicable at the level of the individual than at the level of the instructional group (e.g., classroom). Too little is known about what actually happens in classrooms, (e.g., what teachers do to improve problem-solving performance, the nature of student-student and teacher-student interactions, and the types of classroom atmospheres that enhance performance). The use of "teaching experiments" in the sense described by Kilpatrick & Wirszup (1969–75) holds great promise for helping us establish sound principles of problem-solving instruction. Furthermore, when I was teaching the seventh graders in the study described earlier, the observations I made of students working on problems in regular classroom settings sometimes provided very different kinds of data about students' abilities, beliefs, and attitudes than would have been obtained by means of interviews or observations of individuals under less natural conditions. The students felt at ease with me, they expected me to observe and comment on their efforts, and they were working in what was for them a relatively nonthreatening environment.

Taking a Closer Look at Cooperative Learning Groups

Despite the impressive research evidence supporting the use of small groups in problem-solving instruction, we must be careful not to infer from these results that problem-solving instruction can only be effective if students are organized in small groups. In fact, it is not at all difficult for me to imagine situations in which forcing students to work "cooperatively" may have a debilitating effect on performance, in terms of both short-term and long-term learning. The instructional methods I have advocated for some time include individual, small group, and whole class activities. As Silver (1985) points out, we need to learn much more about the conditions under which small group problem solving enhances learning.

REFERENCES

Brown, A.G. (1978). Knowing when, where, and how to remember: A problem of metacognition. In R. Glaser (Ed.), *Advances in instructional psychology.* (Vol. 1, pp. 77–165). Hillsdale, NJ: Lawrence Erlbaum Associates.

Brown, C., Brown, S., Cooney, T., & Smith, D. (1982). The pursuit of mathematics teachers' beliefs. In S. Wagner (Ed.), *Proceedings of the Fourth Annual Meeting of the North American Chapter of the International Group for the Psychology of Mathematics Education* (pp. 203–215). Athens, GA: University of Georgia, Department of Mathematics Education.

Charles, R., & Lester, F. (1982). *Teaching problem solving: What, why and how.* Palo Alto, CA: Dale Seymour Publications.

Charles, R.I., & Lester, F.K. (1984). An evaluation of a process-oriented mathematical problem-solving instructional program in grades five and seven. *Journal for Research in Mathematics Education, 15,* 15–34.

Garofalo, J., & Lester, F.K. (1985). Metacognition, cognitive monitoring, and mathematical performance. *Journal for Research in Mathematics Education, 16,* 163–176.

Garofalo, J., Kroll, D.L., & Lester, F.K. (1987, July). *Metacognition and mathematical problem solving: Preliminary research findings.* Paper presented at the annual meeting of the PME, Montreal.

Kilpatrick, J., & Wirzsup, I. (Eds.), (1969–75). *Soviet studies in the psychology of learning and teaching mathematics* (14 vols.). Stanford, CA: School Mathematics Study Group.

Lesh, R. (1983). *Metacognition in mathematical problem solving.* Unpublished manuscript available from the author. WICAT Corp., Orem, Utah.

Lester, F.K. (1987, July). *Why is problem solving such a problem?* Paper presented at the annual meeting of the PME, Montreal.

Lester, F.K., & Garofalo, J. (1982, March). *Metacognitive aspects of elementary school students' performance on arithmetic tasks.* Paper presented at the meeting of the AERA, New York.

Lester, F.K., & Garofalo, J. (1986, April). *An emerging study of sixth graders' metacognition and mathematical performance.* Paper presented at the meeting of the AERA, San Francisco.

Lester, F.K., & Garofalo, J. (1987, April). *The influence of affects, beliefs, and metacognition on problem-solving behavior: Some tentative speculations.* Paper presented at the meeting of the AERA, Washington, DC.

Lin, H. (1979). Approaches to clinical research in cognitive process instruction. In J. Lochhead and J. Clement (Eds.), *Cognitive process instruction: Research on teaching thinking skills* (pp. 11–32). Philadelphia: The Franklin Institute Press.

Schoenfeld, A.H. (1985). *Mathematical problem solving.* Orlando, FL: Academic Press.

Silver, E.A. (1985). Research on teaching mathematical problem solving: Some underrepresented themes and needed directions. In E.A. Silver (Ed.), *Teaching and learning mathematical problem solving: Multiple research perspectives* (pp. 247–266). Hillsdale, NJ: Lawrence Erlbaum.

Stengel, A., LeBlanc, J. F., Jacobson, M. & Lester, F. (1977). *Learning to solve problems by solving problems: A report of a preliminary investigation* (Technical Report II.D. of the Mathematical Problem Solving Project). Bloomington, IN: Mathematics Education Development Center.

Sternberg, R.J. (1986). Cognition and instruction: Why the marriage sometimes ends in divorce. In R. F. Dillon & R. J. Sternberg (Eds.), *Cognition and instruction* (pp. 375–382). Orlando, FL: Academic Press.

Thompson, A.G. (1985). Teachers' conceptions of mathematics and the teaching of problem solving. In E.A. Silver (Ed.), *Teaching and learning mathematical problem solving: Multiple research perspectives* (pp. 281–294). Hillsdale, NJ: Lawrence Erlbaum.

FOOTNOTE

1. I am grateful to Beatriz D'Ambrosio, Joe Garofalo, and Diana Lambdin Kroll for their helpful reactions to an earlier version of this paper.

Uses of Macro-Contexts to Facilitate Mathematical Thinking[1]

John Bransford, Ted Hasselbring, Brigid Barron, Stan Kulewicz,
Joan Littlefield, Laura Goin

Vanderbilt University

The National Council of Teachers of Mathematics (1980) has identified problem solving as the recommended focus of school mathematics in the 1980s and beyond. The council emphasizes that students must learn to "formulate key questions, analyze and conceptualize problems, define the problem and the goal, discover patterns and similarities, seek out appropriate data, experiment, transfer skills and strategies to new situations, and draw on background knowledge to apply mathematics" (NAEP, 1983). These are important aspects of what we shall call "mathematical thinking." The major question we shall address is the degree to which typical mathematics instruction is ideal for developing mathematical thinking. We argue that it is not, and we provide some initial data showing the success of alternate approaches. However, we emphasize that our initial findings leave a number of questions unanswered. We close by suggesting further studies that should be conducted in order to clarify ways in which mathematics instruction might be improved.

BACKGROUND

The ideas presented in this paper have developed from several studies conducted with fifth and sixth grade students who were having difficulty in mathematics. Most of the research was conducted as part of the Vanderbilt dynamic assessment project, a project that focused on alternative assessments of handicapped children (e.g. Bransford, Delclos, Vye, Burns, & Hasselbring, 1986; Vye, Burns, Delclos, & Bransford, in press; Bransford, Delclos, Vye, Burns, & Hasselbring, in press).

The term "dynamic assessment" refers to attempts to assess individuals' responsiveness to teaching (Feuerstein, Rand, & Hoffman,1979) or "zone of sensitivity to instruction" (Vygotsky, 1978; Wood, Wood, & Middleton, 1978; Wood, 1980). The methods of assessment are different from those used in standardized, "static" assessments, such as intelligence tests and achievement tests, where instruction on the part of the tester invalidates results. An important component of dynamic assessment is a systematic attempt to actively change various components of tasks and approaches to teaching in order to find the conditions that are most effective for each child. When one does this, it is common to see students achieve in ways that are surprising (e.g. Feuerstein et al., 1979; Bransford et al., in press). These findings emphasize the importance of instruction in helping students learn.

CREATING ALTERNATE PATHWAYS FOR LEARNING

Our work in dynamic assessment has motivated us to attempt to create alternate pathways to important competencies such as mathematical and scientific thinking, the ability to read effectively, the ability to critically evaluate evidence, and so forth. An article by Burton, J.S. Brown, & Fischer (1984) provides an interesting illustration of the importance of this goal. They discuss the problem of helping people learn to ski effectively. The development of the "Graduated Length Method" (GLM) of teaching skiing a number of years ago was a breakthrough that made successful and enjoyable skiing available to thousands of people who had not previously been considered candidates for participation in the sport. In the GLM method, several elements of the task are carefully and systematically manipulated by a skillful coach so that the learner skis in a series of increasingly complex situations, each requiring an extension of the skills learned in the previous, less complex environment. So, a novice skier is given very short skis, no poles, and is put on a gentle slope. The short skis make turning easier and allow practice in developing rhythm, an essential component of successful control. The lack of poles helps the student to focus on balance and on the movement of the skis. The gentle terrain greatly reduces the frightening speed that novices often experience on steeper slopes and allows them to build confidence and to practice important movements that are critical for success on the more demanding slopes.

In the course of training, the GLM coach analyzes the performance of the learner at each level of instruction and makes decisions about when and what to change, based on the successes and failures of the student. Gradually, longer skis are introduced; wider, narrower, or steeper slopes are presented; the snow conditions are also varied; poles are added. An important characteristic of the GLM method is that, even at the simplest level of instruction, the student is actually skiing rather than engaging in isolated exercises (e.g. balancing on a wooden beam) that have dubious relevance for the actual performance of complex skilled behavior and that are often not motivating to pursue.

The GLM method also depends on effective teaching. For example, changes in the types of skis, types of slopes, and so forth are made at points when the coach decides they will help either to advance the student to the next level or to make the student aware of current errors that need to be debugged. The coach might have the student ski in soft, powdery snow so that a lack of rhythmic turning could be clearly visible in the tracks left by the skis, or, if the student was not using the skis properly in negotiating turns, the coach might move the location to an icy area, where the proper use of edges of the skis is critical in staying upright. Overall the GLM method is designed to make it easier for instructors to teach.

For present purposes, the important point involves the relationship between (a) people's abilities to develop an important competency (skiing) and (b) cultural practice regarding established methods of teaching. Prior to the GLM approach, many people had great difficulty learning to ski. It was tempting to conclude that some people simply had the ability and many others did not. Given the GLM method, however, thousands of persons who would otherwise have failed were able to succeed.

Several colleagues have informed us that the GLM method has been replaced by ones that are even more effective. However, this does not negate the basic arguments of Burton and colleagues about the role of new developments in skiing instruction. It is still the case that the older approaches to teaching skiing represented a cultural practice that blocked many people's chances for success. We believe that there may be analogous barriers to the development of mathematical skills.

INITIAL WORK WITH FIFTH AND SIXTH GRADERS

As noted earlier, a portion of our work in dynamic assessment involved attempts to work with fifth and sixth graders who were at least 1½ years behind their peers in mathematics and who qualified for special education services in Tennessee (we shall refer to these students as LH, which stands for "learning handicapped"). The opportunity to work with these students—especially in the context of an 8-week "mathematics camp" held during the summer at Vanderbilt—has suggested several features of performance that we feel are important and may have implications for the design of new learning environments. We also feel that the implications may hold for regular education as well as special education students.

Strategies for Avoiding Mathematics

Many of our LH students showed evidence of sophisticated mathematics-related strategies. The strategies were designed to enable the students to avoid mathematical tasks or to get the teacher to provide them with the answers. For example, in one exercise involving a computer-based assessment of the speed of answering basic mathematics facts (e.g. $7 + 8 = ?$), several students tried to act very relaxed and purposely took a great deal of time pushing the keys so as to avoid a true assessment of their mathematics abilities. Similarly, when given word problems and asked to represent the problems visually, students often tried to get out of the task or to focus on the goal of providing detailed drawings of some of the items mentioned in the problems. Other students simply looked for some numbers in the word problems, generated an answer with little thought, and then expected the teacher to provide the correct answer. Strategies similar to these have been described elsewhere (e.g. Holt, 1964; McDermott, 1986, personal communication). The strategies often involved sophisticated ways to help students avoid problems that they do not like to face.

Lack of Fluency in Basic Mathematics Facts

Almost every one of our LH students had great difficulty with basic mathematics facts (e.g. 6 + 4 = ?). Data from several other studies also emphasize these types of difficulties (Allardice & Ginsburg, 1983; Russell & Ginsburg, 1984). Our data indicate that even when students are accurate on basic facts, they have frequently failed to follow the normal developmental sequence of automatizing their abilities to recall this information (Hasselbring, Goin, & Bransford, 1987). In order to generate correct answers, our LH children needed to rely on counting strategies, a procedure that is slow, cumbersome, and often embarrassing to the child. We believe that the lack of fluency in the area of basic mathematics facts can seriously hamper the development of subsequent skills such as addition with columns of numbers and the ability to solve simple word problems (e.g. Resnick, 1986). The cumbersome nature of these strategies probably also contributes to students' negative attitudes towards mathematics tasks and towards their abilities to do mathematics.

The report of the National Council of Teachers of Mathematics places much more emphasis on problem solving than on fluency in basic mathematics skills. It is possible that, at least for special education students, we may need to rethink the importance of fluency in computational skills because a lack of fluency may provide a bottleneck that retards the development of more sophisticated skills. In fact, we believe that fluency may also be an issue for students in regular education.

Data from a study comparing special education and regular education students across the elementary grades are illustrated in Figure 1 (from Hasselbring, Goin, & Bransford, 1987). The study assessed the speed with which students could add two numbers that ranged from 0 to 9. Answers given in less than ¾ of a second (a reasonable time for adults) were considered fluent or "automatized." Measurements of time took into account differences in students' abilities to quickly press the appropriate computer keys.

Several aspects of the data are particularly noteworthy. First, by the first grade the special education students have fewer instances of fluent addition than do regular education students, and the differences become greater with age. Second, even the regular education students are much less fluent at basic addition than one would like. For many facts, these students have to count to themselves rather than simply retrieve the appropriate answer from memory. This requires attentional resources that are often needed for other aspects of complex mathematics tasks.

Difficulties with Word Problems

As one would expect, our LH children have great difficulty solving simple word problems. Part of the reason is their lack of fluency in basic mathematics, plus the fact that they have difficulty in areas such as fractions.

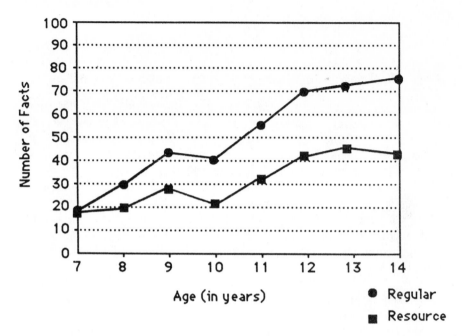

Figure 1. Number of "automatized" facts for students in regular education and special education

However, Russell, and Ginsburg (1984) report that these difficulties persist even when computational errors are not counted and credit is given for specifying the correct mathematical operation. Similar results were found in our research where credit was given for producing correct visual representations of problems irrespective of the accuracy of the calculations (Kulewicz, Barron, Goin, Hasselbring, & Bransford, 1986). Studies conducted by Littlefield & Rieser (1985) show that many regular education fifth and sixth grade students also have great difficulty in solving word problems. Inspections of students' locus of gaze while solving word problems suggest that many simply looked from one number to another without really attempting to understand the nature of the problems they were being asked to solve. Especially interesting were data indicating that many less successful students began to work with numbers before they ever read the questions that defined the problems. When problems contained irrelevant numbers, these students were especially likely to make errors in selecting the numbers that were relevant to the task. In general, the results of the Littlefield and Rieser study suggest that academically less successful students frequently have erroneous ideas about the nature of word problems. As DeCorte and Verschaffel (1985) argue, students' "word problem schemas" are frequently inaccurate or incomplete.

Less Than Optimal Teaching

Observations of the type of instruction students receive suggest that there may be considerable room for improvement. This is true both with respect to basic mathematics facts and with respect to problem-solving skills.

Fluency. Consider first the type of teaching that students typically experience with respect to mastery of basic facts. Students often receive drill and practice on basic facts (either through paper and pencil exercises or on a computer). Hamann & Aschraft (1986) note that the amount of practice of particular facts varies greatly within typical mathematics texts. Some problems, especially those containing the numbers 2, 3, or 4, are presented frequently whereas other facts rarely occur.

Data collected at Vanderbilt also show that typical approaches to drill and practice do not help many students who are relying on procedures such as finger counting (Hasselbring et al., 1987). In particular, drill and practice does not produce a qualitative shift in strategies from finger counting to memory retrieval. Students simply keep counting on their fingers and get a little faster at this as a result of practice. However, their reliance on counting procedures does not change.

We should note that LH students can learn basic facts very well when provided with special computer programs that are designed to produce these qualitative shifts in strategies (Hasselbring, Goin & Bransford, 1987). Furthermore, students can learn about general problem-solving strategies while learning basic facts. Thus, students can be helped to focus on the goal of increasing their score on a mathematics-based computer program and then be helped to define the problems that are keepiing them from reaching this goal (e.g. having to rely on finger counting for some problems). In short, students can be helped to take a "higher order approach" to the development of "lower order skills" (Bransford et al., 1986; Resnick, 1986).

Word Problems. Instruction that students receive in solving word problems also leaves room for improvement. Several investigators argue that the types of word problems presented in texts are not sufficient to develop the types of skills necessary for transfer to real-life examples (e.g. Lesh, 1981). In addition, the instruction for how to solve problems is often too terse.

In our Nashville studies, we found that the instruction provided to our LH students usually involved one or two example problems that were worked out by the teacher, followed by seatwork. The instructional procedures seem similar to the "chalk and talk" procedures observed in regular education classes by Crosswhite (1986) and Stodolsky (1985). Stodolsky argues that this approach to instruction represents a restricted set of paths to learning and often produces less than adequate problem-solving skills.

We are especially concerned about the degree to which typical approaches to teaching word problems are related to problem solving. Students may be introduced to problem-solving strategies in order to solve the problems, but the problems are still ends in and of themselves rather than means to some larger end. As Figure 2A illustrates, the relationship between "mathematics" and problem solving is one of set to subset. Figure 2B illustrates a different relationship. Here, mathematical thinking is viewed as an important component of general problem-solving skills. It is also important to differentiate word problems that emphasize general problem solving from those that emphasize algorithms. Van Hanaghan & Baker (in preparation) note that many word problems are introduced as "addition problems," "subtraction problems," and so forth. These problems focus on the development of number algorithms rather than on problem solving per se.

A. PROBLEMS AS ENDS IN AND OF THEMSELVES

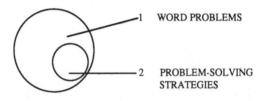

1   WORD PROBLEMS

2   PROBLEM-SOLVING STRATEGIES

B. PROBLEMS AS MEANS TO LARGER ENDS

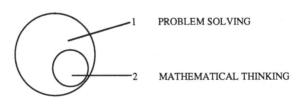

1   PROBLEM SOLVING

2   MATHEMATICAL THINKING

Figure 2. Two different relationships between word problems and problem solving

We believe that both sets of relationships depicted in Figure 2 are important. However, those depicted in Figure 2B are especially important because they help students understand the function of mathematical tools for simplifying problem solving.

The idea that mathematical inventions provide powerful sets of "helps" or tools for enhancing general problem solving seems to be very important. Based on our experiences, students often do not view mathematical concepts from this perspective. For example, we have asked a number of college students majoring in education or arts and science to explain why logarithms are useful. In what ways do they make it easier to solve various problems? Despite remembering something about logarithms, the vast majority of the students were surprised when told that logarithms represent an important invention that greatly simplifies problem solving.

We have encountered many additional examples of situations where students have memorized facts and theories with very little appreciation of how they make it possible to comprehend otherwise perplexing phenomena. In order to become useful for thinking, these facts and procedures must be transformed into conceptual tools (e.g., Bransford & Stein, 1984; Hanson, 1970). In addition, students must develop fluency in the use of these skills, otherwise their attentional resources will be overwhelmed by the complexities of the task (e.g. Schneider & Shiffrin, 1977, 1984).

Different Approaches to Teaching Word Problems

It is useful to consider how approaches to teaching word problems might differ if one emphasized the relationships depicted in Figures 2A and 2B. As an illustration of Figure 2A, imagine that students receive word problems such as the following in mathematics class:

A waterboy for a softball team brings 1 quart of water for each player. If there are 9 players, and each quart of water weighs 2 pounds, what is the total weight of the water?

It seems clear that the ability to solve this word problem requires problem solving. The relationship between the problem and problem-solving skills is the one illustrated in Figure 2A. We argue that, in this approach, problem solving is emphasized only in a restricted sense.

In order for Figure 2B to become applicable, the waterboy problem plus others would need to be incorporated into a larger context (we will call it a macro-context) that provides richer experiences with problem solving. Although there is a variety of ways to create such contexts, we shall focus on an approach that utilizes the power of interactive videodiscs. Videodiscs provide a powerful medium for learning because they allow access to individual segments almost instantaneously.

One way to create macro-contexts is to use existing movies such as *Raiders of the Lost Ark*, *Star Wars*, and so forth. These are available on random access video and are quite inexpensive to buy. They are also legal to use as long as schools (a) buy rather than rent them and (b) use them for education rather than for entertainment (Becker, 1985). Our initial work has involved the use of these types of videos although, currently, we are beginning to make our own videodiscs.

The first 10 minutes of *Raiders of the Lost Ark* provides an excellent macro-context for teaching mathematical thinking. In this segment, Indiana Jones goes to South America in the hopes of finding a golden idol. A lesson using this segment could focus on the idea of planning for a trip to the South American jungle that is similar to the trip taken by Indiana Jones. In order to plan for the trip, students need to anticipate problems that they might encounter, problems such as the need for food and water. When students attempt to determine the exact amount of food and water needed, they are generating word problems that they need to solve. This is quite different from solving problems that other people provide (e.g. Bransford & Stein, 1984). We noted at the beginning of this paper that goals stressed by the NAEP include helping students learn to "formulate key questions." An especially important aspect of mathematical thinking includes the ability to generate key questions that need to be asked.

A problem relevant to the goal of planning for a trip might be analogous to the waterboy problem discussed above:

> Indiana Jones needs to bring enough water to drink. Each person should have at least 1 quart of water a day, and Indiana needs enough for 3 people for 2 days. If water weighs a pound per pint, how many pounds of water will Indiana need?

There are several reasons why the Indiana Jones problem seems preferable to the waterboy problem. First, the Indiana problem can help students think about information that is useful rather than arbitrary. How much water do we really need per day? What is the weight of water? In the waterboy problem, one is less likely to learn useful facts such as this.

The Indiana Jones problem also becomes more meaningful because it is related to other problems involved in planning. Thus, problems involving the weight of water can be related to other problems such as the weight of food, the weight of kerosene for the torches, and so forth. Rather than being exposed to only an unrelated set of word problems, students can see each problem as a subproblem related to an overall goal. Furthermore, when students begin with a general goal such as planning for a trip and then generate specific subgoals, they begin to see how mathematical problem solving (including problem generation) facilitates real-world adaptation. In this sense, the experience illustrates the kinds of relationships depicted in Figure 2B.

AN INITIAL STUDY

Our goal in this section is to discuss the results of an experiment in which we attempted to teach problem solving within a larger macro-context such as the Indiana Jones trip to South America. We were motivated to take this approach to mathematics instruction because middle school teachers with whom we have worked had expressed serious doubts about the ability of their learning handicapped students to solve anything but the most rudimentary word problems. In addition, most of the students with whom we worked expressed similar doubts.

Our study was designed to investigate the usefulness of using macro-contexts to teach mathematical problem solving (Kulewicz, Barron, Goin, Hasselbring, & Bransford, 1986). For this project we worked with fifth and sixth graders who were approximately 1½ years behind their peers in mathematics. The environment involved the use of videodiscs to provide a macro-context that helped students formulate meaningful problem-solving goals. To develop this environment we utilized the first 10 minutes of the film *Raiders of the Lost Ark* presented on videodisc. This segment shows Indiana's trip to a South American jungle to capture the golden idol. This segment enabled us to formulate the following goal: One might want to return to the jungle to explore the region or to get the golden gong that Indiana left behind. If so, it could be important to know dimensions of obstacles such as the size of the pit one would have to jump, the height of the cave, the width of the river and its relationship to the size of the seaplane, and so forth. Since this information is on film, it does no good to measure sizes directly (e.g. the pit is only several inches wide on the screen). However, one can use known standards (e.g. Indiana Jones) to estimate sizes and distances that are important to know.

The general goal of learning more about important dimensions of potential obstacles and events guided the selection of mathematically based problems that were based on scenes from the 10-minute movie segment. Through the use of random access videodisc we were able to isolate and quickly access the sequence of frames that specified each problem situation. For example, at one point Indiana comes to a pit and must attempt to get over it. He jumps. How wide is the pit? Could humans possibly jump something that wide?

The width of the pit can be estimated by finding another, earlier scene where Indiana uses his bullwhip to swing over the pit. Through the use of freeze frame we are able to show a scene of Indiana swinging and extending halfway across the pit. Measurement on the screen (either by hand or through the use of computer graphics) allows students to see that the pit is two Indianas wide. If Indiana is 6 feet tall, the pit is 12 feet wide. Students can be helped to determine this information for themselves and, subsequently, to see if they could jump something that was 12 feet wide. In our initial studies, the problems that we worked with involved finding the length or width of an object, given its proportional relationship to a standard with a known length or width. Our aim was to facilitate children's comprehension of the problem situations and thereby improve their motivation to solve various problems plus increase their understanding of the relationships between the known and unknown quantities expressed in the problems. The use of the video provided an especially rich macro-context from which to begin. The video was supplemented with effective teaching (mediation). For example, students were encouraged to create visual and symbolic representations of problems, and they received individualized feedback about the strengths and weaknesses of their approach to each problem. All instruction was one-on-one.

Effects of learning in the video context were compared to the effects of learning in a control condition in which students received teaching that was similar in format but more individualized than the teaching they received in school. For example, in one-on-one sessions that included a great deal of encouragement, students in the control group worked on problems and were shown correct solution strategies after attempting to solve each problem. They therefore received more attention and more immediate feedback than they received in class.

As will become apparent, there are a number of differences between our video group and control group. Our study was not designed to specify the exact ingredients that might be responsible for differences in performance. For our initial study the goal was to (a) provide the best teaching context that we could envision in order to see if there was any hope for our LH students and (b) compare this approach to one that was close to the classroom procedure except that it involved one-on-one rather than group instruction.

Method

Twenty fifth and sixth grade students participated in the study. All children were enrolled either part or full time in a special education classroom or received their instruction in mathematics from a resource teacher. Prior to being assigned to a teaching condition each child was tested with the Key-Math test. Total Key-Math scores provided the basis for a stratified random assignment to one of the two teaching conditions. Thus the two groups were equivalent with regard to average grade-level achievement in mathematics (mean = 3.7).

Similarities of the Two Methods

All children were given two word-problem pretests, two posttests, and participated in seven individual teaching sessions. The first pretest consisted of problem situations similar to those found in textbooks. The other consisted of problems taken from the macro-context provided by the film. These problem situations were the same as those used during the teaching sessions. However, the proportional relationships and the value associated with the standard were changed. Before this second pretest children in both groups watched the first 12-minute segment of the film. Those objects that would be involved in the problems were pointed out while the children watched the film. We were interested in whether children would do better on the problems presented in the macro-context even before any instruction had taken place.

The two posttests differed on the same dimensions as the pretests. The first posttest consisted of problems taken from unrelated contexts (problem situations of the type found in textbooks). These problems had never been seen by the students. The problems on the second posttest were the same set given in the pretest and used during the teaching sessions. However, again both the proportional relationship and the value associated with the standard were changed.

Over the seven teaching sessions three problem types were introduced. These types differed in the calculations required for solution, and consequently in problem difficulty. In the first problem type the relationship of the numbers involved only whole numbers (e.g. The pontoon is 3 times as long as Indiana Jones). The second problem type involved finding a fractional amount of the standard (e.g. The golden gong is $\frac{1}{3}$ as high as Indiana Jones). The third and final problem type involved whole numbers and fractions (e.g. The cave entrance is $1\frac{1}{2}$ times as high as Indiana Jones).

Within each teaching session the first problem presented was taken from the Raiders context. the experimenter showed students how to solve the problem, including how to make a visual representation of that problem. Each child then represented and solved three problems independently. Of these three problems the first two were taken from the Raiders context. The third was a problem of the same type taken from an unrelated context. Feedback was given directly after the child completed each problem solution. All students received the same sequence of problems across the seven teaching sessions.

Instruction for the Control Group

As noted earlier, our goal for the control group was to simulate, and to some extent improve upon, the type of instruction these students were receiving in the classroom. In general, their classroom teachers would demonstrate how to solve a particular type of word problem and then ask students to solve similar problems at their seats. After solving various problems, students' answers were scored as correct or incorrect, and students received feedback about the accuracy of their work.

In our control group, experimenters worked individually with children. Students first read a problem and the experimenter demonstrated the solution, including how to represent the problem visually and how to set up and perform the computation. Students then worked on problems on their own and, after each problem, received feedback. The feedback consisted of information about how to represent the problem visually, how to set up the correct mathematical equation, and how to compute the correct quantitative answer. We will refer to the feedback given to control students as "generic" because it was presented as a model solution rather than explicitly tailored to the exact strengths and weaknesses of each student's representations and solutions. Students were given a great deal of praise and encouragement in an attempt to keep their motivation high. As will be discussed in more detail below, the effect of our control group instruction was very similar to the effects of the classroom instruction; neither worked very well. The teachers noted that students in the classroom made very little gains in learning to solve word problems and the same was true of the students in our individual sessions. Based on this type of instructional environment, it is easy to reach the conclusion that the ability to solve word problems was beyond the grasp of these children.

Instruction for the Video Group

Instruction for the video group differed from the control students in terms of: (a) representation of specific video scenes relevant to each problem to be solved (only the video group saw these scenes), (b) level of explanation provided during the daily demonstration problem, and (c) the type of feedback given. These are described below:

Initial video presentation. In order to provide an enriched presentation of each problem situation, the children in the video group were shown the individual film segment on which the current problem was based (e.g. a scene of Indiana swinging across the pit was shown prior to a problem involving the width of the pit). This was done for the demonstration and also before the students attempted independent solutions of each macro-context problem. The children in the control group saw the 12-minute video segment prior to the first pretest, but did not see individual scenes before each problem.

Explanation during demonstration. Demonstrations for the control and video groups were similar in that both included a representation of the problem, restatement of what was being asked, and identification of the information that would be used to find the answer. In addition, the correct equation was set up and carried out. The explanations differed in that the demonstration for the video group was elaborated by including an explanation of why certain steps were carried out (e.g. "we are writing down Indiana's height next to our picture of him so that it will be easy to remember when we are ready to find out how tall the statue is"). Although further research is needed to confirm our beliefs, we think the video context helped motivate students by creating an interest in the problems and their solutions.

This increased interest led to students paying more attention to the elaborated explanation than they may have if the elaborated explanation had been presented in the absence of the video context. In addition, we feel that the video context made it easier for students to see how each problem related to previous ones, thus making it relatively easy to help students understand connections between previous solutions and the problems they were attempting then. In this way, students become relatively fluent at problem representation and at the selection of appropriate algorithms.

Feedback following performance. The final difference between the groups consisted of the type of feedback received. We noted earlier that, after the children in the control group completed a problem, regardless of the child's solution, the experimenter demonstrated a correct representation and solution. The feedback in the video group was tailored toward each child's attempt at representation and solution, and identification of errors made. Any specific errors were discussed and immediately corrected by the child before continuing.

Results. In order to evaluate the effectiveness of the two teaching programs, two major types of analyses were completed for the pretest and posttest data (more detailed analysis is provided in Kulewicz et al., 1986). The first examined differences between the two groups in the percentage of problems in which the child's final answer was correct.

As shown in Figure 3, students in both groups did very poorly on both pretests. The children in the control group also did quite poorly on the posttests. However, children in the video group solved significantly more problems on both posttests than on the pretests. On the posttest, the difference between the in-context and unrelated context problems was not significant. Thus, the problem-solving skills acquired by students in the video group could be readily applied to problems that they had never seen before and that referred to new and unrelated contexts.

The second analysis assessed differences in the overall quality of children's representations. The problem representation generated for each of the pretest and posttest problems was evaluated on five dimensions: content, proportion, information, use of brackets, and equation. Each dimension was scored as being correct or incorrect (1 or 0). A representation score was determined for each problem by summing across the number of points given for the five dimensions. Thus for each problem, subjects received a representation score ranging from 0 to 5. As shown in Figure 4, the pattern of results found for representation scores was the same as that found for the percentage of problems answered correctly. That is, the quality of all children's representations was poor at pretest. The quality of the representations of the control group did not change significantly on the posttests. In contrast, the mean representation scores of children in the

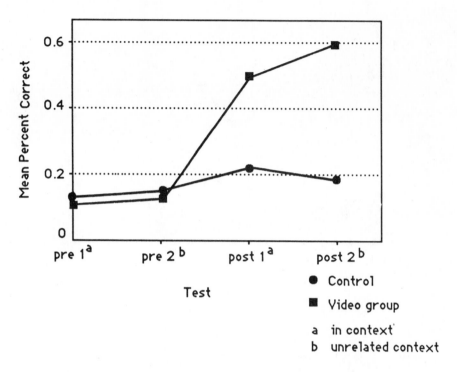

Figure 3. Pretest and posttest scores on quantitative answers to word problems

video group were significantly higher on both posttests than on either pre-test.

Analyses of student performance during the daily teaching suggest that the superior posttest performance of students in the video group did not suddenly emerge at the end of the experiment. Instead, students in the video group were performing better each day.

Overall, it is clear that the instruction used for our control group, one-on-one instruction that provided demonstrations of correct problem-solving procedures, practice, feedback and encouragement, was not effective in teaching our learning handicapped children to correctly represent and solve this set of word problems. In contrast, the instruction that the video group received was effective. Students showed significant improvements, and both the students and their teachers seemed excited by the results. Students in the experimental group would have performed even better if they had known more about fractions. Many of the more difficult problems involved situations where the to-be-measured object was 1½ or 2⅓ as large as the standard. Students who did not know how to add and multiply fractions had special difficulties with problems such as these.

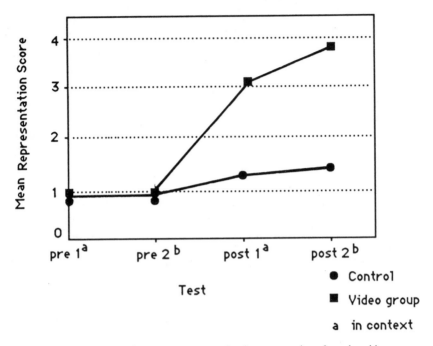

Figure 4. Pretest and posttest scores on visual representation of word problems

BEYOND THE INITIAL STUDY

We noted in the introduction to this chapter that our initial attempts to facilitate mathematical thinking were preliminary. Our goals in this section are twofold. First, we discuss our plans for isolating the instructional components that were responsible for our initial findings. Second, we explore additional aspects of mathematical thinking that were not emphasized in our initial studies but seem important to pursue.

Isolating the Effects of Instructional Components

Consider first the issue of the instructional components that helped students learn in our experimental condition. We suspect that the emphasis on visual representations of problems, plus the use of tailored feedback, played an important role in learning. It is possible, in fact, that these are the only major variables and that the video-based macro-context played no additional role.

We believe that the video environment has a number of potentially important functions. First, it seems to facilitate students' abilities to comprehend the problems they are being asked to solve. In addition, it seems to help them catch their own errors because it is easier to estimate the reasonableness of their answers. Third, it enables students to link their work on individual problems with an overall goal such as planning a trip into new territory. Fourth, as we discuss later it provides a context for teaching problem-finding and problem representation.

Studies investigating the importance of each of these factors are currently being designed. For example, we will compare the effects of working with problem types that all involve a common goal in a common video context (e.g. measuring various objects and artifacts in the Indiana Jones context) with the effects of working with semantically unrelated sets of problems like the ones that normally appear as exercises in classrooms and texts. Measures will include assessments of problem comprehension plus the ability to spot and correct errors.

Facilitating Additional Aspects of Mathematical Thinking

Although it is important to attempt to isolate those components of our instruction that were most useful to students, we do not want to focus on this issue entirely. A major reason is that our instruction was still far from ideal. There are a number of elements of mathematical thinking that, at least from our perspective, are important to emphasize and that we plan to pursue. We consider some of these here.

1. It is important to emphasize general aspects of measurement. Why don't humans simply use individual people as standards rather than use rulers and yardsticks? Why do we have so many different measures along a dimension (e.g. length) rather than only one?

This latter issue is especially interesting in light of the fact that many students with whom we have worked do not really understand why they have to learn different measures such as inches, feet, yards, miles, and so forth. They need to realize that the use of different measures actually simplifies problem solving. If everything were measured in inches, for example, we would have to deal with extremely large numbers to find distances between cities.

The general idea that mathematical discoveries and inventions actually simplify problem solving is very foreign to many students (e.g. Sherwood, Kinzer, Hasselbring, & Bransford, 1987). They need to understand the types of problems that the invention of new units helps us solve. This kind of information helps students learn when to use various units of measurement. A number of theorists note that knowledge remains inert unless people know when to use it (e.g. Simon 1980; Whitehead, 1929). Ideally, people choose units of measurements that allow them to be precise, yet deal with numbers of a reasonable size.

2. It is important for students to experience how problem solving can be simplified through the use of mathematical notation. The following statements are elegant: 1P (for Pit) = 2I (for Indiana); 3I = 1Ptn (for pontoon).

These expressions provide a simpler way to communicate essential information than do sentences created from words.

Can the use of notation be experienced as useful? One approach is to imagine the need to use standards to measure items in a video where the exact size of the standard is not yet known; it must be determined later. Since one cannot compute an exact answer, the expression of relationships is needed.

Another, more complex way to motivate the use of mathematical notation might be to compare the relationships found in a situation involving actual life (e.g. measurements of Johnny and of a marked-off pit on the ground) with a photograph of the situation. Clearly, the actual size of Johnny and the pit in the picture is much smaller than in real life, but what about the relationship between the elements? If 1P (pit) = 2J (for Johnny) in the actual situation, it should be the same in the picture, too.

It is interesting to note in this context that many college students have difficulties relating actual situations to appropriate mathematical representations (e.g. Soloway, et al., 1982). If students in earlier grades are helped to experience the usefulness of representations, and are encouraged to actually use them as means for achieving interesting ends, errors should be less likely to occur.

3. Instruction should explicitly emphasize the role of argument and evidence in mathematical thinking. An important concept that many students fail to learn involves the difference between inductive and deductive approaches to knowledge acquisition. Imagine, for example, that we measure Johnny standing by a marked-off pit and measure a photograph of the same situation. If the general relationships between Johnny and the pit are invariant across the two conditions, will these also be invariant for a new set of circumstances? We could keep finding new examples and measuring them, but we would still be relying on induction. A more powerful approach would be to prove the necessity of the invariant relationships. Many students fail to realize the power of proofs for substantiating knowledge claims.

An emphasis on proof versus induction also has other advantages. In algebra, for example, researchers such as Sleeman (1984) note that many high school students "solve" the problems by simply picking a number to be the unknown (e.g. "assume X = 3") and calculating the answer. If the equation doesn't balance, students pick another number for X (e.g. 6) and try again. Part of the students' problem may stem from the fact that they do not understand the uses of algebra. Why have mathematicians heralded it as such a powerful invention?

In his book on mathematics, Jacobs (1982, p. 39) provides an excellent illustration of the use of algebraic notation. He begins with a number trick like the following:

Choose a number (one person chooses 7, the other 4)

Add 5	12	9
Double the result	24	18
Subtract 4	20	14
Divide by 2	10	7
Subtract the number first thought of	3	3
The result is 3		

Jacobs notes that the trick works (i.e. it ends in a 3) when one begins with a 7 or a 4. Will it work if one begins with a 6? A 10? A 23? One approach to solving this problem is to begin with different numbers and work through the puzzle. This is an inductive approach to knowing and, although it can be powerful, it has limitations as well. Jacobs then shows that a more powerful approach is to represent particular numbers as variables and prove whether any beginning number will result in the same answer. Examples such as this seem excellent for helping students use mathematical tools as means for interesting ends.

4. Students need to see how complex problems must often be broken down into a set of word-problem-like subproblems. In our initial studies we emphasized to some degree that each individual word problem was really a subproblem for an overall survival problem. Nevertheless, we could have made the link between mathematical problem solving and general issues, such as planning, much more explicit. This should increase the likelihood that students will realize the value of mathematical thinking for their everyday lives.

5. The problems students solve should allow them to acquire useful content knowledge. Our pits, pontoons, rivers, and so forth were from a movie set. A more useful measurement task would help students learn actual values that are realistic. For example, one could take scenes from *King Kong* (this is on videodisc) in which King Kong fights with various prehistoric animals such as pterodactyls. How big do scientists estimate these to be, and how big are they when one uses standards from the movie to estimate their length?

At a more general level, learning might be made more efficient if we adopted an integrated approach to instruction that provided important content while also teaching mathematical thinking. In particular, the problems typically found in mathematics texts usually involve arbitrary information. They can rather easily be recast to teach about important aspects of science (e.g. the weight of water on earth, the density of metals), social studies, and so forth. By doing so, students can learn more in a given time period. This issue is discussed in more detail in Bransford, Sherwood, & Hasselbring (in press).

6. Instructors need to emphasize problem finding and problem defining. These aspects of problem solving are extremely crucial yet are rarely taught

(e.g. Bransford & Stein, 1984). Instead of finding and defining their own problems, students are usually given prepackaged sets of problems to solve.

The goal of emphasizing problem finding and defining provides the major reason for our use of video to create macro-contexts. Students can watch a segment from *Raiders of the Lost Ark* (or any other video) and look for spots where they would like more information in order to achieve an overall goal (e.g. information about the width of the pit could be important if one were planning a journey to the spot visited by Indiana). Students can then try to define their problem mathematically rather than have it defined for them.

In our work with middle school students who were having difficulties in mathematics, we have emphasized problem finding informally and find that (a) children like to find their own problems and (b) they become good with practice. Our forthcoming studies will include measures of students' abilities to find and generate problems that are relevant for achieving particular goals.

Informal evidence for the importance of an emphasis on problem finding comes from our work during the summer with a group of mathematics-delayed students. They worked with problems in the Indiana Jones context, but they also were given the opportunity to find their own problems in other contexts such as King Kong. As we walked across the campus with these students after class, we observed that they spontaneously began to generate their own problems. For example, they would use themselves as standards to estimate the height of trees and buildings, the length of trucks, and so forth. these examples of spontaneous mathematical thinking are the kinds of activities that we want to promote.

7. Effective performance requires fluency and not just accuracy. Instruction that develops fluency is an important component of teaching mathematical thinking. If students are not fluent at basic processes, their attention is overtaxed. Imagine trying to carry on a conversation when you were first learning to drive a car. Until driving skills become fluent, people cannot talk and drive.

Earlier we presented data indicating that, even for students in regular education, there was a surprisingly large number of simple number facts that students could not access with fluency. This lack of fluency can get in the way of developing higher order skills. In our research, we find that short amounts of time such as 10 minutes per day for developing fluency can result in significant improvements in performance. Students also feel good about their noticeable improvements.

Fluency needs to be developed in a number of areas. We believe that one of the major reasons for the success of our videodisc-based instruction is that students received a considerable amount of practice drawing representations and calculating answers for problem types that were very similar to one another. They became fluent at this process, in part because they were easily able to perceive the similarities among the particular problems that they attempted to solve. In future studies we also plan to help students become fluent in other activities such as matching mathematical equations (e.g. 1 Pit = 2 Indys) with visual representations of these equations. Fluency at these activities should free students' attention so that they can perform other aspects of mathematical thinking that otherwise would be extremely difficult to accomplish.

SUMMARY

We have argued that instruction in mathematical problem solving can be strengthened by focusing on relationships between general issues of planning and problem solving and the specific nature of word problems. The use of videodiscs to create macro-contexts for problem solving appears to be particularly promising, especially for helping students learn to find and define their own problems, rather than simply to practice solving problems that others supply to them. Video-based contexts can also increase interest levels so that students receive enough practice to become fluent at solving particular problem types. Without a sufficient degree of fluency, their attentional resources will be overtaxed.

We presented data from an initial study which indicate that the use of macro-contexts can be especially beneficial for students who are having difficulty in mathematics. The progress made by our students represents only a small step toward the development of mathematical thinking. Nevertheless, we believe it to be an important step. Ideally, all students will come to view themselves as problem solvers who have a special edge because they have the ability to think mathematically. In order to develop this type of attitude, students need to be helped to find and define issues and to see how mathematical inventions and discoveries simplify their problem solving. Current methods of teaching tend not to develop this kind of attitude. Our planned studies will involve instruction that focuses on problem finding and problem defining in the context of complex, problem-solving activities. We will assess the degree to which this type of instruction helps students increase their appreciation of mathematics as well as increase their problem-solving skills.

FOOTNOTE

1. Preparation of this chapter was supported, in part, by grants G008300052 and G008730072 awarded to John Bransford and Ted Hasselbring. Aspects of the work with videodiscs was also supported by a grant from the IBM Corporation. We are very grateful to Bob Sherwood and Jim Van Hanaghan for helpful comments and suggestions regarding this manuscript.

REFERENCES

Allardice, B.S., & H.P. Ginsburg (1983). Children's psychological difficulties in mathematics. In H.P. Ginsburg (Ed.), *The development of mathematical thinking* (pp. 319–350). New York: Academic Press.

Becker, G. (1985, November-December). A question of copyright. *Electronic Education,* p. 19.

Bransford, J.D., & Stein, B.S. (1984). *The IDEAL problem solver.* New York: W.H. Freeman & Co.

Bransford, J.D., Delclos, V., Vye, N., Burns, S., & Hasselbring, T. (in press). Approaches to dynamic assessment: Issues, data and future directions. In C. Lidz (Ed.), *Dynamic assessment: Foundations and fundamentals.* New York: Guilford Press.

Bransford, J.D., Delclos, V.R., Vye, N.J., Burns, M.S., Hasselbring, T.S. (1986). *Improving the quality of assessment and instruction: Roles for dynamic assessment.* Paper presented at American Psychological Association. Washington, D.C.

Bransford, J.D., Sherwood, R.S., Hasselbring, T.S. (in press). Effects of the video revolution on development: Some initial thoughts. *Constructivism in the Computer Age.* Hillsdale, NJ: Erlbaum.

Bransford, J.D., Sherwood, R., Vye, N.J., Rieser, J. (1986). Teaching thinking and problem solving: Suggestions from research. *American Psychologist,* 41 (10), 1078–1089.

Burton, R.R., Brown, J.S., & Fischer, G. (1984). Skiing as a model of instruction. In B. Rogoff & J. Lave (Eds.), *Everyday cognition* (pp. 139–150). Cambridge, MA: Harvard University Press.

Crosswhite, J.F. (1986, October). Better teaching, better mathematics: Are they enough? *Arithmetic Teacher,* 54–59.

de Corte, E., & Verschaffel, L. (1985). Beginning first graders' initial representation of arithmetic word problems. *Journal of Mathematical Behavior,* 4, 3–21.

Feuerstein, R., Rand, Y., & Hoffman, M. (1979). *The dynamic assessment of retarded performers: The learning potential assessment device: Theory, instruments, and techniques.* Baltimore: University Park Press.

Hamann, M.S., & Ashcraft, M.H. (1986). Textbook presentations of the basic addition facts. *Cognition and Instruction,* 3(3), 173–192.

Hanson, N.R. (1970). A picture theory of theory meaning. In R.G. Colodny (Ed.), *The nature and function of scientific theories* (pp. 233–274). Pittsburgh: University of Pittsburgh Press.

Hasselbring, T.S., Goin, L.I., & Bransford, J.D. (1987, April). *Assessing and developing math automaticity in learning disabled students: The role of microcomputer technology.* Paper presented at the annual meeting of the American Educational Research Association, Washington, D.C.

Hasselbring, T., Goin, L., & Bransford, J. (1987). Effective mathematics instruction: Developing automaticity. *Teaching Exceptional Children,* 19(3), 30–33.

Holt, J. (1964). *How children fail.* New York: Dell.

Jacobs, H.R. (1982). *Mathematics: A human endeavor* (2nd ed.). New York: W. H. Freeman & Co.

Kulewicz, S., Barron, B., Goin, L., Hasselbring, T., & Bransford, J.D. (1986). *The effects of video-context and mediation on mathematical problem solving.* (Technical Report No. 86.1.6). Nashville, TN: Vanderbilt University, Learning Technology Center.

Lesh, R. (1981). Applied mathematical problem solving. *Educational Studies in Mathematics,* 12, 235–264.

Littlefield, J., & Rieser, J.J. (1985). *Differentiation of information: Locus of gauge pattern in mathematical story problems.* Poster presented at biannual meeting of Society for Research in Child Development. Toronto, Canada.

McDermott, R. (1986). *Not getting caught not knowing.* Colloquium. Nashville, TN: Vanderbilt University.

National Assessment of Educational Progress (NAEP). (1983). *The third national mathematics assessment: Results, trends and issues* (13-MA–01). Denver, CO: Educational Commission of the States.

National Council of Teachers of Mathematics (1980). *An agenda for action: Recommendations for school mathematics of the 1980s.* Reston, VA: The Council.

Resnick, L.B. (1986). The development of mathematical intuition. In M. Permutter (Ed.), *Minnesota symposium on child psychology* (Vol. 19). (pp. 159–194). Hillsdale, NJ: Erlbaum.

Russell, R. & Ginsburg, H.P. (1984). Cognitive analysis of children's mathematics difficulties. *Cognition & Instruction,* 1, 217–244.

Schneider, W., & Shiffrin, R.M. (1977). Controlled and automatic information processing: I. Detection, search and attention. *Psychological Review,* 84, 1–66.

Schneider, W., & Shiffrin, R.M. (1984). Automatic and control processes revisited. *Psychological Review,* 91(2), 269–276.

Sherwood, R.D., Kinzer, C.K., Bransford, J.D., & Franks, J.J. (1987). Some benefits of creating macro-contexts for science instruction: Initial findings. *Journal of Research in Science Teaching,* 24(5), 417–435.

Sherwood, R., Kinzer, C., & Hasselbring, T., & Bransford, J. (1987). Macro-contexts for learning: Initial findings and issues. *Journal of Applied Cognitive Psychology,* 1, 93–108.

Simon, H.A. (1980). Problem solving and education. In D. T. Tuma & R. Reif (Eds.), *Problem solving and education: Issues in teaching and research* (pp. 81–96). Hillsdale, NJ: Erlbaum.

Sleeman, D. (1984). An attempt to understand students' understanding of algebra. *Cognitive Science,* 8, 387–412.

Soloway, E., Lochhead, J., & Clement, J. (1982). Does computer programming enhance problem-solving ability? Some positive evidence on algebra word problems. In R. Seidel, R. Anderson, & B. Hunter (Eds.), *Computer literacy* (pp. 171–185). New York: Academic Press.

Stodolsky, S.S. (1985). Telling math: Origins of math aversion and anxiety. *Educational Psychologist,* 20, 125–133.

Van Haneghan, J.P., & Baker, L. (in preparation). *Cognitive monitoring in math.*

Vye, N.J., Burns, M.S., Delclos, V.R., & Bransford, J.D. (in press). Dynamic assessment of intellectually handicapped children. In C. Lidz (Ed.), *Dynamic assessment: Foundations and fundamentals.* New York: Guilford Press.

Vygotsky, L.S. (1978). *Mind in society.* Cambridge, MA: Harvard University Press.

Whitehead, A.N. (1929). *The aims of education.* New York: Macmillan.

Wood, D. (1980). Teaching the young child: Some relationships between social interaction, language, and thought. In D. Olson (Ed.), *The social foundations of language and thought.* New York: W.W. Norton & Company.

Wood, D., Wood, H., & Middleton, D. (1978). An experimental evaluation of four face-to-face teaching strategies. International *Journal of Behavioral Development,* 1, 131–147.

Choosing Operations in Solving
Routine Story Problems[1]

Larry Sowder

San Diego State University

Story problems are an important part of the curriculum, inasmuch as they represent the interplay between mathematics and reality and give a basic experience in mathematizing. What more respected authority can there be than Polya?

> *Why word problems?* I hope that I shall shock a few people in asserting that the most important single task of mathematical instruction in the secondary schools is to teach the setting up of equations to solve word problems. Yet there is a strong argument in favor of this opinion.
>
> In solving a word problem by setting up equations, the student *translates* a real situation into mathematical terms: he has an opportunity to experience that mathematical concepts may be related to realities, but such relations must be carefully worked out. . . . (1962, p. 59).

Notwithstanding the quote, Polya no doubt would be pleased with the post-1962 progress in, or at least the rhetoric about, the inclusion of nonroutine problem solving as an important part of the present curriculum.

ASPECTS OF SOLVING A STORY PROBLEM

Figure 1 outlines some of the elements which presumably enter into the solution of a story problem. The implied near-linear sequence is, of course, a simplification. The considerable work with representations (e.g., Janvier, 1987) suggests that the distinction between things external and internal to the solver is worthwhile. Figure 1 reminds us that where the problem is being encountered (the setting) can influence a solution: Is the problem being presented in school? Is the student solving it alone, during seatwork, on a test, . . .?

Some elements of Figure 1 show areas in which deliberate instruction is often missing. For example, rarely does one hear teacher directions like, "Be sure you can explain why you know that addition, subtraction, or whatever, is the correct operation for the problem," in an effort to establish an intent on the part of the learner.

Many of the elements in Figure 1 require no elaboration. Some have received considerable attention already; for example, the many variables in the tasks themselves were the theme for a monograph (Goldin & McClintock, 1980). The focus in this paper will be on a key step: Deciding what operation(s) to use.

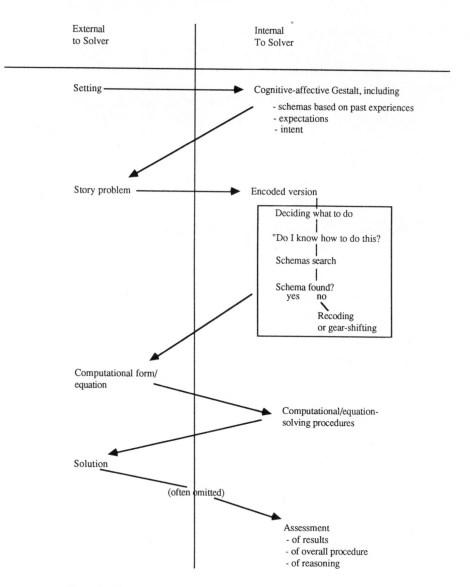

Figure 1. Elements involved in solving a story problem (cf. Sowder 1985)

DECIDING WHAT TO DO

Given that a student has sufficient reading comprehension skill to encode a story problem, a major stumbling block is to link the information to a correct choice of operation(s). This section presents the argument that many students approach this decision point without a proper mental set or make their choices on flimsy, unreliable bases.

Do I Know What to Do?

If solvers *think* they cannot solve a problem, they unfortunately often give up at that point. We have all observed such behavior as this one, noted by Lester and Garofalo (1987): A group of seventh graders stopped working on a (nonroutine) problem involving percents because "we can't do percents." Even though they had done prior work with percent and the percents in the problem were easy (20% and 50%), "we haven't done percent yet this year" convinced them they could not solve the problem. There is encouraging anecdotal evidence that extensive work with nonroutine problems may liberate students from such defeatist or "I can't do it until you show me how" attitudes (e.g., Charles & Lester, 1984). Studies of instruction in nonroutine problem solving should examing whether an improvement in attitude toward the solution of story problems is indeed a by-product of the instruction.

Schema Search

Evidence from recent national assessments in mathematics (Carpenter, Corbitt, Kepner, Lindquist, & Reys, 1980; Lindquist, Carpenter, Silver, & Matthews, 1983; National Assessment of Educational Progress, 1983) have indicated that performance on one-step story problems involving whole numbers in general is adequate. Recent interview studies of students' strategies, however, suggest that even students who are correctly solving whole number story problems, let alone those involving rational numbers, may be using strategies of little value in more complicated problems and certainly little of long-term value. These strategies are summarized next.

Interviews of sixth and eighth graders in my recent work have supplemented and confirmed reports from several sources on strategies that students use (Greer, 1987a; Greer & Mangan, 1984; Kalmykova, 1975; Lester & Garofalo, 1982, 1987; Noddings, 1985; Sherrill, 1983; Sowder, 1986; Sowder, Threadgill-Sowder, Moyer, & Moyer, 1984; Stevenson, 1925; Trafton, 1984). Here is a list (Sowder, 1988), not comprehensive but nonetheless representative of the variety of approaches that students, or even a single student, might take:

1. Find the numbers and add (or multiply or subtract . . .; the choice may be dictated by what has gone on in class recently or by what operation the student feels most competent at doing).
2. Guess at the operation to be used.
3. Look at the numbers; they will "tell" you which operation to use (e.g., ". . . if it's like, 78 and maybe 54, then I'd probably either add or multiply. But [78 and] 3, it looks like a division because of the size of the numbers").
4. Try all the operations and choose the most reasonable answer.

5. Look for isolated "key" words to tell which operations to use (e.g., "all together" means to add).

6. Decide whether the answer should be larger or smaller than the given numbers. If larger, try both addition and multiplication and choose the more reasonable answer. If smaller, try both subtraction and division and choose the more reasonable.

7. Choose the operation whose meaning fits the story.

The first four strategies, of course, are not taught and would be amusing if they were not used by real learners. Although most often the students who use these strategies are not successful students, there are exceptions. One seventh grader in a gifted program used strategy 4; her computational facility made the strategy quite feasible with one-step problems.

Strategies 4–6 do involve at least a bit of number sense, a minimal semantic processing, and a very minimal awareness of the meanings for the operations. The key-word strategy (#5) unfortunately is occasionally taught by well-meaning teachers who are not aware of its limits. Sherrill (1983) noted a "pervasive" use of this key-word strategy in an interview study, and Nesher and Teubal (1975) found that even primary school children were using key words. Note that strategies 4 and 6 may be effective with some whole numbers, but less useful when large whole numbers, fractions, or decimals for which the student has less number sense are involved.

All but the last strategy (#7) are extremely difficult to apply to multistep problems. Again, note the implications for the NAEP findings, since the poorest performances on story problems there occurred on problems requiring more than one calculation, involving extraneous data, or requiring an interpretation of a calculation. The relatively poor performance on the more complicated problems may be explained by the over-reliance on immature strategies. If that explanation is correct, then of course the relatively good performance on one-step problems is specious.

What is most disappointing is the rarity of the meaning-based strategy 7. In interviews, even students who make frequent correct choices of operations rarely can give any justification for their choice of operation. "I just know" is a common explanation, as is a recital of why the other operations would not give correct solutions (usually based on the anticipated size of the answer). Zweng, in her report of her interview work on problem solving with elementary school students (1979), noted that the typical curriculum of that time did not provide the students with language for describing generically the common applications of the operations. This lack is remedied in some text series coming out now; for example, language like "division tells you how many 18s are in 1746" might be used. It will be interesting to see whether children who use such series for two or three years adopt a meaning-based strategy.

Nonconservation of Operation

An indirect confirmation of the limits of students' meanings for the operations, and evidence of the influence of strategy 6 (decide whether the answer should be larger or smaller, if larger, try both + and ×, etc.), is given by what has been called "nonconservation of operation" (Greer & Mangan, 1984): Students who correctly decide that an operation will give the solution to a problem involving whole numbers may then change their minds when the same problem is given with fractions or decimals less than 1 in place of the whole numbers. For example, consider, "A pound of cheese costs $2.46. How much will 3 pounds of the cheese cost?" A student might correctly choose to multiply on that problem but then, when the next problem involves 0.82 pounds of cheese ("A pound of cheese costs $2.46. How much will 0.82 pounds of the cheese cost?"), the nonconserver of operation will often opt for subtraction or division! Nonconservers' explanations usually show that they realize that the correct answer should be less than the cost for one pound. Their years of computing with whole numbers have given them the unintended generalization: Multiplication makes bigger, division makes smaller (MMBDMS). Thus, in their minds certainly multiplication is *not* called for, but some operation (or sequence of operations) that will give a smaller answer is in order. (Again, note that for whole numbers that appear in one-step story problems, MMBDMS is all right and makes Strategy 6 a successful one, unless the numbers are so large that the student has little number sense for them.)

Several recent reports have noted the nonconservation phenomenon with various levels of students (e.g., Bell, Fischbein, & Greer, 1984; Ekenstam & Greger, 1983; Fischbein, Deri, Nello, & Marino, 1985; Hart, 1981; Greer, 1987a; Mangan, 1986; Sowder, 1986; Tirosh, Graeber, & Glover, 1986). Mangan's extensive work included the testing of groups from age 10 through preservice elementary teachers (Mangan, 1986, Experiment 3; cf. Greer & Mangan, 1986). In each group, including the preservice teachers, a change of multiplier from a whole number to a decimal less than 1 resulted in a drop in performance of roughly 40%.

Gear-Shifting

Although the findings about strategies is depressing, there is a positive note from the interview work. Some students "shift gears" when confronted with a multistep problem and, apparently realizing that the immature strategies are inadequate, adopt some unknown strategies to arrive at a solution. What these strategies are, and whether the students adopt meaning-based strategies, has been difficult to tease out. One could hypothesize a means-end analysis, but I cannot offer any evidence to support that idea.

That some students do shift gears is encouraging. Perhaps for these students the immature strategies are only shortcuts. Since K–6 one-step story problems yield to and perhaps invite the immature strategies, the strongest indictment of one-step story problems might be not their criticizable) forms but rather their prevalence. Certainly there would seem to be profit in including many more multistep problems in the curriculum. An instructional study along these lines could show whether more extensive work with multistep problems discourages a dependence on the weak strategies.

WHAT SCHEMAS *SHOULD* STUDENTS HAVE?

After a large scale evaluation program in England (Concepts in Secondary Mathematics and Science), project workers concluded, "Thus one can say that of children at the *end of the first year* in the secondary school, about 30 percent will have a sound understanding of the number operations" (Hart, 1981, p. 39), a figure based only on work with *whole numbers*. Unfortunately, there is no reason to expect that American students perform better than this. The English report on fractions does not offer any such statistic (Hart, 1981, chap. 5), but all evidence points a fortiori to a bleaker performance for many English and American students when problems involve fractions or decimals. For example, even though 60% of the 13-year-olds in the third NAEP could correctly calculate 7/8 × 3/2, only 17% were correct on this problem: "George has 3/4 of a pie. He ate 3/5 of that. How much pie did he eat?" (National Assessment of Educational Progress, 1983, p. 26).

Why don't students have better meanings for the operations? Baroody and Ginsburg, having worked extensively with young children and with informal (out of school) mathematics, argue that "For the most formal mathematics to which they are exposed, children are not given either the time or the incentive to develop stronger schemas" (1986, p. 106). Do they even have the opportunity? Although recent text series are showing improvement, examination of some series suggests that there is a shortage of material on the meanings for the operations, even when a series attempts to make problem solving a more central focus and a source of meaning.

Work with young children has shown how complex it is to deal with several situations which involve only addition and subtraction (Briars & Larkin, 1982; Carpenter, Moser, & Romberg, 1982; Riley, Greeno, & Heller, 1983). Vergnaud's more mathematical analysis of multiplication and division (1983), and the nonconservation phenomenon, suggest that these operations are also complicated psychologically. Thornton's title, "Four operations? Or ten?" (1985), is symptomatic of the complexity one encounters in trying to link the operations to their uses in story problems.

What schemas, then, should the curriculum seek to foster? Following are four analyses that give us different directions to look in planning research on story problems. Each approach demands considerably more time than most curricula now spend on story problems, but a movement away from a curricular emphasis on computation will allow more time for such treatments.

The Conventional Taxonomy, Refined

How might the links between the operations and their applications be organized in the curriculum? Perhaps closest to current curricular approaches is the taxonomy provided by Greer (1987b). His approach follows the now-common type of analysis for addition and subtraction (e.g., Carpenter & Moser, 1982; Riley, Greeno, & Heller, 1983) but represents a refinement of the usual treatments of multiplication (into repeated addition, Cartesian product, part of an amount, scaling) and division (sharing, repeated subtraction). Greer, for example, distinguishes between symmetrical and asymmetrical types of multiplication (and division) problems. Asymmetrical multiplication occurs in situations in which the multiplication is "psychologically noncommutative;" 3-sets-of-5 is not the same psychologically as 5-sets-of-3, even though $3 \times 5 = 5 \times 3$. Greer's labels for the types are fairly self-explanatory. He calls the asymmetrical types multiple groups (the example just given), iteration of measure, change of scale, rate, and measure conversion. The symmetrical cases are labeled rectangular array, combinations ($=$ Cartesian product), and area. One might expect the curriculum to give attention to each of these interpretations, with a close linking of interpretation to operation.

A Psychological Approach

Work such as that underway by Marshall (1987a, 1987b), represents a psychological approach and may prove to be especially important. Marshall has identified five schemas which have semantic bases (i.e., are meaning-based) and, if used, should enable a student to categorize story problems. For example, her "change relation" schema includes problems in which an amount is dynamically transferred from one agent to another. Her other schemas are based on a combine relation, a compare relation, a transform relation, and a vary relation. Although her pilot work has been promising, there is still much work to be done, of course. For example, will instruction aimed toward a schema based on the vary relation eliminate the problem of nonconservation of operation by overriding MMBDMS? Too, a semantically-based categorization is an important first step, but linking operations to a category may prove troublesome for students.

Dimensional Analysis

The recent efforts (cf. Kaput, 1985; Kaput, Schwartz, & Poholsky, 1985) to build on a distinction between types of *quantities*, intensive (e.g., 30 miles per hour) and extensive (e.g., 30 miles), give a third approach which must be studied and analyzed for its implications for story problem instruction. Dimensional analysis is very useful in scientific areas by people who are already familiar with the operations. Its use as a determiner of operation seems however, at first glance, to be only a sophisticated version of key words, so it is not clear where it should best be brought into the curriculum. For example, it is not likely that multiplication would be introduced via dimensional analysis. But dimensional analysis serves such useful purposes in science and in other areas where conversion among units is common that it and its infuence on problem solving should receive attention.

Use Meanings

A fourth framework in which the meanings for the operations can be cast is that of Usiskin and Bell (1983). This piece of work analyzes the applications of arithmetic in a nonconventional fashion. In contrast with the usual curricular development, in which what types of numbers the children know dictate the "uses," Usiskin and Bell have identified categories which do not depend on the numbers involved but rather represent major subsuming categories of uses. Here are their basic "use meanings" (p. 146):

Operation	Use Meanings
Addition	putting together
	shift
Subtraction	take-away
	comparison
Multiplication	size change
	acting across
Division	ratio
	rate
Powering	change of dimension
	growth

Usiskin and Bell also list "derived use classes" as opposed to these "basic use classes." For example, their "recovering addend" category is the commonly labeled "missing addend" type, in which the action of the problem is an addition action but the operation needed to solve the problem is subtraction. (Example: Bobby needed 3.8 gallons of gas to fill up a 5-gallon can. How much gas was in the can before she filled it?)

The "acting across" category for multiplication is a new one; their analysis uses it to include area and volume, Cartesian product, the fundamental counting principle, and the multitude of physical relationships giving "compound" units (e.g., 150 watts for 6 hours gives 900 watt-hours). Not visible is the repeated-addition use for multiplication so common in the curriculum. Usiskin and Bell argue against its inclusion since its fit to situations depends on the first factor being a whole number, and their search was for categories that were independent of the numbers involved. They properly decry approaches which give *only* repeated addition as an interpretation for multiplication (p. 231).

Building a whole curriculum around these use meanings is an awesome task. Like dimensional analysis, the framework is more likely to be realized in some sort of summarizing work in junior or senior high school, with subsequent evaluation efforts to clarify how the framework helps students in attacking story problems.

FINAL WORD

Some instructional studies *have* given good results with story problems (e.g., Cohen & Stover, 1981; Good, Grouws, & Ebmeier, 1983; Charles & Lester, 1984). Identifiable elements of the instruction in these studies include devoting additional time for the possible development of meanings for the operations and for specific story-problem-centered activities, and giving instruction in translating among representations. It is, admittedly, less clear how much, if any, direct instruction in meanings for the operations was actually included. Nor did the studies examine the particular strategies used by the students on routine story problems. But it would appear on the face of it that more students were at least partially equipped to use strategies other than the immature ones given above. So there is hope that with more research and a redirection of the operations part of the curriculum, students can approach story problems with confidence and with the proper tools.

FOOTNOTE

1. The interview data described were gathered with the support of the National Science Foundation (SED 8108134, MDR 8550169, and MDR 8696130). Any interpretation of the dta are not necessarily those of the Foundation.

REFERENCES

Baroody, A., & Ginsburg, H. (1986). The relationship between initial meaningful and mechanical knowledge of arithmetic. In J. Hiebert (Ed.), *Conceptual and procedural knowledge: The case of mathematics* (pp. 75–112). Hillsdale, NJ: Lawrence Erlbaum.

Bell, A., Fischbein, E., & Greer, B. (1984). Choice of operation in verbal arithmetic problems: The effects of number size, problem structure, and context. *Educational Studies in Mathematics, 15,* 129–147.

Briars, D., & Larkin, J. (1982). *An integrated model of skill in solving elementary word problems* (A.C.P. #2). Pittsburgh: Carnegie-Mellon University.

Carpenter, T., Corbitt, M., Kepner, H., Jr., Lindquist, M., & Reys, R. (1980). Solving verbal problems: Results and implications from National Assessment. *The Arithmetic Teacher, 23,* 8–12.

Carpenter, T., & Moser, J. (1982). The development of addition and subtraction problem-solving skills. In T. Carpenter, J. Moser, & T. Romberg (Eds.), *Addition and subtraction: A cognitive perspective* (pp. 9–24). Hillsdale, NJ: Lawrence Erlbaum.

Carpenter, T., Moser, J., & Romberg, T. (Eds.). (1982). *Addition and subtraction: A cognitive perspective.* Hillsdale, NJ: Lawrence Erlbaum.

Charles, R., & Lester, F., Jr. (1984). An evaluation of a process-oriented instructional program in mathematical problem solving in grades 5 and 7. *Journal for Research in Mathematics Education, 15,* 15–34.

Cohen, S., & Stover, G. (1981). Effects of teaching sixth-grade students to modify format variables of math word problems. *Reading Research Quarterly, 16,* 175–199.

Ekenstam, A., & Greger, K. (1983). Some aspects of children's ability to solve mathematical problems. *Educational Studies in Mathematics, 14,* 369–384.

Fischbein, E., Deri, M., Nello, M., & Marino, M. (1985). The role of implicit models in solving verbal problems in multiplication and division. *Journal for Research in Mathematics Education, 16,* 3–17.

Goldin, G., & McClintock, C. (Eds.). (1980). *Task variables in mathematical problem solving.* Columbus, Ohio: ERIC/SMEAC.

Good, T., Grouws D., & Ebmeier, H. (1983). *Active mathematics teaching.* New York: Longman.

Greer, B. (1987a). Nonconservation of multiplication and division involving decimals. *Journal for Research in Mathematics Education, 18,* 37–45.

Greer, B. (1987b). Understanding of arithmetical operations as models of situations. In J. Sloboda & D. Rogers (Eds.), *Cognitive processes in mathematics* (pp. 60–80). New York: Oxford University Press.

Greer, B., & Mangan, C. (1984). Understanding multiplication and division. In J. Moser (Ed.), *Proceedings of the sixth annual meeting, PME-NA* (pp. 27–32). Madison, Wisconsin.

Greer, B., & Mangan, C. (1986). Choice of operations: From 10-year-olds to student teachers. *Proceedings of the tenth international conference, PME* (pp. 25–30). London.

Hart, K. (Ed.). (1987). *Children's understanding of mathematics: 11–16.* London: John Murray.

Janvier, C. (Ed.). (1987). *Problems of representation in the teaching and learning of mathematics.* Hillsdale, NJ: Lawrence Erlbaum.

Kalmykova, Z. (1975). Productive methods of analysis and synthesis. In M. Kantowski (Ed.), *Analysis and synthesis as problem-solving methods.* (T. Merz, Trans.) Vol. XI of *Soviet studies in the psychology of learning and teaching mathematics* (pp. 121–168). Chicago: University of Chicago. (Original work published 1955)

Kaput, J. (1985). *Multiplicative word problems and intensive quantities: An integrated software response* (Technical Report 85–19). Cambridge, MA: Educational Technology Center.

Kaput, J., Schwartz, J., & Poholsky, J. (1985). Extensive and intensive quantities in multiplication and division word problems: A preliminary report and a software response. In S. Damarin & M. Shelton (Eds.), *Proceedings of the seventh annual meeting, PME-NA* (pp. 139–144). Columbus, Ohio.

Lester, F., & Garofalo, J. (1982, March). *Metacognitive aspects of elementary school students' performance on arithmetic tasks.* Paper presented at the annual meeting of the American Educational Research Association, New York.

Lester, F., & Garofalo, J. (1987, April). *The influence of affects, beliefs, and metacognition of problem solving behavior: Some tentative speculations.* Paper presented at the annual meeting of the American Educational Research Association, Washington, DC.

Lindquist, M., Carpenter, T., Silver, E., & Matthews, W. (1983). The third national mathematics assessment: Results and implications for elementary and middle schools. *The Arithmetic Teacher, 31,* (Dec.), 14–19.

Mangan, M. C. (1986). *Choice of operation in multiplication and division word problems.* Unpublished doctoral dissertation, Queen's University, Belfast, Northern Ireland.

Marshall, S. P. (1987a). *Schema knowledge structures for representing and understanding arithmetic story problems* (Technical Report). San Diego: Center for Research in Mathematics and Science Education.

Marshall, S. P. (1987b, April). *Knowledge representation and errors of problem solving: Identifying misconceptions.* Paper presented at the annual meeting of the American Educational Research Association, Washington, DC.

National Assessment of Educational Progress (1983). *The third national mathematics assessment: Results, trends and issues* (Report No. 13–MA–01). Denver: Education Commission of the States.

Nesher, P., & Teubal, E. (1975). Verbal cues as an interfering factor in verbal problem solving. *Educational Studies in Mathematics, 6,* 41–51.

Noddings, N. (1985). Small groups as a setting for research on mathematical problem solving. In E. Silver, (Ed.), *Teaching and Learning mathematical problem solving: Multiple research perspectives* (pp. 345–359). Hillsdale, NJ: Lawrence Erlbaum.

Polya, G. (1962). *Mathematical discovery, vol. 1.* New York: Wiley.

Riley, M., Greeno, J., & Heller, J. (1983). Development of children's problem-solving ability in arithmetic. In H. Ginsburg (Ed.), *The development of mathematical thinking* (pp. 153–196). New York: Academic Press.

Sherrill, J. (1983). Solving textbook mathematical word problems. *The Alberta Journal of Educational Research, 29,* 140–152.

Sowder, L. (1985). Cognitive psychology and mathematical problem solving: A discussion of Mayer's paper. IN E. Silver (Ed.), *Teaching and learning mathematical problem solving: Multiple research perspectives* (pp. 139–145). Hillsdale, NJ: Lawrence Erlbaum.

Sowder, L. (1986). Strategies children use in solving problems. *Proceedings of the tenth international conference, PME* (pp. 469–474). London

Sowder, L. (1988). *Concept-driven strategies for solving story problems in mathematics* (Grants MDR 8550169 & MDR 8696130). Washington, DC: National Science Foundation.

Sowder, L., Threadgill-Sowder, J., Moyer, J., & Moyer, M. (1984). *Format variables and learner characteristics in mathematical problem solving* (Grant SED 8108134). Washington, DC: National Science Foundation. (ERIC Document Reproduction Service No. ED 238 735)

Stevenson, P. R. (1925). Difficulties in problem solving. *Journal of Educational Research, XI,* (No. 2), 95–103.

Thornton, E. B. C. (1985). Four operations? Or ten? *For the Learning of Mathematics. 5*(2), 33–37.

Tirosh, D., Graeber, A., & Glover, R. (1986). Preservice teachers' choice of operation for multiplication and division word problems. *Proceedings of the tenth international conference, PME* (pp. 57–62). London.

Trafton, P. (1984). Toward more effective, efficient instruction in mathematics. *The Elementary School Journal, 84,* 514–528.

Usiskin, Z., & Bell, M. (1983). *Applying arithmetic, a handbook of application of arithmetic.* Chicago: University of Chicago.

Vergnaud, G. (1983). Multiplicative structures. In R. Lesh & M. Landau (Eds.), *Acquisition of mathematics concepts and processes* (pp. 127–174). New York: Academic Press.

Zweng, M. (1979). *Children's strategies of solving verbal problems* (Grant NIE-G–78–0094). Washington, DC: National Institute of Education.

Assessing Problem Solving: A Short-Term Remedy and a Long-Term Solution

Sandra P. Marshall

San Diego State University

The purpose of this paper is to discuss some current approaches to the assessment of problem solving. As the title indicates, I offer suggestions about how we can make short-term modifications that will improve our assessment practices now, and I also outline the steps that can be taken to make substantial gains in assessment methodology.

Adequate assessment of mathematical problem-solving skills and knowledge has continually perplexed mathematics educators and psychometricians. The fundamental issue is how to estimate what a person knows from a small sample of his or her behavior. This is the basic question in any testing situation, but it is aggravated in the domain of mathematical problem solving because there is no widespread or universally accepted definition of problem solving. Two tests of problem solving don't necessarily assess the same thing. Moreover, we usually face additional constraints of time, test format, media, and cost, making our task even more difficult. Currently, almost all problem-solving assessment consists of paper-and-pencil tests, each test containing a set of traditional story problems. The problems usually require one or two arithmetic computations each, and individuals' responses are recorded as multiple-choice answers. It is generally agreed that these are inadequate measures of problem-solving ability.

Given recent heightened interest in problem solving in mathematics and science, we ought to provide a better means of assessing problem-solving performance. One way to do so is to lessen the constraints that impinge upon the problem-solving situation. Another is to develop new models of testing that more perfectly address the needs of problem-solving evaluation.

Both of these means are discussed here. First, I show how we can modify existing testing situations to garner more and better information from the individuals we are assessing. Several examples are included from one existing standardized test. Second, I sketch a new model of problem-solving evaluation that allows us to ask very different questions about individuals' knowledge and skills. This model is grounded in cognitive psychology and focuses on acquisition and retrieval mechanisms of long-term memory.

Before turning to either of these topics, however, we should first set some guidelines about what we mean and do not mean by the phrase *problem solving*. Further, it is necessary to talk about objectives: What do we hope to achieve from our assessment techniques?

PROBLEM SOLVING AND ITS ASSESSMENT IN MATHEMATICS

Let us begin by characterizing problem solving as a response of an individual to a new experience or situation that demands some action by the individual. In the everyday world, an individual acquires some knowledge or some skills that are relevant for operation within a designated domain. The individual's proficiency in organizing the knowledge and coordinating it within a new, unfamiliar situation is termed "problem-solving ability."

A distinction usually is made between situations in which an individual does not know what to do and those that are merely repetitions of previous experiences. According to the extent that an individual can be placed in a novel experience (relevant to the domain) and can use information he or she already knows to make sense of the new experience, we characterize the individual as a good or poor problem solver. Good problem solvers can recognize important similarities and differences between the novel situation and other already-encountered problems; good problem solvers have several options of response available to them; good problem solvers know when and how to acquire more information if it is necessary.

One difficulty in assessing problem-solving ability is that it is usually hard to conjure up a novel situation that will adequately test an individual's problem-solving skill. In arithmetic, the standard format is a story problem that requires the individual to organize the information given in the problem, to understand the question that is asked, to decide which pieces of the given information to use, and to carry out appropriate arithmetic operations. In large part, mathematics teachers and text developers have adopted a view of novel situations in which the novelty lies in changing text details of the story. Thus, arithmetic texts have numerous instances in which several items are given as a group, all of them virtually identical (Marshall, 1985). The only differences are in the names of the actors in the stories or the locations in which the stories take place. Having solved one of these as a novel situation, an individual will not need to engage in true problem-solving behavior on the others. It is sufficient to repeat the solution steps derived for the first one.

There is an alternative view of a novel situation. In this view, it is not the details of the story that makes the problem a *problem*. Rather, it is the whole problem-solving situation itself. As I explain below, we can take a routine problem and ask a novel question, demanding of our students the ability to look at the story problem in a nontraditional way and forcing them to demonstrate their understanding by responding to questions about the structure and information contained in the story.

If we are to modify the evaluation process of problem solving, we must first be explicit about what we want to know from the evaluation. Three aspects seem predominant: (a) We need to know whether the individual has enough facts about the domain to be operating within it; (b) we need to know that the individual has the requisite behavioral alternatives or "tools" that are appropriate within the domain; and (c) we want to know whether the individual can call upon the knowledge and skills in a nonpredetermined order to make sense of a new experience. Most of our testing procedures are aimed at the first two of these aspects. The third is virtually ignored.

One way to be more specific about the nature of these aspects is to examine them from the perspective of information-processing theory. In terms of memory organization, many cognitive psychologists posit two distinct types of memory structures: declarative and procedural. These correspond roughly to the dichotomy of semantic and episodic memories. The mechanisms for acquiring and retrieving information from these two memory stores are quite different (cf. Wickelgren, 1979).

The first aspect of the evaluation process, whether or not the individual knows the relevant factual knowledge of the domain, refers to an assessment of declarative knowledge. There are certain domain-specific details that must be acquired before an individual can engage in problem solving. In mathematics, these are facts and concepts such as addition facts, multiplication facts, and knowledge of the order of operations. These facts are stored in declarative memory and are static pieces of information that can be related by means of a semantic network.

The second aspect of evaluation has to do with procedural knowledge. To engage in problem solving, one needs a set of skills or techniques that are appropriate for the domain. These are the "tools" that an individual develops in order to function within the domain. Procedural knowledge is characterized as a set of rules that can be applied to a situation whenever specific conditions are satisfied. Each rule has the form of an "if-then" statement: *If* certain conditions are met, *then* some specified action can be performed. In arithmetic, the algorithms for carrying out arithmetic operations are good examples. Given a problem such as: $13 \times 27 = ?$, most of us call upon a set of rules that are executed one at a time. These same rules can also be used for the problems of: $156 \times 289 = ?$ or $2365 \times 34769 = ?$. The rules can be used regardless of the numerical values given in the problem.

Finally, there must be an agency for knowing which facts and which procedures are germane to a given situation. Such knowledge resides in a *schema*, a form of knowledge that relates a set of declarative facts to a set of procedural rules. For example, we expect students to develop a schema for multiplication. The declarative aspects of the schema are recognition of the operation symbol and the necessary addition and multiplication facts that apply to the problem. The procedural aspects of the schema are the procedural rules for executing the multiplication algorithm. One advantage of unifying the declarative and procedural knowledge into one knowledge structure is that all of the related information about the concept *multiplication* can be easily accessed, no matter what its origin in memory. In addition to knowing how to multiply, it is imperative that an individual knows when, why, and what the results mean. These aspects are captured in the general schema.

A primary distinction among the three knowledge structures is that it is easier to acquire declarative knowledge than procedural or schematic knowledge. It is also easier to access and assess this type of knowledge. One only needs to ask the individual a question that forces the retrieval of the particular information from long-term memory. Consequently, much of the current assessment in mathematics is directed at declarative knowledge.

The remainder of this paper addresses the ways in which all three types of knowledge may be assessed, with emphasis upon procedural and schematic knowledge. In the next section, I illustrate how we may make modifications of existing tests. In the last section, the focus is upon a new model for assessing the components of a schema.

MODIFYING EXISTING TESTS

Assume we have a typical problem-solving test that consists of a set of story problems. These items usually have a format similar to the following:

(1) Mary needed 2 cups of sugar to make 4 dozen
    cookies. How many cups of sugar will she need
    to make 6 dozen?
    a. 12 cups
    b. 6 cups
    c. 4 cups
    d. 3 cups

Before considering how and where to make changes, we need to consider the existing status of story problems. What is the purpose of an item such as (1)? What information is gained by presenting a student with this problem? How is this information used?

Tests serve several purposes. They may provide numerical estimates of how successful an individual is in solving story problems. Such tests are called achievement tests, and they are usually given within a fixed time and to a group of individuals. Comparisons are made among individuals. We can think of these tests as measuring individuals.

Tests may also be used to determine how well concepts are taught (or learned). These tests are typically given to a large number of individuals, with the individuals receiving different sets of items. The purpose here is to estimate which concepts are known by the population being assessed and which are not. Typically, individual scores are not released. Indeed, since individuals have not necessarily answered the same set of items, comparisons of total test scores among individuals are meaningless. Comparisons are made among the concepts that are tested. These comparisons are based on performance on one or two items that evaluate a particular concept.

Finally, tests may be diagnostic in function. The focus in this case is on aspects of the problems that are troublesome for individuals. The emphasis is upon the individual student, not upon comparisons with other students. Rather than total test scores, we look for a pattern of responses that characterizes the way that an individual solves a set of problems. The types of mistakes that an individual makes are important.

It should be evident that not all items are equally well-suited for achievement, assessment, and diagnostic testing. In general, almost any test that provides assessment or diagnostic information could also be used as an achievement test. The reverse is not necessarily true. Some achievement tests provide little or no diagnostic information and do not measure a sufficient range of concepts to be of value as assessment tests. With this in mind, I shall focus primarily on assessment and diagnostic tests with the understanding that many of the items discussed could also serve on achievement tests.

Given a story problem such as (1) above, we can make three basic alterations to gain more information about students' problem-solving abilities. These are:

1. We can retain the general structure of the problem statement and change the nature of the distracters.

2. We can retain the multiple-choice format of the response and change the type of question asked.

3. We can change the response format from multiple choice to open ended or free response.

The first proposed modification is the easiest to implement. A large number of existing story problems on standardized tests have associated multiple-choice distracters that provide little or no diagnostic information. In many instances, the distracters reflect only errors in the execution of algorithms, ignoring the possiblity of errors in the selection of algorithms. A problem requiring addition, for example, might have three distracters corresponding to errors of arithmetic fact (such as $4 + 7 = 12$) or errors in executing the addition algorithm (such as failing to regroup).

The objection to such distracters is that they allow expression of only one aspect of problem solving, following steps of an arithmetic algorithm. They cannot assess the degree to which the individual understood the question, the extent to which he or she formed a correct mental representation of the problem, or the amount of attention given to irrelevant parts of the problem. In terms of knowledge structures, these distracters evaluate only a limited aspect of procedural knowledge and do not assess schema knowledge at all.

One standardized assessment instrument, developed by the California

Assessment Program, has begun to make systematic changes in the distracters for story problems. Recent research has demonstrated the importance and usefulness of having diagnostic distracters (Marshall, in press a, in press b). An example of a CAP item is the following:

> (2)** It is 1.3 kilometers from Sharon's house to school. She rides her bicycle to and from school every day. How far does she ride in 5 days?
> a. 6.3 kilometers
> b. 6.5 kilometers
> c. 10 kilometers
> *d. 13 kilometers

The correct response is indicated by the asterisk.

Each of the distracters is based upon an alternative way to represent and solve the problem. If an individual added the Arabic numerals in the problem, he or she would obtain the first distracter. Multiplication of the same values would yield the second distracter. The third distracter corresponds to ignoring the first value given and multiplying the other two.

A large majority of sixth-grade students cannot solve this problem. Eighty percent of them select one of the three distracters as their response. A classroom teacher, presented with the information that students cannot solve the problem, might infer that the difficulty lies in using decimals or in understanding kilometers. Instead, the major misunderstanding seems to be in recognizing that one must compute distance for a round trip. Sixty-seven percent of the students answering this question on the CAP test selected distracter b. Without the information contained in the distracters, a teacher would not know to focus on the need to translate verbal statements such as "to and from" into mathematical relationships.

The second modification proposed above is to change the nature of the questions posed in the problems. By changing the questions, we can focus on the student's acquisition and organization of schema knowledge. Many different aspects can be examined. For instance, we can ask whether students recognize the underlying structure of a problem by having them identify similar problems. We can have them recognize restatements of information in the problem. We can ask them to identify the same information given in two different forms, such as verbal and graphical. And, very simply, we can ask them directly which operations they would use to solve a problem. If the goal is to probe students' understanding of story problems, we should minimize the amount of time they spend doing computations. Testing time should be spent in evaluating other aspects of problem solving.

What will these problems look like? Below are several examples taken from the California Assessment Program *Survey of Basic Skills* for grades 6 and 8.

Recognizing the Underlying Structure

The objective here is to present several items that have surface similarities but require different means of solution. Example 3 demonstrates this:

(3)†† PROBLEM:
        One packet of gelatin weighs 20 grams. What is the weight of 10 packets of gelatin?

        Which of the following problems can be solved in the same way as the problem above?

        a. Juanita runs 10 miles in 90 minutes. How long does it take for her to run each mile?

        b. A felt pen costs $.49 and a ballpoint pen costs $.99. How much would it cost to buy both pens?

        c. It takes 4 ounces of orange juice to fill a glass. How many glasses can be filled from a 64-ounce bottle of orange juice?

       *d. A pencil costs $.10. How much would 10 pencils cost?

An alternative way to test the same knowledge is to present several items that have different surface characteristics. All but one of the items have the same underlying relationships and require the same problem-solving strategy for solution. Thus:

(4) Which of the following problems is different from the rest?

        a. Joan has 12 pieces of candy. She plans to give them equally to her three friends. How much candy will each friend get?

        b. The five members of the school basketball team each scored the same number of points. If the whole team scored 80 points, how many points did each player make?

      *c. Bob has 4 dogs. Each dog eats 12 ounces of dog food every day. How much dog food must he buy each week to feed his dogs?

        d. I bought 15 apples for $2.85. How much did each apple cost?

These problems are testing more than choice of arithmetic operation. Two problems may require the same operation but have different relationships. For example, both of the problems below require the operation of subtraction. However, they are conceptually very different problems.

(5) Joe kicked the football 20 yards. This was 5 yards further than his friend Ed kicked the ball. How far did Ed kick the ball?

(6) There are 50 children in my class at school. Twenty of them are boys. How many are girls?

In problem (5), students must recognize that they have been given two ways to express how far Ed kicked the ball. First, he kicked it 5 yards shorter than Joe. Second, he kicked it some particular distance that can be expressed as yards. The objective here is to figure out a numerical value for the second way of expressing the distance by using the first way.

In problem (6), a specific form of the part-whole relationship is developed. One category is given (e.g., children) together with two subcategories (e.g., boys and girls). Since these two subcategories exhaust the category of children, knowing "the whole" (e.g., how many children) and knowing something about one of "the parts" (e.g., how many boys) allows us to know how many girls as well.

Now suppose we have another problem:

(7) Pat can throw a baseball 30 feet. Her brother can throw it twice as far as she can. How far can her brother throw the baseball?

Is the football problem more similar to the children problem than it is to the baseball problem? I submit that it is not. Problems (5) and (6) have little in common except the use of subtraction. Problems (5) and (7) share a common structure. In each case, an unknown quantity is expressed in relative terms of another quantity ("twice as far", "5 yards further"). The similarity of the two problems lies in the fact that some quantity can be expressed in some unit of measure (such as number of yards) and also as a relative amount in terms of some other quantity. This relationship is missing from problem (6). Good problem solvers understand or at least sense this affinity. As demonstrated in these examples, basing judgment of problem similarity on operation alone can be misleading.

Recognizing the Same Information in Several Forms

One objective of assessment may be to determine whether an individual's understanding of story problems is tied to particular expressions or modes of delivery. We expect students with genuine understanding of problem structure to demonstrate flexibility in interpreting information, regardless of its format. Two forms of items are relevant here. The first presents some information and asks the student to identify a restatement of it. The second presents information in one form, such as verbal, and asks the student to identify the drawing or graph that represents the same information. Problem (8) illustrates the first of these forms, and problem (9) is an example of the second.

PROBLEM:
(8)†† Scott collected some old coins.
      Curt collected half as many as Scott.
      Which statement contains the same information?
        a. Scott has half as many coins as Curt.
        b. Curt has twice as many coins as Scott.
     *c. Scott has twice as many coins as Curt.
        d. Curt has as many coins as Scott.

PROBLEM:

(9)** Harry and Al live the same distance from the school but in opposite directions. They found that they lived 500 meters apart. Which drawing shows this?

    a.   Harry
       250m
       school
       250m
         Al

    b. Harry_____ school_____Al
        500m   500m

  *c. Harry_____ school_____Al
        250m   250m

    d. school_____ Harry_____Al
        250m   250m

These items are not easy for students to solve. Roughly 54 percent of sixth graders and 38 percent of eighth graders cannot answer problem (9) correctly.

Specifying the Operation

Traditional story problems focus upon computations and the operations that generate the computations. In many instances, we are not really interested in whether the computations are done correctly. These can be tested quickly and more efficiently by computational tests. Our interest is in whether individuals can determine which operations to use and, for multiple-step problems, in what order. The knowledge of how to carry out an algorithm is procedural knowledge. Knowledge of when to use a particular algorithm is schematic knowledge. It is the latter that we wish to assess.

Problems that test operation identification are perhaps the easiest of all items to write, because the distracters are simply a list of the arithmetic operations. Thus, we have:

(10)†† Russia produces about 3/20 of the world's oil. The Middle East countries produce about 2/3 of the world's oil. What is their combined production?

How would you solve this problem?

    a. multiply
    b. divide
    c. subtract
    d. add

There are several possible variations on this theme. One could write mathematical expressions or equations for the distracters. For multiple-step problems, the distracters could have the form of "add then divide" or "add, multiply, and subtract." The difficulty with the latter is that not all options can be captured by a four-alternative, multiple-choice format. To test simple one-step problems, one can list all four arithmetic operations. Since a student must carry out one of these, we are confident that we are testing the student's problem-solving skills. For the multiple-step ones, there must be several combinations of operations that are not listed as distracters. We are faced with the same problem here that we face when trying to write distracters for computational items: How certain can we be that the incorrect answers we provide as response alternatives are the ones that correspond to responses by students who cannot solve the problem?

Rather than asking the student to identify the operation(s) to use in a particular problem, it is useful to present the student with the problem and a possible solution and to ask whether the problem has been worked correctly. With this format, we can determine whether the student can recognize errors in using algorithms as well as errors in selecting which algorithms to use. We can also find out whether students detect the use of improper values in computations. Thus, with a single item we can examine aspects of declarative, procedural, and schematic knowledge. For example:

PROBLEM:

(11)** Martha bought two shirts at $7.99 each and three sweaters at $10.49 each. How much change should she get back from $50.00?

Bill solved the problem in the following way:

Step 1	Step 2	Step 3	Step 4
$7.99	$10.49	$15.98	$50.00
× 2	× 2	+ 20.98	− 36.96
$15.98	$20.98	$36.96	$13.04

What can you say about Bill's work?

  a. He should have first added $7.99 and $10.49.

*b. He should have multiplied $10.49 by 3.

  c. He subtracted incorrectly in step 4.

  d. There is no mistake.

The third and final modification suggested here is to change the response format altogether. The most widely suggested replacement is the open-ended or free response. Such a format simulates as closely as possible the situation that occurs in most problem-solving situations. When solving real problems, we rarely have several known solutions against which we can compare our answers. Instead, we must decide independently when the problem is solved.

From a cognitive psychological perspective, one impact of moving to a free-format response is that students can no longer utilize the strategy of means-end analysis. When distracters are present, students frequently use means-end analysis to work backwards in a problem, starting with a possible answer (one of the multiple-choice options) and figuring out how to obtain it. If they are successful, this becomes the chosen answer for the problem. If they are unsuccessful, they move to another option and repeat the strategy. In the absence of a list of possible answers, this strategy must be discarded. Thus, we begin to see other problem-solving strategies.

The advantage of the free-response problem is that we are no longer limited by our set of distracters. Even with careful planning, we cannot be sure that we have captured the best distracters for every individual. As a case in point, consider the following problem:

> (12) John has 12 baseball cards. He gives ⅓ of them to Jim. How many cards does John have left?
> > a. 4
> > b. 6
> > c. 8
> > d. 9

Although no longer a part of the CAP test, this item was on the sixth-grade assessment test for many years and yielded consistent patterns of responses for boys and girls at every administration. The problem is very difficult for California children; only about 30 percent of them solve it correctly. Most students select alternative (a), which corresponds to the first step in solving the problem.

Several years ago, as part of a study on differences between boys and girls in solving story problems, I used this item in interviews with sixth-grade students and allowed them to respond freely. The most common response from the 90 children was the value "11 2/3", an incorrect response that is not reflected in the distracter list of (12). The incorrect answer "4" was the second most common response.

What happens when children work a story problem and find that their solution is not among the response alternatives? Either they conclude that they have solved the problem incorrectly and they try again or they give up. One suspects that students who initially subtract 1/3 from 12 and fail to find their answer in the list of response alternatives next try another operation. In this case, a large number of them apparently multiply the two numbers rather than subtract one from the other.

Some students may give up when their own solution is not a response option. They may decide to make a random selection from the possible responses or they may elect to leave the item blank. Many items are left unanswered on standardized tests by children. We have no way of knowing why, but failure to obtain one of the response options may be a contributing factor.

Impact of Changing the Test Items

The modifications described here have to do with changing the test format. The most immediate impact of these changes is on the time needed to answer the items. It takes longer for students to respond to nonstandard, noncomputational items. Therefore, tests which incorporate the features described here must have fewer items or testing time must be lengthened.

A second effect is on the cost of testing. If a multiple-choice format is used, more time must be spent upon developing meaningful distracters. This translates into higher cost for producing the test. If free-response items are used, there will be additional cost for scoring.

The effects of changing the nature of test items will be felt in different ways, according to whether the testing situation is achievement, assessment, or diagnostic. For example, if the items provide more information about what a student does or does not know about a particular concept, the number of items needed to test the concept is not important. Thus, a few well-developed items may have greater diagnostic or assessment value than a larger set of many traditional ones.

It is easier to use nontraditional formats for diagnostic testing than for achievement testing. Several situational constraints are lifted. First, the number of students to be evaluated is usually smaller in the diagnostic setting. The amount of time that can be used in testing is usually larger. The scope of the test is frequently narrower. Many diagnostic tests begin at a general level and attempt to focus on the particular difficulties of the individual as the testing progresses. As a result, students need not respond to identical sets of items.

DEVELOPING A NEW MODEL OF TESTING: SCHEMA ASSESSMENT

One requirement of the present approach to problem-solving assessment is an analysis of the domain in which problem solving is to be examined. If we are to measure an individual's expertise in the domain, we must be able to describe the fundamental knowledge structures that can and should be used by the individual. Our focus in this analysis is upon the highest level concepts, sometimes called "higher-order thinking skills."

There may be many ways to characterize the higher-order skills for a domain. For example, in the domain of arithmetic story problems, one can characterize problems according to the semantic relations expressed (e.g., Marshall et al., 1987; Riley, Greeno, & Heller, 1983), according to the operational uses required (e.g., Usiskin & Bell, 1983), or according to the nature of the quantities used in the problems (e.g., Greeno, Brown, Foss, Shalin, Bee, Lewis, & Vitolo, 1986). While all may be sound classifications, some may have more instructional validity than others. The choice of the defining characteristics of a domain must reflect the instructional objectives for that domain. Assessment and instruction must coexist on the same dimensions of the domain.

As discussed in the previous sections, several distinct types of knowledge may be required in a problem-solving task. These different types of knowledge, declarative, procedural, and schematic, have been the focus of much research in the fields of science, mathematics, and reading (cf. Anderson, 1983; Shoben, 1980). We are now at the point that we need to consider how best to evaluate their presence or absence in an individual. It is particularly important that we consider how to assess schematic knowledge. Procedural and declarative knowledge structures alone can be assessed through traditional means, as demonstrated in the previous section. Schema evaluation requires new psychometric procedures.

The knowledge structure in long-term memory that corresponds to a higher-order skill or concept is the schema. Recall that within a schema are embedded both declarative and procedural knowledge. To assess schematic knowledge, one must be able to assess the other two types as well.

At this point, we need to become more specific about the structure of a schema. Although many researchers posit schematic knowledge in their theories of learning and instruction, most fail to give it explicit definition. A notable exception is Nancy Stein's theory of schematic knowledge for reading (see, for example, Stein & Trabasso, 1982).

A problem-solving schema can be hypothesized as having four distinct components. The first is a body of facts or declarative knowledge that describes the general situation to which the schema applies. A second component is a set of conditions that must be satisfied for the schema to be instantiated. A third feature of schematic knowledge has to do with the mechanisms for setting goals related to its instantiation. Other problems may need to be solved before it can be used. Finally, the fourth part of schematic knowledge is the collection of procedural rules that can be applied as the schema is implemented. These are the possible actions that can be taken within the schematic framework. Examples of these four components for schematic knowledge in the domain of arithmetic story problems are given in Marshall and others (1987).

An important feature of a schema is that it is a collection of differing types of knowledge. There is no specified order in which information related to the schema is accessed or implemented. Any specific instance of a schema will involve only a sample of the elements that characterize the full schema, and the way in which these elements are used will depend upon the situation. Consequently, a schema is more reasonably represented as a network than a hierarchy of related concepts or rules.

As I have pointed out elsewhere, there are three important questions to be asked of an individual to demonstrate his or her understanding and use of a schema (Marshall, 1986b). First, how competent is the individual in mapping from a novel situation to a particular schema? When we ask this question, we are seeking to determine if the individual recognizes the definitive aspects of the situation. Second, does the individual have the critical components of the schema as part of his or her knowledge base? As we evaluate schematic knowledge, we need to know whether we are observing errors based upon incomplete knowledge or upon use of an inappropriate schema. Finally, we ask whether the components of the schema are linked together or exist in long-term memory as isolates or unrelated elements.

These three questions are addressing different concerns about an individual's use of short-term and long-term memory. The first question of mapping accuracy relates to efficiency in coding incoming stimulus information in short-term memory and in pattern matching between short-term and long-term memory. Tangential questions arise about whether the incoming test stimulus is too taxing for short-term memory capacity, whether we can structure items to facilitate this pattern matching, and whether the order of presentation of information influences the accuracy of the pattern match. As of now, we lack good procedures for measuring this aspect of schema use. Several experimental paradigms exist, such as having individuals pick out items that have similar characteristics or explain why one item does not fit into a designated group. Additional methods need to be developed. This question is not addressed by the present paper.

The second and third questions regarding schema use are of more immediate concern here. The second one focuses on whether the individual has acquired the critical elements for that schema. The third emphasizes the connectivity among these elements. Both of these questions are issues of how knowledge is stored in long-term memory and can be answered by evaluating the organization of that knowledge.

Assume that we have a well-defined subject domain that can be characterized by a distinct number of schematic knowledge structures. We can think of each schema as a graph containing nodes and links between the nodes (see Figure 1). Each declarative fact that is pertinent to the schema is a node, as is each procedural rule that may be required. Many of the declarative nodes may be linked together, forming a tight cluster of facts that are associated. Similarly, many procedural rules may be joined, indicating that when one is required, the others may also be needed.

The importance of connectivity may be seen by considering the psychological concept of activation, which is found in most cognitive theories of memory. Under this concept, any particular node may be accessed as a result of stimulation. For example, when we see a dog, the memory node that corresponds to dog should be activated. If other nodes are connected to that one, they also will receive some measure of activation, so we might think of a pet dog, or of the stuffed dog purchased for a child, or of a cartoon dog in the morning newspaper.

If some links or arcs are not present in a schema, a node may be limited in the ways it receives activation. Suppose a schema contains six nodes, all linked directly to each other as in Figure 1a. The access of any node results in activation of all nodes within the schema. Access is direct and rapid. Now

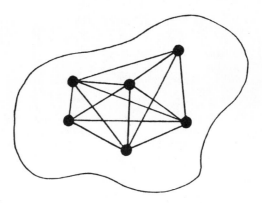

(a) completely linked graph

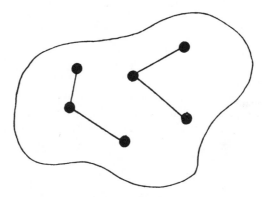

(b) partially linked graph

Figure 1. Graphs representing schematic knowledge

consider the schema represented in Figure 1b. Again, there are six nodes, but in this case they are divided into two distinct components. To activate all nodes in the schema, at least two nodes, one from each component, must be directly accessed. Access in this situation would be slower than in the first, since two pieces of information must be processed and two paths in memory traversed.

   In general, a well-formed schema will have many links so that any relevant piece of information activates the entire set of nodes within the schema. In such a situation, access of the schema is rapid and all possible related knowledge is available for problem solving. When several distinct and separate components are present, each will need to receive separate activation. If any component is not activated, necessary knowledge may not be retrieved from memory and problem solving may be more difficult.

One goal of instruction and hence of assessment is to determine which links are critical to a well-constructed schema. Instruction should aim at creating those links, and assessment will consequently focus on estimating whether they have been formed as desired.

As an individual builds up knowledge about the domain, he or she acquires schematic structures that should be similar to those of the competent problem solver. If we are truly interested in whether or not individuals have schematic knowledge, we ought not to leave the creation of such knowledge to chance. One articulated objective of instruction is to foster the development of appropriate schematic knowledge structures in the individual's long-term memory. That is, instruction ought to lead to the development and modification of a schema in well-understood and specific ways.

There are two questions of interest that may be asked about an individual's schematic knowledge. First, does the individual have all of the requisite nodes that are needed to use the schema in a problem-solving situation? That is, does the individual already possess each of the declarative pieces of information and each of the if-then rules that are pertinent to the schema? Second, do these different elements of information exist independently or are they linked together? How cohesive is the set of knowledge that comprises the schema? For a schema to work effectively as an organizing factor of long-term memory, it should be a unified structure rather than a loosely knit one. Psychological research has demonstrated repeatedly that items which are tightly linked in memory are retrieved more quickly and have a greater number of access paths than those which exist as isolates.

These two questions can be answered by constructing test items that evaluate for an individual either the number of nodes or the number of links between nodes. Such assessment requires a model of the knowledge base for a hypothetical competent problem solver and a model of the knowledge possessed by an individual. To determine what an individual knows or doesn't know, the model of the individual is matched against the model of the competent problem solver. In artificial intelligence and cognitive science studies, this is referred to as an *overlay model*.

Both models are expressed as graphs with nodes and arcs (i.e., the links between the nodes). Using statistical procedures developed for graph theory, we can make systematic samples from the target graphs (i.e., those of the competent problem solver) and can estimate the size and complexity of the graphs of the individual student. The statistical techniques, based upon the statistical graph theory of Frank (1971), have been presented elsewhere (Marshall, 1986b). My objective here is to present a general outline of how this theory can influence assessment of problem solving.

As a simple example of the use of this approach to measure schematic knowledge, consider the case for the addition schema. What declarative knowledge is required? First, the individual must know simple addition facts. Depending upon the level of sophistication of the individual, these may be facts relating to whole numbers, fractions, and so forth. The individual must know what several words mean, such as "add," "plus," "find the sum," "how much altogether." The individual must recognize the addition symbol "+" and know that the statement of "2 and 3" can be interpreted as "2 + 3."

There are also related preconditions or prerequisites that must exist if the addition schema is instantiated. For example, there must be at least two numbers. The things to be added must be "summable." If more than single-digit numbers are involved, the individual must have concepts of place value and alignment. We can easily extend this list. The point is: There are many declarative facts and concepts that are related to this schema. Not all of them will be required for a single problem-solving situation. Only a sample will be used. Our task is to make meaningful samples that will demonstrate what knowledge the individual possesses and what is missing.

The advantage of considering the relevant knowledge to have a graph structure is that we can test many nodes simultaneously rather than each one individually. Thus, each test item will represent an assessment of many distinct nodes. In theory, we can determine the optimal number of nodes to include in one item. In practice, the number will depend upon the particular schema being assessed. For sparse schematic structures, it may be preferable to examine each node independently. For structures with many nodes, it seems reasonable to look at groups of nodes. By constructing items in this way, we register a gain in testing efficiency. Only a few items may be needed to provide adequate assessment of a complex schema.

In a similar way, it is possible to assess whether there are links between nodes. Not only do we want to determine the number of different nodes, we also want to estimate the degree of connectivity among them. In practice, each assessment item should be developed so that a correct response demonstrates knowledge of several specified nodes and explicit connections between them. At the moment, protocol analysis or interview techniques are the best means we have for conducting this form of assessment. One anticipates that this type of testing will be available in the future through computer evaluation.

The importance of this approach, and others like it, is that it forces us to consider explicitly which knowledge structures are being assessed and how an individual test item calls upon these structures. If the items are constructed specifically to test a set of nodes and a set of interconnections within them, we can gather a great deal of information that is unavailable to us now. Unless we have a means of testing the connections explicitly we can only infer that such links exist if an individual makes a correct response. If the individual makes an incorrect response, we frequently cannot assess why. By modeling his or her knowledge organization, we can make hypotheses about the level of understanding and can test these hypotheses directly. The individual's response to each item should provide information that allows us to modify the model and make it more detailed.

SUMMARY

The procedures discussed here require us to consider how knowledge is accessed, stored, and retrieved in human memory. In most testing situations, we want to know whether an individual "knows" a domain. This means that we want to know whether the individual has a good understanding of the basic principles that govern the domain and whether the individual can use the knowledge of the domain. It is not sufficient to evaluate an individual's possession of isolated facts and algorithms. Our testing procedures must be aimed at larger and broader conceptual structures. At the moment, our best bet is to focus on the schema.

The two approaches outlined in this paper represent a shift from assessment procedures based upon statistical or psychometric models to procedures based upon cognitive models of learning and memory. This is a significant change, and it affects all aspects of the testing process. The development of tests, the interpretation of results, and the use of the test results must all undergo modification. As demonstrated here, test development needs to reflect the definition and organization of the knowledge base to be tested. Items can be constructed to measure declarative, procedural, and/or schematic knowledge. Once these items are incorporated into a test, we can begin to look at student performance in terms of how much a student knows and also in terms of how well the student has organized the information in his or her long-term memory. Having this information about a student allows us to modify existing instruction and create new instruction with the objective of helping the student to learn more efficiently. In short, we now have explicit and direct links among the testing, teaching, and learning processes.

FOOTNOTES

1. Items marked with ** are reproduced from the *Annual Report* of the California Assessment Program, 1982. Items marked with †† are reproduced from the *Rationale, Grade 8, Survey of Basic Skills*. Both documents are available from the California Assessment Program, California Department of Education, Sacramento, California.
2. I have developed this particular classification more thoroughly than can be presented here. Interested readers are invited to pursue the topic in another paper (Marshall, Pribe, & Smith, 1987).

AUTHOR NOTES

Some of the research discussed in the paper was sponsored by the Office of Naval Research under Contract N00014-K-85-0661.

REFERENCES

Anderson, J. R. (1983). *The architecture of cognition.* Cambridge, MA: Harvard University Press.

Frank, O. (1971). *Statistical inference in graphs.* Stockholm: FOA Repro Forsvarets Forskningsanstalt.

Greeno, J. G., J. S. Brown, C. Foss, V. Shalin, N. Bee, M. Lewis, & T. Vitolo (1986). *Cognitive principles of problem solving and instruction* (Project No. N–00014–82–K–0613). Washington, DC: Office of Naval Research.

Marshall, S. P. (1985). *An analysis of problem-solving instruction in arithmetic textbooks.* Paper presented at the meeting of the American Psychological Association, Los Angeles, CA.

Marshall, S. P. (in press a). Assessing knowledge structures in mathematics: A cognitive science perspective. In R. Freedle, *Advances in discourses processes.* New York: Ablex.

Marshall, S. P. (in press b). Selecting good diagnostic items. In N. Frederiksen, R. Glaser, A. Lesgold, & M. Shafto (Eds.), *Diagnostic monitoring of skill and knowledge acquisition.* Hillsdale, NJ: Lawrence Earlbaum Associates.

Marshall, S. P., C. A. Pribe, & J. D. Smith (1987). *Schema knowledge structures for representing and understanding arithmetic story problems* (Contract No. N–00014–K–85–0661). Washington, DC: Office of Naval Research.

Riley, M., J. Greeno, & J. Heller (1983). Development of children's problem-solving ability in arithmetic. In H. Ginsburg (Ed.), *The development of mathematical thinking* (pp. 153–196). New York: Academic Press.

Shoben, E. J. (1980). Theories of semantic memory: Approaches to knowledge and sentence comprehension. In R. Spiro, B. Cruce, & W. Brewer (Eds.), *Theoretical issues in reading comprehension* (pp. 309–330). Hillsdale, NJ: Lawrence Erlbaum Associates.

Usiskin, Z. & M. Bell (1983). *Applying arithmetic: A Handbook of applications of arithmetic. Part II: Operations.* (Project No. SED 79–19065). Washington, DC: National Science Foundation.

Wickelgren, W. (1979). *Cognitive psychology.* Englewood Cliffs, NJ: Prentice Hall.

Testing Mathematical Problem Solving

Edward A. Silver
University of Pittsburgh
Jeremy Kilpatrick
University of Georgia

The topic of testing mathematical problem solving lies at the intersection of two powerful educational movements. In 1980 "problem solving" was chosen to be the focus of school mathematics for the remainder of the decade (National Council of Teachers of Mathematics, 1980). Although some would argue that the focus has remained more rhetorical than real, many teachers have made genuine efforts to include more problem-solving activities in their instruction, and curriculum materials have been revised to incorporate such activities. At the same time, national reports on the status of education (Stanic, 1984) have stepped up efforts to compare student performance by state, by district, by school, and even by teacher, and such efforts have often resulted in more instructional time than ever before being given over to testing. Mathematics educators concerned about increasing the attention given to problem solving in school mathematics instruction have sought instruments that would convince teachers and students alike that the students were improving their problem-solving performance. Testers concerned about measuring all the desired outcomes of instruction have sought to develop instruments that would tap problem solving as one of the "higher order skills" in which many students are presumably deficient. The result has been a flurry of activity to improve the measurement of problem-solving performance in mathematics.

Amid this activity, there has been too little reflection on how the testing of problem solving operates and what signals it may be sending to students, teachers, parents, administrators, and the general public. In this paper, we discuss two functions that the testing of problem-solving performance serves—to inform instructional decision making and to signify important educational values. Although testing serves many functions, these two have received less attention in recent years than they deserve. We end the paper by addressing some of the steps that need to be taken if testing is to carry out these functions in a more positive and productive way. Throughout, we have attempted to find ways of linking problem-solving assessment more closely to research and to identify assessment topics on which fruitful research might be done.

TESTING AND INSTRUCTIONAL DECISION MAKING

An important function of testing is to provide information that teachers can use in making instructional decisions. Except for tests that mathematics teachers might develop for their own use, current tests are not generally

178

helpful to teachers in deciding how problem-solving instruction should proceed. Many standardized tests of mathematics achievement contain a section, and offer a subscore, entitled "Problem Solving." The items in that section, however, usually involve rather simple, routine applications of well-practiced algorithms; they seldom require original thought or deep reasoning. The subscores, furthermore, do not tell teachers what difficulties their students are having with problem solving and give no instructional guidance.

A major testing program that attempts to evaluate problem-solving performance is the National Assessment of Educational Progress. Nevertheless, when the items and results from the Third and Fourth National Mathematics Assessments are examined, we find that even though considerable effort had been made to assess the higher-order thinking involved in mathematical problem solving, there is little information in the data that teachers could use for instruction. Although clusters of items on arithmetic computation show the types of common errors students might make and hint at some useful instructional procedures, there are few clusters of interrelated items that deal with noncomputational skills or knowledge.

It can easily be argued that the National Mathematics Assessments were never intended to provide information directly for the improvement of mathematics instruction. Therein lies a major part of our concern, for we can think of no large-scale testing effort that is designed to provide the kind of information that would be useful for instructional decision making in general, let alone about problem solving. How is it that such an important function of testing is going unmet?

The tests that teachers construct themselves appear to be increasingly more oriented toward emulating both the form and the content of multiple-choice standardized tests. A serious study might well be undertaken of the tests teachers construct and how they treat problem solving in those tests. Our impression is that teacher-constructed tests are not nearly as useful as they might be in providing information to guide problem-solving instruction. Psychometric theory has provided powerful techniques for analyzing the results of students' performance on multiple-choice tests. Unfortunately, there is far less technology associated with the construction of useful items. Most psychometric techniques (e.g., item discrimination indexes, scaling, norming) can be applied only after items have been written and administered. More effort needs to be given to techniques that would help teachers (and others) construct instructionally useful test items and assessment tasks.

How might tests provide instructional guidance to problem-solving instruction? Glaser (1987) has suggested that cognitive psychology may provide some help in this regard. In particular, he suggests that cognitively guided testing might be able to provide detailed error analysis information for well-known classes of procedural errors and misconceptions. Another aspect of Glaser's view is that testing ought to be able to provide information about the automaticity of component processes of a complex performance.

The automaticity of processes in mathematical problem solving is a topic that has tended to be undervalued by researchers (Gagné, 1983) and that ought to be given more attention in research. Finally, Glaser argues that testing ought to be able to provide detailed information concerning the cognitive structures and abilities associated with expertise in the domain being tested (e.g., complex pattern recognition, perception of deep structures). These represent some useful suggestions for researchers to explore in efforts to improve the assessment of problem-solving performance.

TESTING AND EDUCATIONAL VALUES

Another function of testing is to signal to students, teachers, and the general public those aspects of learning that are valued. When students ask, "Is that going to be on the test?" they are inquiring as to the value of the knowledge in question. In general, current tests place greater emphasis on those aspects of the curriculum that are relatively easy to assess than on those aspects that are highly valued by professionals in the field of mathematics education. As a result, the tests oversample basic skills in arithmetic and algebra and undersample problem-solving and other higher-order processes. If we are to communicate the values associated with a serious intellectual engagement with mathematics, we must find ways to assess that engagement, and we must regularly include such assessment as part of our mathematics testing.

An example of a testing program that has attempted to deal seriously with problem solving is the California Assessment Program (CAP). It has become one of the finest examples of useful large-scale testing in the United States. The CAP Tests, which are administered to every student in Grades 3, 6, 8, and 12 in California, provide school-level and district-level reports that can be useful in determining the extent to which schools and districts are achieving the instructional objectives specified by the state. Considerable attention has been devoted to the creation of innovative assessment items for the sixth-grade, eighth-grade, and twelfth-grade tests. The CAP tests, however, have been constrained to consist of only multiple-choice items with four choices. Sandra Marshall (this volume) provides further information about and commentary on the CAP tests.

There is widespread agreement that CAP is able to test some of the most important aspects of problem solving with the multiple-choice format and that it represents a substantial improvement over commercially available standardized tests. In fact, CAP has served as a model that several other states have used in redesigning their state assessment programs particularly with respect to testing higher-order cognitive skills. Nevertheless, CAP is part of a confusing message that is being sent to teachers and students in California. On the one hand, the California state curriculum guide (California State Department of Education, 1986) asserts that problem solving is an important instructional goal that should be demonstrated in classroom activities involving explorations and situational problem solving, problem creation and generation, sharing multiple solutions, discussing processes, and evaluating and interpreting proposed solutions. On the other hand, the CAP test is able to assess this goal with only a few multiple-choice items.

The limitations of multiple-choice items and the message they send to students, teachers, and the general public about the character of knowledge that is valued make such items a powerfully conservative force in any effort to improve the quality of mathematics education. A reliance solely on the sleek efficiency of multiple-choice (and other short-answer) formats will severely hinder efforts to help students develop a reflective and interrogatory stance toward their learning.

For progress to be made in transcending the limits of multiple-choice items, much experimental work will need to be done. Although the past two decades of research have produced many careful analyses of pupils' behavior in solving various novel and routine problems, little of that research has directly influenced the way problem solving is assessed. Research results need to be examined for suggestions of innovative assessment techniques that match proposed goals for problem solving in the mathematics class-room. For example, if one wants to influence how pupils organize their mathematical knowledge so that it can be used productively to solve problems, one can examine research (e.g., Silver, 1979) that has utilized techniques (e.g., free sorting) for uncovering the structure a pupil imposes on a set of mathematical problems. Researchers might then explore how teachers could use such techniques as assessment tools.

Some of the more elusive goals that teachers hold for instruction deal with processes such as monitoring or evaluation, with pupils' beliefs about mathematics, or with their beliefs about the problem-solving process. Schemes and techniques have been developed by researchers to concep-tualize and measure some of the metacognitive components of problem solving (Garofalo & Lester, 1985; Schoenfeld, 1985). More research needs to be undertaken that explores these schemes and techniques for their utility and validity as assessment tools. For other instructional goals, such as will-ingness to engage in problem solving and persistence in the face of problem difficulty, schemes and techniques are lacking and will need to be devised and their effectiveness investigated. In general, just as instruction and test-ing should be more closely integrated, so also should research and development efforts be merged and directed toward the creation and eval-uation of innovative assessment tools that are appropriate for the important instructional goals associated with mathematical problem solving.

WHAT TESTING NEEDS TO BE

The formal assessment of mathematical problem solving has changed little over the past 25 years. If the goal of developing proficiency in problem solving is to be realized, its importance must be communicated to students, teachers, and the general public through the tests that are given. For example, some tests should contain tasks that measure the more subtle aspects of problem solving, such as recognizing when problems have a similar mathematical structure or observing that a given mathematical model (e.g., equation, graph, diagram) can be used to represent a problem. Moreover, there need to be open-ended problems for students to solve in which they generate numerous conjectures based on a set of given data or conditions. Problems need to be provided for which students must develop and fit a mathematical model to the task.

Some efforts have been made to put such tasks into tests. The California Assessment Program has begun to develop such tasks (Marshall, this volume), and as the designers of the CAP tests move away from a strictly multiple-choice format, they may be able to assess many more facets of problem solving. The change needed, however, is more drastic than an evolution in item format. Creighton Buck (1959), reviewing mathematical competitions, once noted the difference between assessments of routine competence in mathematics and assessments of mathematical ingenuity and insight. Competitions that test routine competence and achievement ask the student to respond to a large number of short-answer questions in a relatively short period of time. A premium is placed on memory and on skill in manipulating numerical or algebraic expressions. The American High School Mathematics Examination (Berzsenyi, 1987) is an example of such a competition. Although most of the problems in the competition are challenging and many are quite elegant, the timing (30 questions to be answered in 90 minutes) does not allow for much reflection. Competitions that test ingenuity and that require students to demonstrate research ability in mathematics necessarily give students more time for each question. For example, in taking the Stanford University Competitive Examination in Mathematics (Polya & Kilpatrick, 1974), students responded to three to five questions in three hours. It has not been demonstrated that time pressure contributes to the accurate assessment of problem-solving performance. In fact, the speed with which one can solve a nonroutine problem may be unrelated to the quality of one's solution.

Tests in which students respond with written or oral statements rather than by filling in bubbles on answer sheets are neither as efficient nor as reliable as the current ideology of testing in the United States demands. In our view, however, there is an inherent conflict between that ideology and efforts to assess problem-solving performance. As long as test construction remains dominated by traditional views that put a premium on efficiency of measurement, including single scores for unidimensional measures having high internal consistency, problem solving will not be adequately assessed by tests.

An approach that merits careful consideration is the increased use of examinations. According to Resnick and Resnick (1985), a distinction can be drawn between examinations and standardized tests. Standardized achievement tests are generally rather loosely linked to the local curriculum. Examinations, in contrast, are closely tied to a syllabus and its associated learning goals. Resnick and Resnick claim that "American school children are the most tested in the world and the least examined" (p. 17). Most standardized testing assesses general rather than course- or curriculum-specific knowledge and skills, and much of it is superficial, rather than challenging students to think deeply about what they have learned (Halberstam & Peressini, 1987). An examination system similar but not necessarily identical to those used in many European countries would allow for a closer match between large-scale assessment and instructional goals and objectives. We are aware that the European examination systems may have certain negative features (e.g., use of a single indicator to make critical educational decisions, increased student stress). Nevertheless, some positive features of these systems (e.g, use of syllabuses and copies of previous examinations to guide instruction, raised expectations and standards, flexibility of examination format) may suggest adaptations that could serve some assessment needs in North America. Data from examinations—especially when those examinations are constructed and graded through a moderation process (Resnick & Resnick, 1985)—can provide useful feedback to educational practitioners making decisions about syllabus revision or other forms of pedagogical change. In fact, the widely acknowledged success of the Advanced Placement Program of the College Board in Calculus AB and BC strongly supports the potential value of an examination system.

On the horizon, there are some promising signs of approaches and techniques that may lead to better assessment of mathematical problem-solving performance. The Joint Matriculation Board (JMB), together with the Shell Centre for Mathematical Education in Nottingham, England, have for some years been experimenting with a modular approach to syllabus and examination change (Burkhardt, 1987). Examination questions have been prepared that assess students' ability to deploy their mathematical knowledge in solving nonroutine problems. These questions are being incorporated into the JMB's examinations at the rate of about 5% each year as a way of gradually encouraging teachers, and students, to give serious consideration to problem solving in mathematics.

The National Assessment of Educational Progress (NAEP) has completed a pilot study of alternative ways of assessing higher-order thinking in science and mathematics (Blumberg, Epstein, McDonald, & Mullis, 1986) and has published a manual that teachers can use to assess their students' ability to do such thinking (NAEP, 1987). Although most of the investigations involve science rather than mathematics, the general approach can be adapted for use in any mathematics course. Also, the College Board has begun some pilot work to develop modular materials for teachers to use in assessing their students' preparation for the study of algebra. These materials, termed "Algebridge," consist of a set of diagnostic assessment instruments, together with suggestions for instruction that would help students overcome their misconceptions about algebra. Several of the proposed modules deal directly with problem solving and contain questions of various types, including open-ended questions.

THREE DIRECTIONS FOR THE FUTURE

Efforts to construct improved instruments for assessing problem-solving performance in mathematics ought to proceed in any and all of three directions. The first is to refine our *technique* for assessing problem solving by continuing to develop current approaches to assessment. For example, the CAP problem-solving items and similar items developed for some other state testing programs use a multiple-choice format in creative ways to test some important components of problem solving. Such developmental work should continue, but it should be accompanied by a careful analysis of the content validity of such items. In other words, we need to understand how students' performance on innovative multiple-choice items, such as those assessing the ability to match a diagram with a problem or those asking students to judge the reasonableness of a solution, relates to their performance in actual problem-solving situations.

Marshall (this volume) has outlined a long-range program to develop a new model of testing that promises to improve current assessment techniques. It requires a thorough and detailed analysis of the domain to be assessed, an analysis that unfortunately has yet to proceed beyond a rudimentary stage. Goldin (1982) has raised some other issues that should be considered in attempts to improve assessment techniques. Although current approaches to assessment have their limitations, they have not been pursued sufficiently far to suggest that they be abandoned. Nitko (in press) discusses a variety of ways in which current assessment techniques, including both internal and external testing, could be better integrated with instructional activities and goals.

The second direction is that of *technology*. Advances in artificial intelligence promise that (within limits) open-ended responses to assessment questions may soon be machine scorable. The currently available technology of tailored testing permits each student to receive questions by computer that are suitable for his or her level of ability and allows the student to spend more time on each question with no loss in measurement efficiency. The technology of intelligent videodiscs can present students with realistic situations to explore mathematically in ways that are not possible using pencil and paper. One should not, however, get carried away by the promise of this direction for improving assessment in problem solving. All of our experience with technology in education over the past several decades suggests that any new assessment technologies will be very slow to find their way into classrooms. At best, they may be used for large-scale programmatic testing. Their use by teachers in instructional testing is likely to be severely limited for the foreseeable future, although there may be many promising opportunities for research in this area.

The ultimate instrument for assessing problem solving, and the ultimate direction in which improvement efforts, including research and development efforts, ought to be aimed is the *teacher*. Many aspects of problem-solving performance, including such matters as one's seriousness in undertaking the task and one's appreciation of the elegance of one's solution, seem likely to elude our best efforts to improve testing through technique and technology. Their assessment requires the skills of a sensitive, informed teacher. The teacher who can conduct a problem-solving lesson can also assess how students have responded to it and how their performance has improved as a consequence. Unfortunately, recent attempts to control what teachers are doing in instruction have had the consequence of *deskilling* them—convincing them that they lack the expertise to assess how their students are learning and thinking. What is needed are serious efforts to reskill teachers, to provide them not only with tools such as sample problems and scoring procedures that they can use to construct their own assessment instruments but also with the confidence they so often lack in their own ability to determine what and how their students are doing in solving mathematical problems. Such efforts set a challenging agenda for future research and practice.

REFERENCES

Berzsenyi, G. (1987, December). AHSME. *Consortium: The Newsletter of the Consortium for Mathematics and Its Applications*, p. 4.

Blumberg, F., Epstein, M., MacDonald, W., & Mullis, I. (1986). *A pilot study of higher-order thinking skills assessment techniques in science and mathematics* (Final report). Princeton, NJ: National Assessment of Educational Progress.

Buck, R. C. (1959). A look at mathematical competitions. *American Mathematical Monthly, 66*, 201–212.

Burkhardt, H. (1987). Curricula for active mathematics. In I. Wirszup & R. Streit (Eds.), *Developments in school mathematics education around the world* (pp. 321–361). Reston, VA: National Council of Teachers of Mathematics.

California State Department of Education. (1986). *Mathematics framework for California public schools, grades K–12*. Sacramento: Author.

Gagné, R. M. (1983). Some issues in the psychology of mathematics instruction. *Journal for Research in Mathematics Education, 14*, 7–18.

Garofalo, J., & Lester, F. K., Jr. (1985). Metacognition, cognitive monitoring, and mathematical performance. *Journal for Research in Mathematics Education. 16*, 163–176.

Glaser, R. (1987). The integration of instruction and testing. In D. C. Berliner & B. V. Rosenshine (Eds.), *Talks to teachers* (pp. 329–341). New York: Basic Books.

Goldin, G. A. (1982). The measure of problem-solving outcomes. In F. K. Lester, Jr. & J. Garofalo (Eds.), *Mathematical problem solving: Issues in research* (pp. 87–101). Philadelphia: Franklin Institute Press.

Halberstam, H., & Peressini, A. (1987). On the value of examinations. In I. Wirszup & R. Streit (Eds.), *Developments in school mathematics education around the world* (pp. 476–493). Reston, VA: National Council of Teachers of Mathematics.

National Assessment of Educational Progress. (1987). *Learning by doing: A manual for teaching and assessing higher-order thinking in science and mathematics* (Report No. 17–HOS–80). Princeton, NJ: Educational Testing Service.

National Council of Teachers of Mathematics. (1980). *An agenda for action: Recommendations for school mathematics of the 1980s*. Reston, VA: Author.

Nitko, A. J. (in press). Designing tests that are integrated with instruction. In R. L. Linn (Ed.), *Educational measurement* (3rd ed.). New York: Macmillan.

Polya, G., & Kilpatrick, J. (1974). *The Stanford mathematics problem book: With hints and solutions*. New York: Teachers College Press.

Resnick, D. P., & Resnick, L. B. (1985). Standards, curriculum, and performance: A historical and comparative perspective. *Educational Researcher, 14*(4), 5–21.

Schoenfeld, A. H. (1985). *Mathematical problem solving*. New York: Academic Press.

Silver, E. A. (1979). Student perceptions of relatedness among mathematical verbal problems. *Journal for Research in Mathematics Education, 10*, 195–210.

Stanic, G. M. A. (1984). Un esprit simpliste—Five current reports. *Journal for Research in Mathematics Education, 15*, 383–389.

Teaching as Problem Solving

Thomas P. Carpenter
University of Wisconsin

In the last ten to fifteen years there have been significant advances in our understanding of how children and adults solve problems in a variety of content domains; however, there has been relatively little progress in applying this knowledge to improve instruction. Although a great deal of the research addresses issues that appear to have direct implications for instruction, this research has had limited impact on the teaching of mathematics.

One reason that the research has had such little influence on the mathematics curriculum may be that it does not directly address the central problems of classroom instruction. Much of the problem-solving research has focused on the problem-solving processes of individuals and has not investigated learning or instruction. The studies that have considered problems of learning, often have been conducted in controlled laboratory settings involving individuals or small groups for limited periods of time. Brophy (1986) has argued that such research fails to take into account the reality of typical classrooms in which one teacher must teach a diverse group of 25 to 40 students. It is a valid point that an understanding of the problem-solving processes of novices and experts does not translate directly into prescriptions for classroom instruction, and instruction that is successful with individuals or small groups in controlled experiments may not work with 30 students in a typical mathematics class. However, it would be premature to dismiss such research out of hand as irrelevant for classroom instruction. Problem solving is a complex process, and we are having enough difficulty truly understanding the problem-solving processes of individuals. Unless we can understand how individuals learn to solve problems, it is unlikely that we will make much progress in understanding how such learning takes place in classrooms. Furthermore, this research may generate the knowledge base to ask more appropriate questions in studies of classrooms. This knowledge base may also provide a framework for teachers to make more informed instructional decisions. Although knowledge of individual problem-solving processes may not translate directly into classroom practice, classrooms are composed of individuals, and such knowledge may provide teachers with a basis to more effectively assess their students' knowledge and make decisions about appropriate instruction. This point is discussed in greater detail later in the paper.

Although case studies and controlled experiments will continue to make significant contributions, we also need to begin to consider the problems of problem-solving instruction in classrooms. It is not only a question of coming to grips with the problems of instructing groups of 30 students; it is also a question of taking into account the entire picture. Learning to become a good problem solver is not like learning an isolated skill that can be decomposed into its essential elements. If we take seriously the constructivist notion that all learning is essentially problem solving, our study of problem solving cannot simply focus on isolated aspects of the curriculum. Problem solving is involved in the way that students try to make sense out of instruction in light of their existing constructs; it is involved in the way that they attempt to put structure on the knowledge they acquire and to relate it to their existing knowledge; it is involved in how they learn skills as well as how they learn to apply those skills.

Students' success in problem solving is not simply a function of how successfully they have learned a collection of problem-solving procedures; it is also a question of the understanding they have developed for the mathematics involved in solving the problems. One of the most significant differences between expert and novice problem solvers is the nature of the knowledge possessed by each group (Chi, Glaser, & Rees, 1982). Thus, it is not possible to focus only on problem-solving processes. In order to effect comprehensive change in problem-solving instruction, research must ultimately address the complexity of problem solving within the mathematics curriculum as well as the complexity of classroom instruction.

Unfortunately just as research on problem solving generally has not addressed issues of classroom instruction, research which has been most directly concerned with the investigation of classroom instruction has not for the most part seriously considered problem solving as a goal of instruction. For the last decade research on classroom teaching has been dominated by the process-product paradigm (Brophy & Good, 1986). Process-product research attempts to establish relationships between teacher actions and student outcomes. Teacher actions that are positively correlated with student achievement are identified by observation of typical classrooms. Principles for improving instruction derived from the correlational studies are subsequently validated experimentally.

A major criticism of process-product research is that because most studies rely on standardized achievement tests as measures of student outcomes, teacher processes that are related to gains in problem-solving performance are overlooked (Romberg & Carpenter, 1986). Some studies have attempted to include a measure of problem solving as a dependent variable (Good, Grouws, & Ebmeir, 1983), but it is difficult to construct good tests of problem solving that meet the psychometric requirements of process-product research.

In theory, if one is committed to the process-product paradigm, it should be possible to apply it to the study of problem solving. However, if one begins with different assumptions about problem solving and the current state of instruction in problem solving, the process-product paradigm appears to be severely limited. The correlational-experimental loop that characterizes current process-product research is based on the assumption that principles for effective instruction can be derived from current practice. In the case of problem solving, this assumption is highly questionable. Results from the mathematics assessment of the National Assessment of Educational Progress (Carpenter, Lindquist, Matthews, & Silver, 1984) suggest that even at its best, current instruction in problem solving may fall far short of the ideal.

The assumptions about learning and problem solving upon which traditional process-product research are based may present an even more fundamental obstacle (Confrey, 1986). In general, most process-product researchers appear to operate from a transmission perspective of teaching and learning both in their analysis of classroom teaching and in their statements of principles for effective teaching. There seems to be at least the tacit assumption that what students learn is a direct function of what teachers teach, and there is a parallel assumption that principles of effective teaching can be communicated directly to teachers in the form of propositions. If one adopts a constructivist perspective that is consistent with much of the recent research on problem solving, an alternative paradigm for the study of classroom instruction in problem solving is needed.

AN ALTERNATIVE PERSPECTIVE

One way to conceive of teaching is that teaching is a skill. From this perspective, the goal of research is to identify principles of effective teaching that can be followed almost algorithmically. It would be unfair to characterize process-product research in general as operating from this perspective, but some programs for effective teaching come very close to it. I propose that a more appropriate model for studying the teaching of problem solving conceives of teaching as problem solving. This is essentially the approach that was proposed in a report by Panel 6 of the National Conference on Studies in Teaching (National Institute of Education, 1975) and is discussed in detail in Clark and Peterson (1986).

From this perspective, teachers do not simply engage in classroom behaviors; they make decisions and generally attempt to solve problems of instruction. One consequence of conceiving of teaching as problem solving is that it makes sense to consider applying the same techniques to the study of teaching that have proved effective in studying problem solving in general. In particular, the focus shifts from teacher behavior to teacher thinking.

In the last decade, research on teacher thought processes has burgeoned. Comprehensive reviews of this work can be found in Shavelson and Stern (1981) and Clark and Peterson (1986). The research summarized in these reviews supports the conclusion that teaching involves decision making and problem solving. Not surprisingly, teachers exhibit the same characteristics in solving problems of instruction that are employed by problem solvers in other contexts. Just as behaviorist analyses of problem solving proved to be inadequate to capture the complexity of the problem-solving process, viewing teachers simply as actors who exhibit certain behaviors is severely limiting. They do not blindly follow lesson plans in teachers' manuals or prescriptions for effective teaching. They interpret them in terms of their own constructs and adapt them to fit the situation as they perceive it. Teachers' beliefs and knowledge have a profound effect on the way that they teach and as a consequence on the learning of the students in their classrooms. Although the research on teachers' thought processes has clearly documented the critical role that teacher thinking plays in instruction, the research that has been completed to date does not provide an adequate model for research on the teaching of problem solving. In general, research on teacher thinking has focused on generic processes: whether teachers use the rational planning model; whether they plan in terms of lessons, units, or some other segment of time; what factors they attribute students' successes and failures to. For the most part, this research has not seriously examined the subject matter taught as a variable to be investigated. Shulman (1986b) calls this the "missing paradigm" problem.

A major focus of recent cognitive science research in problem solving has been on problem solving in semantically rich content domains, and a primary concern has been with the analysis and representation of the knowledge and problems within these content domains. In spite of the fact that research on teachers' thought processes was in part a response to the advances made in cognitive science, research on teacher thinking generally has not followed this lead. Although cognitive science provides rich descriptions of the knowledge and problem-solving processes within a number of areas that could be applied to the study of teaching, for the most part neither traditional research on teaching nor the research on teacher thought processes has drawn on this analysis.

What is needed is a paradigm that blends the concern for the realities of classroom instruction that is found in research on teachers' thought processes with the rich analysis of the structure of knowledge and problem solving that is found in cognitive science research. A critical question for this research to address is what the nature of teachers' knowledge is and how it influences their instructional decisions.

KNOWLEDGE AND PROBLEM SOLVING

Adopting the perspective that teaching is problem solving suggests that teachers' knowledge should be a major focus of research on teaching. Research on problem solving in complex, semantically rich domains has found that there are fundamental differences between expert and novice problem solvers in the nature and organization of knowledge within the content domain (Chi et al., 1982). Experts tend to have a richer knowledge base that is more highly structured than novices'. This implies that success in teaching problem solving may be related to teachers' knowledge about the problem-solving process, the relevant mathematical content, their students' conceptions and misconceptions, and/or a variety of other variables.

Traditional studies of teachers' knowledge have not been particularly successful in establishing relationships between teachers' knowledge and students' performance. In fact, the inability to find significant relationships between student achievement and to presage variables like teacher knowledge lead researchers to abandon the study of such variables in favor of process-product studies. One limitation of most of the early studies of teachers' knowledge is that they employed relatively global measures of teacher knowledge, like number of courses completed or performance on a standardized test.

Recently, Shulman (1986a, 1986b) has proposed a much more fine-grained analysis of teachers' knowledge. He distinguishes between three categories of knowledge: content knowledge, curricular knowledge, and pedagogical knowledge. Content knowledge, which is also referred to as subject matter knowledge, is the knowledge of the subject per se as it is held by experts in the field. It is the conceptual and procedural knowledge of arithmetic, algebra, geometry, and the like, that are the focus of the content courses that teachers take in their academic disciplines.

Curricular knowledge is knowledge of the range of instructional materials available to teach a particular subject. It is more than knowledge of what is taught in a particular course. It is knowledge of the alternatives available for instruction and an understanding of the basis for the differences among the alternatives. Curricular knowledge generally receives less emphasis in preservice education than content knowledge, but it is a major focus of inservice education and the publications and activities of professional groups like the National Council of Teachers of Mathematics.

Shulman (1986a) defines pedagogical knowledge as follows:

> The understanding of how particular topics, principles, strategies, and the like in specific subject areas are comprehended or typically misconstrued, are learned and likely to be forgotten. Such knowledge includes the categories within which similar problem types or conceptions can be classified (what are the ten most frequently encountered types of algebra word problems? least well-grasped grammatical constructions?), and the psychology of learning them (p. 26).

Pedagogical knowledge includes knowledge of how to represent ideas in order to make them comprehensible to the learner. It also includes knowledge of the difficulties that students are likely to encounter in learning a particular topic as well as strategies for overcoming those difficulties. It includes knowledge of the conceptual and procedural knowledge that students bring to the learning of a topic, the misconceptions they may have developed, and the stages of understanding that they are likely to pass through in moving from a state of having little understanding of the topic to mastery of it. It also includes knowledge of strategies that can be used to connect the knowledge that students are learning to the knowledge that they already possess and to strategies to eliminate their misconceptions.

Pedagogical knowledge is addressed in preservice methods courses and inservice programs, but often in very superficial ways. Pedagogical knowledge frequently is presented as isolated bits of information rather than a coherent theory of learning and instruction. Cognitive science research is beginning to provide some coherence to our understanding of children's learning and problem solving that could serve as a basis for organizing pedagogical knowledge, but this information infrequently finds its way into preservice and inservice programs for teachers. Although distinctions are drawn between the three kinds of knowledge, there is a certain amount of overlap, and the interrelationships among them are critical. Pedagogical knowledge and curricular knowledge both build upon content knowledge. The nature of students' conceptions and misconceptions generally is related to the structure of the content they are learning, and studies of children's concepts and misconceptions often begin with a thorough analysis of the content. In a similar way content knowledge provides a basis for understanding differences between alternative curriculum materials when the alternatives represent fundamental distinctions in the interpretation of the content or address different goals of instruction. Pedagogical knowledge also provides a framework for curricular knowledge. A clear understanding of the concepts and misconceptions that children hold and the instructional strategies that may be effective for teaching children with particular understandings or misconceptions provides another basis for making distinctions between instructional materials. Curricular knowledge also influences how pedagogical knowledge can be applied. Strategies that may be effective to teach concepts or eliminate misconceptions are only viable if the teacher knows about appropriate curricular materials that incorporate them.

One of the features of all three kinds of knowledge as Shulman characterizes them is the prominence given to knowledge that is highly specific to the subject matter that is being taught. Content knowledge includes knowledge of content that is directly relevant to the topic being taught, not just broad, general knowledge of mathematics. Curricular knowledge is concerned with the specific alternatives available for teaching a topic. Pedagogical knowledge is more than knowledge of general theories of learning and development; it includes specific knowledge of students' understandings and misconceptions and the strategies that are effective for dealing with them.

Research on teaching generally has employed global measures of teachers' knowledge, and for the most part pedagogical and curricular knowledge have been ignored. Shulman (1986a) observes: "There have been no studies of teachers' (pedagogical) knowledge, of the schemata or frames they employ to apprehend student understandings or misconceptions" (p.26). Clearly this is a strategic site for research on the teaching of problem solving, and it offers one of the best possibilities for integrating cognitive science research on problem solving with research on teaching and teachers' thought processes. The advances that have been made in the last decade in our understanding of children's mathematical thinking and problem solving provide a coherent basis for examining teachers' pedagogical knowledge and how they apply this knowledge to make curricular decisions.

A MODEL FOR RESEARCH AND CURRICULUM DEVELOPMENT

A general model for research and curriculum development is presented in Figure 1. This model serves as the framework for a program of research that I am engaged in with Elizabeth Fennema and Penelope Peterson, which is based on the premise that teaching is problem solving. We are attempting to integrate the perspectives of cognitive and instructional science to study teachers' pedagogical knowledge in the area of elementary arithmetic and how that knowledge influences classroom instruction and students' learning.

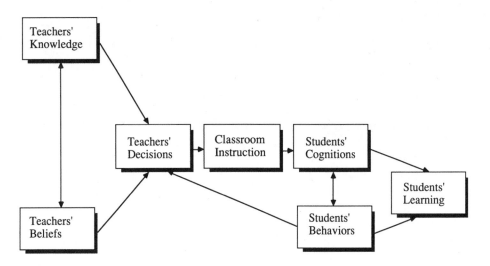

Figure 1. Model for research and curriculum development

The model assigns a central role to teachers' and students' thinking. Classroom instruction is based upon teachers' decisions, and the effects of instruction on students' behaviors and learning are mediated by students' cognitions. As indicated in the figure, teachers' decisions are presumed to be based upon their knowledge and beliefs as well as their assessment of students' knowledge through their observation of students' behaviors.

THE RESEARCH PROGRAM

We are currently in the second year of a four-year research project that is applying the model represented in Figure 1 to study instruction in addition and subtraction in first grade. Research in addition and subtraction provides a highly structured, detailed analysis of the development of addition and subtraction concepts and skills as reflected in children's solutions of different types of word problems. For reviews of this research see Carpenter (1985), Carpenter and Moser (1983), or Riley, Greeno, and Heller (1983).

The research is based on a detailed analysis of the problem space. Addition and subtraction word problems are partitioned into several basic classes, which distinguish between different types of action or relationships that represent different interpretations of addition and subtraction. Within each class three distinct problem types can be generated by systematically varying the unknowns. This scheme provides a highly principled analysis of problem types such that knowledge of a few general rules is sufficient to generate the complete range of different types of problems.

The analysis is also consistent with the way that children think about problems and solve them. Empirical research on children's solutions of addition and subtraction problems has documented that young children initially solve word problems by directly representing the action or relationships in the problems. Thus, the taxonomy of problem types provides a framework to identify the processes that children are likely to use to solve different problems and to distinguish between problems in terms of their relative difficulty. The research also has identified the major levels that children pass through in acquiring more advanced procedures for solving addition and subtraction problems, and models have been proposed of the procedural and conceptual knowledge underlying performance at each level (Briars & Larkin, 1984; Riley et al., 1983).

Thus, there is a highly structured, coherent body of pedagogical knowledge regarding the development of addition and subtraction concepts and skills in children. This body of knowledge provides a basis for relating each of the components of the model in Figure 1 to one another. Teachers' pedagogical knowledge and beliefs, classroom instruction, students' cognition and learning all can be evaluated in terms of this basic framework. In our studies, teachers' knowledge is assessed in terms of their ability to distinguish between different problem types, their knowledge of the relative difficulty of different problems, their knowledge of the different strategies that children use to solve different problems, and their ability to identify the relation between problem types and the strategies that children use to solve them. We also are testing teachers' ability to assess students' knowledge and teachers' knowledge of whether their own students can solve particular problems and the processes they use to solve them.

Teachers' beliefs are assessed in terms of some of the fundamental assumptions that underlie the constructivist perspective that is represented by our interpretation of the current research on addition and subtraction and our analysis of how it should be applied to instruction. We have constructed four belief scales, and we are also evaluating the same beliefs using structured interviews.

> Scale I goes from the belief that children construct their own knowledge to the belief that children receive knowledge.
>
> Scale II goes from the belief that instruction should facilitate children's construction of knowledge to the belief that teachers should present knowledge.
>
> Scale III goes from the belief that skills should be related to understanding and problem solving to the belief that skills should be taught in isolation.
>
> Scale IV goes from the belief that the natural development of children's mathematical ideas should provide the basis for sequencing instruction to the belief that the sequence should be based on the formal structure of mathematics. Note that this scale essentially addresses the issue of the relative importance of content knowledge and pedagogical knowledge for sequencing instruction.

We are studying classroom instruction using separate coding systems to code teachers' actions and students' behaviors. The coding systems have categories for mathematics content and the strategies used to solve problems that are derived from the basic analysis of children's solutions of addition and subtraction problems. The analysis has had to be simplified to make coding of classroom behavior possible, but the coding system is able to pick up the relative emphasis on word problems and distinguish between four distinct categories of strategies for solving problems. The coding system for the teachers' behavior is also designed to identify teachers' attempts to diagnose their students' understanding of a topic and the kinds of grouping decisions they might make on the basis of that diagnosis. The coding system also differentiates between teachers' actions that focus on answers to problems and teachers' actions that focus on the processes that students use to get answers.

Finally, the assessment of students' learning and cognition is based on the same principles that guide the rest of the research. The taxonomy of problem types and the characterization of children's problem-solving processes provide a framework to evaluate learning and problem solving. The analysis of problem types and the development of children's problem-solving abilities make it possible to select critical problems that differentiate between levels of performance. The techniques developed to investigate children's problem-solving processes also make it possible to assess students' knowledge and understanding at a deeper level than whether they can answer a problem correctly or not. As a consequence, it is possible to characterize children's performance in terms of whether they have acquired particular concepts or skills rather than simply in terms of scores on a test. The analysis of problem types and children's solution processes also provides a basis to develop measures of transfer and problem solving that are clearly related to the knowledge and skills that are being investigated. This makes it possible to develop measures of problem solving that are relatively sensitive to the effects of instruction.

The common framework which is used to characterize the knowledge and/or performance within each of the components of the model in Figure 1 makes it possible to examine specific relationships between different components of the model with a much higher degree of specificity than has been possible in previous studies. For example, it is possible to attempt to establish links between teachers' knowledge and how that knowledge is translated into specific classroom activities that are related to that knowledge or to investigate how particular instructional activities are reflected in students' learning of the concepts and skills being taught.

Assessing Students' Thinking

One of the key relationships in the model in Figure 1 is the relationship between teachers' decisions and teachers' assessment of students' thinking. In the figure, this relationship is represented by the arrows joining students' cognitions, students' behaviors, and teachers' decisions. A key assumption that our research is examining is that one of the principal ways that teachers might apply pedagogical knowledge is in the assessment of their own students' knowledge and abilities.

A primary focus of our test of teachers' knowledge is on teachers' ability to assess students' problem-solving processes and their knowledge of how their own students solve different problems. The principle that assessing students' knowledge is important is embedded in at least two of the belief scales, and several categories within the system for coding classroom behavior are designed to identify teachers' actions that are intended to assess children's thinking. A major component of the experimental treatment that is part of our research attempts to help teachers develop procedures to use the pedagogical knowledge they have learned to assess their own students' knowledge and abilities and use that knowledge to make instructional decisions.

There is not a great deal of evidence that teachers can successfully assess their students' knowledge and use that information to make instructional decisions. Studies of children's thinking generally deal with individuals, and most teachers find it difficult to evaluate 30 students with anything but a paper and pencil test. Furthermore, the research on teachers' decision making has found little evidence that teachers take into account the assessment of individual students when planning for instruction (Clark & Peterson, 1986). On the other hand, the Beginning Teacher Evaluation Study found that teachers' ability to predict individual students' success in solving specific problems on a standardized achievement test was positively correlated with student achievement in the teachers' classes (Fisher et al., 1980). Our own data also indicate that teachers' knowledge of their own students' abilities to solve different problems is positively correlated with performance of the teachers' classes. Generally the students of teachers who were more successful in predicting student success in solving a series of word problems had higher levels of achievement on a test of problem solving than students of teachers who were less successful (Carpenter, Fennema, & Peterson, 1987).

Furthermore, the fact that teachers do not currently use knowledge about students in planning for instruction does not necessarily imply that they would not do so if appropriate knowledge were available. Most teachers can distinguish many of the critical differences between different types of problems when asked to do so, and many of them have a reasonable intuitive feel for problem difficulty. In fact, most teachers know a great deal about their own students' abilities to solve different types of problems. But in general much of this knowledge is impressionistic; it is not principled, and it lacks coherence and structure (Carpenter et al., 1987). The research on children's thinking and problem solving provides the kind of structure that may make it possible to develop routines for assessing children's abilities and knowledge and to use the information about students provided by such assessments in planning for instruction.

A Focus on Process

A distinguishing feature of cognitive science research is the concern for the cognitive processes that are involved in solving problems. In the research on children's addition and subtraction concepts, the primary distinctions between stages of development are drawn on the basis of the processes that children at each stage use to solve different problems, and even problem difficulty is interpreted in terms of the processes that are required to solve different problems. One of the unifying themes of our research is a focus on the processes that children use to solve problems. Process measures are used in our assessment of students' learning, and teachers' knowledge of the processes that students use to solve different problems is a primary component of the assessment of teachers' pedagogical knowledge. The classroom observation scheme includes codes that distinguish between whether a teacher's instruction is concerned with specific processes used to solve problems, whether they are assessing the processes a student used to solve a problem or simply the answer, and whether they are giving feedback about the process used to solve the problem or about the answer.

The processes that children use to solve problems is also a unifying theme for the experimental treatment. The teachers learn that it is necessary to be concerned with the processes that students use to solve problems, not just whether they can get a correct answer. The understanding of children's thinking and problem solving is developed in terms of the processes that children use to solve different problems and how those processes evolve over time. This basic knowledge provides the framework to develop principles of assessment and instruction. The emphasis in assessment is on how children solve problems. A primary goal of instruction is to build upon the informal modeling and counting processes that children naturally use to solve problems and to teach children to use processes that involve symbolization and greater levels of abstraction. Teachers in the experimental treatment group learn that children solve problems in many ways, and the different solutions reflect very different levels of understanding and very different levels of ability to apply skills to solve problems or learn more complex calculations.

Our initial studies suggest that teachers typically may not consider the processes that children use to solve problems as a matter of primary concern, and as a consequence their instruction is not significantly affected by their knowledge of how students solve problems (Carpenter et al., 1987). Although teachers' knowledge of their students' abilities to answer problems correctly was found to be positively correlated with student performance, no correlation was found between teachers' ability to predict the strategies that students would use to solve problems and student performance. Again, this may reflect the fact that teachers traditionally have not had a sufficiently rich knowledge base to assess the processes that their students use to solve problems and differentiate between different solutions in planning for instruction. Until we have been able to evaluate the performance of our experimental teachers, we will not know whether teachers are able to use general knowledge about the processes that children use to solve problems to assess their own students and make instructional decisions that translate into achievement gains.

Cognitively Guided Instruction

Conceiving teaching as problem solving is not only important for understanding teachers' planning and classroom instruction, it also provides a perspective to analyze the impact of teacher training programs and the implementation of new curricula and a basis for designing programs of instruction and teacher education. Teachers' beliefs and knowledge not only have a profound effect on the decisions they make regarding instruction; they also influence how teachers respond to teacher education programs and new programs of instruction.

The instruction for teachers in our experimental treatment focuses on teachers' pedagogical and curricular knowledge. Rather than attempting to prescribe a program of instruction or even a series of principles for instruction, we are attempting to help teachers to use knowledge from cognitive science to make instructional decisions. This approach, which we call "Cognitively Guided Instruction," is based on the premise that the teaching-learning process is too complex to specify in advance, and as a consequence, teaching essentially is problem solving. Instruction necessarily needs to be mediated by teachers' decisions, and ultimately the most significant changes in instruction will occur by helping teachers to make more informed decisions rather than attempting to program them to perform in a particular way.

The guiding principle for Cognitively Guided Instruction is that instructional decisions should be based upon careful analyses of children's knowledge and the goals of instruction. This requires that teachers have a thorough knowledge of the content domain and that they can effectively assess their students' knowledge in this domain. Knowledge of the content integrates content and pedagogical knowledge. It includes an understanding of distinctions between problems that are reflected in children's solutions at different stages in acquiring expertise in the domain. This involves knowledge of problem difficulty as well as knowledge of distinctions between problems that result in different processes of solution. The ability to assess their own students' knowledge also requires that teachers have an understanding of the general stages that children pass through in acquiring the concepts and procedures in the domain, the processes that children use to solve different problems at each stage, and the nature of the knowledge that underlies these processes.

The initial goal of instruction was to familiarize teachers with research on children's solution of addition and subtraction problems. They learned to classify problems, to identify the processes that children use to solve different problems, and to relate processes to the levels in which they are commonly used. Although the taxonomy of problem types and the models of children's cognitive processes were simplified somewhat, teachers were expected to acquire thorough understanding of the research. This knowledge provided the framework for everything else that followed, and over a week of the four-week workshop was spent on it. During the remainder of the workshop, teachers were to derive principles of instruction from this research and design their own programs of instruction based upon those principles.

Although instructional practices were not prescribed, broad principles of instruction were discussed. The basic principle was that insofar as possible, instruction should be appropriate for each child. This was taken to mean that problems, concepts, or procedures being learned should have meaning for the child. For a task to have meaning, the child should be able to relate it to the knowledge that he or she already possesses. This implies that instructional decisions be based upon regular assessment of each child's knowledge throughout the course of instruction.

Other broad principles that were discussed were that instruction should be organized to involve children to actively construct their own knowledge with understanding and that instruction should stress relationships between concepts, skills, and problem solving. Specific issues were identified that teachers needed to address in planning their instruction, but they were not told how they should resolve them. These issues include the following:

How should instruction initially build upon the informal and counting strategies that children use to solve simple word problems when they enter first grade?

Should specific strategies like counting on be taught explicitly? These strategies represent a major transition between children's initial direct modeling strategies and the learning of number facts, but they are not essential for skilled performance.

How should symbols be linked to the informal knowledge of addition and subtraction that children exhibit in their modeling and counting solutions of word problems?

Another goal of the workshop was to familiarize teachers with the procedures and materials available for instruction. Teachers were encouraged to evaluate curricular materials on the basis of the pedagogical knowledge they acquired earlier in the workshop. Principles of assessment were also identified. The central principle that was discussed is that it is important to assess not only whether a child can solve a particular problem but also how the child solves the problem. Research on addition and subtraction has effectively identified the processes that children use to solve problems by watching them solve the problems and listening to them explain how they were solved. The techniques used in this research provide a model for classroom assessment. Although a typical teacher has to deal with students at the same time rather than a single child in a clinical study, teachers do find time to talk to individual children during the course of instruction. By judiciously selecting problems, teachers can assess children's knowledge during the course of instruction. Because the taxonomy of problem types clearly scales problems, problems can be selected that are appropriate to assess each child's knowledge based on the child's responses during previous interviews. Responses to several carefully selected problems can provide a reasonable basis for deciding whether a child has progressed to a more advanced level or whether a particular activity would be appropriate for the child.

We are currently studying how the teachers in the workshop use their knowledge to make instructional decisions. We anticipate a great deal of variety in the implementation of the program. The common thread that we would like to see run through all classes is the regular assessment of children's knowledge and the use of the information from these assessments to make instructional decisions.

CONCLUSION

A little more than three years ago at another San Diego conference on problem solving, Doug Grouws (1985) proposed that the teacher and classroom instruction were neglected themes in problem-solving research. This paper reiterates the view that problem-solving research must be concerned with the problems of classroom instruction. It is not just a question of taking into account the complexity of real classrooms; it is also a question of taking a more comprehensive, long range view of the teaching and learning of problem solving in schools. Significant gains in problem solving are going to require comprehensive changes in instruction that address the learning of concepts and skills as well as the learning of problem solving. The gains are going to come slowly over extended periods of time.

This paper suggests that the traditional paradigms for studying problem solving and the paradigms for studying classroom instruction are inadequate for the task of studying problem solving in classrooms, and an alternative model for studying problem-solving instruction is proposed. The model provides a different way of thinking about curriculum and teacher education as well as a new perspective of research on teaching and problem solving. The primary thesis of the model is that teaching is problem solving. Rather than attempting to derive prescriptions for teaching, the focus is on teachers' knowledge and beliefs and how teachers solve problems of instruction. Teachers' knowledge of their own students' concepts and abilities and how this knowledge is used to plan for instruction play a central role in this conception of teaching. One of the most positive features of the model is that the conception of teaching that is derived from it is consistent with the conception of learning and problem solving that is represented in most of the current problem-solving research. As a consequence the model offers an opportunity to integrate research on teaching and research on problem solving.

NOTE

The research reported in this paper was supported in part by a grant from the National Science Foundation (Grant No. MDR–8550236). The opinions expressed in this paper do not necessarily reflect the position, policy, or endorsement of the National Science Foundation.

REFERENCES

Briars, D. J., & Larkin, J. H. (1984). An integrated model of skill in solving elementary word problems. *Cognition and Instruction, 1*(3), 245–296.

Brophy, J. (1986). Teaching and learning mathematics: Where research should be going. *Journal for Research in Mathematics Education, 17*(5), 323–346.

Brophy, J., & Good, T. L. (1986). Teacher behavior and student achievement. In M. C. Wittrock (Ed.), *Teaching and learning mathematical problem solving: Multiple research perspectives* (pp. 17–40). Philadelphia: Franklin Institute Press.

Carpenter, T. P. (1985). Learning to add and subtract: An exercise in problem solving. In E. A. Silver (Ed.), *Teaching and learning mathematical problem solving: Multiple research perspectives* (pp. 17–40). Hillsdale, NJ: Lawrence Erlbaum.

Carpenter, T. P., Fennema, E., & Peterson, P. L. (1987). *Teachers' pedagogical content knowledge in mathematics: A new domain for research.* Paper presented at the annual meeting of the American Educational Research Association, Washington, D.C.

Carpenter, T. P., Lindquist, M. M., Matthews, W., & Silver, E. A. (1984). Achievement in mathematics: Results from the National Assessment. *The Elementary School Journal, 84* (5), 485–495.

Carpenter, T. P., & Moser, J. M. (1983). The acquisition of addition and subtraction concepts. In R. Lesh and M. Landau (Eds.), *The acquisition of mathematical concepts and processes* (pp. 7–14). New York: Academic Press.

Chi, M. T. H., Glaser, R., & Rees, E. (1982). Expertise in problem solving. In R. Sternberg (Ed.), *Advances in the psychology of human intelligence* (pp. 7–75). Hillsdale, NJ: Lawrence Erlbaum.

Clark, C. M., & Peterson, P. L. (1986), Teachers' thought processes. In M. C. Wittrock (Ed.), *Third handbook of research on teaching* (pp. 255–296). New York: Macmillan.

Confrey, J. (1986). A critique of teachers' effectiveness research in mathematics education. *Journal for Research in Mathematics Education, 17*(5), 347–360.

Fisher, C. W., Berliner, D. C., Filby, N. N., Marliave, R., Cahn, L. S., & Dishaw, M. M. (1980). Teaching behaviors, academic learning time, and student achievement: An overview. In C. Denham & A. Lieberman (Eds.), *Time to learn* (pp. 7–32). Washington, D.C.: United States Department of Education.

Good, T. L., Grouws, D. A., & Ebmeier, H. (1983). *Active mathematics teaching.* New York: Longman.

Grouws, D. A. (1985). The teacher and classroom instruction: Neglected themes in problem-solving research. In E. A. Silver (Ed.), *Teaching and learning mathematical problem solving: Multiple research perspectives* (pp. 295–308). Hillsdale, NJ: Lawrence Erlbaum.

National Institute of Education. (1975). *Teaching as clinical information processing: Report of Panel 6, National Conference on Studies in Teaching.* Washington, D.C.: National Institute of Education.

Riley, M. S., Greeno, J. G., & Heller, J. I. (1983). Development of children's problem-solving ability in arithmetic. In H. Ginsburg (Ed.), *The development of mathematical thinking* (pp. 153–200). New York: Academic Press.

Romberg, T. A., & Carpenter, T. P. (1986). Research on teaching and learning mathematics: Two disciplines of scientific inquiry. In M. Wittrock (Ed.), *The third handbook of research on teaching* (pp. 850–873). New York: Macmillan.

Shavelson, R. J., & Stern, P. (1981). Research on teachers' pedagogical thoughts, judgments, decisions, and behavior. *Review of Educational Research, 51,* 455–498.

Shulman, L.S.(1986a). Paradigms and research programs in the study of teaching: A contemporary perspective. In M. Wittrock (Ed.), *Handbook of research on teaching* (pp. 3–36). New York: Macmillan.

Shulman, L.S. (1986b). Those who understand: Knowledge growth in teaching. *Educational Researchers 15*(2), 4–14.

Teaching Mathematical Problem Solving: Insights from Teachers and Tutors

Richard J. Shavelson
University of California, Santa Barbara and The Rand Corporation
Noreen M. Webb
University of California, Los Angeles
Cathleen Stasz
The Rand Corporation
David McArthur
The Rand Corporation

In this paper, we think about teaching mathematical problem solving. The primary source of our thinking is research on (human) teaching, especially studies contrasting expert and novice teachers. Our premise is that expert teachers and tutors have invented practical theories[1] (e.g., Shulman, 1986, 1987) of teaching mathematical problem solving that have withstood the acid test of the classroom or other "real-world" settings (e.g., tutoring). These practical theories offer considerable insight into teaching mathematical problem solving that is not available from studies of student problem solving, or from instructional manipulations that test a theory of student problem solving. Nevertheless, many features of these practical theories appear to be consistent with recent cognitive research. An understanding of how expert human teachers and tutors teach mathematical problem solving will enable us to do a better job of educating other teachers in how to teach students to solve mathematical problems, be they other teachers human or "intelligent" machines.

Before proceeding, two caveats are in order. First, by modeling the master teacher, we run the risk of learning "what is," rather than what can or should be. This is a small risk because of the diversity of approaches we take to examine teaching of problem solving. The likelihood of an important discovery is still high.

The second caveat is that the master teachers or "experts" chosen for study largely determines what is discovered. If experts are identified by high (residual) mean scores on achievement tests of students' basic skills, we are more likely to find expert teachers using direct instruction than if tests of creative problem solving were the criterion for expertise. However, this does not seem an insurmountable problem. By casting our net widely—teachers, teacher tutors, and even students tutoring one another—and by presenting research that used a variety of criteria for identifying expertise, the findings presented here may suggest new insights into teaching mathematical problem solving. The purpose of this paper, then, is to develop hypotheses about how to teach mathematical problem solving, drawing on the research on teaching literature and some of our recent research.

We begin by briefly pointing out why even the best, most relevant process-product research is, in the end, only indirectly relevant to teaching mathematical problem solving. Then we review research on classroom teaching that characterizes how individual teachers teach mathematical problem solving, drawing out hypotheses about the critical features for teaching problem solving. Next, we report some very preliminary work with expert tutors where our intent is to develop a "theory" of an expert tutor in first-year algebra. Again, the focus is on how the tutor teaches mathematical problem solving. Subsequently, some new research on small-group mathematical problem solving is presented, with the intent of understanding how peers explain to one another how to solve problems. Finally, we conclude by bringing together a set of hypotheses about teaching mathematical problem solving, and briefly pointing to their relevance for teaching teachers to teach mathematical problem solving.

Before turning to our task, note that by focusing on teaching mathematical problem solving we largely ignore a new and informative literature on teachers' subject-matter knowledge (e.g., Leinhardt & Smith, 1985; Shulman, 1985), and teachers' pedagogical knowledge (e.g., Berliner, 1986; Calderhead & Miller 1985; Leinhardt & Greeno, 1986; Shavelson, 1986). Nevertheless, as will be seen below, to teach mathematical problem solving assumes a rich and accurate mathematics knowledge base. Moreover, this knowledge base must also include a firm understanding of what students know about mathematics and what excites them; of the structure, substance, activities, and physical arrangement of a lesson that can be used to teach problem solving, and of the classroom (and other) routines that create the environment in which teaching problem solving can take place. A complete exposition of research on teaching mathematical problem solving, then, should also include this literature. But the result would be a monograph, not a paper, and so goes beyond our purview.

PROCESS-PRODUCT RESEARCH ON TEACHING[2]

Most research on teaching over the past 20 years falls within the process-product framework. Measures of teacher behavior are (usually) correlated with residualized standardized-achievement-test measures (Shavelson et al., 1986), and behavior found to be systematically related to these outcomes may become the object of further research, most notably in randomized experiments (e.g., Brophy & Good, 1986). These studies have had a profound influence in teacher training, evaluation, and/or policy, and have gone a long way in convincing policy makers that there is a knowledge base for teaching that goes beyond simply subject matter (Berliner, 1986).

We regard the series of studies by Good, Grouws, and their colleagues

(Good & Grouws, 1975, 1979; Good, Grouws, & Ebmeier, 1983) as the best of process-product studies of classroom mathematics teaching. In their work, instructional practices of teachers with high-achieving fourth graders ("high-achieving teachers") were identified relative to instructional practices of teachers with low-achieving fourth graders ("low-achieving teachers"). This analysis led to the development of a script for teaching fourth-grade mathematics with the following sequence: daily review, development of a new concept, seatwork with uninterrupted successful practice, and assignment of homework (see Brophy & Good, 1986 for details). In a subsequent randomized experiment, fourth grade students taught by teachers using the derived guidelines showed substantial gains, and performed better than students in the control condition. Similar, though less dramatic results were reported for students in grades 6–8 (see Good, Grouws, & Ebmeier, 1983).

As good as this series of process-product studies is, we contend, as in the past (see e.g., Shavelson, 1973), that by the nature of its language and its variables, process-product research cannot speak to questions such as how to teach mathematical problem solving. Questions such as what goal was the teacher trying to attain in a particular teaching episode, how did the teacher explain a tricky concept, and what did the teacher consider to be signals for monitoring progress toward that goal are examples of the kinds of questions relative to teaching mathematical problem solving that are not in process-product research.

COGNITIVE ANALYSIS OF EXPERT CLASSROOM TEACHING[3]

To answer the question of how to teach mathematical problem solving, a much richer description and analysis of teaching is needed than that typically provided by process-product research[4]. This rich description should include teachers' intentions, subject-matter and pedagogical knowledge, substantive classroom explanations, and classroom routines and overt behavior. The analysis should provide a representation of the development of the lesson sequence that reproduces the essential features of explanations of mathematical problem solving, preferably at varying levels of abstraction (from a quite detailed representation of, say, subtraction with regrouping using symbols such as sticks and numbers, to a general planning network for the entire sequence of lessons on regrouping).

Leinhardt (in press, ab; & Greeno, 1986; & Smith, 1985) has carried out the kind of analysis envisioned here, studying expert and novice teachers teaching subtraction with regrouping. Her description and analysis of one of the experts (Leinhardt, in press, a, pp. 31–32; in press, b) provides an example of the kind of studies we believe research on teaching mathematical problem solving should pursue. It also provides a basis for generating hypotheses about how to teach students to solve problems involving subtraction with regrouping.

We observed Dorothy [Patrick] teach a sequence of eight lessons on subtraction with regrouping. On the first day of the sequence, she quickly reviewed sums with ten ($10 + 4$, $10 + 8$, $10 + 3$, etc.) . . . [Patrick] then switched to a series of two-digit subtraction problems done at the board with students giving choral support. Finally, she gave them two problems that required regrouping. By rehearsing the simple two-digit column response for subtraction, [she] prevented students from counting up—a clumsy way of getting the answer that does not require regrouping. Specifically, given the problem, 34 minus 17, the students could "count on" from 17, which would focus on the answer, but not on the need for adjusting the algorithm (you cannot take 7 from 4).

[Patrick] had students label these last two problems as "foolers." Then she went to banded sticks, felt strips, and renaming two-digit numbers, each time pausing just before the solution to see if the children could come up with a way of doing it.

Patrick's first lesson can be represented by node-link diagrams at different levels of abstraction. These diagrams represent concepts and their labeled relationships, as presented in a lesson. Figure 1 [Leinhardt's (in press, a) Figure 1] represents lesson 1 at a very general level. The central node is subtraction. It is both an arithmetic operation that may include renaming, and a problem class. The concept of subtraction can be represented in a number of different ways, ranging from concrete objects (e.g., sticks, felt strips) to abstract symbols (numbers). Figure 2 [Leinhardt's (in press, a) Figure 2] provides a considerably richer account of the lesson. Subtraction is shown as a problem class with two distinct problem types: "regular" and "foolers" (require renaming or regrouping). Note that the students know that foolers are subtraction problems where the top number in the one's column is smaller that the bottom number, but, at this point, they are not certain that foolers can be solved. Subtraction is also shown as an operation that produces an answer that can be checked, and one part of the subtraction operation is renaming. Further, subtraction can be represented in three ways: in written form, by sticks, and by felt strips. And each representation provides a somewhat different perspective on subtraction. For example, sticks are partitioned: a ten's bunch into ten sticks; felt strips are traded, a ten's strip for ten ones.

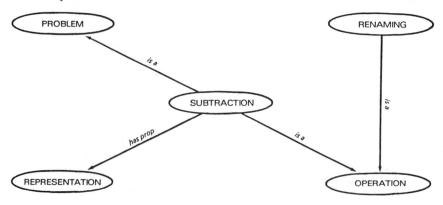

Figure 1. Core semantic net (Leinhardt, in press a)

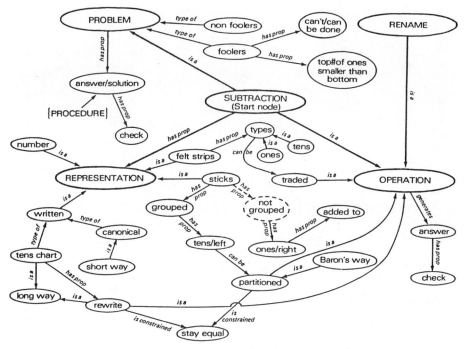

Figure 2. Lesson One, Teacher (Leinhardt, in press a)

Figure 3 shows the diagram for lesson two where the renaming concept was expanded to encompass the trading representation of felt strips. More strips were generated, but the equality of the number's value was retained. This was the key to dealing with "foolers." Moreover, the "rename operation [was shortened] to its canonical form [crossing out numbers in ten's column] and [linked] . . . to the fooler problem. Operations . . . depended upon written forms of numbers as the principle representation system with an introduction that reviewed felt strips" [Leinhardt (in press, a), p. 20]. Figure 4 shows the renaming concept as a procedure in the form of a set of nested condition-action (production) systems that call one another.

In the remaining lesson, Patrick's students "explored subtraction in increasingly complex and ambiguous contexts: word problems, money, with addition and 'regular' subtraction, and by correcting other students' work" (Leinhardt, 1986, p. 32).

Leinhardt (1986, p. 32) concluded from her analysis of this lesson sequence of finely tuned teaching that: (a) multiple representations of the subtraction procedure provided students with a "glitch free" understanding of subtraction skills, (b) rehearsal of the concept and skill in multiple contexts provided mastery to all students and a list of constraints on subtraction, and (c) offering informal proofs develops "sophisticated mathematical ideas" in students (Leinhardt, 1986, p. 32).

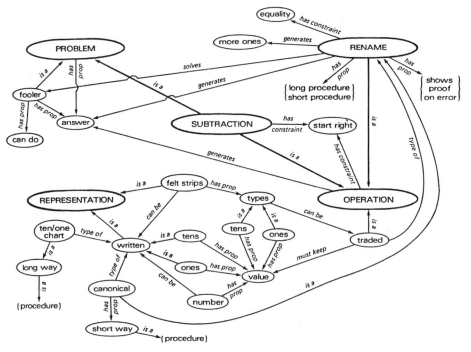

Figure 3. Lesson Two, Teacher (Leinhardt, in press a)

This description and analysis of an expert teacher's lesson goes a long way in telling us how to teach a sequence of classroom lessons that results in students being able to solve a variety of subtraction problems with regrouping (cf. Leinhardt, in press, a). Or, at least, this research on teaching leads us to formulate the following hypotheses about how to teach mathematical problem solving. Problem solving performance will be enhanced by:

1. Activating students' prior knowledge (e.g., addition with accent on base ten: $10+3$, $10+8$) relevant to teaching a new concept (e.g., subtraction with regrouping).

2. Sequencing from relevant prior knowledge (addition) to relevant prior knowledge more closely related to the lesson goal (i.e., "regular" subtraction) to the lesson-sequence goal (subtraction with regrouping, or solving "foolers").

3. Multiple representations of a mathematical concept, some concrete and some symbolic (e.g., representations of subtraction with regrouping using numerical symbols, sticks, and felt strips). Indeed, the initial lesson set up the problem and used three ways for students to think of subtraction before they were taught the solution (Leinhardt, 1986; Shavelson, Webb, & Lehman, 1986b).

4. Coordination and later translation among alternative mental rep-

---

Procedures

Rename

    A.) If want to rename

         then write original number as tens and ones

         then write new number tens decremented by 1 ten

         then write new number ones incremented by ten

    B.) If want to rename

         then write new number as tens and ones

    C.) If want to rename (short)

         then cross out tens' number

         then decrement tens' number by 1

         then write new tens' number above old

         then cross off ones

         then increment ones by 10

         then write new ones' number above old

    D.) If want more ones

         then rename

Test

    If want to check rename

         then add new tens to new ones if equal in value to old then checks

                 or

         then count sticks or felt if equal in value to old then checks

Subtraction Foolers

    If want to subtract fooler

         then rename

         then subtract

Figure 4. Procedures (Leinhardt, in press a)

resentations. For example, in teaching regrouping with sticks (two bundles of tens and six loose ones), Patrick led her students to discover that the rubber band could be taken off a bunch of (ten) sticks, while the usual number procedure (26–8) required that 1 be subtracted from the ten's place, and ten added to the one's place.

5. Evaluation of problem-solving performance through group choral responses or having students correct one anothers' work.

6. Rehearsal, not only of a particular problem type (e.g., subtraction with regrouping), but with other problem types (e.g., including "regular" subtraction and addition algorithms). Leinhardt (1986, p. 32) pointed out that "this practice reembedded subtraction into the matrix arithmetic the students already knew, blocking the over-use [sic] of the regrouping procedure and thus, recasting the new skill as a now familiar and friendly old one."

7. Informal proof (e.g., of the equality of alternative representations of a two-digit number: 42 or 4|2 or 3|12).

8. Establishing that a particular mathematical concept (e.g., subtraction) is both a type of arithmetic problem and an operation. By distinguishing the problem type and operation, the students can link the particular mathematical procedure with the appropriate problem type. For example, dividing the problem-solving domain into "regular" subtraction (without regrouping) and "foolers" (subtraction with regrouping) provides students with algorithms for the subtraction operation and distinguishes the algorithm for "regular" from "regrouping" and addition algorithm.

These hypotheses are obviously incomplete; there is more to teaching mathematical problem solving. Nevertheless, they do seem to capture something about how to teach mathematical problem solving. Bolstered with concrete examples from the rich description of Patrick's teaching, the hypotheses would be even more informative. By stating the hypotheses one at a time we also lose the sense of well orchestrated teaching in which all hypotheses are integrated into a smoothly flowing sequence of lessons. Again, coordinating the rich description from this research with the hypotheses would help. Also missing is a description and analysis of the pedagogical knowledge that underlies the orchestration of this sequence of lessons (but see Berliner, 1986; Leinhardt & Greeno, 1986), and the subject-matter knowledge (Leinhardt & Smith, 1985; Shulman, 1987) that enables Patrick to explain the concept of subtraction with regrouping. Finally, general abstract versions of many of these hypotheses can be found in the mathematics learning and problem-solving literature. However, previous research, unlike Leinhardt's does not provide us with enough detail for us to say how to teach problem solving. For example, it is very easy to say, "present informal proofs," but Leinhardt's analysis of Patrick enables us to understand what the process of presenting such proofs entails, and the conditions under which different actions should be taken. Leinhardt's analysis doesn't view actions as separate factors that should be thrown into the teacher's bag of tricks. Instead, she observes them in context, paying attention not only to the structure of the processes, but also to the conditions under which they may be useful (cf. Shavelson, 1973; 1976).

COGNITIVE ANALYSIS OF EXPERT TUTORING

Expert tutoring might just be to cognitive research on teaching what the microscope is to the biologist. Tutoring magnifies the teaching of mathematics by its intense concentration on solving problems, by speeding up the teaching process through one-on-one interaction, and by eliminating a large number of the administrative routines required to run a classroom. However, in spite of its potential importance as a rich source of information about teaching, we are only now beginning to learn about the cognitive processes of the tutor (e.g., Putnam, 1987).

Recently, we have begun a systematic analysis of the knowledge and information processing skills of tutors in the area of high-school algebra. Our approach to studying tutoring is shaped by a larger research project aimed at developing an intelligent computer tutor for algebra. This goal forces us to understand the teaching of problem solving at an even more microscopic level than Leinhardt provides. Automating tutoring expertise in an intelligent computer system requires a highly detailed description of the specific cognitive processes and structures involved in making tutorial decisions.

To describe tutoring activities in algebra, we use a knowledge engineering method that extracts detailed information about a target subject from a "domain expert," and then formalizes the information so that it can be implemented as "rules" in an expert system (Duda & Gashnig, 1981). In our tutoring study, we videotape and carefully analyze half-hour sessions with local expert tutors and high school students. The teachers have been selected on the basis of their experience and recognition by their peers. All are highly regarded by their peers, and one has recently received the teacher-of-the-year award from the local school district. To analyze the tapes we use a variant of interaction analysis, a method employed by anthropologists studying group behavior (e.g., Evertson & Green, 1986).

Although our analysis is far from complete, we have identified several distinct types of knowledge that contribute to tutoring expertise, including knowledge of the subject matter (Putnam, 1987), knowledge of the student (Brown & Burton, 1978; Matz, 1982; Sleeman & Smith, 1981), and specific tutoring skills. Knowledge of tutoring skills itself divides into several levels or "tiers", as shown in Table 1. Each tutoring session consists of a sequence of problems worked by the student and tutor. At the highest level, tutors appear to control the selection or generation of problems using a set of knowledge goals (kgoals) they have for the student. Once a problem is selected, tutors use information about the student, and the current problem-solving state, to choose a general kind of tutoring activity or purpose to engage in. In working a single problem, the tutor may engage in several different kinds of activities. Finally, once an activity is decided on, tutors draw on a wide repertoire of local techniques or tactics to accomplish their purposes. We briefly discuss each of these knowledge levels below.

Table 1
Different Levels of Pedagogical Knowledge in Tutoring

Knowledge Type	Main Role
Algebra and problem solving knowledge goals (kgoals).	Generate or select problems for the student.
Strategic purposes in tutoring a problem and the conditions for invoking them.	Control general kinds of tutoring activity in force within a problem.
Tutoring tactics.	Generate a specific tutoring action to fulfill a tutoring purpose or activity.

Knowledge Goals in Tutoring

Most tutoring sessions are organized around a series of problems generated by the tutor. Problems are rarely generated at random; instead each appears to have a "point." Points typically involve one or more "knowledge goals" (kgoals)—concepts that the tutor wants the problem to exemplify and with which the student must come to terms, if he or she solves the problem correctly. The excerpt below demonstrates this level of tutoring expertise in action.

   T: O.K. Let's try another one. O.K. And we want to solve it for a positive X. [T writes $-x > 5$]
   S: Put a + X?

3   T: Yeah, you could. Let's try this one instead. We'll go back to that one. Let's try this one. And you want to solve it for positive X. [T writes $-x = 15$]
   S: [Hesitates].

6   T: O.K. Let me give you another shot at it. I'm thinking of a number and its opposite is -7. What number am I thinking of? [T writes $-x = -7$]
   S: $+7$.

9   T: Great. O.K. I'm thinking of a number and its opposite is -11. What number am I thinking of? [T writes $-x = -11$]
   S: $+11$.

12   T: Good. I'm thinking of a number and its opposite is 21. [T writes $-x = 21$] Don't get caught.
   S: $+21$, no -21.
   T: That's right. So what you did is you just changed the signs in your head and that was perfect.

15   All right. What you could have done is to multiply both sides by negative 1. It doesn't have to be written down but [T writes $(-1)(-x) =$
18   $(-1)(21)$] that's what you could have done. Because if you did that,

the negative 1 and the negative X gives you a positive X and the negative 1 times the 21 gives you [T writes x = −21] a −21. O. K. But you knew how to do that in your head. Now tackle that problem. Back to −X = 15.

S: I would go by negative 15.

21 T: Yeah. O.K. And the way you're reading this is, "I'm thinking of a number and its opposite is 15."

S: So I would do that with 15X?

24 T: No—just what you did when you said it—you did it just fine. "I'm thinking of a number equals . . ."

S: Negative 15. [S writes x = −15]

27 T: That's correct.

S: Oh, I see—O.K.

30 T: O.K. It's opposite of the positive 15 so the number itself is −15. Perfect. O.K. Now, there was a trick to working with inequalities and it was if you multiplied by a negative or if you divided by a negative, the sign changes its direction. So with that in mind let's look at that one [T refers back to the original problem −x < 5].

33 S: [Student writes x < 5]

T: Better look at it one more time. O.K. Put it on the number line.

36 [Student draws correct number line] And this is saying, "I'm thinking— you're thinking of a number, or I'm thinking of a number and its opposite is larger than 5." So the number you're thinking of is less than −5 because they're opposites. It's perfect. O.K., do you want to try some more?

In this excerpt the tutor generated four problems (−x > 5, −x = 15, −x = −7, −x = 11), suspending the first two to do the last two, and returning to the suspended problems when the interpolated problems were completed. The generation of this sequence of problems appears to involve two main kgoals: dealing with implicit −1 coefficients and reversing the inequality sign when multiplying through by a negative number. The original problem, −x > 5, exemplifies both concepts. However, when the student fails to readily answer the problem, the tutor seems to simplify her kgoals for the student using a very general heuristic: If the student has difficulties solving problems that exemplify several significant kgoals, back off to consider problems that exercise each kgoal separately. Thus, the following problems focus only on the kgoal involving negative coefficients. When the tutor judges this kgoal to be accomplished by the student (line 31), both initial kgoals are reinstated, and the first problem is resumed.

Several types of kgoals were observed to impart a continuity to the tutorial sessions. The most obvious ones in the above excerpt involve strictly algebraic concepts, such as changing the direction of the inequality when multiplying through by a negative number. The presentation of these kgoals tends to be relatively rigidly ordered. Some concepts are logically based on others and so should never be tutored before the student is exposed to the prerequisite skills. However, these logical constraints do not completely limit the tutor's generation of problems. The current excerpt, for example, shows that the kgoals the tutor chooses is a joint function of the logical structure of the algebra concepts and the tutor's assessment of which concepts the student misunderstands. We observed several cases where the tutor's kgoals changed during a session apparently because the tutor discovered different algebra concepts that the student did not understand.

In addition to kgoals involving strictly algebraic concepts, we noted the tutor focusing on higher-order problem-solving concepts, or "metacognitive" skills within the algebra domain. Among the kinds of kgoals that fall into this class are: translating problem solutions into alternate representations (to suggest a different approach or perspective), learning skills for self-diagnosis and debugging, answer checking by inserting the solution back into the equation, dividing a problem into subparts, recognizing that there are alternate ways to solve a problem, and hypothesis generation, testing and prediction skills. The tutors' adoption of metacognitive kgoals appears less ordered and more opportunistic than decisions about strictly algebraic goals. Tutors just seem to keep such kgoals in mind and look for opportunities to drive them home. In the current excerpt, for example, the tutor demonstrates the value of rethinking symbolic problems as word problems (lines 6, 9, and 12), and also has the student represent the solution on a number line (line 34). Thus, within a single problem, the tutor may have several different kgoals in mind, and will bring them into play as the opportunity arises.

Tutoring Tactics

Once the problem has been submitted to the student, the flow of control in tutoring changes from a relatively orderly process to an opportunistic one, in which the tutor strikes a balance between meeting the kgoals set for the problem and dealing with local student responses. We see tutoring within each problem as involving two distinct kinds of knowledge. At the lowest level, tutors appear to have a wide repertoire of local techniques for dealing with student problems. Following Ohlsson (1985) we refer to them as *tutoring tactics*, since they are actions aimed at treating specific student difficulties as they arise. The following excerpt from the tapes, with a different tutor and student, exhibits several interesting tutoring tactics and techniques.

Teacher: O.K., do you want to start on number 17? I don't know, have you done these before ever? [The problem is $x/3 = b/2 + c/6$]

3   Student: I think we have, I don't remember.

T: Now usually the thing that bothers most students is fractions. They could do without them. So let us get rid of the fractions.

6   S: O.K.

T: Let us multiply every single term by what we refer to as the least common multiple, something that can divide evenly into all. What do you think that would be?

9   S: 6.

T: 6. So I'm going to divide . . . multiply this by 6, multiply this by 6.

12   And then it will turn into something you'll feel more comfortable with. [S writes $x/3 = b/2 + c/6$] O.K. Now when I   say multiply each term by 7, I'm going to write in parentheses next to the object 6, O.K.? [T writes (6) above and to the left of each of the three division terms in the equation] I'm multiplying each thing by 6. 3 into 6 goes how many times? [T points to the 3 under x, then the parenthesized 6 above it]

15   S: 2.

T: So what are you going to have left?

S: . . .

18   T: 2x [S writes 2x below the x/3]

S: 2x

T: 2 equals . . . 2 goes into 6 how many times? [T points to the 2 under the b, then the parenthesized 6 above it]

21   S: 3

T: So you'll have . . .

24   S: 3b [S writes 3b below the b|2]

T: That's right.

T: 6 into 6 goes . . . [T points to the 6 in 6/c, then the parenthesized 6 above it]

27   S: Once.

T: So, you'll just have a c. [S writes c below the c/6. S now has constructed a new line equation: $2x = eb + c$]

T: See now you'll feel much more comfortable with that, you've just been doing that all along.

30   Right?

S: Right.

T: So now once you eliminate the fractions, everything else is like what we've been doing before.

33   The only other thing remaining to do is to do what to both sides?

S: Divide?

T: By . . .

36   S: 2. [S writes x = (3b + c)/2]
     T: Good.

In this excerpt, the tutor is coaching the student to complete a single step in a problem. The excerpt's most salient property is the remarkable intensity of the interaction. The discussion does not focus directly on obtaining the right answer, or even on the correct next visible step in the solution (i.e., going from x/3 = b/2 + c/6 to 2x = 3b + c). Instead, the student and tutor join in a discussion of the reasoning processes required to make the next algebraic transformation.

Reasoning discussions appear to be focused on the several kinds of problem features and cognitive objects including:

- Problem conditions. The properties of the current algebraic expression that should be attended to in deciding upon the next thing to do.
- Procedures. The specific procedure that should be invoked at a point in solving the problem (e.g., "factor this expression").
- Concepts. Mathematical concepts, like the notion of an additive inverse of reciprocal of a fraction. Concepts are usually mentioned when they are relevant to the current reasoning.
- Hierarchical goals structures. The goals and subgoals that should, or could, be adopted at a particular point in problem solving. Figure 5 gives an abbreviated representation of the goal structure for the current excerpt.

The excerpt exemplifies several important tactics concerning how goal structures are used by tutors to guide reasoning discussions. First, the tutor uses the tactic of organizing discussions of goal structures in a top-down fashion. In discussing the goals for the next step, the tutor does not begin with a low-level description of the mathematical transformation to effect (e.g., multiplying each term by 6). Rather, she begins (in lines 4–5) by mentioning the higher-level goal—eliminating fractions—that should be achieved. Moreover, several intermediate levels in the goal structure may be mentioned before the tutor begins to discuss the actual algebraic manipulations.

Second, the tutor demonstrates several tactics that vary the relative contributions of the tutor and student in deciding and satisfying each goal. The goal of eliminating fractions is simply given by the tutor, presumably because she thinks that decision may be difficult for the student. On the other hand, finding the least common multiple is prompted for by the tutor, but is satisfied by the student (lines 8–9). Similarly, the goal of reducing terms is shared by the student and tutor, with the tutor mentioning the terms to divide, and the student simply carrying out the divisions and writing the results (lines 13–27).

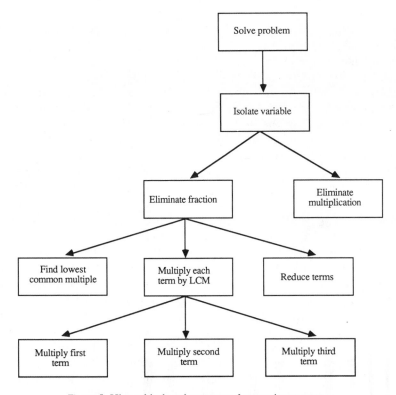

Figure 5. Hierarchical goal structures for tutoring excerpt

Third, once the tutor and student have collectively discussed and implemented the goals, arriving at a new step in the solution (line 28), the tutor
does not simply go on to the next step, but reminds the student of the reason
for the low-level multiplications and simplifications, namely to get rid of the
fractions (line 32). In other words, once the student and tutor have proceeded down the hierarchical goal structure for this step, the tutor again
focuses the discussion on higher-level goals. This time the tactical intent
behind discussing the high-level goals is not to help the student determine
which lower-level actions to do next, but rather to provide a *justification* for
the reasoning that has just been accomplished.

It is apparent from the different tutoring interactions we have observed
that the richness of the hierarchical goal structures affords varied kinds of
reasoning discussions. Different tutors adopt distinctly different tactical
styles or default levels of coaching or support. Similarly, a single tutor may
change the tactical level of coaching between or within problems.

Strategic Tutoring Purposes

The previous section briefly analyzed local tutoring exchanges and
attempted to point out some of the tactics tutors use to control the sessions

on a local basis. However, this level of analysis does not explain why they adopt the different actions, or how they decide when to adopt one tactic and not another. Our observations suggest that tutors choose tactics by first deciding upon a particular strategic tutoring purpose. The purpose is determined by attending to various conditions in the tutoring situation, such as the current state of the student (e.g., Did the student just make an error?), and past history (Has the student made several mistakes in a row?). Once a tutorial purpose is selected, that decision is gradually refined into the selection of a specific tutoring tactic.

The long excerpt above exemplifies three tutoring purposes. In lines 1–3 the tutor is engaged in *knowledge assessment*, or adding to her understanding of the student's general level of competence and specific skill deficits. In this case, it appears the tutor has inferred (or supported an existing inference) that this student may be unfamiliar with the manipulation of algebraic fractions. Inferences about student knowledge can be used for many purposes. One use in evidence here is to support the *kgoal modification*. As noted above, the tutor may begin a session with some predetermined knowledge goals for the student, but may decide to refine, or more radically change them, on the basis of the student's performance within the session. In this case, the tutor may have decided, on the basis of the brief discussion (lines 1–3), that the student's skills for removing fractions were weak, or the tutor may have simply confirmed an expectation she already had at the beginning of the session. Thus, steps involving fractions will receive much more discussion in tutoring. Once this activity is terminated, the remainder of the excerpt comprises what we refer to as a *reasoning support* activity. Consistent with the tutor's knowledge assessment and kgoals, most of the support is directed at helping the student reason about fractions. As noted above, several tactics are deployed for this purpose.

In addition to knowledge assessment, kgoal modification, and reasoning support, we have observed the following strategic tutoring activities:

- Problem solution. When the tutor begins a problem we assume he or she solves it mentally before presenting it to the student, or is so familiar with the problem type that the solution is automatic and the solution path(s) well known. The tutor's solution probably tags particular steps as problematic, and may also incorporate information about the common types of errors the students might make (see Clark, Snow, & Shavelson, 1976; Stein, Brown, & Berliner, 1986).

- Performance maintenance. Performance maintenance refers to tutoring responses designed to orient the student, maintain the pace of the tutoring session, and maintain the student's affect and level of motivation.

- Performance evaluation. Performance evaluations provide the student with feedback regarding the correctness of his or her action.

- Reasoning remediation. Remedial activities are highly interactive tutoring exchanges where the main goal of the tutor appears to be to help the student fix his or her most recent reasoning step.

Many tutoring tactics can be used for several strategic tutoring purposes. Table 2 lists some of the tutoring tactics used for remedial tutorial purposes. Many of the same tactics can be used when the tutor is supporting, as opposed to fixing, the student's reasoning, or when the tutor is simply describing his or her own solutions.

Table 2
A Partial List of Remedial Tutoring Tactics

Tactic name	Description
Modeling exemplary reasoning	The tutor does the reasoning for the step. This includes detailed discussions of the goals satisfied, the properties of the problem that would trigger their selection, as well as the algebraic transformation that results.
Coaching exemplary reason	The student and tutor share in the construction of the goal structure for the next step. Depending on how much help the tutor believes the student needs, the student may take more or less responsibility for establishing and implementing goals.
Redirecting student goals	The tutor suggests the student adopted the wrong goal (e.g., isolating the variable rather than collecting terms), and suggests the correct one.
Explaining negative reasoning consequences	The tutor tells the student that the low-level action the student took actually satisfies an inappropriate higher-level goal (e.g., "Well, b/x would be correct, but we want the x to stand alone. If put b/x it would turn into a 1, I want x to stand alone, so it would simply be simply b/1.")
Comparing question and reasoning similarities	The tutor suggests to the student that a previous question, and the reasoning and goals that were used to solve it, are appropriate for the current problem. Specific aspects of the reasoning or the question may be referenced.
Modifying questions	The tutor highlights the student's error by changing the question so that the student's reasoning is now correct. Often this helps the student see the nature of their slip.

Strategic tutoring purposes appear to be largely data-driven in character. Specifically, they appear triggered mainly by events that arise in the tutoring session (e.g., a specific student error), and are less governed by enduring constraints (e.g., a lesson plan). This contrasts with classroom teaching, where activities seem much more controlled by long-term plans (e.g., Shavelson & Stern, 1981; Leinhardt & Greeno, 1986) and little opportunistic learning and tutoring arises.

Some Hypotheses

While this research is still in the formative stage it seems to offer promise in telling us how to tutor mathematical problem solving, or at least it leads to some testable hypotheses about teaching, including:

1. Explicitly discussing the goals students should be pursuing while solving a problem will lead to better problem-solving performance than if just the visible steps they must produce are discussed.
2. At least for beginning students, discussing goals in a top-down fashion from higher-level concepts (e.g., eliminate fractions) to intermediate goals, to lower level algebraic manipulations, will result in better problem-solving performance than if discussions proceed from bottom-up or are randomly organized.
3. As the student proceeds down the hierarchy of goal structures in solving the problem, reinforcing the higher-level goals as a means of justifying lower-level goals or manipulations will produce better problem-solving performance than if such justifications are omitted.
4. Fading, or decreasing the coaching of the student as a function of the student's increasing proficiency, produces better problem-solving performance than more abrupt removal of support, as it enables the student to gradually take on more of the problem-solving activity and practice new or relearned skills.
5. Sharing problem solving with the student, assigning the student certain key decisions, while the tutor takes care of other operations of less pedagogical importance, will lead to better performance than if the student is required to make all problem-solving decisions himself or herself.
6. Modeling exemplary reasoning, by discussing goals and the properties of the problem that suggest those goals, will produce better problem-solving performance than if the tutor just shows correct answers to problems.
7. Engaging in multiple tutorial purposes, including knowledge assessment, reasoning support and remediation, and others will produce better student performance than if the tutor just provides the students feedback about the correctness of their solutions.
8. Selecting simpler problems that exemplify one knowledge goal at a time, when the student has recently made errors on complex problems will result in better learning than if the tutor persists in giving additional complex problems.
9. Opportunistically demonstrating metacognitive kgoals in the course of working towards structured domain-specific goals (e.g., tutoring specific algebraic concepts) will produce better problem-solving performance than simply focusing on the domain-specific kgoals.
10. Translating among alternative symbolic representations of a problem (math symbols and number line) will lead to better problem-solving performance than working with just one symbolic form.

COGNITIVE ANALYSIS OF TEACHING DURING SMALL-GROUP PROBLEM SOLVING

The study of small-group problem solving provides another lens for a microscopic analysis of teaching mathematical problem solving. It has many attributes of tutoring research and some of classroom teaching, and more. It is an excellent setting to study students' problem-solving processes because it avoids directions to "think aloud": students freely verbalize their thoughts to one another. Having just solved the problem themselves, some students are in an excellent position to understand what their peers don't know—perhaps better than teachers and tutors.

Although small-group problem solving shares some features with expert classroom teaching and expert tutoring, it is a different setting in fundamental ways. First, "teacher" and "student" roles are not assigned, or formalized during group processes, although some studies have shown that the most able student in a group often assumes a "teacher" role (Webb, 1982). Instead, students are typically given instructions to help each other, and to ask each other for help. Second, although some group members may be more proficient than others, there is usually no formally recognized "expert." Students may be quick to assess each others' competence (usually correctly) even when they don't know each other (see Webb, 1980a) and may even designate some group members as helpers, but expert roles are not publicly announced in advance. And third, unlike expert teachers and tutors, students in small groups do not receive training in teaching. Teaching occurs spontaneously.

Small-group problem solving might not involve formal teacher-learner relationships, but teachers establish small groups in the classroom with the intent of having students learn from each other. Given the differences between small-group problem solving and expert classroom teaching and tutoring, analyses of small-group problem solving may yield some insights into teaching mathematics problem solving that do not appear in these other, structured teaching situations.

None of the studies on small-group problem solving have explored in detail how students teach each other. Instead, the most detailed analyses of small-group teaching behavior from audio or videotaped records or detailed observations have only distinguished between kinds of helping behavior at a general level: explanations describing how to solve a problem (consistently found to be beneficial for the explainer's learning but not necessarily the receiver's) and nonelaborated comments or answers to questions that typically provide an answer to a problem without any description of how to solve the problem (found to be unrelated to the help-giver's learning and detrimental to the help-seeker's learning (see Webb, 1982). These analyses give few insights into how to teach mathematical problem solving.

Consequently, we undertook new analyses to reveal the kinds of "teaching" behavior that student peers engage in spontaneously. The intent here is to show whether and how peer teaching shares common elements with expert classroom teaching and expert tutoring and to show teaching activities that may be unique to the peer setting.

The Small-Group Setting and Mathematical Task

The data on peer interaction comes from a study of small groups of 11th-grade students assembled to learn a novel mathematical task (see Webb, 1980a, 1980b, 1980c). The two groups used here for illustration consisted of four students each (all females) with mixed ability levels: one high, two medium, and one low. All students were above-average on national norms, however, so the ability designations are relative. These students, then, represent a select portion of the student population.

These groups were selected specifically because they were known from previous analyses to give frequent explanations and were expected to reveal interesting teaching behavior. We looked at many group protocols from other studies with students that were more representative of national populations (e.g., wider range of ability, varied ethnic and cultural backgrounds; Webb, 1984; Webb & Kenderski, 1984, 1985). But, for a variety of reasons, including poor descriptions of the problems students were supposed to solve and lack of skills among the students in many groups, students in these groups exhibited little teaching. Instead, the interaction in many groups demonstrated the "blind leading the blind" often with incorrect or incomplete explanations (see also Noddings, 1985). Even though the groups analyzed here have unusual characteristics—mixed-ability groups of bright students who all had considerable mathematical skill—recall that we are looking for unique examples of teaching and not attempting to generalize from sample to universe of teaching in small problem-solving groups.

The mathematical task for each group was to calculate an algebraic expression for the nth polygonal number. The nth polygonal number is the total number of dots in an array of polygons, in which the outermost polygon has n dots on each side. A sketch of the array for the nth triangular number appears in Figure 6. The smallest triangle has two dots on each side, and each successively larger triangle has one more dot on each side. The nth triangular number is the total number of dots in an array of triangles in which the outermost triangle has n dots on each side. The number of dots forms an arithmetic series: $1 + 2 + 3 +$ series. The complete algorithm that students were taught to use appears in Table 3. Prior to group work, students were trained very well individually on parts of the problem as separate tasks (e.g., how to draw the array, how to calculate the sum of an arithmetic series). During group work, students had to put together the pieces that they had learned to find the nth hexagonal, nth pentagonal, and nth triangular numbers.

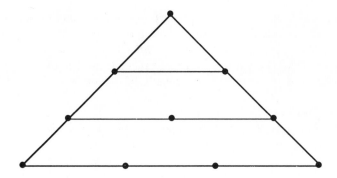

Figure 6. Array for the *n*th triangular number (Reprinted from Webb [1980c] with permission)

Table 3
Algorithm for Calculating the nth Triangular Number

Step I.	Draw the array of triangles.
	(1) Draw a triangle.
	(2) Starting at one vertex, draw a line from the vertex to an adjacent vertex and continue the line past the adjacent vertex for a short distance.
	(3) Starting at the vertex in (2), draw a line from that vertex to the other adjacent vertex, and continue the line past the adjacent vertex for a short distance.
	(4) Connect the ends of the lines drawn in (2) and (3) with a straight line.
Step II.	Mark the correct number of dots on each side.
	(1) On the innermost triangle mark a dot at each vertex.
	(2) On the second triangle, add dots such that each side has three dots on each side.
Step III.	Decompose the array of dots into layers of dots.
	(1) The first layer is the dot on the vertex common to both triangles.
	(2) The second layer contains all dots in the innermost triangle except the dot in the first layer.
	(3) The third layer contains all dots in the second triangle except the dots in the first and second layers.
Step IV.	Calculate the difference *d* between consecutive layer ($d = 1$).
Step V.	Calculate the formula for the nth term of the arithmetic series whose terms are the layers in III.
	(1) The general formula is $a + (n-1)d$, where *a* is number of dots in the first layer, and *d* is the difference calculated in step IV. No number is substituted for *n*. (The n_{th} term of the series is $1 + (n-1)1$ or *n*.)
Step VI.	Calculate the formula for the sum of the arithmetic series.
	(1) The general formula is $\dfrac{(a + n^{th} \text{ term})}{2} \times n$
	where *a*, n^{th} term, and *n* are defined in Step V.
	(The sum of the series is $\dfrac{(1 + n)}{2} \times n$ or $\dfrac{n + n^2}{2}$)

Reprinted from Webb (1980c) with permission.

Structure of Small-Group Problem-Solving Process

The groups generally showed two phases in their interaction. The first phase consisted of problem solving, in which group members worked on the problem until at least one of them obtained a solution or understood the solution procedure. Groups tended to start immediately to try to solve the problem, with little planning or description of the goal. Typically, one or two members of the group talked aloud as they solved the problem. Little teaching occurred during this phase. Although there were some elaborated answers to questions, students seemed to give these elaborations to justify their solution or problem-solving procedures, rather than to teach another student.

The only aspect of work in the first phase that was noteworthy was the constant interruptions between students, which is reminiscent of the frequent interruptions during expert tutoring described in the previous section. In contrast to expert tutoring settings, however, the interruptions did not always have a monitoring function. Rather, they consisted of questions of clarification ("Why did you do that?"), challenges of another student's work ("No, it can't be that"), or offers of alternative answers ("No, the first one is one").

The second phase started when at least one group member obtained the correct solution or understood how to do so. The demarcation between phases was usually clear (for example, "Ahhh. I get it. They put the two equations together. They put this one . . . whatever that solves, and then they also stuck it in that $a + (n-1)d$."). This phase consisted of explanations to other students so that they could solve the problems. Most of the teaching activity between students occurred during this phase. The intent of many explanations during this phase was clearly to help another group member understand how to solve the problem. The peer teaching activities described below, then, come from the second phase of group work.

Peer Teaching Activities

By and large, the peer teaching activities observed in small-group problem solving consisted of many of those discussed earlier for expert classroom teaching—including activating prior knowledge, using multiple representations of the mathematical concepts, coordinating and translating between representation, evaluating problem-solving performance, rehearsing with other problems or problem types, and informal proofs; and for expert tutoring—including immediate interruptions of students' problem-solving performance, requests for justification and remedial feedback.

Many kinds of teaching activities occurred even within a single teaching episode. For example, the following episode demonstrates, first, the use of multiple representations of the same concept—"$n-1$" is algebraic, the drawing of the triangles is geometric, the specific example of "$4-1$" is numeric—and coordination between them. Second, the "teacher" used the example of a different (and simpler) problem type as illustration (triangles instead of hexagons). Third, she generalized from specific numerical relationships ("if you had 5 dots, then you'd just have 4 drawings") to the general principle (the number of dots on a side is one more than the number of polygons in the figure) in an inductive fashion:

A: n − 1 is the total number of hexagons?

B: Yeah. Remember, like if you have a triangle like that (draws picture) . . . And then you have a triangle like that, right? So you have four sides, I mean dots on side, right. n equals the number of dots. 4 − 1 is gonna equal how many triangles you have. That triangle in there, and you have this one, and then you have that one. Three. Now it works the same for hexagons.

A: That's triangles?

B: See this thing right here?

A: Yeah, yeah.

B: That's a triangle. Then there's this thing . . . is a triangle.

A: So that's 3 − 1 and 2 − 1.

B: Yeah, that will work for anything. For every time you put figures connecting all the dots.

A: Then, what's the n? Then the n is just n.

B: Is just the number of dots on one of the sides.

A: Yeah.

B: So, if you had 5 dots, then you'd just have 4 drawings.

C: So . . . then n − 1 will give you how many hexagons you have.

A: Just the number of hexagons. O.K., I get it.

Although much of the behavior observed in peer teaching activities was similar to that observed in expert teaching and tutoring situations, the groups showed unique aspects as well. Perhaps most important, although not specifically a teaching activity, is the freedom students felt to (a) admit that they did not know how or understand how to solve the problem ("You can write it out but I still don't understand it"), (b) control the pace of group problem solving and teaching when they did not understand ("Wait, I'm lost", "Wait, stop, wait a second"; see also Noddings, 1985), (c) control the content of explanations ("So why do they have n − 1?"), and (d) challenge other students' work and explanations ("That can't be right"). These activities are seldom, if ever, observed in expert teaching and tutoring settings.

Another unique aspect of small-group problem solving is that students were well "tuned into" each others' problem-solving processes (Vedder, 1985). Because they had just solved the same problems, or were in the process of doing so, they easily understood where others went wrong or didn't understand. "Tuning into pupils' problem-solving processes to a very detailed level" is one of the fundamental conditions for good teaching and for efficient cooperative learning, a variation of small-group problem solving, according to Vedder (1985, p. 40). When a student asked a question, the others understood immediately what was meant. When a student made an error, other group members immediately challenged and/or corrected it. Furthermore, students translated mathematical or unfamiliar terms into their own language (for example, referring to a "bunch of hexagons" or drawing a picture instead of using the term "array" that was used in the problem) so that they could readily understand each other (see also Noddings, 1985, for discussion of the importance of interpreting the vocabulary of the problem).

In addition to looking at teaching activities that probably are beneficial for learning, it is also important to look at activities that occur during small-group problem solving that may be detrimental to learning. First, evident in these groups (and informally observed in most other groups) was the failure to assess whether students really understood the explanations. The explainers often seemed to rely on students' own admission of whether they understood ("O.K., I get it", "Oh, right"), which might not have been accurate. The most accurate indication of another student's understanding may have been the ability to solve a problem correctly by herself. Yet students (like expert tutors) rarely allowed students to solve a problem without "help."

Another detrimental set of activities that often occurs in small-group problem solving is the failure to give students adequate help when they need it, which is consistently shown to be negatively related to achievement (Webb, 1982, 1983). The kinds of events that fall into this category include asking a question and receiving no response, making an error and either not being corrected or being told the correct answer without being given an explanation of how to obtain it, and asking for an explanation and receiving only a brief response (e.g., the correct answer) without any elaboration.

The analyses of small-group problem solving, then, lead to the following hypotheses. Problem solving will be enhanced by:

1. Using and coordinating multiple representations of a problem within an explanation of a specific concept (e.g., algebraic, numeric, and geometric representations of "$n - 1$ = number of hexagons"). It is less clear whether multiple representations flexibility should be maintained in explanations of procedures. Students stayed within a single symbolic representation (e.g., algebraic) when explaining or modeling multiple steps.

2. Using specific examples to illustrate general concepts (e.g., illustrating "$n - 1$ equals the number of hexagons" with a single hexagon, two hexagons, and so forth).

3. Constructing the learning setting in such a way as to encourage students to freely control the pace and content of the teaching activities.

4. "Tuning into" students' problem-solving processes, so that errors and gaps in understanding can be corrected immediately (e.g., pro-

ceeding through the problem solution immediately before trying to monitor a student's solution process or explaining the solution process; see Vedder, 1985).

5. Translating unusual or unfamiliar vocabulary into language that students are familiar with (e.g., "drawing" or "bunch of hexagons" instead of "array"; see Noddings, 1985).

6. Assessing whether students understand how to solve the problem by giving them opportunities to solve problems by themselves, without interruptions (see Vedder, 1985).

7. Responding to all questions.

8. Responding to all indications of misunderstanding or incomplete understanding (errors, statements of confusion—"I don't get this", and questions—"How did you get d = 4?") with explanations (elaborated descriptions) instead of brief responses or only the correct answer.

We have only begun to capture the richness of teaching in small problem-solving groups. Although there is much overlap with expert teaching and tutoring settings, we have observed some unique aspects as well.

CONCLUSIONS

We set out to discover important aspects of practical theories of teaching mathematical problem solving, in an attempt to address the question, "How do you teach mathematical problem solving?" We studied expert teachers and tutors, reasoning that experts have invented theories that have withstood the acid test of the classroom or other real-world settings. We also studied students teaching one another in small problem-solving groups, reasoning that these students, being closer to the difficulties of learning to solve new classes of problems than adults, might come up with some unique teaching techniques. Our research sites, then, included classrooms, teacher-student tutorials, and small problem-solving groups.

We found a number of things that experts did to teach problem solving that appeared to be important. Hence, we hypothesized that if teachers taught in the manner suggested, their teaching of mathematical problem solving would be improved over what they currently do (unless, of course, they already do these things). Certain important features of teaching problem solving appeared in all three research sites, suggesting their stability and robustness. These features included:

1. Activating students' prior knowledge relevant to teaching a new concept (e.g., activating addition concept with accent on base 10 in preparation to teaching subtraction with regrouping).

2. Using multiple representations to teach a mathematical concept

(e.g., using mathematical symbols, numbers, geometric figures as alternative representations of a concept).

3. Coordinating and translating among alternative representations so that students see a concept in multiple ways (e.g., base 10 notions by translating back and forth between bundles of (10) sticks, felt strips, and numbers).

4. Evaluating problem-solving performance in an ongoing manner.

5. Providing informal proofs (e.g., the equality of alternative representations of a two-digit number: 42 or 4|2 or 3|12).

6. Providing detailed explanations and justifications of reasoning in problem solving (e.g., discussing various goals involved in deciding the next step in solving an equation).

7. Using specific examples to illustrate a general concept (e.g., illustrating "$n - 1$" equals the number of hexagons with a single hexagon, two hexagons, and so on).

8. Tuning into students' problem-solving processes so that errors and gaps in understanding can be corrected immediately.

These features of teaching mathematical problem solving are obviously incomplete. Stating the features one at a time loses the sense of well orchestrated teaching and tutoring, and the richness of the descriptions provided by the research and so needed in helping teachers acquire the knowledge and skills to teach problem solving. Moreover, these features are stated generally without the conditions that lead to their activation, conditions also available in research protocols. Bolstered with concrete, well contextualized examples from research protocols, we suspect these features of teaching problem solving would prove quite helpful to teachers trying to improve how they teach mathematics.

FOOTNOTES

1. We speak of theories and not theory because there are probably as many invented theories of mathematical problem solving as there are expert teachers. Nevertheless, we suspect there is overlap among these theories and that, at some level of abstraction, they can be integrated into a more general theory. But we are years away from the general practical theory, and to force the many theories into some common framework would block progress. We need to understand individual experts' practical theories very well before attempting to build a more general theory.

2. A number of recent reviews of the research on teaching are more or less relevant to teaching mathematics (e.g., Brophy & Good, 1986; Romberg & Carpenter, 1986; Bell, Costello, & Kuchemann, 1980; Cooney, 1980; Romberg, Small, & Carnahan, 1979; Suydam & Osborn, 1977); few reviews are relevant to teaching mathematical problem solving (but see Silver, 1985).

3. This section draws heavily on the work of Gaea Leinhardt. Note that she used residualized achievement-test means, as well as other criteria, to identify her expert teachers.

4. Some process-product research provides parallel qualitative analyses that begin to answer the "how" question (e.g., Berliner & Tikunoff, 1976, 1977; Good et al., 1983).

REFERENCES

Aronson, E. (1978). *The Jigsaw Classroom.* Beverly Hills, CA: Sage.

Bell, A. W., Costello, J., & Kuchemann, D. E. (1980). *A review of research in mathematics education.* Nottingham, England: Shell Centre for Mathematical Education.

Berliner, D. C. (1986). In pursuit of the expert pedagogue. *Educational Researcher, 15,* 5–13.

Brophy, J. (1986). Teaching and learning mathematics: Where research should be going. *Journal for Research in Mathematics Education, 17,* 323–346.

Brophy, J. E., & Good, T. L. (1986). Teacher behavior and student achievement. In M. W. Wittrock (Ed.), *Handbook of research on teaching* (Third edition). (pp. 328–375). New York: Macmillan.

Brown, J. S., & Burton, R. R. (1978). Diagnostic models for procedural bugs in basic mathematical skills. *Cognitive Science, 2,* 155–192.

Calderhead, J., & Miller, E. (1985, September). *The interaction of subject matter knowledge in student teachers' classroom practice.* Paper presented at the annual meeting of the British Educational Research Association, University of Sheffield.

Clark, C. M., & Peterson, P. L. (1986). Teachers' thought processes. In M. W. Wittrock (Ed.), *Handbook of research on teaching* (Third edition). (pp. 255–296). New York: Macmillan.

Clark, C. M., Snow, R. E., & Shavelson, R. J. (1976). Three experiments on learning to teach. *Journal of Teacher Education, 27,* 174–180.

Collins, A., Brown, J. S., & Newman, S. E. (in press). Cognitive apprenticeship: Teaching the craft of reading, writing, and mathematics. In L. B. Resnick (Ed.), *Cognition and instruction: Issues and agendas.* Hillsdale, NJ: Lawrence Erlbaum.

Cooney, T. (1980). Research on teaching and teacher education. In R. Shumway (Ed.), *Research in mathematics education* (pp. 433–474). Reston, VA: National Council of Teachers of Mathematics.

Duda, R., & Gashnig, J. (1981). Knowledge-based systems come of age. *Byte, 6,* 231–281.

Everston, C. M., & Green, J. L. (1986). Observation as inquiry and method. In M. C. Wittrock (Ed.), *Handbook for research on teaching* (Third edition). (pp. 162–213). New York: Macmillan.

Good, T., & Grouws, D. (1975). *Process-product relationship in fourth grade mathematics classes.* (NIE Final Report). Columbia, MO: Center for Research in Social Behavior.

Good, T., & Grouws, D. (1979). Teaching effects: A process-product study in fourth grade mathematics classrooms. *Journal of Teacher Education, 28,* 49–54.

Leinhardt, G. (1986). Expertise in mathematics teaching. *Educational Leadership, 43,* 28–33.

Leinhardt, G. (in press, a). The development of an expert explanation: An analysis of a sequence of subtraction lessons. *Cognition and Instruction.*

Leinhardt, G. (in press, b). Math lessons: A contrast of novice and expert competence. *Journal for Research in Mathematics Education.*

Leinhardt, G., & Greeno, J. G. (1986). The cognitive skill of teaching. *Journal of Educational Psychology, 78,* 75–95.

Leinhardt, G., & Smith, D. A. (1985). Expertise in mathematics instruction: Subject matter knowledge. *Journal of Educational Psychology, 77,* 247–271.

Matz, M. (1982). Towards a process model for high school algebra errors. In D. H. Sleeman & J. S. Brown (Eds.), *Intelligent tutoring systems* (pp. 25–50). New York: Academic Press.

McArthur, D., Stasz, C., Hotta, J., Peter, O., & Burdorf, C. (in preparation). Skill-oriented lesson control for basic algebra.

Noddings, N. (1985). Small groups as a setting for research on mathematical problem solving. In E. Silver (Ed.), *Teaching and learning mathematical problem solving: Multiple research perspectives* (pp. 345–359). Hillsdale, NJ: Erlbaum.

Ohlsson, S. (1985). Some principles of intelligent tutoring. *Instructional Science, 14,* 293–326.

Putnam, R. T. (1987). Structuring and adjusting content for students: A study of live and simulated tutoring of addition, *American Educational Research Journal, 24,* (1), 13–48.

Romberg, T. A., & Carpenter, T. P. (1986). Research on teaching and learning mathematics: Two disciplines of scientific inquiry. In M. W. Wittrock (Ed.), *Handbook of research on teaching* (Third edition). (pp. 850–873). New York: Macmillan.

Romberg, T. A., Small, M., & Carnahan, R. (1979). *Research on teaching from a curricular perspective* (Theoretical Paper No. 81). Madison, Wisconsin: Research and Development Center for Individualized Schooling.

Shavelson, R. J. (1973). What is the basic skill of teaching? *Journal of Teacher Education, 14*, 144–151.

Shavelson, R. J. (1976). Teacher's decision making. In N. L. Gage (Ed.), *The psychology of teaching methods,* Seventy-fifth Yearbook of the National Society for the Study of Education, Part I. (pp. 372–414). Chicago: University of Chicago Press.

Shavelson, R. J. (1983). Review of research on teachers' pedagogical judgments, plans, and decisions. *The Elementary School Journal, 83*, 392–413.

Shavelson, R. J. (1986, June 19). *Interactive decisionmaking: Some thoughts on teacher cognition.* Invited address, I Congreso Internacional, "Pensamientos de los Profesores y Toma de Decisiones," Seville, Spain.

Shavelson, R. J., McDonnell, L., & Oakes, J. (in press). *Considerations in developing a national indicator system for monitoring mathematics and science education.* Santa Monica: The RAND Corporation.

Shavelson, R. J., & Stern, P. (1981). Research on teachers' pedagogical thoughts, judgments, decisions and behavior. *Review of Educational Research, 51*, 455–498.

Shavelson, R. J., Webb, N. M., & Burstein, L. (1986). Measurement of teaching. In M. W. Wittrock (Ed.), *Handbook of research on teaching* (Third edition). (pp. 50–91). New York: Macmillan.

Shulman, L. S. (1985). On teaching problem solving and solving problems of teaching. In E. Silver (Ed.), *Teaching and learning mathematical problem solving: Multiple research perspectives* (pp. 439–450). Hillsdale, NJ: Erlbaum.

Shulman, L. S. (1986). Those who understand: Knowledge growth in teaching. *Educational Researcher, 15*, 4–14.

Shulman, L. S. (1987). Knowledge and teaching: Foundations of the new reform. *Harvard Educational Review, 57*, 1–22.

Silver, E. A. (Ed.). (1985). *Teaching and learning mathematical problem solving: Multiple research perspectives.* Hillsdale, NJ: Erlbaum.

Sleeman, D. H., & Smith, M. J. (1981). Modeling student's problem solving. *Artificial Intelligence, 16*, 171–188.

Stein, P. A., Brown, P., & Berliner, D. (1986). Teacher estimation of student knowledge: Accuracy, content and process. In D. Berliner (chair), *Differences in the information processing of expert and novice teachers.* Symposium presented at the annual meeting of the Rocky Mountain Educational Research Association.

Suydam, M., & Osborne, A. (1977). *The status of pre-college science, mathematics, and social studies education: 1955–1975* (Vol. 2, Mathematics education). Columbus: The Ohio State University Center for Science and Mathematics Education.

Vedder, P. (1985). *Cooperative learning: A study on processes and effects of cooperation between primary school children.* Westerhaven Groningen, Netherlands: Rijkuniversiteit Groningen.

Webb, N. M. (1980a). A process-outcome analysis of learning in group and individual settings. *Educational Psychologist, 15*, 69–83.

Webb, N. M. (1980b). An analysis of group interaction and mathematical errors in heterogeneous ability groups. *British Journal of Educational Psychology, 50*, 266–276.

Webb, N. M. (1980c). Group process and learning in an interacting group. *The Quarterly Newsletter of the Institute for Comparative Human Cognition, 2*, 10–15.

Webb, N. M. (1982). Student interaction and learning in small groups. *Review of Educational Research, 52*, 421–445.

Webb, N. M. (1983). Predicting learning from student interaction: Defining the interaction variables. *Educational Psychologist, 18*, 33–41.

Webb, N. M. (1984). Stability of small group interaction and achievement over time. *Journal of Educational Psychology, 76*, 211–224.

Webb, N. M., & Kenderski, C. M. (1984). Student interaction and learning in small-group and whole-class settings. In P. L. Peterson, L. C. Wilkinson, & M. Hallinan (Eds.), *The social context of instruction* (pp. 153–170).

Webb, N. M., & Kenderski, C. M. (1985). Gender differences in small-group interaction and achievement in high- and low-achieving classes. In L. C. Wilkinson, & C. B. Marrett (Eds.), *Gender differences in classroom interaction* (pp. 209–236). New York: Academic Press.

Welch, W. (1978). Science teaching in Urbanville: A case study. In R. Stake & J. Easley (Eds.), *Case studies in science education*. Urbana, IL: University of Illinois.

Learning to Teach Mathematical Problem Solving: Changes in Teachers' Conceptions and Beliefs

Alba G. Thompson
Illinois State University

Despite the large amount of research on mathematical problem solving relatively few studies have addressed instruction in problem solving, and of these only a few have considered the role of the classroom teacher. For the most part, studies related to problem-solving instruction have been based on the writings of Polya (1957, 1981) and have focused on instructional methods designed to develop global thinking and reasoning processes, specific skills, and general and task-specific heuristics (Lester, 1980; 1985). Because the purpose of such studies has been to determine the relative effectiveness of instructional methods, there has been a tendency to control for the effect of the teacher. Reports of instructional studies in problem solving have generally lacked good descriptions of what actually happened in the classroom (except for those in which programmed instructional booklets were used) and have often failed to assess the direct effectiveness of instruction. Rather than assessing whether or not students exhibited thinking and behaviors modeled in instruction, instead they have assessed the number of problems solved correctly on a posttest (Silver, 1987). As a result, our knowledge of desirable instructional practices in problem solving is mostly of folklore rather than research evidence.

In the first part of this paper I summarize some very general notions about instruction that have come out of research on mathematical problem solving. The remainder of the paper is devoted to issues related to the preparation of teachers. I devote a considerable amount of space to the description of a study whose purpose was to document changes in teachers' conceptions of problem solving. This description provides the context for raising some pertinent issues and arguing for their inclusion in our research agenda.

WHAT WE KNOW ABOUT TEACHING PROBLEM SOLVING FROM RESEARCH

In a retrospective account of research on teaching mathematical problem solving, Kilpatrick (1985) noted that "research over the last two and a half decades has not provided much explicit guidance to the teacher in matching teaching techniques to goals, but it has clearly shown that one cannot expect to accomplish one goal in problem solving by teaching for another" (p. 11). He acknowledged that we have gained a better understanding of the highly complex nature of problem solving, and how difficult it is to improve problem-solving performance. We have become aware of the importance of getting students to shift to an active role and of providing a congenial environment for problem solving (Kilpatrick, 1985).

There is a consensus among mathematics educators that improving students' problem-solving performance requires more than simply giving students lots of problems to solve. Schoenfeld (1985) suggests that much of the complexity of learning and teaching problem solving is due to the fundamental interconnections that the learner must make among:

- his/her mathematical resources (e.g., knowledge of concepts, facts, and procedures);
- heuristics (methods and rules of mathematical invention and discovery);
- control mechanisms necessary to manage these resources and processes;
- beliefs the learner holds about the nature of mathematics, in general, and of problem solving in particular; and,
- a variety of contextual and affective factors that bear on problem-solving performance.

If teaching for problem solving involves more than providing students with problems, then we must answer the question of how to help students in each of the above areas and help them establish the necessary interconnections among the areas. While research has shed light on the cognitive demands problem solving places on an individual, ensuing hypotheses and issues related to effective classroom instruction remain in need of thoughtful study. Furthermore, research on teaching, in general, has not been enlightening in providing guidance about effective instructional techniques for developing problem-solving competence in mathematics. The main reason is that problem solving, itself, has rarely been the focus of the teaching that was studied. Another reason is that reports of process-product studies, which constitute the bulk of the literature on research on teaching, have focused on global teacher behaviors and thus lacked the level of specificity (in their analysis of what the teacher actually does when explaining mathematics) necessary to be helpful (see Shavelson, Webb, Stasz, and McArthur, this volume).

PREPARING TEACHERS FOR THE TASK: THEIR VIEWS ABOUT PROBLEM SOLVING

One of the greatest challenges I have faced as a mathematics educator has been, and continues to be, that of helping teachers learn ways to improve their students' problem-solving competence and enhance their mathematical thinking. Why is it so difficult? It is not that I am lacking in good suggestions to pass on to the teachers. On the contrary, I often have more suggestions than I can reasonably pass on. Perhaps the answer lies in the fact that I am attempting to teach them an art, or should I say a double art? Polya (1981) noted that problem solving is a practical art. Teaching, too, I regard as a practical art. In my view teaching is an activity that cannot be prescribed; it cannot be reduced to a sequence of predetermined steps to be learned as one learns, say, an algorithm. As I reflect on my own teaching, I cannot agree with the view that teaching mathematical problem solving can be learned as a skill. As Stanic and Kilpatrick (this volume) noted, teaching problem solving is "a human activity that requires [among other things] experience, taste, and judgment."

According to Polya the teacher must illustrate techniques of problem solving, discuss them with the students, and practice them in an insightful, nonmechanical way (Stanic and Kilpatrick, this volume). This requires that the teacher not only be knowledgeable about and feel comfortable "doing" mathematics, but the teacher must also have an understanding of the learners, of the mathematics they already know, of how to motivate and guide them, and of the classroom activities and arrangements most conducive to problem solving. Clearly, the design of courses and experiences to help teachers become competent teachers of problem solving is not a trivial task, and deserves much more attention from researchers in mathematics education than it has so far received.

Teachers' Views About the Nature of Problem Solving

In working with teachers, the main difficulties I have encountered have been related to the teachers' views of what constitutes a problem in mathematics, their views about the nature of mathematics in general and of problem solving in particular, their attitudes towards problem solving, and their beliefs about what it means to do mathematics. This has been true of elementary teachers as well as of secondary teachers. While secondary teachers tend to be stronger than elementary teachers in their knowledge of the subject matter, I have found secondary teachers generally more resistant to introducing changes into their teaching. Elementary teachers, for the most part, tend to react enthusiastically to new techniques, but their generally weaker mathematics background, and resulting feelings of inadequacy to handle mathematical problem solving, become serious obstacles.

How does one remove those obstacles? How should we go about helping teachers increase their knowledge and confidence to teach problem solving? How do we go about modifying teachers' misconceptions about problem solving? An attempt to seek answers to these questions was part of a study designed to document changes in the conceptions of mathematical problem solving of 16 elementary school teachers over a three-week summer course on problem solving and after a year of teaching problem solving in their classrooms (Thompson, 1985). Because a complete description of the study would be beyond the scope of this paper, I briefly describe some of the main features of the summer course and some of the findings of the study.

Initial data indicated that 5 of the 16 teachers conceived of a problem task as essentially the description of a situation involving stated quantities, followed by a question about some relationship among the quantities whose answer called for the application of one or more arithmetic operations. Consistently, these teachers used the terms "story" or "word" problems in their responses and gave these as examples of a problem task. In discussing the nature of problem solving these teachers referred to the presence of a problem statement, "the application of computational skills," the importance of readily identifying the operation or the steps necessary for the solution," and "the right method." Implicit in their responses were the notions that:

1. It is *the answer* that counts in mathematics, once one has an answer, the problem is done.
2. One must get an answer in *the right* way.
3. An answer to a mathematical question is usually a number.
4. Every context (problem statement) is associated with a unique procedure for "getting" answers.
5. The key to being successful in solving problems is knowing and remembering what to do.

These views are not unlike those held by many students. Is it that teachers successfully communicate their views to their students? Or is it that these views, in both teachers and students, stem from a common source, say, the curriculum? Or is it a combination of the curriculum and the teacher? Where do these views originate, and how are they formed? If it is the case that teachers' views are the result of their own schooling experience with mathematics, and years later they return to school to pass them on to a new generation of students (thus perpetuating a cycle), then where do we break into the cycle, and how do we go about modifying those views? These are essential questions in need of attention by mathematics education researchers.

Fortunately not all teachers have such limited conceptions of the nature of mathematical problem solving. As I mentioned earlier, the views discussed above were manifested in the responses of only 5 of the 16 teachers studied. The responses of the other 11 teachers reflected a more generalized view of what constituted a mathematical problem. In their descriptions these teachers alluded to a variety of tasks, including "puzzles," "mazes," and "optical illusions." These teachers referred to problem solving as an activity that called for the application of "reasoning skills," "logic," "trial and error methods," and "a variety of approaches to the finding of solutions"; as involving the processes of "searching for and discovering new ideas"; as requiring "inventiveness and creativity" to successful performance; as "not being as dependent on learned skills as other mathematical activities"; and as "being the form that mathematics takes in life." These teachers referred to the "challenging," "fun," and "frustrating" nature of problem solving.

One would expect the teachers in this second group to approach problems differently and act differently from those in the first group when teaching problem solving. Yet, it was not just their views of what constitutes a problem in mathematics that appeared to influence their performance and instructional actions, but also their perceptions of their own competence as problem solvers and of their ability to teach problem solving. At the beginning of the course, all the teachers, reportedly, thought that teaching mathematics was an easy or fairly easy task. Yet, they indicated that mathematics was the subject the students generally had the most difficulty learning. All but one teacher indicated that they found problem solving difficult to teach, and all agreed that students generally found problem solving difficult to learn.

The summer course focused on principles of heuristic teaching in mathematics. The main purpose of the course was to enhance the teachers' confidence and competence in solving problems, in the use of heuristics, and in the use of pedagogical techniques for enhancing students' problem-solving performance and mathematical thinking skills.

The class met daily for three hours during a period of three weeks. The first half of the period was devoted to posing and solving problems. The initial focus was on modeling the use of heuristics in solving nonroutine problems. The teachers were given a variety of problems to try to solve, and by the third day, they led the class in discussions of problems that had been assigned. The second half of the class period dealt with pedagogical methods and issues related to problem solving. Suggestions for planning and implementing whole-group and small-group problem-solving sessions and lessons employing a problem-solving approach to the content were presented and discussed. The problems discussed during the first half of the period often provided a basis for the discussions during the second half. As one may expect, instructional issues were frequently raised in the context of solving problems, so the separation of topics between the two periods was not rigid. The main issues addressed during the second period were related to the role of the teacher in using a problem-solving approach and in conducting problem-solving sessions (e.g., questioning techniques, assisting students, extending problems). Other issues were planning, using instructional resources, evaluating students' problem-solving performance, and using assessment methods and instruments that support a problem-solving teaching approach. The teachers were given readings throughout the course.

The data were gathered through three questionnaires that were administered at the beginning and end of the summer course, and at the end of the school year following the course; daily entries in journals the teachers kept throughout the course; informal interviews; classroom observations; and four follow-up sessions held throughout the school year.

By the end of the summer session the teachers had become aware of different problem types. Labels for various categories of problems had been encountered in the readings and their purpose in the curriculum had been discussed in class. This terminology enabled the teachers to make distinctions among problems that, reportedly, they were not aware of, had overlooked, or simply were unable to articulate before. All of the teachers indicated finding the terminology useful, particularly in planning for the inclusion of different types of problems in their teaching.

There was evidence, both from our class discussions and from the questionnaire responses, of an emerging notion of problem solving as a general process for generating mathematical knowledge, involving the search for and discovery of patterns and regularities, conjecturing or making reasonable assumptions, testing assumptions and generalizing. Inductive discovery strategies had been used frequently in solving problems in the course. Some teachers alluded to a new awareness on their part of the role of proof in the generation of mathematical knowledge. An inductive activity that led to a false conjecture had triggered a class discussion on the notion of mathematical proof. It became apparent from the discussion that many of the teachers had been willing to accept the validity of a statement on the basis of a few examined cases.

The teachers also indicated that prior to the summer session they had conceived of problem solving (in the context of teaching mathematics) as an activity requiring a written statement of a problem, and that they were "beginning to see it also as an approach to teaching mathematics" in which all that may be needed "is a question from the teacher." Two teachers stated having used this approach in teaching other subjects, but not much in teaching mathematics.

Some journal entries were as follows:

- As I reflect on my years of teaching I have used much of the same methodology in my teaching (social studies, art, etc.), but not so much in math. Yet, problem solving, as I see it now, is applicable to all facets of teaching in varying degrees, but particularly to math.

- I sit in class and find myself reexamining my teaching style. Something that has struck me is that I have typically accepted all students' answers (without giving clues to whether they were right or wrong) in all areas of the curriculum, but not very much in math. Probably because I felt there were right and wrong answers in math.

- I have realized that to teach problem solving I don't need to have a problem to give to my students. It is a way of teaching that I can use in many of my lessons. What is not crystal clear is whether I will be effective in doing this, but I am going to try it.

By the end of the second week of the course, several teachers reported feeling more confident and competent in solving problems, although "not totally at ease." The comments below show the salience of the teachers' affective concerns:

- I have experienced more affective than cognitive changes. The affective changes are releasing the already present cognition. I am much more able to give myself permission not to know everything immediately. It's amazing to me how great it feels and how quickly it came after 50 years of not being able to do it. I can now make progress towards a solution even if I can't completely solve the problem.
- I know now that there are definite strategies that one employs. These are developed with practice and "everyone" uses them (it's not a mystical clairvoyance that one needs to begin a problem).
- Some of the problems we've done have really blown my mind. I have been challenged greatly in my thinking skills by solving the problems presented in this class. I see many deficiencies in my own logical thinking, but I am willing to do everything I can to improve.
- My fear of mathematics is lessening. My concept of the value of mathematics has been tremendously broadened. I feel a need to go back and study mathematics for myself—in school (as a student) I managed to avoid it as much as possible—I'm beginning to feel it within my grasp.

With respect to their ability to teach problem solving, all the teachers reported that they felt more confident to teach problem solving and were more knowledgeable of ways in which to help students. An aspect of teaching problem solving that the teachers admitted not having thought about before the summer session was planning. They commented on the importance of selecting problems according to some rationale and planning appropriate questions in advance, noting that this would help them feel more confident in their discussions with students.

In relation to the use of a problem-solving approach to teaching the prescribed content of the mathematics curriculum, several teachers expressed concern about their ability to "think of the right question at the right time" in order to engage students in discussions. They remarked that the use of such an approach places greater demands on the teacher and noted the need for a thorough understanding of the topic on the teacher's part. A few illustrative comments were:

- Thinking about my approach to teaching math, I see a need to incorporate much more of the problem-solving approach. I feel that my teaching approach has been greatly influenced by policies of proficiencies in basic skills and pressures to accomplish this with my students. I need to strike a better balance. But, will I be able to ask effective questions? I think this is the key.

- My big problem is in coming up with good questions—not the ones I can take my time to think about, but the ones that I will need to use in reacting to students in class. This won't be easy.

Changes in Teachers' Instructional Practices

At the beginning of the summer course the teachers were asked (via questionnaires and interviews) about their teaching of problem solving dur-ing the previous school year. Four teachers reported teaching problem solving approximately once a week, and two of them indicated using supplementary materials in problem solving. Four teachers indicated having taught problem solving as a separate unit lasting anywhere between two to three weeks. Eight teachers stated not having taught problem solving per se, but occasionally assigning word problems from the textbook.

Data on the teachers' instructional practices during the school year following the summer course were obtained through classroom observations, the teachers' reports during the follow-up sessions, and the final questionnaire. Classroom visits were scheduled to observe each teacher once teaching a nonroutine problem, once teaching a word problem, and once when the students were engaged in some independent or small-group problem-solving activity. Observations forms were used, and each teacher was given a score (0–20) based on the observations. Complete data were available for 14 teachers; two teachers were transferred to another district in midyear.

The data showed that six of the teachers taught problem solving in a systematic way, allowing for some type of daily activity in problem solving that did not necessarily require direct teaching. They explained that at times they just briefly discussed an assigned problem or allowed students to present problems to the class or work independently, while other times they presented and discussed problems in great detail and with much care. When asked if they felt more confident in teaching, they noted:

- Much more than before. At the beginning of the year I felt I needed to prepare thoroughly, now I am more relaxed. If I haven't solved the problem myself I let the students know.
- Yes. I tell my students if I don't know the solution ahead of time; this seems to make them more interested for some reason. I wouldn't have thought of trying this before.
- Not always. I felt that I was learning along with the students. I found that I had to work the problems backward to have a complete understanding of the solution before I presented them to the class. Recognizing that I have limitations in solving problems, I forced myself to learn all I could before teaching a certain aspect. Also, I had to instill the idea, in my students, that new challenges can be fun. Sometimes they actually agreed with me! I have learned to enjoy

math, and as I got better at solving problems, I was able to do a better job of teaching my students.

- I honestly don't mind to have children see me attack a problem I do not have the answer to. I, of course, try to prepare with problems that I have to take a second, third and fourth (or more) looks at. This does not bother me and I feel it teaches children patience and perseverance and the idea of working "with the teacher" rather than working "for the teacher." I feel adequately prepared to the extent that I feel like trying new situations and don't mind taking the risk of not knowing all of the answers or solutions.

- Most of the time, but not always for sure. Some problems were easier to understand and discuss. The most challenging aspect was trying to understand the way some students reasoned their way to a solution. Confidence increased as the year went by, both in me and in my students. I've truly enjoyed doing it and plan to continue. I am not anxious about problem solving anymore. I let the students know if I find that a problem is hard for me too.

The major obstacles that these teachers reportedly encountered were related to: time constraints; some initial "resistance on the part of some students, accustomed to doing mathematics routinely, to try to figure things out"; and having students with a wide range of ability in their classes. One of these six teachers noted having to explain to some parents why her class was not as far along in the textbook as a "less able" sixth-grade class in her school, but that once she had explained, the parents were supportive. Eight teachers stated not having taught problem solving per se, but occasionally assigning word problems from the textbook. The observation scores for the six teachers ranged between 13 and 17 points.

Three of the remaining eight teachers, reported having taught problem solving two or three times a week throughout the year. They noted feeling pressured at times to adhere to the prescribed curriculum. The major obstacles to teaching problem solving that they reported encountering were related to time constraints, and in the case of one teacher, to insufficient student proficiency in basic skills. With respect to their own confidence in teaching problem solving they commented:

- Plenty scares me! I feel comfortable only with the elementary levels. I feel insecure in coming up with general solutions, with equations and formulas, because I lack training and understanding in algebra. I just don't have a really high powered brain. But I have enjoyed problem solving.

- I enjoy teaching problem solving very much and I feel comfortable doing it. I wish that was all I had to teach in mathematics.

- I am most comfortable teaching word problems. Nonroutine problems, I have to prepare carefully before I teach them to my class. I am amazed to see my own improvement in dealing with the more challenging problems.

The observation scores for these three teachers ranged between 11 and 13.

The remaining five teachers reported having taught problem solving on an irregular basis, teaching it once a week at times during the year, and at times letting several weeks go by without having the opportunity to teach it. Four of these teachers referred to time limitations and being under pressure to adhere to the prescribed curriculum as their main reasons for not teaching problem solving more regularly. The other teacher explained that her main problem was "lack of self-discipline and not being too organized." Only one of these teachers indicated feeling confident teaching problem solving. Their comments were:

- I feel comfortable, but not all my students do. Some of them resist thinking.
- I'm still not totally comfortable, mainly because it takes too much time.
- I feel I have better control in guiding and helping students than I did before our class. I wish I could take a follow-up class again next summer. There are aspects of teaching problem solving where I know I could do better if I had more mathematics experience.
- Only when I have thoroughly prepared.
- I am still insecure at times. I need to prepare to make sure that I understand the problem before I present it to my students. I am confident teaching word problems, the challenging problems can still be a problem for me.

The observation scores for these five teachers ranged from 6 to 11.

During the visits to the teachers' classrooms, we observed four teachers leading problem-solving sessions in a somewhat rigid way that seemed to violate the spirit of problem solving. These sessions were characterized by: (a) little spontaneity on the part of the teacher in interacting with the students; (b) failure to probe and capitalize on students' remarks and suggestions; (c) very limited discussion of the mathematics and strategies used in solving the problem; and (d) failure to extend the mathematics beyond the solution. This was due to the teachers' adherence to a format suggested in the instructional materials they were using, which provided them with specific steps and questions for leading the discussion. It was apparent that the teachers were using these materials as a script and, for some reason, felt compelled to follow it closely. While not all the teachers who had curricular materials of this sort available to them used them in the same fashion, this finding does point to the need to examine the effects on instruction of current curricular materials for teaching problem solving. How are they being used and by whom? And are they serving the purpose for which they were intended? Would the teachers who used the materials as a crutch have been better off left to their own resources in teaching problem solving? How much guidance should such materials provide? It seems to me that these are pressing questions for research.

DISCUSSION

I wish to make no claims of working miracles. Indeed, it should be clear that in the case of some of the teachers we were far from succeeding in removing many of the obstacles that stood in the way of their becoming confident and competent problem solvers and teachers of problem solving. But, apparently one can positively affect teachers' beliefs about teaching problem solving and about their relationship to problems. Furthermore, it appears that one can enhance their competence and confidence to solve problems and teach problem solving.

While the teachers appeared to have undergone many cognitive changes, evidence of such changes often appeared only implicitly in remarks that had more of an affective tone. The relationship between the cognitive and the affective is difficult to discern. It is not clear whether it suffices to concentrate solely on the cognitive to bring about necessary changes in the teachers' affect, or if the latter requires separate special attention. What is the role of teacher affect in teaching of problem solving? While, on the surface, affective concerns frequently appeared to be the main obstacles facing the teachers, these concerns seemed to diminish as the teachers gained a broader perspective of the nature of problem solving and as they became more knowledgeable of heuristics and specific techniques. Although it was apparent that the teachers' limited mathematical resources were often a serious obstacle, only a few teachers acknowledged this in their remarks.

What features of the course were most effective in bringing about these changes? Who were the teachers who benefited the most, and why? An essential prerequisite for understanding what happened in the course is a highly detailed understanding of the teachers' conceptions of problem solving and its teaching, before they started the course. One feature of the course that seemed essential in broadening the teachers' conceptions of the nature of problem solving was their active involvement in solving a wide variety of problems and reflecting on their attempts to solve them. The modeling of teaching techniques, followed by a discussion of the rationale for their selection and use, seemed to provide valuable concrete illustrations of the teachers' role in teaching problem solving. I can also point to the readings as another source influencing the changes. But, the answer still remains mostly speculative. The study reported here sought merely to document changes in the teachers. As Shulman (1985) has noted, systematic experimentation with instructional treatments that carefully document the interaction with the teachers over time is necessary.

CONCLUSION

There is no question in my mind that the art of teaching mathematical problem solving can only be mastered, if at all, over a long period of time. The purpose of this paper was to describe an attempt to initiate teachers in this art, and in doing so, raise a few pertinent issues that are in need of systematic study by researchers in mathematics education. As we set up an agenda for research on teaching problem solving, let us make sure we do not leave out of that agenda the preparation of classroom teachers. After all, it will only be through them that the ultimate goal of research on problem solving in mathematics education, namely to improve students' ability to solve problems, will be accomplished.

I hope that ten years from now we will be more knowledgeable about effective ways and techniques of teaching problem solving and have a better sense of how to go about preparing teachers in their use. I also hope that by then we will have had an opportunity to examine curricular materials for teaching problem solving and how they are used by teachers in their classrooms.

REFERENCES

Kilpatrick, J. (1985). A retrospective account of the past twenty-five years of research on teaching mathematical problem solving. In E. A. Silver (Ed.), *Teaching and learning mathematical problem solving: Multiple research perspectives* (pp. 1–15). Hillsdale, NJ: Lawrence Erlbaum Associates.

Lester, F. K. (1980). Research on mathematical problem solving. In R. J. Shumway (Ed.), *Research in mathematics education* (pp. 286–323). Reston, VA: National Council of Teachers of Mathematics.

Lester, F. K. (1985). Methodological considerations in research on mathematical problem-solving instruction. In E. A. Silver (Ed.), *Teaching and learning mathematical problem solving: Multiple research perspectives* (pp. 41–69). Hillsdale, NJ: Lawrence Erlbaum Associates.

Polya, G. (1957). *How to solve it* (2nd ed.). New York: Doubleday.

Polya, G. (1981). *Mathematical discovery: On understanding, learning, and teaching problem solving* (2 vols.; combined ed.). New York: John Wiley & Sons.

Schoenfeld, A. H. (1985) *Mathematical problem solving*. Orlando, FL: Academic Press.

Shulman, L. S. (1985). On teaching problem solving and solving the problems of teaching. In E. A. Silver (Ed.), *Teaching and learning mathematical problem solving: Multiple research perspectives* (pp. 439–450). Hillsdale, NJ: Lawrence Erlbaum Associates.

Silver, E. A. (1987). A window and a frame [Review of Mathematical problem solving]. *Journal for Research in Mathematics Education, 18,* 53–58.

Thompson, A. G. (1985, April). *Changes in teachers' conceptions of mathematical problem solving.* Paper presented at the annual meeting of the American Research Association, Chicago.

Preparing Teachers to Teach Mathematical Problem Solving

Nel Noddings
Stanford University

Why is problem solving so hard to learn and so hard to teach? This is a question that mathematics educators have been asking for a long time, and several tentative answers have been important in developing research programs. I plan to explore five of these answers in the context of teacher preparation; that is, I propose to explore the question of what teachers need to know in order to facilitate problem solving. Problem solving will here be construed mainly as the solution of "word" or "story" problems, but some attention will be given to a larger sense of the term.

READING AND PROBLEM SOLVING

It has long been thought that difficulties with reading affect problem-solving performance. Some studies (Alexander, 1960; Martin, 1963) suggested that reading might indeed be the key skill involved in solving word problems. Later studies, however, showed that even children with normal reading scores experience difficulty with these problems (Balow, 1964; Knifong and Holtan, 1976, 1977), although there were studies that continued to support the importance of reading (Aiken, 1972). Recent research takes a more sophisticated approach and asks what role reading plays in solving word problems (Muth and Glynn, 1985; Threadgill-Sowder, et al., 1985; Grabe and Grabe, 1985) and whether some children use compensating abilities to by-pass their reading problems. Clearly, we need to know more about the ways in which reading interacts with other skills required in problem solving.

Virtually all teacher education programs recognize the importance of teaching reading, and many now require that even prospective high school mathematics teachers learn something about the teaching of reading. Objectives in this area are, for example, mandated in California. Questions arise, however, on exactly what these objectives should be and how they should be met. When state mandates are issued, most programs respond with a course to meet the new requirement. That is what we did at Stanford, and so all of our intern teachers now take a course in reading with an internationally-known psychologist who specializes in reading. This is surely valuable, but more direct connection of reading to the learning of mathematics and, especially, to problem solving is needed, also.

In the Algebra Problem-Solving course that we teach for Upward Bound students each summer at Stanford, we pay considerable attention to reading. Most mathematics teachers, it seems, still advise their students to read the whole problem carefully and then concentrate on the problem: What does the question ask us to find? This advice suggests the typical pattern of attack on math problems, including proofs in geometry; it suggests a backward analysis to be followed by a sequential synthesis. The method is certainly worth a try, we tell our students, but there is something else to do if it doesn't work.

Consider this problem which is typical of a notorious set of time, rate, and distance problems:

> John rides his motorcycle 80 miles at an average rate of 50 miles an hour and 10 miles at an average rate of 25 miles an hour. What is the average rate for the entire trip?

We all know what students do with this problem. They extract the two rates, add them, divide by 2, and report an answer of 37.5. Some are bothered by the fact that they have not used the "80" and "10" that appear in the problem and so tinker about to introduce these numbers, but this is problem solving of a peculiar nature. Students who think this way are savvy about the way we operate in schools. They are not so much reading the problem as they are the school context and their teachers.

Our approach is to connect reading to a task that is receiving attention in current research, that of building a mental representation or creating a problem space. The usual approach to this task is, again, backwards. Advocates of cognitive-processing models get their problem spaces and representations from the finished solution and then seek a reasonable pedagogical approach to its reconstruction. But stymied thinkers simply cannot work this way. They have to build up a space that contains "noise" and "junk" before they can select items for an accurate representation. They have to get a sense of the sort of field on which they are playing. This description is consonant with Lesh's (1985) notion that ideas develop and may be described at intermediate levels of development. Even in individual problems there may be a need to try out ideas and cluster them before deciding on an algorithmic solution.

We, therefore, recommend that students read the problem bit by bit and perform computations just to see what they can find out. After the first sentence, "John rides 80 miles at an average rate of 50 miles per hour," what do we know? We know that $t = 1.6$. In addition to knowing that $t = 1.6$, we know other things: for example, that John would cover 50 miles in 1 hour, 100 miles in 2 hours, 75 miles in 1½ hours, and so forth. This is not a matter of piecemeal translation, a practice that is frequently condemned for its mindlessness. It is, rather, a matter of building a mental problem space, finding out what elements belong in it, how they are related, and how they behave.

With the information derived in this way (t = 2), we can convince students that the problem requires us to consider total distance divided by total time. Consider how far John would ride if he travelled for 2 hours at the rate (37.5) that most students suggest as an answer—only 75 miles.

This method is time consuming, but it reflects a more genuine process of problem solving. A picture is built up little by little, items are deleted, potentially relevant bits are reorganized. The meanings of various words are discussed. (Attention to vocabulary is important, and I will return to this topic later.) Modes of representation are discussed; symbols are defined and agreed upon; consistency of mode is encouraged. In many problems, we perform computations that turn out to be irrelevant, and students often object to all the "extra work." Such complaints suggest that the students have been initiated into a highly artificial way of approaching word problems but the problems themselves are artificial, and that is another tentative answer to our guiding question.

THE PROBLEMS THEMSELVES

A number of studies have been directed to the problems themselves as a source of difficulty. Clearly, this line of research begs the question to some degree, because it leaves unanswered the question why certain features make problem solving hard. Researchers who take this line often have a definite idea about what constitutes problem solving, and their point is that typical word problems ask a great deal more (or a great deal less) of students than genuine problem solving. In a series of studies (Loftus, 1970; Loftus and Suppes 1972; Searle, Lorton, and Suppes, 1974), it was suggested that structural features in the problems themselves account for some student difficulty. These researchers identified the following features as complicating factors: the need for a large number of computations; the need to convert units; complex surface structures; many words; a structure different from that of preceding problems. In a similar line of attack, Williams and McCreight (1965) found that problems in which the question comes at the end are easier; Rosenthal (1971) found that problems in which information is not presented in the order of use are more difficult.

While these studies contributed to our knowledge of how students interact with word problems, they also provided support for pedagogical and curricular changes that are now regarded as questionable. Textbooks have gone too far, it is charged, in cutting down on words, simplifying syntactic structures, presenting problems that require only a single operational or schematic approach. Although these moves make problem solving easier for students, there is justified concern over the value of such problem solving.

Current work on the structural features of word problems concentrates more on the connection between semantic relations and appropriate mental representations (deCorte, Verschaffel, and DeWin, 1985). Studies on the use of writing in understanding word problems (Ferguson and Fairburn, 1985) fall partly into this category also, since the assumption is that the creation of an adequate mental representation requires an understanding of semantic relations and how these may be expressed syntactically. Currently, when we consider simplifying the structure of word problems, we think about how to do this pedagogically (rather than through simplification of the text itself) so that students, too, will learn how to construct and to analyze complex configurations of words.

A second line of attack on the problems themselves charges that the problems are too artificial (Nesher, 1980; Lesh, 1981, 1985). Exposure to stereotypical word problems may actually induce a form of stupidity (Holt, 1964), because students are required to hold back on their natural, intuitive strategies and fish about for a symbolic statement that their teacher will accept as a translation of the words. While there is much truth in this criticism, the greater part of the artificiality may lie in pedagogical processes. Typical textbook problems are, of course, unlike real-world problems; they are already formulated, for one thing. But they can be as challenging and interesting as puzzles in general; they can be real problems if we change the setting to one of genuine problem solving. As Carpenter (1985) has pointed out, even words evoking $9 + 6 = ?$ can be a real problem for a young child. Further, textbook problems are designed to strengthen mathematical techniques and manipulations, and real-world problems cannot meet this need in any systematic way. Textbooks could, however, include problems of both sorts and, thus, achieve an optimal blend.

What is important to teachers in all this? They need to know how research in this area has developed so that they do not repeat moves in their teaching that researchers have already identified as mistakes. I am not recommending that teachers should be taught the current set of facts, "research says . . ." Rather, they should be acquainted with the development of research programs so that they can think critically about applications and modifications. This is a major point of the present paper, and for this reason I have referred to research spread over a twenty-year period, even though it is impossible in a paper of this length to cover the territory exhaustively. The important point is to remind ourselves of how research programs develop and how teachers can use an understanding of this development in their own planning. A teacher who is familiar with the programs described above might hesitate to provide a semantic simplification for a student, for example, and then decide to do it cooperatively with the student. His or her objective would go well beyond solution of the current problem to the more general task of performing such simplifications. The techniques employed might include "reading and doing" as described earlier, writing sample problems, focusing on the meaning of unknown words even if they are irrelevant to the formal mathematics, clustering, and open discussion.

CLERICAL AND COMPUTATIONAL DIFFICULTIES

Just as there has been debate about the contribution of reading to word-problem solving, so there has been debate about the role of computation. There is no question that computational skills are required to complete a problem correctly, but computational errors do not account for a majority of the difficulties in problem solving (see Muth and Glynn, 1985).

It is not always easy, however, to judge exactly where the difficulty lies. In a recent dissertation study, an investigator asked students to solve problems aloud. One youngster selected the correct operation (division) initially and then changed his response to "multiply." He did this and got an outlandish answer which he allowed to stand as his final result. This sort of error would usually be scored as an error of interpretation. When the investigator asked him later why he had changed his response from "divide" to "multiply," the boy answered, "I couldn't remember how to divide these numbers." Thus we cannot always be sure whether errors are due to interpretation or to lack of computational skills.

There are at least two important areas of debate on computation with which teachers should be familiar. One involves the use of drill. Must drill always be meaningful? And what do we mean by *meaningful*? Here I want to draw on years of experience as a mathematics teacher rather than directly on research. It seems to me that drill is meaningful if students understand and accept the fact that something important is coming up for which they will need the skills now being exercised. Before presenting the Pythagorean Theorem, for example, a teacher might provide a few days of practice on the simplification of radicals, learning the squares of numbers from 1 to 25, and extracting square roots. This is probably not the time to make all of these activities structurally meaningful in themselves. The idea is to make the necessary subskills automatic so that students can give their full attention to the new concepts that arise in connection with the Pythagorean Theorem. This way of operating is well supported in both philosophical thinking (Polanyi, 1962) and psychological theory (Norman, 1969), and, of course, much recent research has centered on routines and automaticity (Mayer, 1985). The human brain must give focal attention to the issue perceived as central and significant; subskills are executed in the periphery. It is surely exhausting and discouraging for students to shift their focal attention continually as they struggle with every small step involved in a Pythagorean problem.

This is not, however, an argument for keeping students working at dull computations until they meet some preordained level of competence before even seeing a word problem. In the past fifteen years, this mistake has occurred again and again. Some elementary school children never see word problems because, ostensibly, they have not achieved the requisite computational skill. Computational drill presented in this way becomes an end in itself and comes across to students as truly meaningless. The sort of subskill readiness advocated here requires teachers to think ahead and to analyze the problems and new concepts to be taught, so that the basic subskills can be identified and taught or reviewed efficiently. Then, when the big topic is encountered, teachers should remind their students of how useful their newly-honed skills really are, so that students, too, gain some ability to judge what is important and what is auxiliary.

The other aspect of computation that teachers should think about is its structure-building possibilities. In the sixties, there was great emphasis on structural understanding and little on actual manipulation. The idea was that computation was itself easily mastered if one understood the underlying structure (Bruner, 1960). Today we have reason to doubt the wisdom of this approach. It is, perhaps, better to learn first how to do something and to apply the skill. Then discussion of the underlying structure can take place as the skill is incorporated into more complex algorithmic structures (Case, 1978; Siegler, 1978). Mastery of the basic skill provides an operational structure for the assimilation of elements to be used in the construction of extended structures. Further, mastery of the basic skill provides students with the means of exploring the structures to be understood; they can play intelligently with the objects whose behavior they are probing and, thus, check their own understanding.

Again, this sort of recommendation can be carried too far. I am not suggesting that every topic, every problem, every concept be approached in this fashion (Noddings, 1985a). Sometimes the necessary subskills are so numerous and so indirectly connected to the topic that their practice would do little to enhance understanding of the major idea. The Mean Value Theorem in differential calculus may be an example of this kind. In such cases, it is wiser to start with a structural overview, to induce a Gestalt of the concept. In all cases, students need to attach the new ideas or skills to something.

Discussion of the relations among computation, problem solving, concept building, and understanding is essential for teachers, and they should be encouraged to reflect on these relations and experiment responsibly in their own classrooms. When we teach students a computational skill without bringing them to structural understanding, we are not necessarily committing a mathematical sin. The time for understanding may be somewhere in the future. As Piaget (1970) reminded us, understanding may lag months or even years behind performance. The important thing is to return to an exploration of underlying structure when students have acquired enough skill to participate in genuine investigation. On this matter of returning, we have perhaps been far too negligent.

MOTIVATIONAL FACTORS

Motivation is a topic of enormous concern to teachers, but research on motivation has been comparatively unsophisticated. I have to defend that claim, of course. For a start, I will point to the fact that Marilyn Suydam's (1986) annual review of research on mathematics education does not even include a category for motivation. It does include one labeled "Attitudes and Anxiety," and that is perhaps revealing. Students are generally not enthusiastic about learning mathematics and many are downright frightened by it; yet educators persist in supposing that people should like mathematics and that teachers have a responsibility for inducing favorable attitudes.

There are several topics related to motivation that teachers should think about. The first is a longstanding charge that our instructional methods change bright, curious children into robot-like dullards (Holt, 1964). A second is the very fact of anxiety: Why are people (including many teachers) afraid of mathematics and, especially, of word problems? A third involves the reluctance of many girls to participate in mathematical activity. What I want to explore here is the possibility that these three problems have a common source, that, in fact, they are rooted in a masculine ideology that pervades our culture.

An important aspect of this pervasive ideology is rule following. It may seem odd to relate problems in mathematics learning to our ideological and religious traditions, but I (and many other feminists) believe the relation is real. In the Judeo-Christian tradition, sin is defined primarily as disobedience, the breaking of rules (Daly, 1974), and our culturally acquired sense of self worth depends heavily on our being perceived as law abiding persons. Early in the learning of arithmetic, children detect the importance of obeying rules; arithmetic, like religion, is a rule-governed activity. Children want to please the adults who, it seems, make the rules of arithmetic, and so they watch eagerly for affirmative nods from their teachers. Teachers, trying to be helpful, narrow the field of possible rules: Shall we add or subtract? Multiply or divide? It may be that children left more on their own (and adults, too) would more naturally turn to counting, or sorting, or trying out, or talking with each other than to a dichotomous choice between seemingly arbitrary rules. It may be more comfortable for many students to settle for dull conformity—even stupidity— than to risk becoming a renegade or heretic of sorts. If, further, the rewards for dull conformity are great, then many children will conform. As we now know, girls have been especially vulnerable to pressures to conform. Indeed, their greatest praise has traditionally come from listening politely, doing neat work, following directions, and pleasing teachers with their docility. All this pays off for a while, and girls are successful in the early years of school.

Somewhere along the line, however, boys begin to see that they can modify and even create rules, whereas girls seemingly become even more convinced that they must learn and obey existing rules. This is not at all surprising in a culture that has rewarded women over centuries primarily for service, obedience, and silence. I do not wish to push this theme too far here, but it may be that research on stereotyping and socialization will have to be taken well beyond the mathematics classroom (Boswell, 1985) if we want to understand the motivational factors underlying the decision of so many women to stay out of fields requiring mathematics.

There is a reverse problem also, that teachers should be aware of. When we say to young women, "You're capable and talented, so you certainly should enroll in mathematics classes and plan a career in a field that requires mathematics," we imply that women who do not continue the study of mathematics are lacking in capability and talent. This, too, is an old problem. In medieval days, it was recommended that women could be "more like a man" by remaining virgins and living in convents (McLaughlin, 1974). Now the way to be more like a man (and thus more worthy) is to study mathematics and science. Teachers need to be both well educated and sensitive to the historical problems of women if they are to encourage female students to study mathematics without suggesting that their self worth depends on a positive choice.

The problem of mathematics anxiety in both women and men may be traced in part, as I have suggested, to a pervasive masculine ideology. This is an ideology of individualism and competition. In schools students are forced to work by themselves or in well-defined groups or teams, but competition is often maintained in both settings. Even in cooperative small groups, a great point is often made of competition between groups. The mathematics classroom, thus, contributes to the all-American notion that being "Number One" is what makes life worth living.

In *A Separate Peace*, John Knowles's story of boys in a New England boarding school, we observe rivalry gone deadly. We are also reminded that such rivalry has an adverse relation to genuine learning. When Gene, the unhappy protagonist, deludes himself into thinking that his best friend has become his deadly enemy, he says:

> I became quite a student after that. I had always been a good one, although I wasn't really interested and excited by learning itself, the way that Douglass was. Now I became not only just good but exceptional, with Chet Douglass my only rival in sight. But I began to see that Chet was weakened by the very genuineness of his interest in learning. He got carried away by things; for example, he was so fascinated by the tilting planes of solid geometry that he did almost as badly in trigonometry as I did myself. (Knowles, 1975, p. 46)

Students may be set afire by competition, but their inflamed energies may be directed more toward climbing the hierarchy than toward learning itself. In contrast, students who are disgusted by the spectacle may be afraid to say so. The warrior or competitive model, as William James (1958, p. 284) long ago pointed out, serves as a "bulwark against effeminacy"; the result is an anxiety that turns against mathematics and against the self.

Because I believe these factors really are operating I would like to see mathematics teachers consider radical changes in testing and grading practices. We know that grades greatly affect enrollment in mathematics classes (Chipman and Wilson, 1985; Armstrong, 1985), that they affect career choices, especially for women (Casserly and Rock, 1985), and that mathematics teachers, for whatever reason, grade more stringently than most other teachers (Lantz, 1985).

If grading cannot be eliminated in mathematics classes (and why couldn't all required classes be Pass/Fail?), it could at least be tempered by one or more of the following practices:

(1) retesting without penalty until a satisfactory grade is achieved.

(2) the addition of projects, essays, and presentations to course requirements so that the full range of academic talent might contribute to one's evaluation in math class.

(3) contract grading in which each test passed adds to a cumulative marking-period grade. This practice greatly reduces test anxiety.

(4) elimination of comparisons in grading—no more posting of medians, extremes, and so forth, to show people just where they stand.

(5) a massive professional rejection of the pernicious notion that good teachers produce grades that discriminate more widely and finely than those of poor teachers.

In closing this section, I should connect all this to problem solving. Put simply, it is not likely that students will become effective problem solvers if they hold the tacit belief that problem solving requires the exercise of a magical set of rules possessed only by a dominant ("talented") group of persons. Much of what I have said here applies, of course, to ethnic and racial minorities as well as to women.

PROCEDURAL FACTORS

Now we come to what is considered by many to be the heart of the difficulty in problem solving, factors involving interpretation or procedural factors. There is nothing more disheartening, nor more familiar, to mathematics teachers than the sight of students staring passively at the word problems before them. "I don't know what to do," says the student. When teachers are faced with twenty or thirty students all in this mathematical stupor, the temptation to use didactic methods is understandable. Textbook writers, well aware of the teachers' predicament, cooperate by presenting pages of problems all of a kind (or type) so that, once the teacher demonstrates how to do one problem, students can whisk through ten or twelve with little difficulty and, unhappily, little thought.

How can we avoid this perennially deplored state of affairs? This is a good place to review briefly the factors already discussed in this paper, because three of them are significantly related to procedural difficulties. If students cannot read word problems, they will obviously be unable to solve them. But even when they can read adequately, they may not know where to begin in their own attack on a problem. The central task of a problem solver is to build a representation that will allow an effective search for a solution. In this task, the read-and-do technique described earlier can be very useful. It is a potentially powerful heuristic device that is designed to get the student moving. Half the battle in solving word problems, it seems, is getting started.

Another important set of procedural difficulties may be, as I have noted, affective. Silver (1985) points out that "students' behaviors may be influenced by their feelings of self-esteem, their perceived control—or lack of control—over the situation with which they are faced" (p. 253). In addition to the deep structural issues of stereotyping, socialization, competition, and grading that were discussed under motivational factors, there are affective issues directly related to methods of school problem solving that need some attention.

First, why should students be taught to search immediately for an equation that will translate words into symbols? It is certainly useful to be able to do this for a wide variety of well-defined problem types, but this facility is usually an outcome of experience, of familiarity, practice, and verification. The notion that this is the way to attack even new problems is conducive to the production of a state called learned helplessness. When students cannot perform the magic translation, they confess that they do not know where to begin. It is probably sensible, then, to allow students time to tinker with new problem types and to model this approach in our own teaching. Consider a typical work problem:

> A man can paint a room in 9 hours. His daughter, working alone, can paint the room in 12 hours. How long will it take them working together?

Instead of rushing to the usual equation involving reciprocals (and attendant anguish), teachers might suggest that the situation be studied hour by hour, just the way we would do it in practice if we wanted to make a prediction or work up a bid. How much of the job will the man complete in one hour? How much will his daughter complete? What part of the total job will be done at the end of one hour?

$$(1) \quad 1/9 + 1/12 = 4/36 + 3/36 = 7/36$$

Now there are several things that can be done. Some students may see immediately that an end state of 36/36 is what is sought. How many hours will be required to get there? One way to represent the new problem is with a simple proportion:

$$(2) \quad \frac{1 \text{ hour}}{7/36 \text{ (of the job)}} = \frac{x}{36/36 \text{ (of the job)}}, \quad x = \begin{array}{l} \text{number of hours} \\ \text{required to} \\ \text{complete job} \end{array}$$

or

$$(2') \quad \frac{1}{7/36} = \frac{x}{1}$$

and the solution plus a happy connection to (1) follows.

But if students do not spot this easy solution, they need not be stuck. They can proceed hour by hour:

End of	Man's Part	Daughter's Part	Part of Total Job
Hour 1	1/9	1/12	1/9 + 1/12 = . . . = 7/36
Hour 2	2/9	2/12	7/18
Hour 3	3/9	3/12	7/12
Hour 4	4/9	4/12	7/9
Hour 5	5/9	5/12	35/36
Hour x	x/9	x/12	x/9 + x/12 = 36/36

At logically interesting steps, the teacher can pause to invite student comment and insight. After filling in Hour 5, for example, the teacher might ask, "Shall we go on to Hour 6"? If students say yes, there will have to be a discussion of the result. What does 48/36 tell us about what part of the job has been done? It seems likely that some students will see that father and daughter are very nearly finished at the end of 5 hours. Someone may even say, "They have only 1/36 of the work to finish." "And how long will that take"? the teacher might ask. Even here the response is as likely to be "1/36" or "I don't know" as it is to be "1/7." But we have the machinery to check out or eliminate faulty responses by returning to the chart.

The basic message here is that mathematical thinking is rarely linear and hardly ever abstract in its initial stages. Hermann Weyl's (1956; p. 1836) advice, "Think concretely," is a message that should be modeled continually by teachers. It is an approach recommended by Davis (1984) and one that effectively shows students that they need not remain stuck even though it is perfectly respectable to get stuck now and then and to make errors in the attempt at extricating themselves.

At this stage of the discussion, a problem for teacher educators emerges. In my work with teacher-interns, I encounter very few who are willing or able to take this approach at the outset. Even though they are college graduates, many of them math majors, they, too, search for the infallible equation and are just as afraid as their high school students will be of appearing foolish. Teacher educators, then, have to model and encourage genuine problem-solving behavior.

The depth of understanding required of teachers who can facilitate problem solving by following the developing ideas of their students suggests an intensive mathematical education that concentrates on the topics to be taught. The odd notion that one acquires greater mathematical skill and understanding by simply taking "higher" courses is a half-truth at best. The truth of the notion lies in the obvious fact that continued contact with mathematical topics keeps the door open to the possibility of deeper understanding. The fallacious part is in the implication that more courses in pure mathematics will do the job better than courses that revisit, as it were, basic topics from a more mature mathematical viewpoint.

What else can teachers do to help students with procedural difficulties? A marvelously effective heuristic that we all use in our professional and everyday work is to consult. We talk to each other and try out both ideas and modes of presenting them. It seems reasonable to encourage students to work together on tough problems. Indeed, small groups might even be allowed to tinker with new problems prior to any direct instruction. This is not a nostalgic remonstrance to return to the exclusive use of "discovery" methods, nor was the previous recommendation to model concrete operations meant as such a plea. But dialogue and methods aimed at discovery surely have roles to play. Used properly, both induce engagement, and engagement is required in the construction of representations.

When students work together and try out ideas on each other, several benefits may be expected: (a) There is likely to be a clarification of terms, and vocabularies will be extended. Many students find it uncomfortable to treat merely the formal aspect of word problems (Paige and Simon, 1966); they want to know what sort of objects and real-world activities are involved (Noddings 1985a; 1985b). Further, there is reason to believe that the content of existing problems favors males (Chipman & Thomas, 1986; Donlon, 1973; Donlon, Ekstrom, & Lockhead, 1976; Graf & Ruddell, 1972), so it is imperative to encourage discussion that will help all students to become familiar with the object-domains of word problems. (b) From at least one theoretical perspective (Vygotsky, 1978), it may be predicted that students will internalize group dialogue in the form of more powerful cognitive operations; that is, prompted by the pattern of group exploration and challenge, students will begin to ask themselves powerful questions even when they are working alone. (c) If the groups are homogeneous and the problems both manageable and challenging, students may develop an enhanced sense of their own adequacy as problem solvers (Noddings, 1985b). (d) Students who prefer a relational mode to a competitive one may participate more enthusiastically in a cooperative way of problem solving.

Even in the large group instruction usually found in classrooms, more generous discussion might be profitable. When we present only the finished form of problem solutions, we fail to model mathematical thinking; we demonstrate only mathematical presentation. The latter is not unimportant, and some instruction (and discussion) should be devoted to it, but the two enterprises should not be confused.

SUMMARY

I have suggested several ways in which the preparation of mathematics teachers for problem solving might be strengthened:

(1) Teachers should be reflectively aware of programs of research and not just current results.

    (a) Research on reading and problem solving, for example, shows an increasing sophistication in revealing useful relations between reading and problem solving.

    (b) Research on the structural properties of the problems themselves shows a history of faulty pedagogical inferences drawn from studies that can be used more wisely by thoughtful teachers and curriculum interns.

    (c) Research on computation and problem solving shows some of the same history of faulty inferences but also suggests powerful ideas for both pedagogy and future research.

(2) Mathematics teachers should be broadly educated in philosophy, sociology, and history, particularly in women's history and political ideology, so that they can use this material critically in their choice of curriculum materials, teaching strategies, and methods of evaluation.

(3) Teachers should be intensively educated in mathematics; that is, they should know the material they will actually teach thoroughly, its history, epistemology, applications, multiple forms of solution, connections to other disciplines. Knowledge of advanced mathematics is comparatively less important.

(4) Teachers should be prepared to model both mathematical thinking and mathematical presentation, and they should be taught a variety of ways in which to induce mathematical behavior in their students, for example, use of read-and-do techniques, step-by-step charts, consulting, tinkering.

REFERENCES

Aiken, L. R. (1972). Language factors in learning mathematics. *Review of Educational Research, 42,* 359–385.

Alexander, V. E. (1960). Seventh graders' ability to solve problems. *School Science and Mathematics, 60,* 603–606.

Armstrong, J. M. (1985). A national assessment of participation and achievement of women in mathematics. In S. F. Chipman, L. R. Brush, & D. M. Wilson (Eds.), *Women and mathematics: Balancing the equation* (pp. 59–94). Hillsdale, NJ: Lawrence Erlbaum.

Balow, I. H. (1964). Reading and computation ability as determinants of problem solving. *Arithmetic Teacher, 11,* 18–22.

Boswell, S. L. (1985). The influence of sex-role stereotyping on women's attitudes and achievement in mathematics. In S. F. Chipman, L. R. Brush, and D. M. Wilson (Eds.), *Women and mathematics: Balancing the equation* (pp. 175–198). Hillsdale, NJ: Lawrence Erlbaum.

Bruner, J. S. (1960). *The process of education.* Cambridge, MA: Harvard University Press.

Carpenter, T. P. (1985). Learning to add and subtract: An exercise in problem solving. In E. A. Silver (Ed.), *Teaching and learning mathematical problem solving: Multiple research perspectives* (pp. 17–40). Hillsdale, NJ: Lawrence Erlbaum.

Case, R. (1978). Intellectual development from birth to adulthood: A neo-Piagetian interpretation. In R. S. Siegler (Ed.), *Children's thinking: What develops?* (pp. 37–72). Hillsdale, NJ: Lawrence Erlbaum.

Casserly, P. L. & Rock, D. (1985). Factors related to young women's persistence and achievement in advanced placement mathematics. In S. F. Chipman, L. R. Brush, & D. M. Wilson (Eds.), *Women and mathematics: Balancing the equation* (pp. 225–248). Hillsdale, NJ: Lawrence Erlbaum.

Chipman, S. F. & Thomas, V. G. (1985). Women's participation in mathematics: Outlining the problem. In S. F. Chipman, L. R. Brush, & D. M. Wilson (Eds.), *Women and mathematics: Balancing the equation* (pp. 1–24). Hillsdale, NJ: Lawrence Erlbaum.

Chipman, S. F. & Wilson, D. M. (1985). Understanding mathematics course enrollment and mathematics achievement: A synthesis of the research. In S. F. Chipman, L. R. Brush, & D. M. Wilson (Eds.), *Women and mathematics: Balancing the equation* (pp. 275–328). Hillsdale, NJ: Lawrence Erlbaum.

Daly, M. (1974). *Beyond God the father.* Boston: Beacon.

Davis, R. B. (1984). *Learning mathematics: The cognitive science approach to mathematics education.* Norwood, NJ: Ablex.

de Corte, E., Verschaffel, L. & DeWin, L. (1985). Influence of rewording verbal problems on children's problem representations and solutions, *Journal of Educational Psychology, 77,* 460–470.

Donlon, T. F. (1973). Content factors in sex differences in test questions, *Educational Testing Service Monograph.*

Donlon, T. F., Ekstrom, R. B., & Lockheed, M. (1976). *Comparing the sexes on achievement items of varying content.* Paper presented at the annual meeting of American Psychological Association, Washington, D.C.

Ferguson, A. & Fairburn, J. (1985). Language experience for problem solving in mathematics, *Reading Teacher, 38,* 504–507.

Grabe, M. & Grabe, C. (1985). The microcomputer and the language experience approach, *Reading Teacher, 38,* 508–511.

Graf, G. & Ruddell, J. (1972). Sex differences in problem solving as a function of problem content, *Journal of Educational Research, 65,* 451–452.

Holt, J. (1964). *How children fail.* New York: Dell.

James, W. (1958). *The varieties of religious experience.* New York: Mentor Books.

Knifong, J. D. & Holtan, B. D. (1976). An analysis of children's written solutions to word problems, *Journal for Research in Mathematics Education, 7,* 106–112.

Knowles, J. (1975). *A separate peace.* New York: Bantam.

Lantz, A. (1985). Strategies to increase mathematics enrollments. In S. F. Chipman, L. R. Brush, & D. M. Wilson (Eds.), *Women and mathematics: Balancing the equation* (pp. 329–354). Hillsdale, NJ: Lawrence Erlbaum.

Lesh, R. (1985). Conceptual analyses of problem-solving performance. In E. A. Silver (Ed.), *Teaching and learning mathematical problem solving: Multiple research perspectives* (pp. 309–329). Hillsdale, NJ: Lawrence Erlbaum.

Lesh, R. (1981). Applied mathematical problem solving, *Educational Studies in Mathematics, 12*, 235–265.

Loftus, E. F. J. (1970). *An analysis of the structural variables that determine problem-solving difficulty on a computer-based teletype.* (Report No. 162). Stanford, CA: Institute for Mathematical Studies in the Social Sciences.

Loftus, E. & Suppes, P. (1972). Structural variables that determine problem-solving difficulty in computer-assisted instruction, *Journal of Educational Psychology, 63*, 531–542.

Martin, M. D. (1963). *Reading comprehension, abstract verbal reasoning, and computation as factors in arithmetic problem solving.* Doctoral dissertation, State University of Iowa.

Mayer, R. E. (1985). Implications of cognitive psychology for instruction in mathematical problem solving. In E. A. Silver (Ed.), *Teaching and learning mathematical problem solving: Multiple research perspectives* (pp. 83–112). Hillsdale, NJ: Lawrence Erlbaum.

McLaughlin, E. C. (1974). Equality of souls, inequality of sexes: Woman in medieval theology. In R. R. Ruether (Ed.), *Religion and sexism.* New York: Simon & Schuster.

Muth, D. K. and Glynn, S. (1985). Integrating reading and computational skills: The key to solving arithmetic word problems, *Journal of Instructional Psychology, 12*, 34–38.

Nesher, P. (1980). The stereotyped nature of school word problems, *For the Learning of Mathematics, 1*, 41–48.

Noddings, N. (1985a). Formal modes of knowing. In E. W. Eisner (Ed.) *Learning and teaching the ways of knowing* (pp. 116–132). Eighty-fourth Yearbook of the National Society for the Study of Education. Chicago: NSSE.

Noddings, N. (1985b). Small groups as a setting for research on mathematical problem solving. In E. A. Silver (Ed.), *Teaching and learning mathematical problem solving: Multiple research perspectives* (pp. 345–359). Hillsdale, NJ: Lawrence Erlbaum.

Norman, D. (1969). *Memory and attention.* New York: John Wiley & Sons.

Paige, J. M. & Simon, H. A. (1966). Cognitive processes in solving algebra word problems. In B. Kleinmuntz (Ed.), *Problem solving: Research, method and theory* (pp. 51–119). New York: John Wiley.

Piaget, J. (1970). *Genetic epistemology.* New York: Columbia University Press.

Polanyi, M. (1962). *Personal knowledge: Toward a post-critical philosophy.* Chicago: University of Chicago Press.

Rosenthal, D. J. (1971). *The sequence of information in arithmetic word problems.* Master's thesis, University of Pittsburgh.

Searle, B. W., Lorton, P., & Suppes, P. (1974). Structural variables affecting CAI performance on arithmetic word problems of disadvantaged and deaf students, *Educational Studies in Mathematics, 5*, 371–384.

Siegler, R. S. (1978). The origins of scientific reasoning. In R. S. Siegler (Ed.), *Children's thinking: What develops?* (pp. 109–150). Hillsdale, NJ: Lawrence Erlbaum.

Silver, E. A. (1985). Research on teaching mathematical problem solving: Some underrepresented themes and needed directions. In E. A. Silver (Ed.), *Teaching and learning mathematical problem solving: Multiple research perspectives* (pp. 247–266). Hillsdale, NJ: Lawrence Erlbaum.

Suydam, M. N. (1986). Research on mathematics education reported in 1985, *Journal for Research in Mathematics Education, 17*, 243–316.

Threadgill-Sowder, J., Sowder, L., Moyer, J. C. & Moyer, M. B. (1985). Cognitive variables and performance on mathematical story problems, *Journal of Experimental Education, 54*, 56–62.

Vygotsky, L. (1978). Mind in society. Cambridge, MA: Harvard University Press.

Weyl, H. (1956). The mathematical way of thinking. In J. R. Newman (Ed.), *The world of mathematics*, vol. 3. (pp. 1832–1849). New York: Simon & Schuster.

Williams, M. H. & McCreight, R. W. (1965). Shall we move the question? *Arithmetic Teacher, 12*, 418–421.

Teacher Education and Mathematical Problem Solving: Some Issues and Directions

Randall I. Charles

San Jose State University

For several years after the NCTM issued the Agenda for Action identifying problem solving as the focus of school mathematics, there was concern that too many teachers would view problem solving as a fad and that the teaching of computational skills would remain the priority in mathematics classrooms. That concern no longer exists. Although some teachers have not changed and may never change, a majority of teachers have accepted problem solving as the (or at least a) major focus of mathematics instruction, and they are interested in ways of improving their teaching abilities in this area.

As a result of the increased interest in problem solving, teacher education efforts in this area abound. Inservice and preservice courses, professional workshops and talks, books, and even videotapes are among the means that have been developed to help teachers become better teachers of problem solving. Although it is exciting that teachers are interested in improving their abilities to teach problem solving and that teacher education efforts are plentiful, it is alarming that these teacher education activities have been developed only on the intuitions of the instructors as to what it is they believe teachers should know and be able to do to be effective teachers of problem solving. Teacher educators faced with the immediate task of helping teachers improve their abilities do not have a research foundation upon which to build their programs. The purpose of this paper is to explore some issues involved in building a research agenda relative to teacher education vis-a-vis mathematical problem solving. These issues are explored by examining a teacher education program in mathematical problem solving at Illinois State University (ISU). The description includes the practical aspects of implementing the program and the theoretical underpinnings that guided its development. In the process of describing the program, issues relevant to building a research agenda are discussed.

Before describing this program, it's important to explore some issues concerning goals for teacher education and problem solving.

SETTING GOALS FOR TEACHER EDUCATION RELATIVE TO PROBLEM SOLVING

Shulman (1985) suggests that a teacher education program needs to operationalize answers to two questions : (a) What do we want teachers to know?, and (b) What do we want them to be able to do? Developing answers to these questions is not an easy task for any area, but it is particularly difficult for problem solving. The papers in this monograph make clear that answers to these questions can vary over time and at any given time depending on many factors. That is, different goals can be established for teacher education because different conceptualizations and beliefs exist about the teaching and learning of problem solving. For example, the paper by Stanic and Kilpatrick (this volume) provides an excellent review of the roles problem solving has played in the mathematics curriculum over the years. The answers to the questions posed by Shulman could vary depending on the role one perceives problem solving to play in the curriculum. The papers by Lave, Bransford, and their colleagues (this volume) have challenged our traditional views of the context in which problem-solving instruction might occur. Lave and her colleagues' work suggests that the basic concept of a "teacher" should be examined. Bransford's use of video technology suggests a drastic change for the context in which problem-solving instruction has traditionally occurred.

The implications for teacher education suggested by many of the papers in this mongraph are drastic. Although current hindrances to change in teacher education should not set directions for future research, realities that will probably exist for many years should be considered. One of those realities for both preservice and inservice education is that there is a relatively small amount of time to work with teachers. As a result, choices must be made, choices about what teachers should know and believe about the teaching and learning of mathematics, what they should be able to do in the classroom, and what methods will be used to achieve these outcomes.

The problem-solving, teacher education program at Illinois State University was a three-semester-hour course designed for both preservice and inservice teachers at the elementary and junior high school levels. Based on work with teachers, research on students' problem-solving processes, and research on effective teaching, the following needs for prospective teachers of problem solving were identified:

- Teachers need some competence solving problems.
- Teachers need to know some facts about problem solving and about the school curriculum.
- Teachers need to be able to select, create, and evaluate curriculum material.
- Teachers need ideas for how to direct students' efforts solving problems.
- Teachers need ideas for how to manage instruction (e.g., small group work).
- Teachers need ideas for how to evaluate pupil progress.

The following goals were established for the program:

1. Teachers should be able to solve problems of at least the same level of difficulty that they will use with their students.
2. Teachers' content and curricular knowledge and abilities
   2.1 content knowledge—A teacher should know:
       2.1.1 the meaning of a "problem,"
       2.1.2 the meaning of "problem solving,"
       2.1.3 why problem solving is important,
       2.1.4 what factors influence success,
       2.1.5 the thinking processes involved in solving problems.
   2.2 curricular knowledge—A teacher should know:
       2.2.1 types of problems and problem-solving experiences appropriate for different grade/age levels,
       2.2.2 types of problem-solving skill activities appropriate for different grade/age levels,
       2.2.3 ways to integrate problem solving throughout the mathematics curriculum,
       2.2.4 the roles problem solving has played in the mathematics curriculum over the years.
   2.3 curricular abilities—A teacher should be able to:
       2.3.1 select and create problem-solving experiences appropriate for a given population of students,
       2.3.2 evaluate problem-solving curriculum material.
3. Teachers' pedagogical knowledge and abilities
   3.1 pedagogical knowledge—A teacher should know:
       3.1.1 different roles for the teacher in the classroom,
       3.1.2 teaching actions that can be used to guide problem solving, including their purposes, limitations, ways to use, variations, and so forth,
       3.1.3 ways to manage instruction (e.g., ways to form and manage small groups),
       3.1.4 assessment techniques for performance, attitudes, and beliefs,
       3.1.5 factors that influence the classroom climate for problem solving.
   3.2 pedagogical abilities—A teacher should be able to:
       3.2.1 use teaching actions in a classroom situation,
       3.2.2 write and use questions and hints to guide students as they solve problems,
       3.2.3 implement management practices in a classroom situation (e.g., small group work),
       3.2.4 use assessment techniques relative to performance, attitudes, and beliefs,

3.2.5 build a positive classroom climate for problem solving.

Before discussing these goals, the general organization of the program is described.

ORGANIZATION OF THE PROGRAM AND GETTING STARTED

The problem-solving program was a 1-semester, 15-week, course. The course was scheduled in two ways; one was a 1-night-a-week class for 3 hours; the other was a twice-a-week class of 1 hour and 15 minutes each. Table 1 shows the approximate amount of time devoted to each goal area.

Table 1
Approximate Time Devoted to Major Program Goals/Activities

Weeks	Major purpose
1–3	• develop teachers' problem-solving abilities • explore the role of affect in problem solving
4–7	• develop teachers' problem-solving abilities • develop teachers' content and curricular knowledge • field experience related to students' thinking processes
8–15	• develop teachers' pedagogical knowledge and abilities • field experience related to teaching problem solving

One of the realities quickly confronted when working with teachers relative to problem solving is that many teachers have a great deal of anxiety related to mathematics in general but particularly toward problem solving. To deal with this anxiety, affective issues relative to problem solving are dealt with in the first class session. Problems are solved that are relatively easy for teachers, and problems are solved that are challenging. This setting is used to explore their feelings and their prior experience with problem solving and how those might affect their performance. These issues are then explored with respect to students and how issues related to affect and prior experience can affect their performance. An opening sesssion that focuses on affect has had a very positive impact on the teachers' attitudes. While the role of affect is being explored relative to students, affect relative to teachers is an important topic for a research agenda on teacher education.

TEACHERS AS PROBLEM SOLVERS

It is important to consider separately what it is teachers know *about* problem solving (goal area 2) and what it is teachers can *do* solving problems. The issue of how much mathematics one needs to know (or be able to do) to be an effective teacher of mathematics has yet to be resolved. Previous research has generally found a relatively low correlation between the teacher's knowledge of mathematics and the teacher's performance in the classroom. That research, however, is somewhat flawed in that the knowledge assessed was global knowledge rather than knowledge specific to the topic being taught. Indeed, one of the beliefs guiding the work of Tom Carpenter and others at Wisconsin is that teachers need to be knowledgeable about the nature of addition and subtraction meanings to be effective teachers of addition and subtraction, that their knowledge base must be rich and well organized in this specific domain to be effective teachers in that domain (see Carpenter, this volume).

Teachers need some level of competence as problem solvers before they not only teach problem solving but before they begin to learn about problem solving. The first three class sessions were devoted to experiences solving problems and discussing the teachers' work. The next four class sessions continued to focus on experiences solving and discussing problems but these experiences were used as vehicles for developing the teachers' knowledge related to problem-solving content and the curriculum(see the next section). Throughout the remainder of the course most class sessions began with a discussion of teachers' efforts to solve a problem given as homework the previous week. Sometimes these problems were solved in small groups (particularly at the begining of the course) and later they were solved individually. No grades were assigned to these experiences. Small-group problems and individual problems were assigned during the second half of the course and evaluated with respect to a course grade. Teachers' abilities as problem solvers take time to develop. Extending opportunities to solve problems throughout the semester seems to promote the development of their problem-solving abilities.

An important issue for a research agenda is the teacher's ability as a problem solver. How good a problem solver must a teacher be to be an effective teacher of problem solving? Experience suggests that teachers need some background solving problems and some level of competence as a problem solver prior to teaching students. However, teachers' abilities as problem solvers improve as they teach problem solving. A common maxim is that the best way to learn something is to teach it; this may indeed apply to problem solving. Can teachers become better problem solvers by teaching it? How much do they need to be able to do before they start teaching students? How much experience do teachers need solving problems before they address the teaching of problem solving ? All of these issues need to be considered in a research agenda for teacher education and problem solving.

TEACHERS' CONTENT AND CURRICULAR KNOWLEDGE AND ABILITIES

One of the themes in several of the papers in this monograph is that what students know, that is, their knowledge, and how that knowledge is organized is an important factor influencing problem-solving performance. It is believed that successful problem solvers have a rich store of knowledge organized in sophisticated ways. Carpenter (this volume) extends this idea to suggest that teaching is also a problem-solving activity. He suggests that the more complete the teacher's knowledge relevant to the focus of instruction (e.g., addition and subtraction meanings) and the better organized that knowledge, the better one is able to direct learning experiences of students, that is, to teach.

In designing the ISU teacher education program for problem solving, a knowledge base was identified that might influence one's ability to effectively teach problem solving. That knowledge was separated into two broad areas—content/curricular and pedagogical. This section will examine the content/curricular knowledge introduced in the program.

The content knowledge selected for the program is shown in the list of goals given earlier under items 2.1 and 2.2. Better teachers of problem solving have a clear sense of what problem solving "is all about." They have workable, although often not refined, definitions of what problem solving is and what it is not; they have a sense of what constitutes a problem and how a problem might be defined with regard to an individual or a group. They also have a sense of the role problem solving should play in the mathematics curriculum, and they have a reasonable understanding of the kind of thinking that constitutes problem-solving behavior. Group discussions as a follow-up to teachers' problem-solving experiences were used to develop their knowledge relative to the meanings of problem solving, a problem, and to reasons why problem solving should play an important role in the curriculum. Readings from various sources were also used to influence these discussions. Observations of their peers solving problems together with a field experience involving elementary school students were used to develop the teachers' understanding of the thinking processes involved in problem solving. (The field experience component of the program is discussed later.)

The focus of the program with regard to curricular knowledge and abilities was on making teachers aware of the different kinds of problems and problem-solving experiences that can be used in the elementary/junior high school grades, on developing the teachers' abilities to select and create problem-solving experiences, and on developing teachers' abilities to evaluate curriculum material. Teachers learned that there are different types of problems that can be included in the curriculum (see Charles & Lester, 1982, for a discussion of problem types); they analyzed the nature of those types, and they gained some level of competence writing problems. For example, students were introduced to the problem categorization schemes of Carpenter and others for problems related to the operations of addition and subtraction. They learned to identify the "key actions" associated with the operations and developed some skill writing "one-step" word problems.

A sound problem-solving curriculum is one that presents many different views of problem solving. It was suggested to teachers that the mathematics curriculum should: (a) include activities designed to develop specific problem-solving skills such as determining whether an answer is reasonable or knowing how to make and complete a table; (b) provide ample practice solving different types of problems; (c) have problem solving integrated throughout all aspects of instruction (e.g., to provide motivation for concept and skill learning, to serve as a vehicle for introducing new ideas, to illustrate applications of skills, to serve as a setting for practicing skills).

Teachers developed an understanding of problem-solving skills and ways to integrate problem solving into all aspects of teaching mathematics by completing similar kinds of activities they might use with students and by examining samples of these kinds of experiences in curriculum material. They were also given an opportunity to create problem-solving experiences on their own.

The content and curricular knowledge and abilities selected as the focus for the ISU program were identified based on experience with teachers. Perhaps more time should have been spent on affect or social and personal factors or on the role of technology. Choices had to be made. In the future those choices should emerge not only from experience with teachers but also from research. The challenge for research is to identify the knowledge and abilities in these areas that teachers need to be effective in the classroom.

PEDAGOGICAL KNOWLEDGE AND ABILITIES

For many teachers, teaching mathematics is synonymous with teaching skills. Therefore, it is not surprising that when problem solving was introduced as a major component of the mathematics curriculum , many teachers folded problem solving into their existing beliefs about mathematics—mathematics is skills so problem solving is skills. In fact the NCTM promoted this belief, unintentionally, by including problem solving among its 10 basic skill areas. While it is important that students do learn some skills involved in solving problems (e.g., how to make and complete tables), all too many teachers restrict their problem-solving efforts to this. One of the recommendations for teachers that can be gleaned from papers in this monograph is that more needs to be done in classrooms to promote the art of solving problems. An important question for a research agenda is how can teachers build a classroom environment, a classroom ecology, that promotes mathematical thinking (see Schoenfeld, Stanic & Kilpatrick, Noddings, Lester, this volume). Only when a proper classroom environment for problem solving exists can students begin to develop the art of solving problems.

One way to develop the art of solving problems is through guided practice with reflection on your work, practice where students are not given some mechanistic way to approach a problem or are told what strategies to use to solve it. For the majority of teachers, working with students as they practice solving problems, as they develop the art of solving problems, is their most difficult task, the task for which they feel least competent and most uncomfortable. Therefore, the pedagogical component of the ISU program focused on ways to help teachers direct the practice component of the problem-solving curriculum.

The program concentrated on helping teachers implement a specific teaching strategy for problem solving that was developed as part of an E.S.E.A. Title IV-C curriculum research and development project in West Virginia from 1979–82. Teachers in the program were directed through eight phases in learning to use this strategy.

1) Teachers were given a general overview of the teaching strategy.
2) Teachers heard a description of each teaching action that made up the strategy. Pointers for using each were given.
3) They viewed several videotaped whole-class lessons exemplifying the teaching strategy.
4) They practiced writing hints and questions that could be used as part of the teaching strategy.
5) They practiced using the teaching strategy by teaching small groups of their peers.
6) They viewed more videotapes some exemplary and some poor examples of the implementation of the teaching strategy.
7) They practiced using the teaching strategy with small groups or whole classes of elementary school students.
8) They discussed their experiences using the teaching strategy with children.

The teaching strategy consisted of ten "teaching actions" in the form of a lesson plan. These teaching actions are listed below and the lesson plan is shown in Figure 1. A complete discussion of the implementation of these teaching actions can be found elsewhere (see Charles & Lester, 1982). Recommendations for research on this teaching strategy can also be found elsewhere (Charles, 1985). The remainder of this section will describe the rationale for the use of teaching actions and a lesson plan for educating teachers to direct the practice component of problem-solving instruction and some comments about needed research.

TEACHING ACTIONS

BEFORE students pick up their pencils to start work, have a whole-class discussion with them about the problem. Use the following teaching actions:

1. Read the problem to the students or have a student read the problem. Discuss vocabulary and the setting as needed.

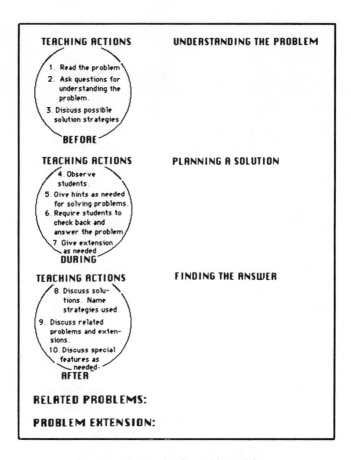

Figure 1. A lesson plan for problem solving

2. Have a discussion related to understanding the problem. Focus on what the problem is asking and the data needed to solve the problem. Be careful not to remove the need for the student to understand the problem on his or her own by asking too many questions.

3. Ask students to suggest possible solution strategies. Do not censor or evaluate students' suggestions.

DURING the time students are solving the problem, move around the room. Use these teaching actions:

4. Observe students as they solve problems. Ask students questions about their work.

5. If students get stumped, provide hints to help them select and implement solution strategies. Repeat understanding questions (from 2 above) as needed.

6. When students get an answer, require them to check their work.

7. For early finishers or, if time permits, for everyone, give an extension of the problem.

AFTER students stop work on the problem, end with a whole-class discussion about the problem. Use these teaching actions:

8. Discuss students' solutions to the problem. If possible, identify different ways (strategies) the problem might be solved. Have students name the strategies used to find the answer.

9. Compare the problem just solved to similar ones solved previously. Discuss the problem extension.

10. Discuss any special features of the problem such as a misleading picture, extraneous data, or a misleading "key word."

Pilot work with teachers as part of the project in West Virginia revealed that even teachers who seemed to have a strong knowledge-base related to the kinds of problems they were to teach and who were good problem solvers themselves had difficulty directing a class of 30 students as they practiced solving problems. In other words, knowing a great deal about the content to be taught seemed necessary but not sufficient to effectively direct a practice session with an entire class. Furthermore, there were many teachers who after an in-depth program aimed at developing their problem-solving abilities, were still very doubtful about their abilities to direct a class as they solve problems.

The idea of a lesson plan was conceived as a vehicle to help teachers get started teaching problem solving. There is often concern when a teaching strategy is given in the form of a lesson plan. One concern is that the strategy becomes a rigid sequence of behaviors that does not allow for individual differences of either teachers or students. Another concern is that a lesson plan may promote the false belief that an algorithm exists for teaching problem solving. Although these concerns are legitimate, experience with the lesson plan given here and research on teachers' planning behaviors and thought processes suggest that a problem-solving lesson plan is not only helpful in getting teachers started teaching problem solving but may in fact be a necessary ingredient in changing teachers' instructional behaviors.

In a study by Charles and Lester (1984), interviews with teachers who used this lesson plan revealed that all of the teachers found it helpful in getting started teaching problem solving. Also, the teaching strategy was considered flexible enough to allow teachers to adapt it to their own teaching styles but structured enough to help less confident teachers feel comfortable teaching problem solving.

Research on teachers' planning behaviors and thought processes provides an explanation for the value of the teaching actions. A major component of teachers' planning is the selection and sequencing of instructional activities (Shavelson & Stern, 1981). In general, teachers do not begin their planning for a lesson by thinking about specific instructional techniques they will use to achieve an objective, but rather they begin by establishing "activity chunks" sequenced in a particular way. Each activity chunk may contain several subactivities. A sequence of activity chunks, provides an "agenda" (Leinhardt, 1983) or a "script" (Abelson, 1976; Shank & Abelson, 1977) for the lesson. The value of the agenda is that it structures the activities of a lesson, making both the teacher's and students' actions predictable and reducing the complexity of the information teachers encounter during instruction. With experience, the agenda becomes internalized or routinized relieving the teacher from having to consciously develop a mental road map for each lesson. Leinhardt (1983) suggests that, "The use of routines [agendas] also reduces the cognitive processing for the teacher and provides them with the intellectual and temporal room needed to handle the dynamic portions of the lesson" (p. 27–8).

The three phases of the lesson (Before, During, and After) and the teaching actions within each phase provide an instructional agenda. The three phases represent activity chunks, and the teaching actions in each phase are subactivities. Experience with this lesson plan shows that teachers initially follow the teaching actions quite closely. With experience, most teachers internalize the teaching actions and refer to the lesson plan only on occasion. Observations and interviews with teachers also showed that only after teachers internalized the teaching actions were they (cognitively) ready to focus on the "dynamic portions" of teaching problem solving (e.g., ways to improve their skills giving hints or ways to improve their discussions with students about problem solutions). Until teachers internalized the teaching actions, they did not feel in control of the lesson and they were not interested in exploring ways to improve individual teaching skills.

What do teachers need to know and be able to do to effectively teach problem solving? Is being a good problem solver adequate preparation for teachers to effectively direct a class of 30 students? Is a set of teaching actions an appropriate way to change teacher behavior? Does it provide too much structure? Does it mechanize problem-solving behavior? teaching behavior? Experience suggests that a strong knowledge-base related to problem solving is not sufficient and that some direction for the teacher's classroom actions is beneficial. However, these issues need to be considered in a research agenda for teacher education. It is also important to consider that the teacher's role in the classroom can (and probably should) vary depending on the kind of problem-solving experience. One of the difficulties that exists in discussing the teaching of problem solving is that these discussions often do not begin by defining the context in which teaching takes place. For the teaching strategy described above, the context was a class of 30 students, working individually or in small groups, practicing to solve problems. If the context for teaching was the videodisc technologies described by Bransford, the role of the teacher might be quite different from the role of the teacher described above. Future research on the role of the teacher should consider the nature of the problem-solving experience and the instructional setting.

FIELD EXPERIENCE

Both the content/curricular and pedagogical components of the ISU program included a field experience for teachers. The first experience occurred about five weeks into the course. The purpose of this experience was for teachers to gain a deeper understanding of the thinking processes involved in solving problems. After teachers had solved problems in class with their peers, several discussions were held exploring the different thought processes that might be involved in problem solving. As a follow up, the field experience provided an opportunity for teachers to observe these behaviors in elementary school students. Each teacher observed students as they solved several problems in a small group. Teachers had an observation form to help them look for certain behaviors as they observed the group, being careful to not intervene and teach the lesson. A discussion of these observations was held among the teachers.

The second field experience occurred near the end of the course. The purpose of this experience was for teachers to practice using the teaching strategy with a small group or whole class of students. After this experience, a whole-class discussion was held with the teachers concerning the implementation of the teaching strategy, its benefits, limitations, and so forth.

Field experiences can be constructed in many different forms and can serve many different purposes. Issues related to field experiences should be considered in building a research agenda for teacher education and problem solving.

PRESERVICE VERSUS INSERVICE EDUCATION

Any mathematics educator who has worked with teachers knows there are obvious and important differences between preservice teachers of mathematics and inservice teachers of mathematics. The teacher education program described above was designed for both preservice and inservice teachers. This was done, as is often the case, for administrative reasons (i.e., to have a sufficient number of students to offer a course). Future research related to teacher education and problem solving should consider the possibility that teacher education programs for preservice teachers of mathematics may need to be fundamentally different from teacher education programs for inservice teachers. One example of an important characteristic of inservice teachers (that may be different from preservice teachers) is suggested by Hall (1986). Hall and his colleagues have shown that inservice teachers move through several phases of use when they are introduced to an innovation (e.g., the introduction of a problem-solving curriculum). Their work suggests that the kind of inservice education program an inservice teacher might experience at the outset of a new program should be different from the kind of inservice education program needed after having one year of experience with the program. Future research needs to consider how the amount of teaching experience one has might influence the nature of a teacher education program.

CONCLUSION

One might hope that the challenge of teacher education programs for mathematical problem solving would be to find activities and experiences that equip teachers with the "ingredients" needed to be effective in the classroom. That is, the focus would be on the *process* of preparing teachers. However, this conference has shown that fundamental questions still exist as to the ingredients needed for effective teaching. This is a critical time in mathematics education relative to problem-solving instruction. Most teachers, administrators, and parents have accepted a change in direction in the curriculum with greater emphasis given to problem solving. Now that they have accepted this change they want results. To get results, the responsibility falls to the quality of the teaching and the quality of the assessments of students' progress. It is time to establish goals for teacher education based on the best knowledge available, to identify effective means to attain those goals, and to develop research plans that enable us to reflect on our efforts. As the research-based knowledge on teaching and assessment evolves from ideas like those presented at this conference, teacher education models so too will evolve.

REFERENCES

Abelson, R. P. (1976). Script processing in attitude formation and decision making. In J. S. Caroll & J. W. Payne (Eds.), *Cognition and social behavior.* Hillsdale, N.J.: Lawrence Erlbaum.

Charles, R. I. & Lester, F. K. (1982). *Teaching problem solving: What, why and how.* Palo Alto, CA: Dale Seymour Publications.

Charles, R. I. & Lester, F. K. (1984). An evaluation of a process-oriented instructional program in mathematical problem solving in grades 5 and 7. *Journal for Research in Mathematics Education, 15* (1), 15–34.

Charles, R. (1985). *Some directions for research on teaching problem solving.* Paper presented at the Research Presession of the Annual Conference of the NCTM, Austin, TX.

Hall, G. (1986). *The inservice challenge.* Paper presented at the conference "Improving science and mathematics education, materials, and teaching: A collaborative effort." Sponsored by the Association of American Publishers, National Association of Research in Science Teaching, and National Council of Teachers of Mathematics, Atlanta.

Leinhardt, G. (1983). *Routines in expert math teachers' thoughts and actions.* Paper presented at the annual meeting of the AERA, Montreal, 1983.

Schank, R. & Abelson, R. P. (1977). *Scripts, plans, goals, and understanding: An inquiry into human knowledge structures.* Hillsdale, N.J.: Lawrence Erlbaum.

Shavelson, R. J. & Stern, P. (1981). Research on teachers' pedagogical thoughts, judgments, decisions, and behavior. *Review of Educational Research, 51* (4), 455–498.

Shulman, L. (1985). On teaching problem solving and solving the problems of teaching. In E. Silver (Ed.), *Teaching and learning mathematical problem solving: Multiple research perspectives* (pp. 439–450). Hillsdale, N.J.: Lawrence Erlbaum.

Teaching and Assessing Mathematical Problem Solving: Toward a Research Agenda

Edward A. Silver

University of Pittsburgh

This volume contains many provocative discussions of important issues in the area of research on teaching and assessing mathematical problem solving. Each of the authors has identified several strategic sites for further research activity in the area, and in many cases they have provided prototypical examples that should prove quite valuable for other workers in the field. The chapters identify and represent several general themes that deserve continued, focused research attention during the next several years. In that sense, these chapters collectively form the intended agenda for research on teaching and assessing mathematical problem solving.

At the conference 25 participants from the United States and Japan, representing a wide range of disciplinary and professional perspectives, including anthropologists, psychologists, mathematicians, philosophers, mathematics educators, and classroom teachers, met for four days to hear invited presentations and engage in discussions about future directions for research in this important area. As one might expect in such a diverse group, no single research agenda—no consensus listing of topics to be researched—was produced at the conference. There was, however, considerable agreement regarding three general themes that dominated the papers and the discussion at the conference: (a) the need to develop effective strategies to capitalize on current knowledge of mathematics teaching and of mathematical problem-solving performance, to improve the teaching and assessment of problem solving, (b) the need to develop an expanded view of mathematical problem solving, and (c) the need for a multi-disciplinary, broad-based effort to develop new knowledge that is directly relevant to classroom teaching and testing.

THEMES FOR A RESEARCH AGENDA

In this section I will consider the three general themes that cut across the presentations and discussions at the conference, and which are represented in the chapters contained in this volume. The identification and discussion of these common themes may serve not only to organize the various perspectives taken by the chapter authors but also to define more clearly some basic directions in which research on the teaching and assessing of mathematical problem solving is likely to proceed.

Using Knowledge from Research on Learning, Performance, and Teaching

One important theme that is evident in many of the papers is that research on teaching and assessing problem solving could be guided by insights obtained from research on mathematics teaching and also from research on problem-solving learning and performance. There are three different aspects of this research literature that might be productively applied to future research on the teaching and assessing of problem solving: results, theoretical constructs, and methods.

Using the results of previous research. One excellent example of a research program that has successfully utilized results from prior research on mathematics learning and performance is the work by Carpenter, Fennema, and Peterson on Cognitively Guided Instruction. Thomas Carpenter's chapter describes how their work began with a foundation of research results dealing with young children's solutions of arithmetic story problems, built a powerful set of teacher enhancement activities on that foundation, and is now examining the effects of these activities on teachers and their students.

In her chapter, Nel Noddings identifies a number of results of previous research on mathematics learning and performance and suggests ways of integrating these findings into the preparation of mathematics teachers. Her paper illustrates the wide range of relevant research as well as the immense complexity involved in trying to prepare future teachers who will be knowledgeable not only about the mathematics they will teach but also about the difficulties their students are likely to have in learning the material. Noddings also stresses the importance of teachers being aware of research programs rather than isolated results.

Using theoretical constructs from previous research. Another example of the way that research on learning and performance can directly affect research on teaching and assessing problem solving is found in the chapter by Sandra Marshall. Previous research on problem-solving performance has demonstrated that problem-solving schemas, or semantic structure categories, are powerful theoretical constructs that help explain not only the organization and encoding of problem-solving information but also the structured recall of the results of a problem-solving episode. Marshall proposes, and gives several useful examples of, ways in which assessment of problem solving could be enhanced by systematically using notions that have emerged from earlier work on problem-solving schemas.

In their chapter, Joseph Campione, Ann Brown, and Michael Connell suggest some possible applications to mathematics of constructs that have been found useful in research on reading. In particular, they point to various aspects of metacognition that appear to have relevance for both teaching and assessing school mathematics. Their discussions of instructional characteristics likely to improve students' disposition toward learning and of dynamic rather than static assessment techniques are both provocative and worthwhile for serious consideration and application to the teaching and assessing of mathematics.

Using the methods of previous research. In his chapter, Richard Shavelson identifies and discusses some methods of research on teaching that could be productively applied to the study of the teaching of problem solving. For example, Shavelson discusses the work of Gaea Leinhardt, who has contrasted expert and novice teachers as they teach lessons aimed at the development of procedural skills. Leinhardt's work provides rich descriptions and analyses of the teachers' intentions, their situated explanations, and their subject matter and pedagogical knowledge. Shavelson argues that Leinhardt's detailed analyses of teachers' plans, goals, knowledge, and actions could be applied to the analysis of skilled teaching of problem solving. Shavelson also gives examples of ways in which work on expert tutoring and small-group learning could be adapted for the study of mathematical problem solving. In her chapter, Alba Thompson offers some additional suggestions for research on teaching problem solving that are obtained from a different research perspective; namely, research on teachers' beliefs. A combination of the perspective taken in Thompson's work with the analytic techniques available from Leinhardt's work on classroom instruction would appear to be a powerful methodology to apply in future research on the teaching of mathematical problem solving.

The literature dealing with research on teaching, however, is not the only literature that may contain suggestions of useful methodology. Edward Silver and Jeremy Kilpatrick in turn, suggest that techniques used in research on problem-solving learning and performance might be adapted for use as classroom assessment techniques.

Viewing Problem Solving within a Broader Context

One of the most prevalent themes cutting across the chapters is that problem solving and problem-solving activity should be viewed within a broader context than traditional school mathematics. There are several different versions of what that broader context might look like, including consideration of a broader domain of mathematical problems and mathematical problem-solving activity, contexts in which mathematics learning involves the social construction of mathematical knowledge, and contexts in which school mathematics is considered as a collaborative practice. A common and persuasive vision of mathematics classrooms as a situated, collaborative practice involving social construction of knowledge and socially-distributed problem solving emerges from the papers. In this view mathematics classrooms would be places where students, working collaboratively and under the tutelage of their mathematics teacher, would engage in doing mathematics rather than having it done to them. Several papers urge consideration of problematic tasks that occur in non-school settings as well as those that are provided in textbooks. One common theme is the need to engage students with problems and problematic contexts in which they can pose and solve their own problems and generate their own conjectures.

Broadening the domain of problems. Some recent analyses have been conducted which demonstrate that school mathematical knowledge is noticeably absent in the skilled performance of many out-of-school quantitative tasks. For example, Scribner's (1984) analysis of the billing and inventory behavior of dairy workers, de la Rocha's (Lave, Murtaugh, & de la Rocha, 1984) study of people measuring food portions in a Weight Watcher's Program, and Carraher, Carraher, and Schliemann's (1985) analysis of child street vendors in Brazil all have demonstrated that functional quantitative competence on tasks in out-of-school settings appears to bear little relation or resemblance to the formal mathematical knowledge related to those tasks. If we look beyond the obvious conclusion that these studies suggest a separation of school mathematical knowledge from everyday practice, we can see another important message that these studies deliver—the importance of situated knowledge. In general, these studies suggest that school mathematics suffers from its dissociation from the contexts in which it might be applicable.

In his chapter, Alan Schoenfeld argues for consideration of the multiple contexts in which mathematical knowledge can be applied. He argues for a consideration of a wide range of contextualized uses of mathematics both in teaching and in research on teaching. The chapter by John Bransford and his colleagues not only reminds us that it is important to consider problematic tasks that occur in non-school settings as well as those that are provided in textbooks but also presents some exciting examples of the use of video and videodisc technology to present problematic situations to students. The situations, excerpts from popular films, are made available to students as contexts in which they can apply mathematical analyses, pose and solve problems, and generate conjectures. Schoenfeld, Bransford and others, and many of the other authors of chapters in this volume advocate consideration of a much broader context for mathematical problem solving than has been considered heretofore in most research.

Problem solving in the context of collaborative practice. School mathematics suffers from an apparent dissociation not only with out-of-school contexts, but also with the discipline of mathematics itself. As Schoenfeld (in press) has argued, school mathematics suffers from its inability to provide students with experience in and an appetite for collaborative mathematical thinking. In their chapter, Jean Lave, Steve Smith, and Michael Butler suggest that school mathematics might be productively viewed within an apprenticeship model.

The apprenticeship notion emerges from the anthropology literature. In particular, much of the current discussion about classroom practice is an extension of Lave's (1977) study of the apprenticeship of tailors in Liberia, in which novices worked with master tailors to learn the skills, habits, and dispositions of these masters toward their work, and novice tailors developed their knowledge and skills by working on "real" tailoring tasks. Applying this view to school mathematics, James Greeno argues that the purpose of the activity of school mathematics might be seen not as the communication of decontextualized and abstract skills and concepts but rather as the development of a richly textured knowledge base, in which the knowledge is situated in important intellectual tasks. This apprenticeship view suggested by Lave and others and by Greeno also implies that a major purpose of school mathematics should be seen as developing in students the habits of thinking and points of view taken by professionals in the field. Their view of an apprenticeship approach to mathematics education is similar to a more general view of intellectual apprenticeship expressed by Collins, Brown, and Newman (in press).

One important consequence of this apprenticeship view for mathematics education is that it implies a view of mathematics classrooms as places in which classroom activity is directed not simply toward the acquisition of the content of mathematics in the form of concepts and procedures but rather toward the situated, collaborative practice of mathematical thinking. This view of mathematics is reminiscent of the writings of George Polya (1954, 1957, 1981), whose work and influence is discussed extensively in the chapter by George Stanic and Jeremy Kilpatrick.

Social construction of knowledge. In her chapter, Lauren Resnick argues that it may be productive to consider mathematics not as a subject that is well-structured and tightly organized but rather as a knowledge domain that is subject to interpretation and meaning construction. She advocates the use of social settings, such as socially shared problem solving, as argument and debate arenas for the development of shared mathematical meaning. Moreover, she argues that this view of mathematics teaching should be applicable to all aspects of mathematics instruction not simply to problem-solving activity. Her chapter discusses some of the theoretical and empirical foundations of such a view. Although she does not rely extensively on the constructivist literature, her arguments should resonate well in that community of mathematics educators committed to a constructivist epistemology.

Tackling the Tough Tasks: Testing, Teaching, and Teaching Teachers

The diversity of the contributors to this volume and the high quality of their contribution attests to the fact there is broad-based interest in the issues of teaching and assessing mathematical problem soving. In fact, there appears to be a surprising enthusiasm in the research community for tackling these tough issues. In the chapters in this volume, a number of important research questions are proposed and discussed, alternative models and approaches are considered, and suggestions are made concerning promising directions for further inquiry. Although many of the ideas represented here are somewhat tentative, the clear message is that the time appears to be ripe for researchers to launch a frontal assault on these issues which are of crucial importance to mathematics education.

Although the focus of the conference was explicitly on teaching and assessment of problem solving, two related issues insinuated themselves into much of the discussion—teacher preparation and teacher enhancement. The need for careful attention to the preparation and continuing professional development of mathematics teachers is evident not only in the papers by Randall Charles, Nel Noddings, and Alba Thompson which deal explicitly with these topics, but also in many of the other papers in the volume. In their chapters, Noddings and Charles each raise fundamental questions about not only the knowledge that prospective teachers will need to have in order to play the role of master teacher but also the needs of current teachers who will need continuing professional development if they are to transform their current teaching approaches. Thompson's chapter reminds us that we also need to pay close attention to the beliefs of prospective and current teachers regarding mathematics, student learning, and their teaching. The need for careful research attention to the preparation and continuing professional development of mathematics teachers becomes immediately apparent when one considers the pedagogical consequences of the apprenticeship view of mathematics education discussed above. As we have noted, this notion implies a view of mathematics classrooms as places where students, under the careful tutelage of their mathematics teachers, engage in doing mathematics rather than having it done to them. A view of mathematics classrooms as environments for collaborative practice in doing mathematics assumes not only that teachers will be skillful in orchestrating the dynamics of such classrooms but also that they will be able to play the role of master mathematical thinker for the apprentice students. Certainly, both of these assumptions need to be tested, and the testing of these assumptions suggests many additional items for a research agenda.

TOWARD A TRANSFORMATIVE RESEARCH AGENDA

What is a research agenda? In common parlance, an agenda is a list of things to be accomplished. Agendas come in many forms: some are printed, some are verbal, and some may even be hidden. In a sense, this volume represents all three forms of agendas. The chapters themselves constitute a printed agenda. Moreover, in the revisions that the authors have made since the conference was held, many have tried to incorporate the comments of others that were made in the conference discussion, thereby including their version of the collective verbal agenda in their individual written chapters. Finally, there appears to be a hidden agenda represented in this volume: reforming the character of precollege mathematics instruction to make it more intellectually stimulating for students. Although it is scientific progress that drives each researcher's agenda, the reform agenda is evident in the background. Given the diversity of disciplinary perspectives represented in the authorship of chapters in this volume, it is quite remarkable that a fairly common reform agenda appears to be represented. In fact, as we have already noted, there is considerable convergence between the suggestions made in this volume concerning research and practice and many of the recent curriculum and evaluation suggestions made by the Commission on Standards for School Mathematics (NCTM, 1987).

This volume represents an important part of a transformative research agenda for mathematics education. The chapters imply a view of school mathematics that differs markedly from the current state of affairs. Instead of dealing solely with the careful study of "what is" happening in the teaching and assessment of mathematical problem solving, the chapters deal more broadly with "what ought to be." The research agenda outlined in this volume should both complement and inform the efforts of mathematics educators to reform current curricular, pedagogical, and assessment practices.

The need to provide opportunities for students to engage in generative mathematical inquiry and activity has recently been more widely recognized in the mathematics education community, and it serves as a cornerstone for much of the current effort to reform the character of precollege mathematics education to make it more intellectually stimulating for students. In California, for example, the *Mathematics Framework* (1985) states: "The ability to analyze situations for potential mathematical relationships and to pose problems whose solution might clarify those relationships or provide new information is a skill to be developed and nurtured throughout the mathematics program" (p. 14). More recently, the NCTM Commission on Standards for School Mathematics (NCTM, 1987) has asserted that "to gain mathematical power, students need to make conjectures, abstract properties and relationships from problem situations, explain their reasoning, follow arguments, validate assertions, and communicate results in a meaningful form" (p. 7). In describing the goals for students in grades 5 and beyond, the Commission also asserted that "Problem solving should be a process that actively engages students in making conjectures, investigating and exploring ideas, discussing and questioning their own thinking and the thinking of others, validating results, and making convincing arguments" (p. 54).

This vision of school mathematics is in stark contrast to the picture of current mathematics teaching, as painted by the most recent NAEP results.

Recent evidence obtained from questionnaires administered as part of the National Assessment of Educational Progress (Dossey, Mullis, Lindquist, & Chambers, in press) confirms that the pattern of activity in mathematics classrooms has changed little from earlier reports (Fey, 1981). In the NAEP survey, student self-report data indicated that (a) teacher explanations constitute most of mathematics instruction, (b) there is extensive reliance on textbooks, and (c) students spend very little time working in small groups or engaging in independent learning activities such as projects or investigations. In general, the NAEP data indicate that daily activity for most students in mathematics classes consists of watching a teacher work problems at the board and then working alone on additional problems provided by the textbook or by a worksheet. Moreover, the pattern of student attitudes and beliefs about mathematics obtained from the NAEP survey suggests that most students view mathematics as consisting mainly of memorizing rules and fail to view it as a creative activity (Brown, Carpenter, Kouba, Lindquist, Silver, & Swafford, in press). The picture that is painted by these data suggests that students are rarely, if ever, given opportunities to experience the intellectual excitement of generative mathematical inquiry. That is, mathematics is done *to* students, and is not done *by* them.

When mathematicians engage in the intellectual work of the discipline, two features distinguish their activity from the experience of students in typical precollege mathematics instruction: they often pose problems for themselves and they frequently encounter ill-structured problems and situations which require the application of problem posing and conjecturing behaviors. In the domain of professional mathematics, problems often arise out of attempts to generalize some already known result, or they represent tentative conjectures. The intellectual activity of professional mathematicians is often aimed at generating novel conjectures or results (Pollak, 1987). Although professional mathematics involves generative and creative cognitive processes, school mathematics almost never provides opportunities for students to generate mathematical ideas. In the domain of school mathematics, problems are almost always stated with well-specified goals, and the students' problem-solving activities are almost always intended to generate results that are already well known to the teacher.

Much of the current reform effort in mathematics education is directed at providing curricular and pedagogical support for students as they engage in mathematical thinking and problem solving. Although there has been considerable research dealing with mathematical problem solving (cf., Schoenfeld, 1985; Silver ,1985), very little of it has examined the kind of problem solving described in the visionary passages cited above. For example, there has been very little attention given to generative mathematical processes, such as conjecturing and problem formulation (Kilpatrick, 1987b). Therefore, a critical item on the transformative research agenda is to examine the nature of these more generative aspects of mathematical thinking, especially as they are represented in the intellectual activity of precollege students and their teachers. Many of the chapters in this volume point to other important related questions for the transformative research agenda.

CODA

The themes of this conference—teaching and assessment—were selected because there appeared to be a need to increase researchers' attention to these areas. Although there has been considerable progress made in the past two decades in understanding the nature of mathematical problem-solving performance (cf., Schoenfeld, 1985; Silver, 1985), far less is known about the areas of teaching and assessing problem solving. In a sense, the goal of the conference was not so much to produce an actual agenda but rather to get the issues of teaching and assessing problem solving on the agenda at all.

As Kilpatrick (1987a) has noted, implicit in the formation of an agenda is the assumption that there will be someone around to carry it out, yet educational researchers tend to operate within their own narrow enclave and appear not to be influenced by agendas set by others. Therefore, he questioned the value of a research agenda in mathematics education. The chapters in this volume, being representative of the general discussion among participants in the conference, give evidence that these topics are definitely on the agenda for research in the next decade. Collectively, the papers demonstrate that there is considerable broad-based interest and enthusiasm in the research community for investigating the areas of teaching and assessing mathematical problem solving. Consensus is fairly strong that an interdisciplinary approach, utilizing the theoretical perspectives afforded by cognitive psychology , the subject matter and pedagogical strengths of mathematics education, and the wisdom of teacher practitioners, is likely to reap substantial dividends in the next decade. The papers in this volume constitute an ambitious research agenda for all those willing to tackle the problems of teaching, teacher preparation, teacher enhancement, and testing and evaluation in the area of mathematical problem solving.

REFERENCES

Brown, C. A., Carpenter, T. P., Kouba, V. L., Lindquist, M. M., Silver, E. A., & Swafford, J. O. (in press). *Results of the fourth mathematics assessment of the National Assessment of Educational Progress.* Reston, VA: National Council of Teachers of Mathematics.

California State Department of Education. (1985). *Mathematics framework for California public schools, grades K–12.* Sacramento: Author.

Carraher, T. N., Carraher, D. W., & Schliemann, A. D. (1985). Mathematics in the streets and in schools. *British Journal of Developmental Psychology, 3*(1), 21–29.

Collins, A., Brown, J. S., & Newman, S. E. (in press). Cognitive apprenticeship: Teaching the craft of reading, writing and mathematics. In L.B. Resnick (Ed.), *Knowing and learning: Issues for a cognitive science of instruction*. Hillsdale, NJ: Lawrence Erlbaum Associates.

Dossey, J. A., Mullis, I. V. S., Lindquist, M. M., & Chambers, D. L. (in press). *The mathematics report card: Are we measuring up?* Princeton, NJ: Educational Testing Service.

Fey, J. T. (1981). *Mathematics teaching today: Perspectives from three national surveys*. Reston, VA: National Council of Teachers of Mathematics.

Kilpatrick, J. (1987a). Editorial. *Journal for Research in Mathematics Education, 18*, 82.

Kilpatrick, J. (1987b). Problem formulating: Where do good problems come from? In A. H. Schoenfeld (Ed.), *Cognitive science and mathematics education* (pp. 123–147). Hillsdale, NJ: Lawrence Erlbaum Associates.

Lave, J. (1977). Tailor-made experiments and evaluating the intellectual consequences of apprenticeship training. *Quarterly Newsletter of the Institute for Comparative Human Development, 1*, 1–3.

Lave, J., Murtaugh, M., & de la Rocha, O. (1984). The dialectic of arithmetic in grocery shopping. In B. Rogoff & J. Lave (Eds.), *Everyday cognition: Its development in social context* (pp. 67–94). Cambridge, MA: Harvard University Press.

National Council of Teachers of Mathematics. (1987). *Curriculum and evaluation standards for school mathematics*. Reston, VA: Author.

Pollak, H. O. (1987). Cognitive science and mathematics education: A mathematician's perspective. In A. H. Schoenfeld (Ed.), *Cognitive science and mathematics education*. Hillsdale, NJ: Lawrence Erlbaum Associates.

Pólya, G. (1954). *Mathematics and plausible reasoning* (2 vols.). Princeton, NJ: Princeton University Press.

Pólya, G. (1957). *How to solve it* (2nd ed.). New York: Doubleday.

Pólya, G. (1981). *Mathematical discovery* (combined ed.). New York: Wiley.

Schoenfeld, A. H. (1985). *Mathematical problem solving*. Orlando, FL: Academic Press.

Schoenfeld, A. H. (in press). On mathematics as sense-making: An informal attack on the unfortunate divorce of formal and informal mathematics. In J. F. Voss, D. N. Perkins, & J. Segal (Eds.), *Informal reasoning and instruction*. Hillsdale, NJ: Lawrence Erlbaum Associates.

Scribner, S. (1984). Studying working intelligence. In B. Rogoff & J. Lave (Eds.), *Everyday cognition: Its development in social context* (pp. 9–40). Cambridge MA: Harvard University Press.

Silver, E. A. (1985). *Teaching and learning mathematical problem solving: Multiple research perspectives*. Hillsdale, NJ: Lawrence Erlbaum Associates.

Working Group on
Teaching and Assessing Problem Solving

San Diego, California   January 9–12, 1987

Joan Akers
San Diego County
Office of Education

John Bransford
Vanderbilt University

George W. Bright
University of Houston

Ann L. Brown
University of Illinois

Thomas P. Carpenter
University of Wisconsin-
Madison

**Randall I. Charles
Illinois State University

Clyde Corcoran
Whittier High School
District

John Donald
San Diego State University

*James G. Greeno
University of California,
Berkeley

*Jeremy Kilpatrick
University of Georgia

Gerald Kulm
AAAS

Jean Lave
University of California,
Irvine

Frank K. Lester
Indiana University

Sandra P. Marshall
San Diego State University

*Douglas B. McLeod
Washington State University

Nel Noddings
Stanford University

Nobuhiko Nohda
University of Tsukuba

Tej N. Pandey
California Assessment
Program

Lauren B. Resnick
University of Pittsburgh

*Thomas A. Romberg
University of Wisconsin

Alan H. Schoenfeld
University of California,
Berkeley

Richard J. Shavelson
University of California, Los
Angeles

**Edward A. Silver
San Diego State University·

*Judith T. Sowder
San Diego State University

Larry Sowder
San Diego State University

George M. A. Stanic
University of Georgia

*James W. Stigler
University of Chicago

Alba G. Thompson
Illinois State University

James W. Wilson
University of Georgia

Working Group on
Effective Mathematics Teaching

Columbia, Missouri   March 11–14, 1987

Heinrich Bauersfeld
Universitat Bielefeld

Jacques C. Bergeron
Université de Montréal

David C. Berliner
University of Arizona

Bruce J. Biddle
University of Missouri

Catherine A. Brown
Virginia Polytechnic Institute

Stephen Brown
State University of New
York-Buffalo

William S. Bush
University of Kentucky

**Thomas J. Cooney
University of Georgia

John A. Dossey
Illinois State University

Elizabeth Fennema
University of Wisconsin-
Madison

Sherry Gerleman
Eastern Washington State
University

Thomas L. Good
University of Missouri

**Douglas A. Grouws
University of Missouri

Celia Hoyles
University of London

Martin L. Johnson
University of Maryland

Mary Koehler
University of Kansas

Perry E. Lanier
Michigan State University

Gaea Leinhardt
University of Pittsburgh

Richard Lodholz
Parkway Public Schools

Marilyn Nickson
Essex Institute of Higher
Education

John Owens
University of Alabama

Penelope L. Peterson
University of Wisconsin

Andrew C. Porter
Michigan State University

Edward Rathmell
University of Northern Iowa

Laurie Hart Reyes
University of Georgia

*Thomas A. Romberg
University of Wisconsin

Janet W. Schofield
University of Pittsburgh

Robert Slavin
Johns Hopkins University

*Judith T. Sowder
San Diego State University

*James W. Stigler
University of Chicago

Working Group on
The Learning and Teaching of Algebra

Athens, Georgia   *March 25–28, 1987*

John E. Bernard
West Georgia College

Lesley R. Booth
James Cook University-
Queensland

Diane J. Briars
Pittsburgh Board of
Education

Seth Chaiklin
Bank Street College

Robert B. Davis
University of Illinois

James T. Fey
University of Maryland

Eugenio Filloy Yague
Centro de Investigacion y
Estudios Avanzados del
I.P.N.

Larry L. Hatfield
University of Georgia

Nicolas Herscovics
Concordia University-
Montreal

Robert Jensen
Emory University

Mary Grace Kantowski
University of Florida

James J. Kaput
Southeastern Massachusetts
University

**Carolyn Kieran
Université du Québec a
Montréal

David Kirshner
University of British
Columbia

Jill H. Larkin
Carnegie Mellon University

Joan R. Leitzel
Ohio State University

Matthew Lewis
Carnegie Mellon University

Tatsuro Miwa
University of Tsukuba

Sidney Rachlin
University of Hawaii

Sharon L. Senk
Syracuse University

*George Springer
Indiana University

*Judith T. Sowder
San Diego State University

*Jane O. Swafford
Northern Michigan
University

David Tall
University of Warwick

Patrick W. Thompson
Illinois State University

John A. Thorpe
National Science Foundation

**Sigrid Wagner
University of Georgia

David Wheeler
Concordia University-
Montreal

Patricia S. Wilson
University of Georgia

Working Group on
Middle School Number Concepts

DeKalb, Illinois   *May 12–15, 1987*

**Merlyn J. Behr
Northern Illinois University

Alan Bell
Shell Centre, Nottingham

Robbie Case
Ontario Institute for Studies
in Education

Karen C. Fuson
Northwestern University

Brian Greer
Queens University, Belfast

Kathleen M. Hart
Kings College, London

**James Hiebert
University of Delaware

Thomas E. Kieren
University of Alberta

Magdalene Lampert
Michigan State University

Glenda Lappan
Michigan State University

Richard Lesh
WICAT

Jack Lochhead
University of Massachusetts

*Douglas B. McLeod
Washington State University

Pearla Nesher
University of Haifa

Stellan Ohlsson
University of Pittsburgh

Joseph N. Payne
University of Michigan

Thomas R. Post
University of Minnesota

Robert E. Reys
University of Missouri

*Thomas A. Romberg
University of Wisconsin

Judah L. Schwartz
Education Technology
Center

*Judith T. Sowder
San Diego State University

Leslie P. Steffe
University of Georgia

Gérard Vergnaud
Greco Didactique, Paris

Ipke Wachsmuth
Universitat Osnabruck

Diana Wearne
University of Delaware

*Advisory Board members and Project Director
**Conference Co-directors